W9-BKJ-277

THE (X) FILES™

I WANT TO BELIEVE™

ABOUT THE AUTHOR

Andy Meisler writes about television for the *New York Times* and several other publications. He is the co-author of *The Secret Life of Cyndy Garvey* with Cynthia Garvey and *I Am Roe: My Life, Roe v. Wade, and Freedom of Choice* with Norma McCorvey. He lives with his wife in Los Angeles.

Other *X-Files* titles published by HarperPrism

FICTION
The X-Files *Goblins*
The X-Files *Whirlwind*
The X-Files *Ground Zero*
The X-Files *Ruins*
The X-Files *Antibodies*

NONFICTION
Trust No One: The Official Guide to The X-Files
The Truth Is Out There: The Official Guide to The X-Files
The X-Files *Book of the Unexplained Volume One*
The X-Files *Book of the Unexplained Volume Two*
The X-Files *1998 Desk Diary*
The X-Files *1998 Wall Calendar*
The Official Map of The X-Files
The X-Files *Postcard Book: The Conspiracies*
The X-Files *Postcard Book: Monsters and Mutants*
The X-Files *Postcard Book: Unexplained Phenomena*

THE OFFICIAL GUIDE TO

THE Ⓧ FILES™

I WANT TO BELIEVE™

Created by Chris Carter

Written by Andy Meisler

with research assistance by Sarah Stegall

HarperPrism

A Division of HarperCollins*Publishers*

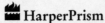

HarperPrism

A Division of HarperCollins*Publishers*

10 East 53rd Street, New York, NY 10022-5299

Thanks to Chris Helcermanas-Benge for the background photograph on poster and to Sarah Stegall for background research on poster.

The X-Files is a trademark of Twentieth Century Fox Film Corporation. All right reserved.

Copyright© 1998 by Twentieth Century Fox Film Corporation. All rights reserved. No part of this book may be used or reproduced in any manner whatsoever without written permission of the publisher, except in the case of brief quotations embodied in critical articles and reviews. For information address HarperCollins*Publishers*, 10 East 53rd Street, New York, NY 10022.

HarperCollins®, ® , and HarperPrism® are trademarks of HarperCollins*Publishers,* Inc.

HarperPrism books may be purchased for educational, business, or sales promotional use. For information, please write: Special Markets Department, HarperCollins*Publishers*, 10 East 53rd Street, New York, NY 10022-5299.

ISBN: 0-06-105386-4

Printed in the United States of America

Front cover photograph courtesy of Fox Broadcasting Company In-House Advertising Department. Photography by Michael Levine.

First printing: March 1998

Cover design: Carl Galian

Interior design: HOTFOOT Studio

Library of Congress Cataloging-in-Publication Data is on file with the publisher.

Visit HarperPrism on the World Wide Web at
http://www.harperprism.com

❖ 10 9 8 7 6 5 4 3 2 1

acknowlegments

Almost without exception, the talented and indescribably busy members of the *X-Files* team were gracious enough to interrupt their work and assist a nosy interloper. A number of non-Xites were of invaluable help, too.

Many thanks to:

Gary Allen, Val Arntzen, Laverne Bashem, Anji Bemben, Anne Bone, Bob Bowe, Jaap Broeker, Tara Butters, Al Campbell, George Chapman, James Charleston, Jodi Clancy, Thierry Couterier, Mark Currie, Chuck Eldridge, Tracy Elofson, Lawrence Farnsworth, Rick Fearon, J. P. Finn, Chuck Forsch (the real one), Connie Frieberg, David Gautier, Vince Gilligan, Gia Gittleson, Gregory Glaser, Sarah Goldstein, Bob Goodwin, Howard Gordon, Louisa Gradnitzer, Jenni Gullett, Nigel Habgood, Ken Hawryliw, Bonnie Hay, Sally Hudson, Shirley Inget, Simon Jori, Laurie Kallsen-George, Marilyn Kapatsky, Peter Kaufman, Louis Landon, Linda Leduc, Toby Lindala, Pearl Louie, Rob Maier, Kim Manners, Valerie and Vivian Mayhew, Steven Melnick, Mike McCabe, Marty McInally, Rick Millikan, Lori Jo Nemhauser, Vivian Nishi, Jim Pate, Mitch Pileggi, Todd Pittston, Paul Rabwin, Joel Ransom, Alan Rich, Bob Roe, Peter Roth, Joanne Service, John Shiban, Francine and Scott Sprigel, Mark Snow, John Solberg, Frank Spotnitz, David Steinberg, Michael Stern, Janice Swayze, Dave Tickell, Anita Truelove, Lyle Tuttle, Helga Ungarait, Alex Ward, Alan Warr, Michael Williamson, Stacy Wise, and Chandra Years.

My deepest respect and admiration to Chris Carter and Mary Astadourian. My heartfelt gratitude to Caitlin Blasdell, my talented editor, and to Maureen and Eric Lasher, my indomitable agents.

the **fifth** season:

tHE DATE: SEPTEMBER 10, 1993. A BUSY NEWS DAY. IN JERUSALEM, THE CHAIRMAN OF THE PALESTINE LIBERATION ORGANIZATION, YASIR ARAFAT, HAS SENT A LETTER TO YITZHAK RABIN, THE PRIME MINISTER OF ISRAEL, RECOGNIZING THE RIGHT OF THE JEWISH STATE "TO EXIST IN PEACE AND SECURITY." IN WASHINGTON, D.C., AIDES TO FIRST-YEAR PRESIDENT BILL CLINTON WORK FEVERISHLY ON THE REVOLUTIONARY HEALTH-CARE BILL THEY HOPE TO PUSH THROUGH THE DEMOCRATIC U.S. CONGRESS—THE FIRST IN A LONG LINE OF LIBERAL REFORMS. IN DETROIT, DR. JACK KEVORKIAN FACES TRIAL FOR PARTICIPATING IN HIS EIGHTEENTH ASSISTED SUICIDE.

The Joy Luck Club and *Sleepless in Seattle* are in the middle of their theatrical runs. The top-rated series on American television include *Roseanne*; *Murder, She Wrote*; and *The John Larroquette Show*.

A new series on the fourth-rated Fox Network, *The X-Files*, is premiering at 9:00 P.M., nestled between the heavily promoted *Adventures of Brisco County, Jr.* and that eagerly awaited late night entrant *The Chevy Chase Show*.

Few TV viewers have heard of *The X-Files'* stars, Gillian Anderson and David Duchovny. However, the name of the series' creator and executive producer, Chris Carter, *is* well known—as that of a talented (and slightly misspelled) wide receiver on the Minnesota Vikings.

Approximately 15 percent of the audience, tearing themselves away from programs like *The Bonnie Hunt Show* ("Bonnie wants to be in a soap ad") and *Step by Step* ("Cody and Carol protest an eviction"), tunes in to watch the painstakingly produced and provocatively plotted pilot episode. They witness the first meeting of FBI special agents Dana Scully and Fox Mulder—in a windowless basement office filled with pictures of UFOs, space aliens, yetis, and other detritus of what most authoritative observers (including network programming executives) consider the lunatic fringe. Of the few and mostly brief reviews the show receives, the majority are cautiously favorable.

The date: May 17, 1997. A fairly slow news day. Rebel leader Laurent Kabila enters Kinshasa, Zaire, and declares himself leader of the "Democratic Republic of the Congo." Lieutenant Kelly Flinn, a female B-52 pilot caught in an adulterous affair, requests an honorable discharge from the air force. The Middle East peace process has long since bogged down. Whatever it is that Dr. Jack Kevorkian is doing this day, he remains very much at large.

Shortly before midnight, a young woman named Lori Jo Nemhauser, in her second year as associate producer of *The X-Files*, finishes her eighteenth consecutive hour on the job and keeps right on working. She is at Encore Video, a state-of-the-art Hollywood production facility, and she is supervising the final stage of post-production on "Gethsemane," the final episode of the show's fourth season. It is an immensely complicated production filmed in—among many other difficult locations—a giant refrigerated warehouse cooled to approximately the same temperature as the surface of Mars. On Friday—way past any realistic deadline—Chris Carter (the executive producer, not the football player) has screened the episode, decided it could be significantly improved, and extensively reedited it. In so doing, he undoes much of the already frantic post-production work of the preceding week.

It is Nemhauser's job to re-mate the reedited sound with the reedited picture, make sure every credit and title is correct, and supervise the final color correction and cleanup of every frame of videotape. She works quickly. The Sunday evening North American time slot of *The X-Files*—perhaps the most anticipated, most fervently watched TV series on this planet—is just eighteen hours away.

Only a few graveyard-shift editors and technicians, plus one sleepy journalist, are present to watch Nemhauser race the clock. Which is a shame, really, because she is putting the finishing touches on a massive and truly amazing entity: the longest, most ambitious, and arguably the best season of the Fox Broadcasting Company's finest and highest-rated show.

One or two parts of the previous paragraph could perhaps be quibbled with, but the great majority of critics—both inside and outside the TV industry—would agree that *The X-Files* has continued to push the envelope. Most long-running television series tend to coast along on recycled plots and/or that easy familiarity between the audience and its characters. Many are produced by stand-ins for the original creators, now busy counting their money and—with scarcely a backward glance—moving on to new projects, new obsessions, and new beach houses.

Not *The X-Files*. As it neared its one hundredth episode, it remained concerned with exploring the possibilities of its original premise: that the world is full of intriguing, frustrating, compelling, tantalizing, and sometimes murderous ambiguities.

Moving through this nightmarish (and often quite funny) world are two passionate believers in totally opposite value systems: the renegade FBI agent Fox Mulder, explorer of outlandish possibilities and firm believer that mankind is blinding itself to the truth, and his partner, Dana Scully, a fiercely skeptical investigator who turns to science and logic in hopes of explaining the unexplainable.

Through the lens of their intensely passionate relationship, a weekly quota of conspiracies, conundrums, depravities, and otherworldly visitations are examined. In contrast to most other television series, each episode takes place in a different locale, tells its story in a different style, and offers different challenges to its creators and

viewers. It's a complicated and infinitely flexible formula that regularly intrigues a steadily growing body of hopelessly addicted fans.

So why does the series still work so well? Perhaps because the several hundred people *behind* the screen feel just as captivated by it. In fact, much more so. They feel a responsibility to the franchise, a duty to resist temptation and avoid compromising their vision.

"We've stayed on the path," says Chris Carter. "We've stayed true to the show—and as a result, the show has gotten better as we've gotten better."

A questioner asks Carter—the former surfer, magazine editor, and struggling TV writer-producer who is now one of the most well-known behind-the-scenes figures in American popular culture—how the passing of four intense years, and the inevitable changes both inside *The X-Files* and out, have affected the series. He squints, hunches his shoulders, and, with a vaguely puzzled expression, leans toward the coffee table in his office.

"The show's original spirit has become kind of the spirit of the country—if not the world," he says finally. "There is a growing paranoia. With the Berlin Wall down, with the global nuclear threat gone, with Russia trying to be a market economy, there is a growing paranoia, because as somebody once said, there are no easy villains anymore.

"On their own, people are starting to say things like 'Trust No One.' 'The Truth Is Out There.' That the world is run by selfish people whose motives are selfish—and as we all buy into the money culture, it is only going to get worse."

"The truth is that this has been my philosophy from the beginning," says Carter, smiling now. "And it's just a wonderful coincidence, isn't it?"

During the 1996–1997 season, *The X-Files'* size and influence grew in just about every way that such things can be quantified. Despite an early-season move from its familiar

Friday-night time slot to Sundays at 9:00 P.M, its total U.S. audience grew 12 percent, to approximately 18 million viewers.

The X-Files was the twentieth rated program of the season, by far the highest-rated series on the Fox Network. It was the fourth-highest hour-long drama, and in the top ten among young adults age eighteen to thirty-four—the viewers that advertisers crave. The X-Files regularly won its time period—in fact, the female-oriented TV movies that CBS programmed on Sunday nights were beaten so soundly that the Eye Network lopped off one night of movie programming and triggered an industry-wide reevaluation of the entire genre.

As one of the crown jewels of Twentieth Century Fox and its parent company, News Corp., it is a prime ingredient in that company's plans to span the globe with direct-broadcast satellites and blanket the Earth with irresistible TV programming. On August 19, 1997, the FX Channel, one of Fox's cable networks, began reruns of The X-Files. The first installment earned the highest rating of any prime-time program on basic cable, helping to nearly triple FX's usual prime-time audience. Ratings have stayed near that level ever since.

The X-Files theatrical movie, which was filmed during the summer of 1997, and which, plotwise, connects the fifth and sixth seasons, was slated to be a major summer release for Fox.

public and media interest in the show—and in David Duchovny, Gillian Anderson, and Chris Carter—continued unabated, to put it mildly. Several national magazines, including TV Guide and Entertainment Weekly, devoted entire issues, or nearly so, to the show. Several others ran cover stories on the show's stars. Last year Chris Carter was declared by Time magazine to be one of "the 25 most influential Americans" and People included him—as well as David Duchovny—in an article on "The 40 Most Fascinating People on Television." The latter piece skimmed over the fact that Carter, strictly speaking, isn't on television—and, shockingly, isn't interested in getting onto it.

"I've been asked to be on Charlie Rose's show once, and on Politically Incorrect about three times," says Carter, "but I honestly don't know what I would talk about. I don't pretend to have any or all of the answers about anything."

Carter adds, "I'm just doing what I know how to do, which is to create these television programs. In fact, because that's about all I do, I feel like I'm one of the dullest people in the world right now. So my opinions are definitely not entertainment."

because it definitely is entertainment, The X-Files frequently spills right over the borders of its time slot. During the fourth season Fox Mulder and Dana Scully made a joint guest-starring appearance on The Simpsons, tracking down an alien apparition that crossed the path of Homer Simpson (it was actually Mr. Burns, the town zillionaire, wandering the Springfield suburbs, glowing radioactively after some unconventional longevity treatments). David Duchovny's guest appearance as "himself" on HBO's The Larry Sanders Show—playing a prime-time star with a same-sex crush on Larry Sanders—won him an Emmy nomination for Best Guest Star in a comedy series.

On the evening of Sunday, September 15, 1997, Gillian Anderson made an impressive, if unscripted, appearance on a top-rated CBS program. During the following week, she took out ads in the Hollywood trade newspapers thanking Chris Carter, David Duchovny, and her other X-Files coworkers for helping her win her first Best Actress Emmy Award. It was one of three Emmys—and one of numerous other awards (see Awards)—won by The X-Files in 1997.

International popularity of the show continued to increase. The show was broadcast in at least fifty-seven separate countries during the 1996-97 season. In many of these countries, the show's ratings were equal or better than any other imported series.

In France, June of 1997, the nationwide elections were popularly know as "The X-Files Elections," because President

Jacques Chirac called them for reasons largely inexplicable to most French citizens.

Several European promoters urged *X-Files* composer Mark Snow to bring himself and his nonexistent orchestra over for a concert tour. On a promotional trip to Dublin, Ireland, supporting actors Mitch Pileggi (A.D. Skinner) and Nicholas Lea (Krycek) were mobbed by screaming fans after a personal appearance.

"We did a signing at a record store," says Pileggi, "and they had to sneak us out the back of the building. Then our car sped off and there were women running down the street chasing us. The car would hit a traffic jam and they would catch up and push against the windows. It was like *A Hard Day's Night*, for God's sake."

By necessity and by design, very little of that hysteria penetrates to the virtually self-contained world from which *The X-Files* emanates.

"We haven't had the chance to experience any of the global phenomena that we've heard about," says Chris Carter. "We all just keep our noses to the grindstone. I think if anything, because of the way I work and because of the way all the people around here work, we just sit around here doing the same work, which has become harder, and try to do it better."

As it has been from the very beginning, the center of the *X-Files* universe is a cluster of ramshackle bungalows and flimsy mobile office trailers in the southwest corner of the sprawling Twentieth Century Fox Studios in West Los Angeles. After all this time, there is still no apparent rhyme or reason to the office assignments, although a frequent visitor will eventually form a mental map of the show's various command posts, brain trusts, think tanks, and crisis centers.

These include: Building 49, the bungalow shared by Chris Carter, his executive assistant Mary Astadourian, his assistant Chuck Forsch, and a constantly rotating collection of tropical fish and wall art (including a proudly framed copy of the "The Ecch Files," the *Mad Magazine* parody of guess what); the offices of the core group of writers-producers—Frank Spotnitz, Vince Gilligan, and John Shiban; the bungalow fiefdom of consulting producers Glen Morgan and James Wong, who, after leaving *The X-Files* after the second season to produce their now-defunct syndicated drama *Space: Above and Beyond*, returned to *The X-Files* as a semi-autonomous writing-producing unit; Rick Millikan's tucked-out-of-the-way casting bungalow; and the narrow little building (located next to a similar one occupied by the production offices used by a stunning succession of unsuccessful Fox motion pictures) festooned with Christmas lights in the shape of a large "X," housing the computerized workspaces of editors Heather MacDougall, Jim Gross, and Michael Stern.

Anyone patient enough to stand around for several days is able to easily see the riveting sights of *The X-Files* in pre- and post-production: worried-looking writers traveling very much alone, in pairs and in packs, lugging index-card covered bulletin boards and/or scripts in progress from office to office; lights burning nonstop in Chris Carter's office as he splits each twenty-four-hour period equally between *The X-Files* and his other Fox Network show, *Millennium*; and, perhaps most importantly, an unending stream of restaurant delivery persons arriving to refuel the entire operation.

As if all this wasn't quite glamorous or exciting enough, the Fox movie studio was undergoing a multimillion-dollar expansion and renovation. Throughout the past season, work was frequently interrupted by blasts of pneumatic jackhammer noise; sudden and supremely inconvenient shutdowns of streets, roadways, and parking lots; and computer-killing weekend power outages.

"We're in the middle of a [expletive deleted] construction site," says coproducer Vince Gilligan, "and I don't think it's ever going to be finished."

He shakes his head, half in anger and half in sheer incredulity, and adds: "In March, I was on my way to Vancouver to do 'Small Potatoes,' and as the limo driver was pulling up to my office to take me to the airport, I walked over to the car, tripped over a bunch of construction debris, and cut the hell out of my hand. I was bleeding all the way to the airport, pressing a wad of tissues in my hand, and elevating it over my head. I had to go get a tetanus shot in Vancouver."

It is an *X-Files* truism that working conditions are a little less chaotic—but no less intense and pressured—at the series' Canadian production office.

"The fact is," says executive producer Robert Goodwin, who on most days is in charge of the several hundred individuals responsible for turning the L.A.-based writer-producers' scripts into exposed color film, "that if you're working on *The X-Files* you've got a job on the best—albeit the most challenging—show of all the ones that are filmed up here. And it's no problem, no problem at all, attracting the best talent when I have an opening."

"I keep a computer list," says Goodwin. "I talk to other producers and directors and production managers and actors, I get recommendations and names, and I put them on my computer list. And when the time comes to, say, find an art director, I look at my list and see if anybody with three stars next to his name is available. Then I call them and ask them to come in for an interview. Then I tell them how our show is different from the other shows they've been

on. Most are eager to try it out. A few work with us for a while and say, 'This is too crazy, this is too hard, and I just don't need this. So thank you very much—but I'm going to go home now.'"

As he has for the past four years, Goodwin—a veteran TV producer, director, and writer who lost more than forty pounds this season thanks to a punishing diet coupled with his punishing work schedule—operates mainly out of a corner office in the ground floor of a small office building at North Shore Studios, a compound that looks—at least from the outside, driving past on Brooksbank Avenue in North Vancouver—more like a suburban subdivision than a movie studio.

The rectangle of offices occupied by *The X-Files*, although relatively bright and new by Hollywood standards, is beginning to show some wear and tear from hundreds of ricocheting production assistants and blizzards of paper tacked and Scotch-taped to the walls. Hopeful actors line up outside Vancouver casting director Coreen Mayrs's office; racks of ski parkas, silver jumpsuits, and other assorted costumes, plus the occasional piece of lighting or camera equipment, line the halls.

Outside the back door, on one fairly typical day, sit three impeccably painted and equipped Providence, Rhode Island, police cars. A few hundred feet away, in a studio building whose exterior resembles a courthouse, set decorator Shirlee Ingett's impossibly cluttered office is filled with, among other things, upended pieces of old furniture, some looking extremely valuable, some not; computers and monitors, some in their boxes, some not; Cubist paintings; toasters; toys; houseplants; household cleaning supplies; Christmas lights; desktop nameplates; Kachina dolls; bowling pins; desktop Buddhas; framed carnival posters; tripods; steamer trunks;

and a complete set of antique surveyors' instruments.

Back in the main building is a receptionist's desk. Behind it is a small ironic shrine to *X-Files* merchandising: on a series of shelves are, among other things, *X-Files* posters, an alien doll, a giant *X-Files* cue ball, and, for some reason, a Cleveland Indians batting helmet. In front of the same desk are large racks holding a mind-boggling assortment of schedules, personnel rosters, scripts, script changes, ratings information, and memos. Hanging on a wall nearby is a box containing dozens of the most important document of all: the daily "call sheet" indicating every cast and crew member's start and finish time and including a hand-drawn map indicating the various locations to be utilized by the film crew throughout the day.

Casually dressed men and women—equipped usually with at least one cell phone, walkie-talkie, and pocket pager apiece—dash in and out the front door at all hours. Since *The X-Files*, unlike most TV dramas, is a virtual anthology series with few important "standing" sets, it is only sporadically filmed in the studio. Its cast and crew spend most of their time at rented locations within a half-hour's drive of North Shore; discrete yellow-and-black "XF" signs mark the active locations—they can be anything from the Vancouver Art Gallery to the Seymour Demonstration Forest to the Versatile Pacific Shipyards to a nondescript office building to the Elbow Room Cafe in downtown Vancouver—and staffers and visitors alike are shoehorned into their parking spaces by corps of radio-wielding PAs.

Parked somewhere nearby is an impressive portion of the series' large collection of production vehicles. The caravan, assembled daily by transportation coordinator Bob Bowe, usually consists of several sixty-five-foot tractor-trailer combinations; several smaller forty-foot trucks; several portable dressing rooms and makeup rooms; one or two "honey wagons" (translation: portable toilets) and mobile production offices; motor homes for the lead actors and prominent guest stars; a few

other miscellaneous vehicles, including the catering truck operated by Edible Planet—the local company that has been feeding *X-Files* personnel for several seasons; and David Duchovny's personal Airstream trailer.

The big trucks are the private preserves of individual production departments (such as lighting, camera, wardrobe, etc.). Inside them is virtually everything needed to make a movie virtually anywhere in the world. The entire rolling inventory is much too extensive to be catalogued, but here is just a tiny part of the contents of one truck assigned to the Props Department: dozens of fake plastic license plates; non-firing machine guns and assault rifles; black rubber pistols for stunt work; hundreds of wristwatches, pipes, and cigarette lighters; Scully and Mulder's personal effects—including their guns, holsters, and FBI wallet and hanging ID's—locked away in a safe to keep them from "curious" fans; on-set Polaroids and crime-scene photos; and a wastebasket full of plastic body bags in eight different colors.

A big diesel generator provides power to the set—which can usually be found by following the thick black cables from the generator truck. The area around the director, cameras, and actors is a jumble of crew members and equipment fairly familiar to regular viewers of TV shows like *Entertainment Tonight* and *Access Hollywood*.

Indeed, the atmosphere on the *X-Files* set is much like that on any other TV show—with the important exceptions that there is very little featherbedding or standing around. Also noteworthy: on top of the constant feeling of intensity and creative tension is a definite overlay of Canadian politeness and ironic humor. NO, YOU CAN'T SMOKE HERE, BUT THANKS FOR ASKING, reads a sign customarily attached to a location wall out of camera range. A bumper sticker on the side of sound mixer Michael Williamson's recording equipment cart reads: I (HEART SYMBOL) AIRPLANE NOISE.

The citizens of Vancouver, long accustomed to film crews in their midst, nevertheless are politely fanatical supporters of *The X-Files*. When the show is shooting at an outdoor daytime location, there is usually a small group of fans—generally carrying umbrellas against the Vancouver rain—standing at a respectful distance and watching patiently as the scene is shot, reshot, then shot again. They do not ask the actors for autographs.

"Oh, no, that would be disruptive," said one spectator, a bit alarmed, when asked one shooting day last spring if she ever asked for an autograph. She added that the rain seemed to be letting up, then craned her neck to see if she could catch another glimpse of Gillian Anderson.

I f the quality and uniqueness of *The X-Files'* fourth season is not always visible from curbside, it is certainly evident in the scope and variety of the episodes that reached the screen.

"I'll tell you this," says Robert Goodwin, "after my first three months I wanted to jump off a bridge, because what we were doing was impossible. I mean, when every script came in it was another huge challenge. Every single one—because they were all so different from the one before. And now, guess what? Those were *easy* compared to the ones we do now."

He adds, "Every year we want the shows to get better. And to get better, that means we have to get bigger. And that means it just gets harder."

As in the previous three years, this *X-Files* season included a mix of three very distinct kinds of episodes. In the first category are "mythology" shows, in which parts of the series' vast, shadowy government/alien conspiracy—as well as the main characters' own hidden pasts—are revealed. The second type is the "stand-alone" episode, where the agents tackle an unconnected crime or conspiracy involving paranormal forces, human greed or evil, or a combination of the two. The third type, not quite as easily categorized, mix large amounts of dark humor with the usual elements; they frequently incorporate subtle self-parody and are best appreciated by long-time fans who have internalized all the plot lines, traditions, quirks, and tics of the show.

As will be seen in the following pages, all three types of shows were well represented in Season Four. Mulder and Scully appeared in meticulously and expensively simulated locales ranging from Siberia ("Tunguska") to Florida ("Terma"); from the United Nations ("Herrenvolk," et. al) to Graceland ("Never Again"); from a corpse-strewn plane crash site ("Tempus Fugit") to a snow cave in the northern reaches of the Canadian Rockies ("Gethsemane").

In their travels, the two agents tracked down serial killers and psychotics, encountered racial prejudice and government venality, and uncovered and battled sinister international conspiracies as well as their own inner demons. They discussed complicated issues of philosophy, religion, and metaphysics—and were shot at, booby-trapped, assaulted, drugged, and threatened with sudden death and the loss of their dreams and careers more times than are healthy even for heroic figures.

Over the course of the ten-month shooting season, sets were built and scenes were filmed in such unlikely and inconvenient places as the bottom of water tanks, on active airport runways, and in a violently shaking airplane cabin. The show's nearly $2 million-per-episode budget increased—but so did the demands on everyone involved with spending it.

Dana Scully finally went on a date. Fox Mulder finally took a vacation. The show's eight-day main-unit shooting schedule stubbornly refused to get any longer.

It would be a mistake, however, to think that logistical heroics and on-screen miracles are the elements that hold the series together. Two of the main pillars upon which the series rests are the show's mythology and—just as importantly—the emotional relationship between the two main characters.

It's no coincidence, Chris Carter concedes with a smile, that the poster behind the desk in Mulder's office reads I WANT TO BELIEVE: Fox Mulder and Dana Scully have very strong—and as noted before, incompatible—belief systems.

But Mulder and Scully believe just as strongly in each other, and thus their struggle to reconcile the irreconcilable provided Chris Carter and his colleagues with much of the creative impetus for the season.

In fact, says Chris Carter, one of his most important creative decisions of the season—to "give" Scully a grave disease—was part of his long-range plan to raise the stakes in their central conflict.

Carter says: "They've dealt with death in an impersonal way, and they dealt with death in a very personal way. As we all do. And now, for various reasons, their own deaths are closer. And by dealing with that in poignant and responsible ways, we can't help but deepen and broaden their characters. And their relationship with one another."

Because of this, adds Carter, the viewers' relationships with Mulder, Scully, and the series' subsidiary characters—several of whom had their own encounters with the Grim Reaper last season—grow closer, too.

Understandably—and very much intentionally—all of these emotional attachments tend to overshadow the considerable amount of growing and changing going on behind the scenes. If you look carefully, however, you can sometimes see evidence of the individual dramas unspooling on the other side of the tube.

For instance, during the fourth season Chris Carter—who last year wrote eleven complete scripts, extensively rewrote an additional thirty-three or thirty-four credited to others, and reached levels of exhaustion unfamiliar even to him—carved out more time for Millennium and the X-Files movie by delegating some of his post-production oversight to relatively junior writer-producers like story editor John Shiban. "It was a great opportunity for me," says John Shiban, "because I got the chance to cut [edit] a lot of shows at the same time I was learning how to do it from people like Chris and Frank [Spotnitz]. It was a little different from film school, that's for sure."

Up in Vancouver, a thirty-five-year-old former X-Files camera operator named Joel Ransom was named to the vital post of director of photography: second in on-set authority only to the director and responsible for the lighting, framing, and shooting of every shot. "A *lot* of sleepless nights," was how he half-jokingly describes his reaction to the unexpected promotion. During the summer of 1996, camera operator Marty McInally, with the help of several local businessmen, invested $100,000 in gyro-stabilized Steadicam equipment and training; he now executes most of those tricky handheld shots for The X-Files.

Other X-Files staffers made new creative statements in the jobs they already held: hair stylist Anji Bemben, for instance, overhauled Fox Mulder's hairstyle—no small matter when the smallest of changes in his appearance are noted by millions of hyper-observant fans. Costume designer Jenni Gullett continued to upgrade Gillian Anderson's Scully wardrobe, selecting clothing by upscale designers and walking the fine line between excessive bureaucratic dowdiness and out-of-character glamour. Props master Ken Hawryliw continues to subtly change Scully and Mulder's ID badges, weapons, and other personal effects, bringing them as close to total authenticity (the FBI-standard Sig Sauer pistols they now carry were *not* the ones used in the pilot, he says disapprovingly) as the exigencies of weekly filming allow. "We've made some progress. But we're not quite there yet," says the bearlike Hawryliw.

Widening the focus a bit, other X-File figures made an impact outside the strict limits of the show. Following the lead of his boss, coproducer Frank Spotnitz divided his time between The X-Files, Millennium, and the X-Files feature film. Coproducer Vince Gilligan, who came to the series from a background of writing theatrical features, sold his script for a big-screen comedy, Home Fries, and saw it turn into a movie starring Drew Barrymore. A year into their very first network writing jobs as staff writers on The X-Files, sisters Valerie and Vivian Mayhew won a promotion to story editors—on the new Fox sci-fi series The

Visitor, where they will work, again as a team, during the 1997–1998 season.

After fifteen years of hard labor in Hollywood, Mitch Pileggi found himself in character-actor heaven, with steady and challenging work as Walter Skinner (he was in thirteen episodes this season); occasional guest-starring roles on other series and TV movies; a featured role in the *X-Files* feature film; and enough time left over to relax and rollerblade near his suburban Los Angeles home.

And this is the best part: "I don't have to go out on auditions any more," says Pileggi delightedly.

Even before she won her Emmy Award, Gillian Anderson found that her status as *The X-Files* leading actress won her new respect in the motion picture community. "People assume that I'm as strong and right-minded and intelligent as the character, which may or may not be true," says Anderson with a laugh. "As a result, it's raised the level of the scripts that I'm sent and the discussions that I've had with people about future projects."

She's looking forward, she says, to actually accepting one or two of them when she gets a few weeks off or when her wild ride on Chris Carter's juggernaut is over.

Which is not to say that the 1996–1997 season was without a measure of frustration, disappointment, and departures. Joel Ransom ably filled the post vacated by John Bartley, the show's original cinematographer, at the end of the third season only after two other directors of photography didn't work out. A similar situation occurred in the vital area of visual effects: not until the hiring of veteran computer wizard Laurie Kallsen-George at mid-season did the situation stabilize.

David Duchovny, while still working with his usual intensity and promising to fulfill his six-year contractual commitment to the series, has, toward the end of Season Four, begun to speak publicly about the physical and mental strains involved in playing one part for so long.

"It's way too long," said the actor last summer to a reporter from the *New York Times*. "There's a point at which it's not challenging anymore. Honestly, I wish they could introduce a new character—not more interesting than me, of course, but interesting—to change the focus a little."

(Some other changes might well be made. By the middle of the fifth season there was serious talk of moving the show's prime filming site—to Los Angeles. It is a move that Duchovny, married to Los Angeles-based sitcom star Téa Leoni, made no secret he desired—as also did, somewhat less publicly, Gillian Anderson.)

"It's not like I want to destroy the show," added Duchovny, "but I need room to think of other things."

but even as he was saying his good-byes, and as the *X-Files* feature film was in production around Los Angeles, preparations were well under way for Season Five. Outsiders' scripts were being read; new writer-producers were being hired; and new episodes, leading the way to the movie and then the perhaps conclusive sixth season, were being planned, plotted, and outlined.

During the summer Chris Carter announced that he was putting Glen Morgan and James Wong in charge of *Millennium*—and that he would devote all of his writing time (except, of course, for the new pilot script percolating in his brain) to *The X-Files*. Then, says Carter, he began working in earnest on the opening episodes of the next season—a heavily mythological two-parter.

"We tie together so many threads," says the *X-Files* creator, his face lighting up. "You're going to see things play out very interestingly."

Carter stops, thinks, smiles, and adds: "But the truth is, as much as we had planned, there are still so many things that we didn't foresee. It's an amazing thing—all of a sudden the show has taken on a life of its own. All of a sudden things are being dictated by the stories which have been told before. Things have their own beautiful symmetry.

"The episodes that begin the fifth season have some amazing things in it that are surprises to me. In the way it all came together it's almost crystalline in its beauty. It all makes me a little giddy actually."

The date: May 18, 1997. Saturday has slipped imperceptibly into Sunday, and at the video editing facility Lori Jo Nemhauser works on. The final color corrections are made; then a final check of the sound and titles; then a final close viewing of "Gethsemane," in real time, from beginning to end.

There are no imperfections visible to the naked eye. Listened to with headphones, the stereo soundtrack reverberates impressively inside an observer's sleep-deprived brain.

Looking only slightly fatigued herself, Nemhauser supervises the making of three high-quality tape copies: one for American broadcast, one for Canada, and a spare "safety master." Shortly after 5:00 A.M., she summons a messenger. At 5:46, the young man, carrying the work of hundreds of people under his arm, leaves Encore Video for the nearby Fox Broadcast Center. Nemhauser shakes hands with and hugs her remaining editing-room colleagues. Outside, in the parking lot, the sun is already bright in the morning sky.

herrenvolk

episode: 4X01

first aired: October 4, 1996

written by: Chris Carter

editor: Jim Gross

directed by: R. W. Goodwin

As Mulder's mother lies dying, he and Scully are
given tantalizing glimpses of a plan to secretly
catalog—and clone—human beings. Only by
putting the pieces together can they hope to
save Mrs. Mulder's life.

guest stars:
Mitch Pileggi (AD Walter Skinner)
William B. Davis (The Cigarette-Smoking Man)
Roy Thinnes (Jeremiah Smith)
Brian Thompson (The Bounty Hunter)
Steven Williams (X)
Laurie Holden (Marita Covarrubias)
Garvin Cross (Repairman)
Rebecca Toolan (Mrs. Mulder)
Vanessa Morley (Young Samantha)
Don S. Williams (The Elder)
Morris Panych (The Gray-Haired Man)
Brendan Beiser (Agent Pendrell)
Casey and Sean Murphy (Young Blond Boy)
Michael David Simms (Senior Agent)
Ken Camroux (2nd Senior Agent)
Liza Huget (Nurse)

principal settings:
Rural Alberta, Canada;
rural Maryland;
Providence, Rhode Island;
Washington, D.C.;
United Nations headquarters,
New York City, New York

On a lonely Canadian back road, a repairman climbs a telephone pole and begins his work. He is stung by a bee, swats it with a grimace of pain, and glances downward. Five identical blond-haired boys, around twelve or thirteen years old, are staring impassively up at him.

"Well, now. Don't you ever take the cake!" he says. "Your mom ever get you mixed up?"

The repairman's expression of surprise turns to distress. He starts to shake and convulse violently, loses his grip on the pole, and falls to the ground. The boys briefly contemplate his death, then turn and walk—without saying a word—into the grasslands beyond.

In a brief flashback from "Talitha Cumi" (3X24), the last episode of Season 3, Mulder and Scully meet Jeremiah Smith—a.k.a. the Healing Man—at a deserted sawmill. Mulder wants Smith to cure his mother, who suffered a massive stroke in this episode. Smith wants to pass along to Mulder his knowledge of a sinister Syndicate/alien conspiracy—which he does at grave risk to his life.

"Mulder, he knows about your sister," says Scully.

"How do I know you're for real?" Mulder asks.

"I can explain everything to you," says Smith.

"First, I want you to come with me," says Mulder. "I want you to come see my mother."

Headlights illuminate the scene. It is the alien Bounty Hunter, stiletto in hand, driving toward them. Smith flees.

"Stay out of his way, Scully," says Mulder. "He doesn't want to hurt you. You can't use your gun."

Mulder pursues Smith. Against Mulder's advice, Scully draws her weapon and aims it at the Bounty Hunter, who—ignoring her warnings for him to stop—moves inexorably toward her.

The action of Episode 4X01 resumes: the Bounty Hunter runs right through Scully, swatting her aside and causing her to fall hard to the ground.

A complicated three-way chase ensues. The Bounty Hunter stalks Smith through the sawmill's interior, but Mulder catches up with him first. Just a step or two ahead of the alien, he leads Smith outside to momentary safety. He calls to his partner to get their car.

Scully runs to the vehicle, starts it, and becomes an unwitting decoy. The Bounty Hunter, believing that Smith is getting away, leaps feet first onto the car's roof.

This gives Mulder enough time to set up an ambush. He leads Smith away and buries himself in a pile of wood chips, leaping out to stab the Bounty Hunter at the base of his neck with the alien stiletto he found in his mother's beach house in "Talitha Cumi" (3X24).

The Bounty Hunter falls, apparently dead. Green ooze bubbles from his puncture wound.

Mulder runs after Smith, who is escaping the scene in a motorboat. Mulder shouts to him: "Jeremiah, stop! What are you doing?"

"There'll be more—right behind him," shouts Smith.

"You can't leave here!"

"They'll kill me!"

"I need your help!" says Mulder. "My mother is dying!"

On the other side of the sawmill site, Scully leaves the car and runs to rejoin Mulder. He is in Smith's boat; they are pulling quickly away from the shore. Scully calls after them, but they do not respond.

She returns to the body of the Bounty Hunter and checks him for vital signs. The hulking figure reaches up, grabs her by the throat with one hand, and squeezes.

"Where are they going?" asks the Bounty Hunter.

"I don't know," says Scully, straining to breathe.

"I need to know," the alien replies.

He pulls the stiletto from his neck, then releases his grip on Scully. She gasps desperately for air.

Mulder and Smith dock their boat at an abandoned pier. Once again, Mulder asks Smith to go with him to help his mother,

but Smith insists that Mulder first accompany him to see "the larger plan."

"The larger plan," says Mulder. "You mean colonization?"

"Hegemony, Mr. Mulder," says Smith. "A new origin of species."

Mulder begs Smith to postpone the trip, but again Smith refuses. He says that "government men" will be waiting to intercept them at the hospital.

"And I will be dead," says Smith. "I won't be able to save your mother. The work will go on. The plan will continue to be executed. Or you can stop it."

"How can I stop it?" says Mulder.

"I can take you to a place, show you the work in progress, where you can see—"

"No! Look! There's no time!" says Mulder.

"Where you can see your sister!" says Smith.

These words hit Mulder with the force of an unanticipated punch. He falls silent, stunned.

In the hospital room where Mrs. Mulder is on life support, the Cigarette-Smoking Man—accompanied by his fellow Syndicalist the Elder, last seen in "Apocrypha" (3X16)—is indeed waiting.

"He isn't coming," says the Elder.

"I told you," says the Cigarette-Smoking Man.

"Then where is he?"

"I don't know," says Cancer Man. "Certainly he anticipated we'd be here waiting for him."

Silently, the Gray-Haired Man, last seen in "Avatar" (3X21), enters the room from its small private bathroom, tucking his weapon back into his shoulder holster.

The Elder suggests that there has been a security leak. He produces some photos of the Cigarette-Smoking Man visiting Mrs. Scully at her beach house and suggests that the unknown photographer be smoked out by leaking some information.

"What information?"

"That Mrs. Mulder's life is in danger," says the Elder. "That left unprotected, she may come to an unnatural end."

The Cigarette-Smoking Man, a bit shaken, agrees.

From a stolen car, Mulder phones Scully—still at the sawmill—to say that he and Smith are in Canada.

"Listen to me," he says. "There are going to be people looking for you. And they're going to think they can get to me through you."

"Mulder—"

"No, no, listen," says Mulder. "There's going to be a record of me going through Canadian Customs, and I need you to cover my tracks. I also need you to know that I'm okay, Scully. I'm fine."

As he says this, we see that the Bounty Hunter is behind Scully, listening. After he hears what he needs to know, he departs rapidly.

"Mulder, he's coming after you!" says Scully.

"Who?"

"The man who you left for dead. He's alive."

Shortly afterward, deep in the Canadian prairie, the stolen car runs out of gas and slows to a stop.

"How much further from here?" asks Mulder.

"Twenty miles," says Smith. "Maybe half that on foot." The pair begin trekking over the rolling green hills.

Back at FBI headquarters, the still-shaken Scully answers a summons to AD Skinner's office. Agent Pendrell is seated at a computer monitor.

Skinner asks Scully the status of her and Mulder's investigation. She lies, telling him that they are still searching for Jeremiah Smith.

Skeptical, Skinner tells her that a computer search has turned up five Jeremiah Smiths—with identical photo IDs—working at Social Security offices around the country. All these men have been missing from their jobs for three days; all were found to have vast amounts of encrypted data on their computer hard drives.

Pendrell shows Scully a small portion of the data: screen after screen of seemingly meaningless letter and number strings, all beginning with the letters SEP. Scully asks Pendrell to download a sample for her.

"There's someone I'd like to run this by," she explains.

Near the end of their long hike, Mulder and Smith reach the dead telephone repairman, still lying where he fell. His face is

"Being grown for what?"

"Pollen," says Smith.

Mulder scans the farm through his binoculars. He is shocked by what he sees. A blond girl, accompanied by one of the blond boys from the opening scene, is tending the plants.

"What is this?" says Mulder. "What's going on here?"

"What did I tell you, Mr. Mulder?" says Smith.

"That looks just like my sister," says Mulder.

He stares at Smith, who says nothing.

"That's not possible," says Mulder. "She's no older than the day she was taken."

Smith still does not reply.

shriveled and withered; ants crawl over his exposed skin.

"What happened to this man?" says Mulder.

"I wouldn't touch the body, Mr. Mulder," says Smith.

They walk over the next rise. In the valley below are a series of green fields. The crop being grown is not immediately recognizable, primarily because the fields are covered by tarpaulins suspended six feet above the ground.

"You're looking at the future, Mr. Mulder," says Smith.

"What is it?"

"A flowering shrub, but its specific epithet can't be found on any of your taxonomic charts."

Mulder runs toward the valley, calling his sister's name. The little girl stands still, waiting for him amid the alien plants, which are swarming with bees.

"Samantha, it's me," says Mulder. "Fox—your brother. Do you remember me?"

Samantha is silent. She is, in fact, completely expressionless.

"She has no language, Mr. Mulder," says Smith, right behind him. "She's a drone. A worker."

"What are you talking about?" says Mulder.

"There's more that you should see," says Smith. "So that you might understand."

Smith shows an anguished Mulder—who grips Samantha's hand tightly—the

rest of the farm. More copies of Samantha and the blond boy work silently among the rundown buildings.

"They're clones," says Mulder, shaken.

"Serial ovotypes," says Smith. "Have you seen enough, Mr. Mulder? We can't stay around here much longer. Let's see if we can find some gas."

In Washington, Scully enters Mulder's apartment and places an X of masking tape on his window. She pores over the computer printouts. Shortly afterward there is a knock on Mulder's door. Scully pulls her gun from its holster.

"Open the door, Agent Scully," says X.

Scully lets him in. The double agent has a message he wants Scully to relay to Mulder. It is a message about his mother.

"Let me just say," says X, nervously, "that she is unprotected."

"From whom?" Scully asks.

X heads for the door. "If you want to involve yourself, Agent Scully," he says, "you'd do well to give this information to your partner."

"Not until you give me some information first," Scully says.

Scully shows X the printouts and presses him for their meaning.

"You're going in the wrong direction, Agent Scully," he says.

Scully stands her ground. "You know what these are," she says. "Confirm or deny."

Reluctantly, X tells her that SEP stands for Smallpox Eradication Program. "But

don't unlock doors you're not prepared to go though, Agent Scully," he adds.

"What is that supposed to mean?" Scully asks.

"Leave it alone," says X. "Protect the mother."

At the farm in Canada, Smith finds a jerrican filled with gasoline. Mulder prepares to leave with him—and Samantha.

"You can't do this," says Smith. "She's not your sister."

"Then who is she?" says Mulder.

Smith shakes his head impatiently. "You have a chance here to understand something so much greater," he says. "To comprehend it and expose it."

"Well, then, explain it to me!" says Mulder angrily. "Explain it to me *now*!"

At this moment the Bounty Hunter, driving a car at great speed, roars up a dirt road toward them. Mulder, Smith, and Samantha run for their lives. They are chased into a field and onto another part of the farm.

Samantha leads them to an underground bunker. It is a giant apiary, filled with huge hanging honeycombs and swarms of infectious bees. Smith says that he and Samantha are immune to them, but that Mulder is not.

Mulder douses himself with gasoline to fend off the insects. The trio enters the apiary. Mulder lays a trap by splashing gas on a honeycomb. It is weakened, and they push it over on the pursuing Bounty Hunter, who writhes in pain as he is swarmed under by the angry insects.

At FBI headquarters, Scully explains to Pendrell that she has partially cracked the computer code: It is based on sequences of amino acids and represents the molecular makeup of the cowpox virus that is the basis of the smallpox vaccine. Every one of the millions of humans who have been vaccinated carries a slightly different code.

Then Scully explains her theory to a gathering of senior agents. Many of them don't understand her; the rest are clearly unconvinced.

"So what you're saying, Agent Scully," says Skinner, "is that we've been cataloged, tagged, and inventoried. By who?"

"I don't know. But it would have to a gov-ernment agency," Scully says.

A senior agent asks: "And to what pur-pose?"

"I don't know," says Scully. "And I think the only man who can answer that is Jeremiah Smith."

A short time later, Smith is sitting with Samantha in the Bounty Hunter's car. Mulder has parked it at a roadside phone booth. He calls Scully and tells her to meet them all at his mother's hospital room.

The Bounty Hunter—his face covered with smallpox sores—roars up in the Canadian telephone repairman's truck. He smashes into the phone booth and caroms to a stop against the car.

Mulder dives for his life. Smith and Samantha cower in the backseat of the smashed sedan. With his massive strength, the Bounty Hunter grabs Mulder and lifts him off his feet.

"Please, you can't kill him," gasps Mulder. "He can't die."

"He must," the Bounty Hunter says impassively.

"That girl is my sister," says Mulder.

"He shows you pieces," says the alien, with what might be contempt. "He tells you nothing of the whole. Because he is incon-sequential. A traitor to the project."

"Kill me," begs Mulder. "Let them go."

"You'd trade your life for his?"

"For my mother's," Mulder pleads.

Smith struggles out of the car. Limping, he tries to get away. The Bounty Hunter looks at Mulder with what might be com-passion.

"Everything dies," he says.

He flings Mulder against the side of the repair truck. The battered agent falls to the ground unconscious.

The alien retrieves his stiletto and sets off to kill Jeremiah Smith. Seeing this, Samantha is suddenly frightened. She screams in ter-ror—an unearthly, incoherent wail.

Five hours later, the corridor outside Mrs. Mulder's hospital room swarms with FBI

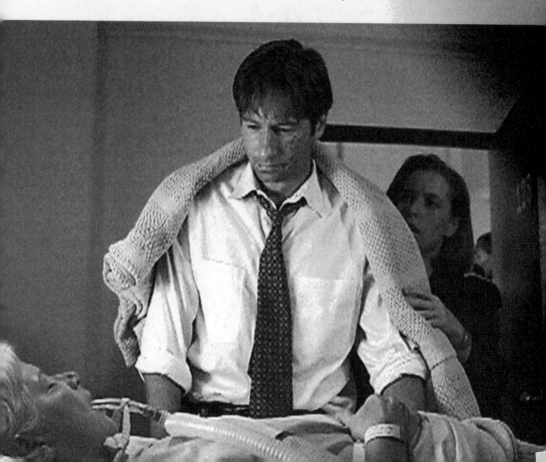

agents. Mulder, exhausted and in shock, arrives.

He brushes past Skinner and Scully, enters his mother's room, and gazes down at her unconscious form.

"She'll never know," he says.

Scully takes him into her arms, and he begins to cry.

At Mulder's apartment, the crossed-tape signal is on the window again. X enters and is alarmed to see that the apartment is dark and empty. He leaves and walks quickly to the elevator. The elevator door opens and a black-gloved hand, holding a silenced pistol, emerges. X is shot in the chest and falls backward to the floor.

In Mrs. Mulder's room, Mulder and Scully sit by her bed.

"I could have saved her, Scully," says Mulder in despair. "I had one chance. And I let it slip away."

"We don't know that, Mulder," says Scully gently. "You can't blame yourself for what you could only hope."

"He took me to a place with green fields. I saw my sister. She was a little girl. I've seen too many things not to believe."

"There are answers to be found now, Mulder. We have hope that there are places to start. That's what I believe."

Mulder says, "You put such faith in your science, Scully. But the things I've seen, science provides no place to start."

"Nothing happens in contradiction to nature," says Scully, her eyes shining with respect and passion for her partner. "Only in contradiction to what we know. And that's a place to start. That's where the hope is."

Mulder looks at her with gratitude. "I feel I came so close," he whispers.

"I feel that, too," says Scully. "I know it. I was warned."

"By who?"

"By a man we both know. Who I believe knows the truth. Who can lead us to a place to start."

In the corridor of Mulder's building, the man known as X lies dying. He gasps and moans with the effort of breathing; blood pours from his wounds and coats his lips.

With his last reserve of strength, X drags himself back to Mulder's door. His last conscious act is to trace the letters "S," "R," "S," and "G"—in his own blood—on the carpet.

It is one month later. At United Nations headquarters in New York, Mulder enters the office of the Special Representative to the Secretary General.

He is met by the representative's assistant, an attractive woman in her late thirties named Marita Covarrubias. She tells him that the representative is too busy to see Mulder, but pursuant to his inquiries, she has determined that the farm in Canada has been abandoned.

"The crops you described were left to die," she says. "But they have been identified as ginseng. No evidence of bee hives or bee husbandry was found. I know it's not the answer you want."

Seeing Mulder's disappointment, she asks why the matter is so important to him.

"I've suffered some very personal losses lately," he says. "I was hoping. . . ."

He turns to leave. As he does so, Covarrubias hands him a file folder. In it is a photograph of Samantha, along with several other identical girls, working the fields in which Mulder had seen her.

"Not everything dies, Mr. Mulder," says the diplomat.

In Mrs. Mulder's hospital room, the Cigarette-Smoking Man and the Bounty Hunter stand over her.

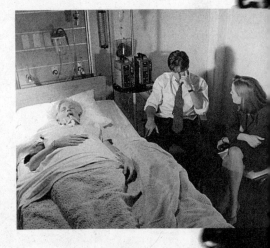

"I need to know the reasons why this should be," says the Bounty Hunter.

"So that the work may continue," says the Cigarette-Smoking Man. "So that the project can go on unabated by removing an unnecessary obstacle."

"What obstacle?"

"Agent Mulder, actually," says the Cigarette-Smoking Man. "If his mother were to die, he—"

"He what?"

"You see, the fiercest enemy is the man who has nothing left to lose. And you know how important Agent Mulder is to the equation."

The Bounty Hunter pauses for a moment. Then he walks to the door and closes it. He places his hand on Mrs. Mulder's forehead, closes his eyes, and concentrates. Mrs. Mulder's own eyes open wide. She looks up at the Cigarette-Smoking Man. She is a healthy, fully conscious woman.

back story:

"Herrenvolk" (translation from the German: "Master Class") is the first installment of another twenty-four-episode marathon. It ties up several significant loose ends from the third season, including the fate of Jeremiah Smith, the "Healing Man"; the survival of Mulder's mother; and the current mission of the alien Bounty Hunter.

"Also," says Chris Carter, "I wanted to bring back Mulder's sister as an important element. She's part of the lifeblood of the show."

On the other side of the ledger, "Herrenvolk" marks the introduction of one of the main

"But we felt that there was only so much we could do with him at this level of involvement. Our big decision was to either escalate him, make him a bigger player in the show—which we were considering—or have him pay the price for collaborating with Mulder."

With X's eradication, Chris Carter and his writing staff saw a chance to introduce yet another variant of the shadowy informant—the alternatively sultry and severe Marita Covarrubias, whose relationship with Mulder seems to extend past strictly professional boundaries. To play her they chose Laurie Holden, an experienced television actress whose binational lifestyle—she was raised in Canada but now lives in Los Angeles (she was in Vancouver filming another TV project when she auditioned for the part of Marita)—seems to oddly echo The X-Files' own.

"I'm not complaining," says Holden, much of whose previous work has been in female-oriented TV movies, "but the whole thing is

themes that runs through the fourth season (and perhaps beyond): the alien/syndicate conspiracy to monitor and control the Earth's population via smallpox-based genetic markers.

Judging from fan mail and Internet reaction, though, the episode will best be remembered for the death of X, an X-Files mainstay since early in the second season. According to coproducer Frank Spotnitz, the decision to eradicate X was made at the close of the third season.

"I personally liked the character," says Spotnitz with considerable feeling. "He actually had some action scenes, as opposed to Deep Throat, whom he essentially replaced, who'd just show up and talk.

so secretive that I really wasn't told much at all about where my character was going. I just went on my instincts—that the key to this character is that she has a secret—and that this secret, which gives my character a kind of through line, would be revealed in the future."

The through line for the Vancouver-based cast and crew was an above-average amount of improvisation and aggravation. To film the enormously complicated chase scenes at night, the show spent a considerable amount of time after sundown at a shut-down Vancouver-area sawmill. The gloomy, rusty structure was torn down completely just a few weeks later.

To get the proper atmosphere for the alien bee husbandry scenes, Chris Carter threw caution to the winds and authorized an unprecedented location shoot near the town of Kamloops, well beyond the radius in which the Vancouver-based production had previously sojourned. "Chris had asked me to find something interesting and different," says locations manager Todd Pittston, "so I went out there scouting and found this very cool ginseng farm. When I drove him down there to show it to him, he said, 'Great!'"

Not so great. According to executive producer Bob Goodwin, who directs the first and last episodes of each season, the company's hair, makeup, and wardrobe truck got hopelessly lost on the three-and-a-half-hour drive from Vancouver. Way beyond the range of cellular phones, it wandered around for three hours—stopping all filming dead in its tracks—before it rejoined the rest of the company. A scene had to be dropped from the Kamloops shooting schedule and expensively reshot back in Vancouver.

While waiting for the missing van, recalls Goodwin, the company members could only gaze at the "two little old beekeepers in shorts" who stood among their swarms of stinging insects. And for all their buzzing menace in the open air, the bees would prove to have the even more horrifying habit of practically disappearing on exposed film. This meant that they would have to be painstakingly and expensively electronically enhanced and "doubled" by the visual effects department in postproduction.

In the meantime, the bees created considerable on-set apprehension. "I used an acting exercise to keep them off me," says Brian Thompson, who played the alien Bounty Hunter. "I said to myself: 'I am concrete. I am not honey. No stings.'"

David Duchovny recalls with some pride that he avoided getting stung, even once. This was not the case, unfortunately, for Vanessa Morley, the child actor who played the eight-year-old Samantha Mulder.

"It happened when were filming the scene at the entrance to the bunker," says Goodwin, "but she was brave. She didn't flinch or yell out until I said 'cut.' She was really wonderful."

Adds Goodwin: "Afterwards, we had a kind of purple heart plaque made up by the props department. It was an award for 'bravery beyond the call of duty.' Gillian presented it to her in a little ceremony two weeks later."

The tagline for this episode is "Everything Dies." This is what the alien Bounty Hunter says to Mulder in a parking lot as he is tracking down Jeremiah Smith.

Ⓧ

In this episode, X becomes the second of Mulder's informants to be shot and killed. Like Deep Throat, he too leaves a dying message for Mulder, scrawling "SRSG" in his own blood. We later learn that the initials stand for "Special Representative to the Secretary General" of the United Nations.

Ⓧ

What's the first name—never uttered on the show—of Mulder's mother? "It's Teena," says Chris Carter.

Ⓧ

To create the massive hanging honeycombs for the underground apiary sequences, the construction coordinator used a Fiberglas composite lattice, used in the aircraft industry, that is, appropriately enough, commonly known as "honeycomb."

Ⓧ

unruhe

episode: 4X02

first aired: October 27, 1996

written by: Vince Gilligan

editor: Heather MacDougall

directed by: Rob Bowman

Someone is abducting, mutilating, and
murdering the inhabitants of a small
town. The primary evidence is a series
of photographs depicting the killer's
psychotic fantasies.

guest stars:
Pruitt Taylor Vince (Gerry Schnauz)
Sharon Alexander (Mary Lefante)
Scott Heindl (Boyfriend)
Walter Marsh (Druggist)
Angela Donahue (Alice Brandt)
William MacDonald (Officer Trott)
Ron Chartier (Postal Inspector Puett)
Bob Dawson (Iskenderian)
Michael Cram (Officer Corning)
Christopher Royal (Photo Tech)
Michele Melland (ER Doctor)
John D. Sampson (Second Cop)

principal settings:
Traverse City, Michigan;
Washington, D.C.

On a rainy day in northwest Michigan, a nervous young couple drives up to a drugstore. The young woman, Mary Lefante, walks inside and asks the elderly druggist to take her picture for a passport.

She smiles. He snaps a Polaroid photo and sets it aside to develop. Another customer, his face obscured by the hood of a yellow slicker, passes behind her.

Mary tells the druggist she has forgotten her money in her car. She exits and is brushed from behind by the hooded figure.

She has been pricked by a sharp object—apparently a drug delivery device of some sort. As the drug takes effect, she staggers to the car. She sees that her boyfriend, blood flowing from a wound in his ear, is dead. His cigarette is still smoldering in his mouth.

Mary falls to the ground and sees the hooded figure, face still obscured, towering over her. His gloved hands cover her mouth with duct tape. Then he zips her, still conscious, into a body bag.

Inside the store, the druggist mutters disgustedly and peels open the Polaroid. The fully developed photo shows Mary, face blurred and horribly distorted, screaming in abject terror.

Mulder and Scully drive into town in their rented car.

"Have the local police been contacted by the woman's abductor?" asks Scully.

Mulder shakes his head.

"No demand for ransom?"

"No," says Mulder. "Unfortunately, it's going on three days."

"Any additional leads?"

"No," says Mulder. "No hair or fiber evidence, either. The rain washed it all away. The autopsy did come back on the dead boyfriend, though. It's a puncture wound through the left eardrum and into the brain. Possibly from a long needle, or awl."

"I'm still not sure how you and I figure into the investigation," says Scully. The obvious solution to the crime, she adds, is that whoever took the photograph of Mary was privy to the woman's abduction.

"That *is* what you would think," says Mulder impatiently.

The agents interview the druggist. He doesn't look like much of an alleged kidnapper: He is gray-haired, mild-mannered, and wears a polio brace on one leg.

"I sure hope you find that young woman safe and sound," he tells the agents.

He limps away to help a customer.

"So, which one of us gets to use the stun gun on Bruno Hauptmann back there?" says Mulder.

"All right. So he doesn't exactly stand out as a suspect," says Scully.

Scully reexamines the photograph, then suggests that the strange image might have been caused by out-of-date film or thermal damage from a nearby space heater. Mulder takes all this in with an expression of pure skepticism.

"All right," says Scully. "What's your theory?"

"I'm not quite sure I have a theory," says Mulder.

A local policeman arrives. He takes them to Mary Lefante's home, where he introduces them to a U.S. postal inspector named Puett.

Puett tells them that the couple—she was a mail sorter, he was a forger—was involved in the theft of unsigned credit cards. The inspector suggests that Mary, afraid of capture, might have faked her disappearance.

"But why would she stab her boyfriend through the ear?" asks Mulder. "The magic was gone?"

Mulder searches Mary's room and finds a cheap Polaroid camera. He covers its lens with his hand while he snaps off several pictures.

"What are you doing?" says Scully.

"In the sixties," says Mulder, "a bellhop named Ted Serios became kind of famous for taking what he called 'thoughtographs.' He claimed that by concentrating on an unexposed film negative he could create a photographic representation of what he saw in his mind.

"He did landscapes, cathedrals, the Queen of England. . . ."

"'Thoughtographs,'" says Scully, taking her turn as the skeptic.

"Also known as 'Skotographs,'" says Mulder. "The literature on thought photography dates almost to Louis Daguerre."

"So that makes it legitimate."

Mulder doesn't answer. He is staring downward at the photographs.

Scully follows his gaze. "Oh, my God!" she says.

As the pictures slowly develop, they each bear the identical image of Mary—screaming in terror and surrounded by frightening, demonlike figures.

"I think he was here, Scully," says Mulder. "Mary Lefante's abductor. I think he stalked her."

Mulder examines the balcony adjacent to the bedroom.

"I think he came in here and he looked at her through the window—this close," he says. "Close enough to affect the film in that camera."

Scully insists that somebody somehow doctored the images and planted them in the camera, perhaps to throw them off the path of the credit card thieves.

"This isn't about mail fraud, Scully," says Mulder. "That's just incidental."

He adds, "What if—what if—someone had this ability. An image like this would be a peek into that person's mind."

"Into their darkest fantasies," says Scully grudgingly.

"The fantasies of a killer," says Mulder.

On a two-lane highway outside of town, Mary Lefante, barefoot and wearing a soiled nightgown, pulls herself out of the underbrush and walks slowly along the shoulder. A police car, siren on and lights flashing, pulls in behind her. Her expression is completely, eerily blank.

Mulder and Scully arrive at the local hospital. An ER doctor tells them that Mary has traces of morphine and scopolamine—the dental anesthetic known as twilight sleep—in her bloodstream.

"Would that account for her condition?" asks Mulder.

"No. It wouldn't," says Scully.

"What would?"

Scully raises Mary's eyelid and stares into her blank blue eye.

"Give her a PET scan," she says.

The machine does its work, creating a multicolored image—a cross-section of Mary's brain.

"Oh, my God," says Scully. "She's been given what's known as transorbital lobotomy. It's what used to be called an 'ice pick' lobotomy. It involves inserting a leukotome through the eye sockets."

"So we're looking for a doctor?" says Mulder. "Someone with training?"

"Not judging by this," says the ER doctor.

"Whoever did this," says Scully, "did it wrong."

As this horrible fact sinks in, Mary's voice comes through the scanner room's intercom system.

"Unruhe. . . unruhe. . . ." she says.

The strange word is spoken in a weird, unearthly moan. A local policeman enters the tomography room to speak to the agents.

"We just got a call," he says. "There's been a second abduction."

At an undetermined location, a woman—she is a secretary named Alice Brandt—peers out of the darkness. She too has been drugged; her mouth has been taped and her arms and legs strapped to an old dentist's chair.

Her kidnapper, whose face we cannot see, shines a light on her and speaks softly to her in German.

Alice's head begins to clear. She looks up with slowly rising comprehension. The kidnapper's hand—holding an ice pick–like object, a leukotome—rises into view. Alice tries to scream for help through the tape. The man sets down the leukotome on an instrument tray. Also on the tray is a loaded hypodermic syringe.

Alice's eyes shine with terror.

At the office from which Alice Brandt was abducted, Mulder and Scully resume their investigation.

They learn that Alice's boss, an accountant, was found dead of a stab wound through his ear. The agents discuss the significance of the word *"unruhe,"* which Scully, who reveals here that she studied German in college, says means "unrest."

Scully examines a series of police photos—apparently normal—and spots an identical construction company sign at both crime scenes. Mulder congratulates her and announces that he is returning to Washington to examine the strange Polaroids.

Scully's expression indicates that she thinks he's wasting his—and the kidnap victim's—time. Mulder points to the Polaroids.

"I still think the answer's in here," he says.

"What if it's not, Mulder?" says Scully angrily. "This woman's time is running out."

"That's all the more reason to fully investigate the one piece of hard evidence that we do have," says Mulder. "I'll be in touch."

In the room where she is being held captive, the faceless kidnapper holds up a new nightgown against Alice's shoulders.

He speaks softly in German again.

Alice shakes her head and loosens the duct tape on her mouth. "Get away from me!" she yells. "Get away from me, you bastard!"

The kidnapper calmly peels off a fresh strip of tape and seals her mouth again.

At FBI headquarters, Mulder works with a photo technician to examine one of the Mary Lefante's Polaroids. The tech scans it onto his computer screen and enlarges it. He concedes ruefully that he can't tell how the photos were doctored.

Mulder asks him to blow up a small facelike blob in the corner of the picture. It becomes a larger facelike blob. After a few rounds of digital enhancement, however, it becomes—still somewhat blurred—the unmistakable face of an old man.

At Traverse City police headquarters, Scully questions a man named Iskenderian, the owner of the construction company whose sign was seen in the crime photos. Scully asks him where the person in charge of the job near the accountant's office is now working.

At the FBI photo lab, Mulder asks the technician to enlarge and enhance a small shadow behind Mary's head. It is the shadow of a man, but strangely elongated.

"It's the kidnapper's shadow," says Mulder. "It's like he's looming over her. Standing over her, he means to pass judgment on her. Like a god."

Scully's rented Ford Explorer stops at an apartment house under renovation.

"Hello?" she shouts through the seemingly deserted building. "Hello?"

She climbs an unfinished stairway to a second-floor corridor. She hears a strange metallic clicking noise from the other end.

A very tall man walks stiffly toward her. "Hi! Can I help you?" he asks.

He identifies himself as Gerry Schnauz, the foreman. In response to Scully's question, he tells her that all the laborers who work for him are at lunch.

Scully's cell phone rings. It's Mulder.

"I may have something about the kidnapper," he says. "It's something about his legs. They're out of proportion. I'm thinking he's either very tall—or not, and wants to be."

Scully puts down the phone and turns to Gerry. He is actually a normal-sized man wearing a pair of metal stilts.

"*Unruhe,*" she says.

A flicker of recognition crosses Schnauz's face. Scully draws her gun.

"Stand where you are," she says.

Schnauz turns and leaps—he is an amazingly agile stilt walker—down the stairway. A warning shot past his head brings him up short.

Scully frisks him. She puts her hand in the pocket of his overalls and pulls it back out with a gasp. Her ring finger has been pricked. It is bleeding.

Scully reaches into the pocket again—slowly and carefully—and pulls out an ice pick–shaped object.

In a police department interrogation room, Scully questions Gerry Schnauz as Mulder looks on. Gerry seems cooperative but sincerely baffled by his arrest; he denies knowing Alice Brandt, Mary Lefante, or the two murdered men. The awl in his pocket, he says, was for starting holes in Sheetrock.

Mulder breaks in. "You want to tell us about the first time you were arrested, Gerry?"

Schnauz's air of innocent bafflement melts away.

"In 1980," says Scully, "you attacked your father with an ax handle. You beat him so severely that he spent the remainder of his life in a wheelchair."

"I was not jailed," says Schnauz. "I was institutionalized. I had a kind of chemical imbalance."

Mulder glances down at a file folder. He reads:

"'Gerald Thomas Schnauz. Diagnosed and treated for a paranoid schizophrenic disorder. Six years in Melvoin Psychiatric Hospital. Released 1986.'"

Mulder looks up. "So, what've you been up to since 1986, Gerry?" he asks.

"Taking care of my father," says Schnauz indignantly. "Looking after him twenty-four hours a day. Making amends. He passed away in January."

"So how'd you feel about that?" says Mulder.

"Sad."

Schnauz sits in sullen silence. Mulder continues.

"It says here you have a sister," he says. "Where *is* your sister, Gerry?

"She passed," says Schnauz, downcast.

"Actually," says Mulder, softly, "it says here she committed suicide in 1980. That was a bad year. What else happened in 1980?"

Gerry snaps out of his funk and sneers at Mulder.

"Well, John Lennon got shot," he says. "Where the hell are you going with this? What are you, Sigmund Freud? Why don't you cut the BS!"

"Why don't we get back to Alice Brandt," says Scully, angrily. *"Where is she?"*

Schnauz stares at the female agent with a hint of fascination. "You seem troubled," he says chillingly.

Mulder moves forward to show him the enhanced photo of the old man.

"Is this your father?" he says.

Schnauz is surprised and badly shaken. "Where'd you get that?" he says.

"You left that for me," says Mulder. "You left it like a fingerprint. Is this what you see when you close your eyes, Gerry?"

Gerry nods.

"Gerry. Tell us where Alice Brandt is."

"She's safe from the Howlers," whispers Schnauz. "She's all right now."

"Gerry. Tell me how I can find her," says Mulder.

Gerry nods.

At the edge of a forest, the agents and local cops briefly search the underbrush. They find Alice Brandt wearing a nightgown, lying on the ground. She has obviously been lobotomized.

Scully reacts with barely suppressed rage and anguish. Mulder seems preoccupied.

"Scully, that word 'unruhe'—unrest. It's bothering me," he says. "Maybe he thought he was curing them somehow. Saving them from damnation. From those things in the picture he called the Howlers."

Scully says, "It's over, Mulder."

Mulder adds, "Then that photo wouldn't be his fantasy, but his nightmare."

"What the hell does it matter?"

"Because I want to understand," says Mulder

"I don't," says Scully angrily.

In the PD booking room, an officer fingerprints Gerry, who is handcuffed to a table. He snaps Gerry's mug shot with a digital camera, then turns to a color printer, which spits out Gerry's booking sheet.

The mug shot on the booking sheet is of the officer—dead. A corona of blood is spattered behind him. As the officer stares at the photo, Gerry reaches from behind and grabs the officer's gun out of its holster. The officer spins around. Gerry aims.

In the booking room afterward, Mulder stares at the photo.

"This wound's in the wrong place," he says. "He was shot in the throat. He wasn't trying to save this victim."

Scully tells him that there's been a strong-arm robbery at the drugstore.

At this newest crime scene, Mulder distractedly feeds a dollar bill into a photo booth near the counter. Mulder has learned from the druggist that the robber—obviously Gerry—has stolen the passport camera and all the film in the store.

Scully says, "He also took morphine, scopolamine, hydrobromide, and insulin syringes. He's making more twilight sleep."

"He wants to continue his work," says Mulder.

As he says this, the flash inside the photo booth goes off.

"You know that job site that I arrested him at, Mulder?" says Scully. "What if he's already picked out his next victim? There were apartment buildings on both sides."

"You think you interrupted his stalking?"

Scully says, "Let's go."

"I'll be right there," says Mulder, deep into his own musings. He tells her that he'll join her after she brings the car around.

Scully rushes out the door, phoning for police backup. As she climbs into the Explorer's driver's seat, a fist grasping a

hypodermic needle extends from below the vehicle. It jabs Scully in the ankle. She cries out in pain, then falls.

Gerry rolls out from underneath the truck and lifts Scully into his arms.

Back in the store, a snapshot drops out of the side of the booth. Mulder picks it up and looks at it. It is of Scully. She is screaming, surrounded by Howlers.

Mulder runs out of the store in time to see the Explorer roar off. He chases on foot, but they are gone.

In the police station later that day, Mulder gazes with desperate concentration at the Polaroid of Scully.

"Six fingers," he says. The demon hand clutching Scully's hair has six fingers.

Mulder asks to see Schnauz's wallet, searches it, and unfolds a worn newspaper clipping—Gerry's father's obituary. A photo shows a modest crowd at a family plot. A military honor guard folds the American flag.

"'Recipient of the Bronze Star during the Korean War, Gerald Schnauz, Senior, DDS'" reads Mulder.

He looks up. "He's a retired dentist," he says.

At Dr. Schnauz's dark and deserted office, Mulder and the police shine their flashlights at old-fashioned fixtures and paraphernalia. A sign on the wall says: TWILITE SLEEP—ASK YOUR DENTIST ABOUT IT!

The room is thick with dust, except for a circle on the floor where the dental chair used to be. Mulder discovers the footprint of a work boot.

"He's been here," he says.

Somewhere else, a dental light snaps on in the darkness. Scully is taped to the missing chair. The leukotome is on the instrument tray. The twilight sleep is wearing off.

"Let me go," she says.

"Shhh," says Schnauz, murmuring to her in German.

"It's over, Gerry. Let me go right now."

He speaks more deceptively soothing words in German, which Scully translates with alarm.

She replies to him in German: "Stop!" she says. "I have no unrest! I don't need to be saved!"

"Yes, you do," says Schnauz, in English. "Everybody does. But especially you."

"Why? Why me, Gerry? Do I remind you of your sister? Why did your sister kill herself, Gerry? What did your father do to her?"

"He didn't do anything to her," say Gerry. "It was the Howlers."

"Okay," says Scully, struggling for control. "Let's talk about the Howlers."

Gerry leans forward until his face is almost touching hers. Scully flinches.

"They live inside your head," he says. "They make you do things and say things you don't mean. And all your good thoughts can't wish them away. You need help."

He touches her forehead with his index finger. "You've got them—right there."

Scully tries to reason with him. "I don't have them, Gerry," she says.

"See!" he says. "They made you say that just now, because they know I'm going to kill them."

Schnauz brandishes the leukotome. Scully reaches the edge of panic.

"What if you're wrong, Gerry? What if there are no such things as Howlers? What if you made them up inside your head? To explain the things your sister said your father did?"

"Great," says Schnauz. "Now they got *you* talking like Sigmund Freud."

He leans toward her again.

"I am on to you! I know your tricks!"

Schnauz places the leukotome against the point of Scully's chin. His voice lowers to a sinister whisper.

"Besides—I've seen them. In that picture that your partner showed me. Pictures don't lie. You saw them, too."

Scully, leaning away desperately from the sharp instrument, says, "If there are such things as Howlers, Gerry, they live only inside your head."

Gerry retreats, comes back with the passport camera, aims it at Scully, and then turns the lens toward himself and snaps his own picture.

At the dentist's office, Mulder is again staring at the Polaroid photo of Scully's photo. Six fingers. A thought hits him.

He pulls out the obituary and counts the tombstones in the picture. There are five—plus one for Dr. Schnauz.

"Let's go," he says to the policemen.

At the Schnauz family plot, Mulder and the policemen fan out. The agent stops and stares into the distance.

Hulking over the dentist's chair, Gerry stares at the Polaroids he's just taken. He shows them to Scully.

"What does this mean?" he asks.

Scully, struggling for control, says, "It means you need help, Gerry."

"No," he replies. "I think what it means is I don't have much time left."

Over Scully's frenzied pleas, Gerry tapes her mouth shut. He grabs the leukotome and moves toward her. A creaking sound of car springs prompts him to move toward a wall and look out a peephole. He sees Mulder.

Mulder circles a parked motorhome, its windows shuttered. He peers inside the driver's window. He spots a key in the ignition. Dangling from the key ring is a plastic molar tooth.

Scully yanks one arm loose and knocks over the instruments. She rips the tape off her mouth and calls Mulder's name.

Mulder begins hammering on the door.

"Scully!" he yells.

He breaks the motorhome's window with a length of loose pipe, then reaches in to unlock the door. Gerry, almost out of time, moves again to lobotomize Scully. The leukotome inches toward Scully's face.

Mulder fires—and Gerry falls.

"Are you hurt?" says Mulder to Scully.

She shakes her head. Mulder looks over at Schnauz.

"Get an ambulance!" he shouts.

Scully pulls herself to her feet and silently, slowly, leaves the motorhome.

Mulder picks up the Polaroid print. On it, Gerry lies on the floor of the motorhome. He is surrounded by darkness: dead.

Back in her apartment in Washington, Scully sits in front of her laptop. She writes:

Addendum to case report: After his death, a diary was found among Gerald Schnauz's belongings. Written in the second person and apparently intended as an open letter to his father, it includes the names of his victims— the women he desired to "save." My name is contained in the last entry.

Scully pauses and looks at the Polaroid photos spread in front of her.

I have no further explanation of the photographs, nor am I confident one is forthcoming. My captivity forced me to understand and even empathize with Gerry Schnauz—my survival depended on it. I see now the value of such insight. For truly, to pursue monsters, we must understand them. We must venture into their minds. Only in doing so, do we risk letting them venture into ours?

back story:

In one interesting respect, "Unruhe" marks a departure for *The X-Files*: It is the very first episode—one of several during the 1996–97 season—that was aired out of order in the series' production schedule.

"Unruhe" was the second episode filmed and the fourth episode aired, part of an elaborate flip-flop designed to get the best episodes into the time slots most likely to attract new viewers.

"We knew at the beginning of the year that we were switching from Fridays to Sunday nights, but it was only after we started shooting that we knew we would be making the switch during the fourth week," says coproducer Frank Spotnitz. "We wanted to pick an episode that was particularly successful as a script and that would be an excellent representative of the show—and we made the decision that 'Unruhe' would be a better episode than 'Teliko' for that purpose."

The seed for the episode itself was planted years ago, when the young Vince Gilligan—whose childhood obsessions, like those of many associated with *The X-Files*, have certainly paid off handsomely— sent away for a *Time-Life* mail-order book chronicling the lives of mass murderers and serial killers.

"I remember a whole chapter on a man named Howard Unruh, the first modern mass murderer," says the writer and coproducer. "In the late 1940s, this guy decided to take a walk through his New Jersey neighborhood with a Luger he'd brought home from the war. He shot, I think it was, thirteen people in twelve min-

utes. Then they took him away with a butterfly net. But the capper on the story was that the book mentioned that 'unruhe' means 'unrest' in German. I thought: 'Gee, you couldn't make that up, could you?'"

Young Gilligan was also fascinated by several *Life* magazine stories on Ted Serios, the "thought photographer" whom Mulder mentions in the episode. The dental angle, Gilligan admits, was pretty much a no-brainer considering many people's terror of the whole subject. (The writer himself has no fear of the dentist's drill, he claims. However, his own dentist, a Dr. Michael Kilbourne, greeted him at his six-month checkup last year by placing a brand-new "Twilite Sleep" sign on his office wall.)

The choice of Pruitt Taylor Vince was an easy one. A well-known character actor who has recently been veering away—in films like *Heavy* and *Beautiful Girls*—from pathetic misfit and deranged-killer roles, Vince had been approached to guest star during *The X-Files'* first season, but had rejected the role as too small. "The first time I saw him was in the movie *Jacob's Ladder*," says Gilligan, "and he stood out even though he had a very small part. I wrote the part in 'Unruhe' with him in mind, and when the casting department contacted him, luckily he was available and wanted to do it."

The plasterers' stilts that Schnauz wears in the episode are notoriously dangerous; when Gilligan, taking personal responsibility for his plot device, tried them out in a Vancouver parking lot, he made sure to have "a bunch of Teamsters" standing around to catch him. Most of the on-camera stilt-walking scenes were done by a stuntman; in the others, Vince was held upright by a safety cable attached to the ceiling. It was later erased in postproduction by the visual effects department.

Schnauz's terrifying thought Polaroids were posed and photographed by the show's prop department; copies and outtakes—especially those including Gillian Anderson—are now prominently displayed in the prop truck that follows the company on location. The brand name on the druggist's instant camera, "ETAP," is—like the brand name on much of the generic equipment seen in the show—the last name of assistant prop master Jim Pate spelled backward.

The razor-sharp lobotomy instrument, or leukotome, used in the show was constructed from scratch and his own imagination by props master Ken Hawryliw. "We called around to various doctors and mental hospitals," he says, "but nobody was willing to lend us one or even tell me what they looked like. I guess that they're not really proud of the whole concept."

Perceptive viewers might notice that Anderson, when playing the scene in which she's held captive in Schnauz's dental chair, seems to come out of the Twilite Sleep zone a little too fast.

"I played it the first time going in and out of consciousness and struggling more with my attempt to make him let me go," says Anderson. "I actually felt very good about that scene, but we reshot it because Chris felt that he wanted the drugs to wear off faster and me to be more aware of the danger."

Still, she felt her scenes with Vince, whom she admires as a person and an actor, were on the whole successful—and that their work was rewardingly intense. The proof of that, she adds, was when she later went to the movies to see *Heavy*, in which Vince stars as a gentle and lovelorn pizza chef.

"It was a little hard for me to let go of the concept of his being an evil person," says Anderson. "Whenever I saw him on the screen, I felt he was going to swing a pick-ax at somebody at any moment."

In this episode Gillian Anderson is proudest of the scene in which, while talking on the cell phone with Mulder, she looks at Schnauz on his stilts and figures out that he's the murderer. "I loved the concept of that," she says.

Ⓧ

episode: 4X03

first aired: October 11, 1996

written by: Glen Morgan and
James Wong

editor: Michael S. Stern

directed by: Kim Manners

guest stars:
Tucker Smallwood (Sheriff Andy Taylor)
Sebastian Spence (Deputy Barney Paster)
Judith Maxie (Barbara Taylor)
Chris Nelson Norris (Edmund Peacock)
John Trottier (George Peacock)
Adrian Hughes (Sherman Peacock)
Karin Konoval (Mrs. Peacock)
Cory Fry (Sandlot Batter)
Neil Denis (Sandlot Catcher)
Lachlan Murdoch (Sandlot Right Fielder)
Kenny James (Radio Singer)

principal setting:
Home, Pennsylvania

home

While investigating the death of an
infant in a close-knit rural community,
Mulder and Scully uncover an even
darker family secret.

On a filthy night of rain and howl-
ing wind, an unlit farmhouse
squats sullenly. Inside, a baby
is being born amid conditions of
indescribable squalor. A haglike
woman screams; a child begins
squalling; an umbilical cord is cut with
rusty scissors.

A trio of quasi-human male figures
shamble out into the storm. One sloppily
dressed being holds the crying infant;
another begins to dig a hole; the third wails
inconsolably. The child is placed into the
ground. As the wailer is clumsily comforted
by his cohort, the remaining man shovels
dirt into the hole.

On an idyllic sandlot baseball field, a
group of youngsters play baseball in the sun.

"All right! Let's play some ball!" says
one boy.

"Swing it in here!" says another.

"Strike!" says the catcher.

"In what league?" demands the batter.

"Hey, quit complaining!" says the pitcher.
"We already had to move home plate
'cause you bitched about the mud!"

The catcher pounds his glove.

"C'mon! Let's hear some chin music!" he
says.

The pitcher winds and delivers. The batter hits a foul ball over a barbed-wire fence
and onto the property of the dilapidated
building in the opening scene.

The children stare at the farmhouse in
fright. Not one of them dares to retrieve the
baseball.

"Here's another one!" shouts the catcher,
holding a ball aloft.

The game resumes. The batter digs into
the dirt near home plate. Blood oozes out
of the ground and over the batter's tennis
shoe. The children stare in horror at the
awful sight. A tiny hand protrudes, grasping upward, from the ground.

At the still beatific crime scene, a nostal-
gic Mulder, using the baseball the fleeing
boys abandoned, works on his pitching
motion while Scully performs a forensic
examination of the baby's grave.

"Compression marks," says Scully, "indicate the shovel blade to be approximately

six and three-quarter inches. Angle of
movement and deeper indentation on the
right side of the mark suggests a left-
handed individual."

As Scully speaks, Mulder tosses the ball
gently into the air, getting the feel of the old
horsehide.

Scully says, "I've collected soil speci-
mens, and although numerous shoe
impressions exist from the sandlot game, a
couple of dental stone casts will prove
invaluable to the investigation."

Mulder works on his knuckleball grip.
Scully realizes he hasn't heard a word she's
been saying.

"Meanwhile," she concludes, "I've quit
the FBI and become a spokesperson for the
Ab-Roller."

Mulder concentrates on the matter at
hand.

"Smell that," he says, shoving the spher-
oid under Scully's nose. "That's perfume.
Eau de ball.

"God, this brings back a lot of memories of my sister," he adds. "All-day pickup games out on the Vineyard, ride our
bikes down to the beach, eat baloney
sandwiches.

"Only place you had to be on time was
home for dinner. Never had to lock your
doors. No modems, no faxes, no cell
phones."

"Mulder," says Scully, "if you had to do
without a cell phone for two minutes, you'd
lapse into catatonic schizophrenia."

Mulder and Scully are joined by the local
sheriff. His name is Andy Taylor.

"For real?" asks Mulder in wonderment.

"Can't thank you and the Bureau enough
for comin' out," says Sheriff Andy. "Just
me and my deputy and—hell, we've never
had anything of this nature."

"Do you have any thoughts or suspects?"

Taylor smiles sheepishly and shrugs. He
tells the agents that the town of Home has
only a few hundred inhabitants; that he
knows each and every one of them; and
that none have had a baby recently.

Mulder asks about the farmhouse in the
distance, adding that several people on its
front porch have been watching them at work.

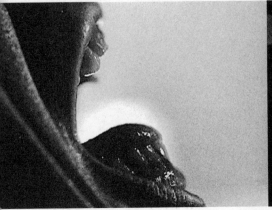

Taylor's mood darkens. Reluctantly, he tells the agents that the house is owned by the Peacocks, three brothers whose parents are believed to have been killed in a car wreck ten years ago. At the time, the brothers refused medical attention for their parents and hauled their bodies back home.

"Have you questioned the men?" asks Scully.

Again, Taylor shrugs.

The farmhouse, he says, was built by the Peacocks' ancestors during the Civil War. It was never equipped with electricity, heat, or running water.

"They grow their own food," says Taylor. "Raise their own pigs. Breed their own cows. Raise and breed their own 'stock'—if you get my meaning."

Taylor adds that he hopes the FBI solves the crime, but without exposing the town to the harsh realities of modern life.

"Look, this town is my home," he says. "It's peaceful. I don't even wear a gun. I've seen and heard some of the sick and horrible things that go on outside my home. At the same time, I knew we couldn't stay hidden forever. That one day the modern world would find us and my hometown would change forever.

"And when I saw . . . *it* in the ground, I knew that day had come. Now, I want to find whoever did this—but in doing so, I'd like it if the way things are around here didn't have to change."

Mulder and Scully go to the sheriff's office to examine the baby's body. They meet Taylor's only deputy, Barney.

"Fife?" asks Mulder hopefully.

"Paster," says Barney, irritated.

The agents are led to a tiny backroom to look at the infant. It is grotesquely malformed.

"Oh, my God!" says Scully.

She adds, "Mulder, it looks as if this child has been afflicted by every rare birth defect known to science. I'm going to have to order DNA typing from the crime lab, but there appears to be abnormalities associated with Neu-Laxova Syndrome, Meckel-Gruber Syndrome, Exstrophy of the cloaca—I mean I don't know where to begin."

"I guess we can rule out murder as the cause of death," says Mulder.

"I don't know about that," says Scully. "There's evidence of occlusion due to dirt in the nose and mouth—indicating the dirt was inhaled."

"There's something rotten in Mayberry," says Mulder.

Disturbed by what they've seen, Mulder and Scully walk outside and sit in the town's charming main square.

Scully says, "Imagine all the hopes and dreams a woman has for her child. Then nature turns so cruel. What must a mother go through?"

"Apparently not much in this case," says Mulder, "if she'd just throw it out with the trash."

"I guess I was just projecting on myself," says Scully.

"Why?" says Mulder, deadpan. "Is there a history of genetic abnormalities in your family?"

"No," says Scully.

"Well," says Mulder, "just find yourself a man with a spotless genetic makeup and a really high tolerance for being second-guessed and start pumping out Uber-Scullys."

Scully smiles despite herself.

"What about your family?" she says.

"Well, aside from the need for corrective lenses and the tendency to be abducted by extraterrestrials involved in an international conspiracy, the Mulder family passes genetic muster."

Getting a bit more serious, Mulder surmises that the child was killed by a pair of frightened young parents—a terrible crime, but not a matter for the FBI or the X-Files.

Scully disagrees. She says that the genetic abnormalities the baby suffered from could not have been the result of a single normal mating. She surmises that the brothers—the products of generations of inbreeding—have kidnapped a woman, impregnated her, and forced her to have their child.

"Kidnapping is a Bureau matter," Mulder concedes.

He has one more thought, albeit not related to the case.

"Scully," he tells his partner, admiringly, "I never saw you as a 'mother' before."

Shortly afterward, the agents approach the Peacock house. A rusty, big-finned old Cadillac convertible is parked in the front yard. Hogs grunt in a nearby sty. Clouds of flies buzz around, attracted by God knows what.

The blacked-out house is uninhabited, and in the dust-filled gloom it's even more disgustingly squalid than before. Dried blood and amniotic fluid cake the floorboards.

They decide to ask Sheriff Taylor to issue an arrest warrant for the Peacock brothers. They bag a pair of bloody scissors as evidence. There's a footprint on the floor; Scully pulls out her tracing of the footprint from the ball field.

"They match," she says.

Under a bed, unseen by the pair, a pair of bloodshot eyes peer out at them. Ragged breaths rasp into the darkness.

Late that night, from his home at 3 Sweetgum Lane, Sheriff Taylor phones Mulder and Scully at their fifties-vintage motel.

He reports that he's phoned in arrest warrants on George Raymond Peacock, approximate age thirty; Sherman Nathaniel Peacock, approximate age twenty-six; and Edmund Creighton Peacock, forty-two. Deputy Paster, he adds, is searching missing person reports for women who've disappeared.

Scully asks Taylor about the white Cadillac: Could it have belonged to the kidnap victim?

"We get so many of those, Agent Scully," says Taylor, wearily. "Car breaks down, they move on."

"We'll check on those in the morning," she says. "You get some sleep, Sheriff."

"You, too, Miss Scully. Good night."

Taylor hangs up, sits down at his desk, sighs, and removes a locked strongbox from his desk drawer. He pulls out a revolver, checks to see that it's loaded, and locks it up again.

At the Peacock house, a screen door creaks. Sherman walks out of the house and down to the Cadillac. He places two crude wooden clubs into the Cadillac's trunk, then—sucking greedily at a rubber hose—siphons gasoline into its tank.

At the run-down motel Mulder is desperately trying to tune in a station—any

station—on an antique black-and-white television. He stands in front of the set, moving a pair of rabbit ears like a divining rod. Scully gets up from her paperwork and walks toward him. When she reaches his side, the snow on the TV screen slackens.

"Don't move! Don't move!" he tells Scully.

The signal fades.

"Damn!"

At the Peacock house the three brothers climb into the front seat of the Cadillac. It roars to life, blowing a cloud of gray smoke from its exhaust pipes. On the behemoth's dashboard radio a Johnny Mathis sound alike is singing "Wonderful, Wonderful."

The driver shifts into gear and moves off.

Sitting on his front porch, Andy Taylor stares gloomily into the distance. His wife joins him and asks him gently what he's doing.

"Just having one last look around before it all changes," he says.

"Oh, honey, come to bed," she says. "It'll still be here in the morning."

She leaves the door unlocked behind her.

The Cadillac cruises down a country road, "Wonderful, Wonderful" still blasting from the radio.

Scully sleeps peacefully in her motel bed.

In the next room, Mulder stares at the only snowbound picture his ancient television can pull in. It is a godawful nature documentary.

"The eldest dominant male of the pack moves in to assure that the prey has been killed," intones the narrator. "Encircling the prey is a signal to the others that it is safe to approach."

Sheriff Taylor lies awake in bed next to his sleeping wife. He hears the strains of "Wonderful, Wonderful" through an open window, gets up, and peers down at the Cadillac. Its engine is running, its doors are wide open, but there is no one inside.

"Andy, what is it?" says his wife.

"Hide. Under the bed," says Andy grimly. "I'm goin' for the gun."

He heads downstairs to his office, but a Peacock brother has already pushed open the unlocked front door. He ducks into a storage closet, grabs a baseball bat, and positions himself behind his bedroom door.

Edmund Peacock opens the door. Andy swings the bat.

Edmund walks right through Taylor's blow, then clubs the sheriff senseless. He is joined by his brothers, who beat Taylor into a lifeless pulp.

The Peacocks stop, catch their breath with loud snorts, smell something—or somebody—and spot Mrs. Taylor's wedding ring gleaming in the moonlight under the bed. They pound the bed with their clubs, collapsing it onto her.

At the Taylor's house the next morning, Deputy Paster sits on the front steps. He is trembling.

Mulder and Scully arrive. Mulder spots fresh tire tracks on the Taylors' lawn.

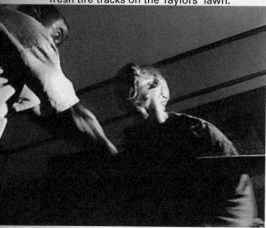

"Big American car," he says.

Barney Paster, clearly in shock, tells the agents that the Cadillac was abandoned by a woman from Baltimore. He hands Scully an overnight report from the federal crime lab.

In the bedroom the agents view the Taylors' corpses.

"His chest is one big hematoma," says Mulder, kneeling over Andy. "There's wood shavings imbedded in what's left of the cranium."

He looks over at the crushed bed frame. Mrs. Taylor's bloody legs protrude.

"They really went caveman on them," he says.

Scully reads the lab report: It contains inexplicable data indicating that the dead child had three genetic fathers. That would only be possible, she says, with a weakened ovum from a female member of the Peacock family—and there are none left.

Paster, carrying a giant automatic pistol, offers to lead Mulder and Scully into the Peacock house to arrest the brothers.

"It's three against three," he says, brandishing his cannon. "And this should give us an advantage."

He jams the gun into his holster and leaves. Mulder and Scully exchange wary glances.

"That," says Mulder, "was a little too 'Chuck Bronson' for me, Scully."

As they start out of the bedroom, Scully pauses.

"Hang on a second, Mulder," she says. "Why would the Peacocks kill Sheriff Taylor? He didn't even question them about the buried child?"

"They probably heard about the warrants issued for their arrest."

"But how did they know?" says Mulder. "He issued the warrants by phone. Unless they overheard us talking about it, how could they know?"

"No, we searched that house, Scully. There was nobody home."

"Exactly. How could they know?"

The pumped-up Paster leads Mulder and Scully—they are all dressed in flak jackets—on a military-style assault on the Peacock house. The agents cover the deputy from the front yard. Paster nervously approaches the front door.

Scanning the entrance with binoculars, Scully spots a tripwire.

"Paster, no!" she shouts.

Paster pushes inside and triggers the booby trap. An ax swings down from the ceiling, decapitating him.

From their hiding places inside the house, the brothers descend on the deputy's body. Sickened, Scully turns to Mulder.

"Paster's dead, she says. "The brothers have moved in like a pack of animals."

Mulder says, in a sober monotone: "The eldest will move in to assure that the prey has been killed. Encircling the prey is a signal that it's safe to approach."

He adds, "What we're witnessing, Scully, is undiluted animal behavior. Mankind, absent its own creation of civilization, technology, and information, regressed to an almost prehistoric state. Obeying only the often savage laws of nature.

"We're outsiders invading the den—trying to take away their only chance of reproducing, which we're going to do."

In an attempt to decoy the Peacocks, the agents decide to release their pigs from the sty. The filthy animals, however, will not budge. Mulder and Scully position themselves behind a couple of the porkers' hindquarters and push.

"Hey, Scully," says Mulder. "Would you

who carefully inserts the wooden board across the threshold.

He trips the trap. A pointed steel rod shoots horizontally across the door frame, knocking the board from Mulder's hand. The two-by-four is speared into the jamb.

The agents draw their guns. Their flashlights stab through the darkness.

"Federal agents! Is there anybody in here?" shouts Scully.

Mulder stumbles across a pile of yellowed newspapers. He picks up the top one. Its headline reads: "Elvis Presley Dead at 42."

"Huh!?" says Mulder, obviously crushed by the news.

think I was less of a man if I told you I was a little excited right now?"

The pigs snuggle up even closer.

"Nah Ram Ewe! Nah Ram Ewe!" says his partner.

"Yeah, that'll work," says Mulder, clueless.

"I baby-sat my nephew this weekend," Scully explains. "He watches *Babe* fifteen times a day."

"People call *me* spooky," says Mulder.

Finally, the hogs spill out of their pen. Sherman Peacock, washing blood off his hands under an outside hand pump, notices. He alerts his brothers, and they all run out of the house in pursuit.

Scully and Mulder proceed quickly toward the back door of the house. Scully finds a two-by-four. She tosses it to Mulder,

They find a series of family photographs hanging on the wall. All the homely, weather-beaten faces show signs of harmful genetic mutations.

Mulder spots some scratches on the floor. He follows them to a woman—grotesquely disfigured—strapped to a kind of wheeled creeper under the bed.

"No! Get the hell out! No! No!" screams the woman in a barely understandable garble.

"It's all right, ma'am!" says Mulder. "We're federal agents! We're here to help you!"

They pull her out from underneath while she screams in protest. The woman recoils from their light. She is in her late forties. Her face is grotesque. She has two stumps for legs. One of her arms is missing.

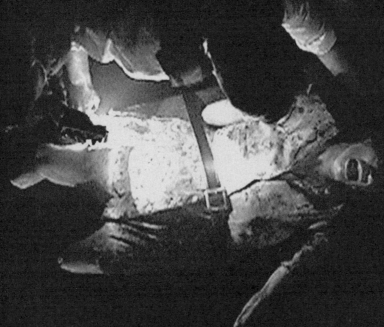

"Take it easy, ma'am!" shouts Mulder. "We're here from the FBI! We're here to help. We're going to make sure you're safe. We're going to make sure you get home."

Scully knows better.

"Mulder, she is home," she says. "This is Mrs. Peacock. This is their mother."

With her remaining arm, Mrs. Peacock pulls herself back under the bed.

Stunned, Mulder and Scully stare at her younger—but still grotesque—likeness on the wall.

Looking out for more booby traps, the agents move to the front window to watch the brothers' hog roundup.

"What about her?" says Scully, nodding toward Mrs. Peacock's bed.

"She's not going anywhere," says Mulder.

"I mean, we may not be able to remove her, Mulder," says Scully. "She doesn't appear to be held against her will. I mean, she *appears* to be, but I'm not sure if she is."

"I'm sure she's an accessory. At least she aided and abetted."

"We're only assuming," says Scully. "We can't prove anything."

Scully sighs deeply. "The way I think it goes here," she says, "is that Edmund is the brother and father of the other two."

Mulder says, "Which means that when Edmund was a kid, he could ground the other two for playing with his things?

"The brothers killed three people, Scully," he adds. "Tell her we're going to bring them in. And try to convince her that she's the one way they can get out of this without her 'boys' getting hurt. And I'll keep an eye on them."

Scully returns to Mrs. Peacock, peers underneath the bed, and gently tries to convince Mrs. Peacock to leave.

"This is our home—why leave it?" says the woman in a terrible rasping voice.

Scully says: "Whatever pain you may feel—"

"Don't feel pain," says Mrs. Peacock. "Runs in the family. Have to check the boys to see if they've hurt themselves."

She adds: "Right arm was torn off. Saw it sittin' there 'cross my dead husband's lap. Boys took me home. Sewn me up like the family learnt in the War of Northern Aggression. Whole time feels same's as if they're makin' breakfast.

"They're such good boys."

"Mrs. Peacock," says Scully, "they murdered Sheriff Taylor and his wife. And Deputy Paster."

Mrs. Peacock bares the yellowed stumps of her teeth. "I can tell you don't have no children," she rasps. "Maybe one day you'll learn the pride. The love. When you know your boy will do *anything* for his mother."

Outside, the brothers spot unfamiliar footprints leading to the house. They gather their forces and run toward the front door.

"Scully!" says Mulder.

He barricades the doorway.

Enraged, the Peacocks break through the barricade. In a desperate melee at close quarters, the agents battle for their lives. It's a close call, even though their assailants are unarmed.

Both Scully and Mulder shoot George before he falls. Sherman accidentally triggers one of his own traps and is impaled on a wooden stake. When the fighting dies down, Scully notices fresh scratch marks on the floor. There is a trap door under the bed.

Mrs. Peacock and Edmund are gone. Scully notifies the Highway Patrol.

"In time, we'll catch them," she says.

Mulder says, "I think time already caught them, Scully."

It is nighttime and the Cadillac sits empty by the roadside. Coming from somewhere inside the car is a reprise of "Wonderful, Wonderful"—and Mrs. Peacock's voice.

"There, there," she says. "Sherman and George were good boys. We should be proud. And you got to know, Edmund, you can't keep a Peacock down. There'll be more. One day. There'll be more.

"But now we have to move on. Start a new family—one we'll be proud of. And find a new place to call ours. A new home. A brand-new home."

The Cadillac's trunk pops open.

To the syrupy sound of that best-loved ballad, Edmund Peacock climbs out, slams the trunk shut, walks around to the driver's seat, and drives away.

back story:

With its semi-gleeful incorporation (celebration?) of blood, gore, incest, genetic nastiness, and one of America's most-beloved TV dads, this episode remains a particularly memorable one—not only to viewers, but to the Fox Network censors.

"Oh, man!" says director Kim Manners. "When (Director of Standards and Practices) Linda Shima-Tsumo first saw that baby, I

thought she was going to just about have a heart attack and die. I shot a *lot* more of it than they ever allowed to get on the air." Other *X-Files* staffers recall several other knockdown battles over the issues of good taste and on-screen bodily fluids.

The lead actors, however, relished Morgan and Wong's teleplay: "I think it was wonderful. One of our best shows," says Gillian Anderson.

David Duchovny says: "I didn't really get 'Home' when I read the script or when we started to do it, but the finished product was really funny and kind of disturbing. I really like that."

Tucker Smallwood, who played Sheriff Andy Taylor, is the first in an astoundingly long line of actors from Morgan and Wong's canceled series, *Space: Above and Beyond,* the pair recruited to guest star in their fourth-season *X-Files* episodes. In the syndicated sci-fi program, Smallwood played Commodore Glen Van Ross; a veteran actor, he also had a nicely visible part last summer as the mission commander in the Jodie Foster movie *Contact.*

The job of filming "Home" turned out to have almost as many weird quirks as the episode itself. This show was a point of pride for special effects makeup master Toby Lindala, who not only transmogrified the actors playing the Peacock brothers, but constructed the genetically deficient baby.

A scene in which Mulder and Scully jostle each other suggestively in the tight confines of Sheriff Taylor's supply closet/ morgue was filmed but ultimately cut. The building that served as the Peacock House—after it was purposely and thoroughly dilapidated by the art and construction departments—served once before on *The X-Files.* It was Harry Cokely's home in "Aubrey" (2X12), and it is located in South Surrey, near the U.S.-Canadian border.

The Johnny Mathis soundalike who croons "Wonderful, Wonderful," over the Peacocks' car radio was *almost*—but not quite—former *X-Files and Millennium* producer-director David Nutter. A professional singer in college, Nutter volunteered to do the deed. But alas, at the last moment

coproducer Paul Rabwin found another man who sang too uncannily like Mathis to pass up.

The hogs appearing in the pig-sty scene with Scully and Mulder were *not* computer generated. They were rented, as dirty and smelly as they looked, and—despite what the script said—at all times eager to escape their confinement and knock off work early. For that reason, while Anderson and Duchovny, in camera range, pushed against the pigs' hindquarters from their end of the herd, a team of pig wranglers, safely out of the shot, pushed them back toward the actors from the other.

The 1958 Cadillac hardtop that served as the murderous Peacock brothers' lead sled was a near-hopeless wreck—painted pink and blown up during the making of another TV show—that was rusting peacefully on a real farm outside Vancouver. It was located, rented, and "restored" by transportation department staffer Nigel Hapgood. Under tremendous time pressure, Hapgood worked frantically to stay one step ahead of the cameras, sawing off its top, then banging into place whatever body panels and/or chrome strips were due to be in camera range on a given day.

However, Hapgood never did get all of the beast's mechanical systems working simultaneously—the brakes were particularly unreliable. Which brings up perhaps the weirdest "Home"-related incident of them all, as recalled by Kim Manners. Shortly after the episode aired, he was shown a letter to *The X-Files* from Cadillac. "They thanked us," says the director, shaking his head in amazement, "for putting one of their products in the show."

Glen Morgan claims to have named the Peacock family after some former neighbors of his parents.

Ⓧ

African-American men are disappearing.
Their bodies, when found, are dead white—
drained of pigment. Were they killed by a
virulent new disease? Were they murdered? Or
does the answer lie elsewhere?

teliko

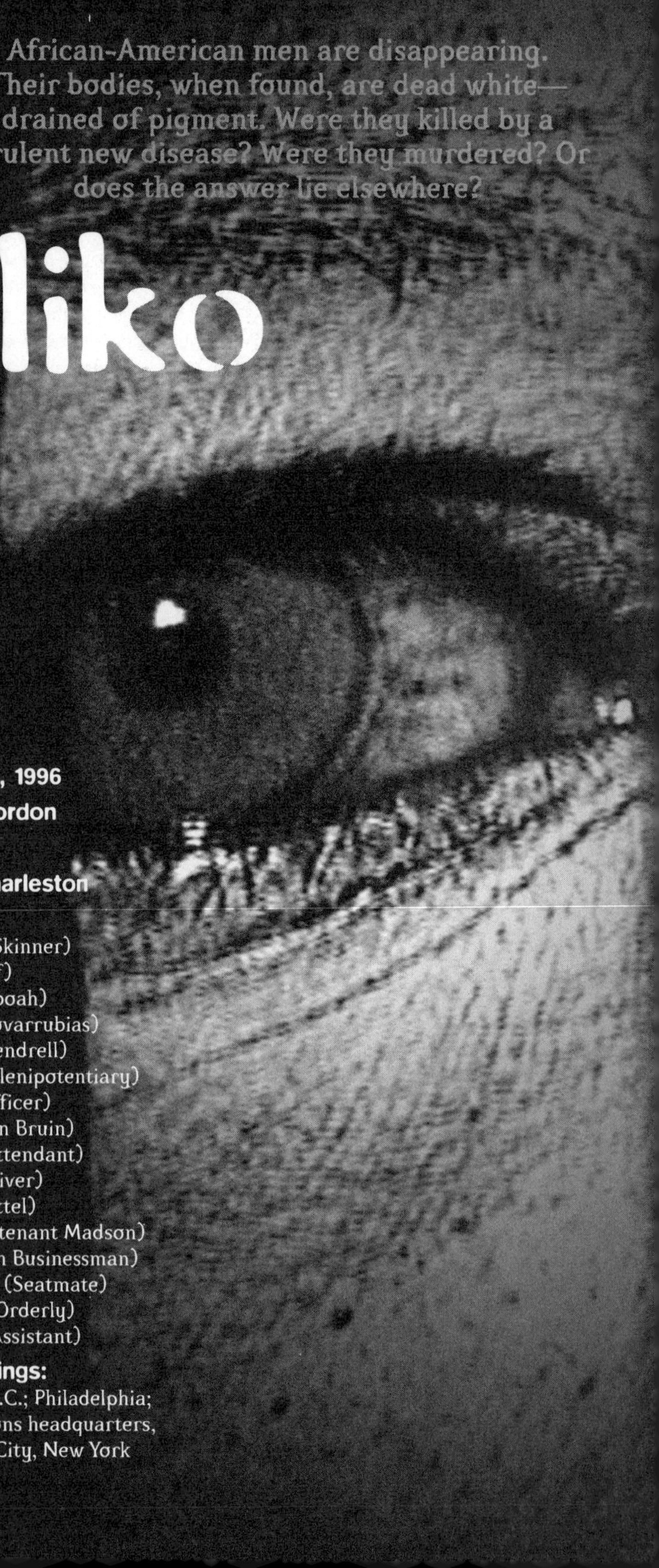

episode: 4X04
first aired: October 18, 1996
written by: Howard Gordon
editor: Jim Gross
directed by: James Charleston

guest stars:
Mitch Pileggi (AD Walter Skinner)
Carl Lumbly (Marcus Duff)
Willie Amakye (Samuel Aboah)
Laurie Holden (Marita Covarrubias)
Brendan Beiser (Agent Pendrell)
Zakes Mokae (Minister Plenipotentiary)
Danny Whatley (First Officer)
Bob Morrisey (Dr. Simon Bruin)
Maxine Guess (Flight Attendant)
Bill Mackenzie (Bus Driver)
Dexter Bell (Alfred Kittel)
Michael O'Shea (Lieutenant Madson)
Don Stewart (African Businessman)
Geoffrey Ayi-Bonte (Seatmate)
Oscar Goncalves (Orderly)
Maria Bitamba (Assistant)

principal settings:
Washington, D.C.; Philadelphia;
United Nations headquarters,
New York City, New York

On a jumbo jet outbound from francophone West Africa, a black African businessman heads to the lavatory to freshen up. Two eyes—their irises strangely pink—stare out through a crack in the lavatory door.

The businessman enters the lavatory, takes off his eyeglasses, looks into the mirror, and sees something terrifying behind and above him. He screams.

As the plane nears JFK Airport, another black man—young and handsome but with a strangely abstracted expression—leaves the lavatory. On final approach a flight attendant checks the lavatory door. It is locked.

She opens the door with a passkey. Inside, the businessman is sprawled dead. His mouth gapes open and his skin is an unearthly albino white.

In AD Skinner's office Scully is introduced to Dr. Simon Bruin, a physician-researcher from the Centers for Disease Control.

"A pleasure, Dr. Scully," says Bruin.

Skinner fixes Scully in his sights. "How familiar are you," he says, "with the series of kidnappings that have taken place in Philadelphia?"

"Only what I've read in the *Herald*," says Scully. "That four young men have gone missing over the past three months. All of them African-American."

Skinner tells Scully that a joint FBI–Philadelphia PD task force has been working on the case, but there have been no good leads to speak of—until the night before.

"What happened last night?" says Scully.

"Owen Sanders, the man most recently reported missing, has been found dead near a construction site."

"How was he killed?" says Scully.

"That's just it, Agent Scully. He wasn't. There was no evidence indicating homicide."

Scully, puzzled, says, "Has a cause of death been determined?"

"No. But I'll let Dr. Bruin give you his thoughts on that."

Bruin hands Scully a photograph. A man with close-cropped hair lies on the pavement, his face a ghostly white.

"This was taken last night," says Bruin, "less than an hour after Sanders's body was found."

Scully does a double take. "I'm sorry," she says. "I thought you said Sanders was black."

"He was."

Bruin shows Scully a newspaper clipping reporting Sanders's abduction. On it is an older photo of Sanders—a normally complected black man. He tells her that he may not be a crime victim. He says that Sanders has suffered complete depigmentation—which might be the characteristics of a hitherto unknown fatal disease.

"It's my opinion, Dr. Scully," he says, "that this investigation should begin and end under a microscope."

"His hope," explains Skinner, "is that someone with a solid medical background like yourself can make a quick and decisive analysis."

Scully says, "Where would you like me to begin?"

In the FBI pathology lab Scully starts her autopsy of Sanders's body. She is joined by Mulder.

"Hey!" he says. "I heard you were down here slicin' and dicin'. Who's the lucky stiff?"

Scully says, "He was the fourth kidnap victim in Philadelphia—until his body turned up like this."

"There's a Michael Jackson joke in here," says Mulder, "but I can't quite find it."

Scully relays her conversation with Bruin and her opinion that—since the body bore no wounds and his wallet was still in his pocket—Sanders died of disease.

"Interesting," says Mulder. "What sort of disease is this?"

"I don't know," says Scully. "There are conditions, like vitiligo, which attack melanocytes and prevent the manufacture of melanin in the skin. Autoimmune disorders that are not clearly understood."

"So he died of a—disorder?" asks Mulder skeptically. "He and four other young black

men, who conveniently contracted the disease in succession and then disappeared without any explanation whatsoever?"

Scully counters that the victims' bodies might already have turned up, but because of the drastic change in their appearance, they are still unidentified.

Mulder remains unconvinced.

"Scully, has it occurred to you that this might just be a little PR exercise?"

"I'm sorry?"

"To divert attention from the fact that young black men are dying and nobody seems to be able to bring in a suspect. The perception being that nobody cares."

"Mulder, not everything is a labyrinth of dark conspiracy. And not everybody is plotting to deceive, inveigle, and obfuscate."

Mulder is unconvinced. He asks Scully if any forensic evidence has been taken from the body. She shows him a container holding hair, fiber, and soils.

He takes it and heads for the exit.

"What are you doing?" says Scully.

"I'm going to join the snipe hunt, if you don't mind," he says. "Before the body count rises."

In a dreary and darkened Philadelphia apartment Samuel Aboah—the strange young black man from the airliner—answers a knock on his door.

It is Marcus Duff, a counselor from the U.S. Immigration and Naturalization Service. Duff announces he is there to help Samuel fill out his naturalization petition.

Aboah is barely responsive, which Duff—who is also black and speaks with a lilting Caribbean accent—interprets as shyness or fear.

"I know how lonely it is, believe me," says Duff. "Being in a strange place, far from your family.

"But once you become a U.S. citizen, I can help you bring over every brother, sister, aunt, uncle, and cousin! It all starts today, Samuel! Know what I'm saying?"

At FBI headquarters, Mulder meets with Agent Pendrell, who's analyzed the evidence from Sanders's body.

"Shouldn't we wait for Agent Scully?" says Pendrell. "Just so I won't have to repeat myself."

"She's not coming," says Mulder.

"Why not?" says Pendrell, disappointed.

"She had a date."

Agent Pendrell looks suicidal.

"Breathe, Agent Pendrell," says Mulder. "It's with a dead man. She's doing an autopsy. Now, you said you found something?"

Pendrell regains his will to live. He tells Mulder that an analysis of Sanders's debris has turned up asbestos fibers and one seed from a rare night-blooming West African plant, *adenia volkensii*.

At an airport pay phone, Mulder calls Scully and tells her that the seed contains a cerebropathic glycoside.

"Does that mean anything to you?" he says.

Scully identifies the substance as a cortical depressant—powerful and possibly lethal if administered in large quantities. No drugs, however, were found in Sanders's blood.

Mulder steps out of the shadows to approach Marita Covarrubias, the UN official from "Herrenvolk" (4X01). There is a definite tension of some kind between the two.

Mulder asks her if she knows anything about the kidnapped black men or the West African poison plant.

"I can't help you," says Covarrubias.

Mulder says, "You can't or you won't?"

He adds, "You made an overture to me. You left an opening. Tell me I'm wrong. Tell me there's nothing here, and I'll just walk away. Either way, I need to know."

Covarrubias says nothing.

On a Philadelphia street, a young African-American man, Alfred Kittel, waits for a late-night bus. He grimaces, slaps his neck

"Could his body have metabolized the substance?" asks Mulder.

"Only if the victim hadn't expired immediately," says Scully.

Scully has also made a discovery: Sanders's pituitary gland, the organ that controls skin pigmentation, has been destroyed.

"Then you've found evidence that this is a disease," says Mulder.

"No," says Scully. "I have identified the effect. I am still looking for a cause."

Mulder tells Scully to keep him informed of her research.

"Where are you going, Mulder?" she says.

"Off," he says, "to water the seeds of doubt."

Outside United Nations headquarters,

as if swatting a mosquito, and pulls a seed-like object from the wound. He slumps, paralyzed but semiconscious, onto a bench.

A bus pulls up. The white bus driver opens the door.

"Hey, I got a schedule," says the driver to Kittel. "You gettin' on or not?"

Kittel sees him, but can neither move nor respond.

"What's your problem? You on drugs or somethin'?" says the driver, closing the door. "Aw, the hell with ya. Damn drugs."

As he pulls away, Kittel sees a man standing in the middle of the street. It is Samuel Aboah, a large portion of his face depigmented, staring at him through translucent eyes.

At the bus stop the next morning, Scully

interviews the bus driver. She asks him whether Kittel looked sick.

"Yeah, now that you mention it," he says guiltily. "I asked him if he needed help, but he didn't say squat. Don't forget to put down I had a schedule to keep."

Mulder arrives. He searches the ground around the bus stop.

Scully tells him that Kittel, who takes the bus to work every evening, was reported missing by his mother. She also relays her conversation with the bus driver.

"It sounds to me," she says, "like some kind of presymptomatic dementia."

"Or a reaction to a powerful cortical depressant," Mulder says.

"What are you suggesting?" asks Scully.

"Find Alfred Kittel and you find another of those rare African seeds," says Mulder.

"What makes you so sure?"

He tells his partner that three months ago, a week before the first disappearance, the New York Port Authority informed the FAA of the bizarre death of an African businessman. The man was flying from Burkina Faso (formerly known as Upper Volta), but that country's embassy refused permission for an autopsy. The cause of death was listed as undetermined.

"Undetermined, Scully," says Mulder, "but not necessarily unknown."

Two Philadelphia policemen, canvassing the neighborhood from which Kittel disappeared, knock on Samuel Aboah's door.

"Aboah!?" says one of the policemen, who is African-American. "What the hell kind of name is that?"

Aboah opens the door.

"Yes?" he says.

They show him Alfred Kittel's picture. "Have you seen him?" asks the cop.

"No," says Aboah.

Kittel—still paralyzed and speechless—is inside Aboah's darkened apartment.

The policemen depart. Aboah returns inside, throws back his head, opens his mouth wide, gagging slightly, and slowly extracts a thin, impossibly long wooden tube.

The terrified Kittel can only watch helplessly.

At Philadelphia INS headquarters Mulder and Scully meet Marcus Duff and ask him to cross-reference his client list with the passenger manifest of the flight from Burkina Faso. Duff protests that he's a social worker, not a police officer.

Scully tells him that they're investigating a possible health crisis.

"What kind of crisis?" he asks.

Duff does not see Mulder's skeptical glance.

Outside Samuel Aboah's apartment, Mulder and Scully sit in their car waiting for him to return home. Scully pores over her notes.

"It's here, Mulder, it has to be," says Scully. "Some evidence of a virus or bacterium."

"I think if you looked up from your microscope," says Mulder, "you'd find what's really missing is a motive."

Scully looks up at him. Not defensive, but simply determined.

"The motive of any pathogen," she says, "is simply to reproduce itself. And my job as a doctor is to find out if and how it's being transmitted."

"*If* this is a health crisis," says Mulder.

"*Death* is a health crisis, Mulder," she says. "*Something* caused Sanders's pituitary to fail, which in turn caused his metabolism to drop, resulting in myxedema coma, and finally in death.

"Sometimes you just have to start at the end to find the beginning. I just hope we don't have to find another dead body to discover what it is."

Mulder glances at the photograph on Samuel Aboah's alien registration form and then at a man climbing out of pickup truck full of day laborers.

"Maybe we won't have to wait," he says.

Mulder leaves the car and calls Aboah's name. He turns and flees.

Mulder and Scully run after him. They chase him down the block and into a blind alley, from which he has seemingly vanished without a trace. Just as they are about to give up, Mulder peers into a small drainpipe on the side of a building.

Aboah has wedged himself into this impossibly small space. He is in a kind of trance state, gasping for air.

"Hey, Scully, look at this," says Mulder, peering into Aboah's eyes.

"Oh, my God!" says Scully.

At a local hospital Scully and Dr. Bruin examine Aboah. Their preliminary tests find nothing out of the ordinary. Scully asks to perform some further, more complicated tests.

Mulder arrives and asks if they've identified Aboah's ailment.

"Not yet," says Scully. "But that doesn't mean he isn't a carrier, or even an index case."

"Well, he's some kind of case," says Mulder, "the way he disappeared down that drainpipe."

Marcus Duff, summoned to act as a translator, arrives. He loudly protests Aboah's detention. He explains that the man's attempted escape from the FBI agents was a justified cultural fear of the authorities. Mulder disagrees.

"That man ran because he's hiding something," he says.

He turns to Scully. "And no amount of tests you run on him—no science—is going to find that."

He turns to leave.

"Where are you going?" asks Scully.

"To find someone I know who plotted to deceive, inveigle, and obfuscate."

At the Burkina Faso Embassy in Washington that evening, Mulder is led into the office of Alpha Diabira, the Minister Plenipotentiary: the number-two man.

Mulder thanks Diabira for receiving him after hours.

"I did not have much of a choice in this matter," says Diabira. "Someone from the United Nations spoke to the ambassador directly. What's so important that it can't wait?"

"With all due respect, sir," says Mulder, "I think you already know."

Mulder asks him about the incident on the airliner and the minister's suppression of the subsequent investigation.

"Even if I tell you what I know," says the diplomat, "you would never believe it."

Mulder says, "You'd be surprised at what I believe, sir."

The minister sighs and leans back in his chair. "I had hoped if I closed my eyes it would go away this time."

"This time?"

"My people, the Bambara, are farmers," says Diabira. "I grew up hearing the old stories—believing them as only a child can believe."

"What kind of stories?"

"The Teliko—the spirits of the air. It was said they rested by day in close, dark places. Deep inside tree hollows and in holes beneath the ground too small even for a child to hide himself. . . ."

In Aboah's hospital room an orderly knocks on his bathroom door. There is no

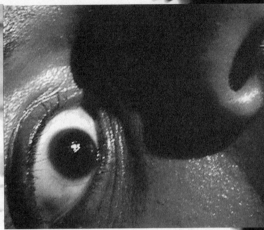

answer. He wheels away a partially enclosed steel food cart.

The minister continues, "Only when the sun fell, when the rest of the world was sleeping, would they come out."

"Come out to do what, sir?" says Mulder.

"I was seven years old, lying awake one night, when I saw him. He was standing over me. His hair was like straw. His eyes like water, staring down at me. I closed my own eyes and screamed, then felt myself being swept up into the air. But when I opened my eyes I saw my father holding me."

Mulder asks, "Then it was a nightmare?"

"That is what my father said," says the minister. "And I believed him. Until the next day. When they found my cousin was dead among his cattle."

Diabira stares at a picture of the dead airline passenger. "Looking exactly like this man," he says.

At the hospital Scully and Bruin examine X rays of Aboah. A large foreign body is lodged in his esophagus. A PET scan indicates that Aboah has no pituitary gland. Both physicians are baffled.

"I can't even begin to explain what we're seeing either, sir," says Scully. "I just hope this patient can provide us with some answers."

"You'll have to find him first," says Mulder, walking up to the pair. "Samuel Aboah's gone. Disappeared."

In an underground parking garage Marcus Duff walks toward his car. Aboah, his hand mottled with white patches, watches him silently—until Duff spots his reflection in his car's sideview mirror.

Startled, Duff wheels and stares into Aboah's eerie gaze.

"Samuel! You scared me!" he says.

Aboah says nothing. He just smiles.

Swallowing his fear, Duff asks Aboah if he's been released from the hospital.

Aboah smiles again and nods.

Duff offers Aboah a lift home. "Lucky for you I was working late," he says.

Aboah smiles, much wider this time. "Yes. Lucky," he says. He holds his blowpipe, already removed from his throat, behind his back.

At the hospital the agents examine the food cart—Aboah's escape vehicle. Mulder looks up in wonder.

"He didn't even *touch* his Jell-O," he says.

Scully tells him that the Philadelphia PD have reported Marcus Duff's car abandoned with keys in the ignition and the hood still warm.

In a dark alley Aboah stands over the paralyzed Duff. He pulls an even thinner tube out of the blowpipe. It is steel, hollow at one end and barbed at the other. He threads it, barbed-end first, up Duff's nostril. Duff's eyes widen in terror.

At the last possible moment, Aboah is interrupted by a patrolling policeman. The policeman's flashlight beam sweeps over the bizarre scene. He sees nobody but the unfortunate Marcus Duff.

From a nearby drainpipe comes the sound of ragged breathing.

Mulder and Scully are at the hospital when Duff, motionless but alive, is wheeled in. They head off to search for Aboah. Mulder is sure he will seek another victim immediately.

"How do you know?" says Scully.

"Because we interrupted him before he could finish."

"Interrupted his killing Duff?"

"No, the killing is just incidental, Scully, to a much more basic need."

"What need?" says Scully.

Mulder posits that Aboah, who was born with no pituitary and lacks the ability to produce melanin, is a member of a lost tribe.

"A clan of sub-Saharan albinos," he says, "linked by a common congenital deficit, who've adapted over generations."

"By stealing other people's hormones?" says Scully.

"Somehow," says Mulder, "Aboah has managed to survive."

They cruise the neighborhood and pass a demolition site. Mulder remembers Pendrell's mentioning of asbestos fibers found on Owen Sanders's body. He stops the car.

Mulder and Scully separate. Flashlights stabbing into the pitch darkness, they search the skeletal remains of the building. Aboah, now completely pigment-free, watches them from his hiding place.

He blows a poison dart into Mulder's neck. The agent manages to cry out for Scully before his paralysis is total.

Scully, reacting to his distress call, crawls frantically through the building's ventilation duct in search of him. She passes the bleached-white body of Alfred Kittel, then locates Mulder.

Aboah crawls up behind her. She whirls and fires her gun in his direction. He vanishes.

Returning to Mulder, she pulls his limp body out of the duct and pulls out her cell phone to call for an ambulance. She doesn't notice that Aboah is behind her, but Mulder makes a supreme effort and shifts his eyes in warning.

Instinctively, Scully whirls, fires, and hits the pouncing Samuel Aboah. He falls, wounded, but still weirdly affectless.

In her office at the FBI Scully types her case notes into her laptop. She writes:

Despite acute trauma to his pituitary gland, Marcus Duff was discharged early this morning from Mt. Zion Medical Center. He is expected to testify before a grand jury in the capital case against Samuel Aboah, who is being charged with five counts of murder. It remains uncertain, however, whether Aboah will live long enough to stand trial. His response to hormone therapy has been poor, his deterioration progressive.

Samuel Aboah lies in his bed at Mt. Zion, connected to all manner of life support apparatus. His face is blanched and drawn, and his pink eyes are enlarged with Graves' disease.

Scully types on:

My conviction remains intact that the mechanism by which Aboah killed— and, in turn, survived—can only be explained by medical science. And that

science will eventually discover his place in the broader context of evolution. But what science may never be able to explain is our ineffable fear of the alien among us. A fear which often drives us not to search for understanding—but to deceive, inveigle, and obfuscate. To obscure the truth not only from others—but from ourselves.

back story:

Like many of executive producer Howard Gordon's episodes, "Teliko" had a long and tortured birth process. "Teliko" was born out of sleeplessness and desperation and anxiety, just like "D.P.O." (3X03) last season and "Sleepless" (2X04) the season before that.

Explains Gordon: "Before I wrote it, I spent about a month working on a story about someone who was immortal—or, at least, appeared to be immortal. With that one I went down the wrong road entirely."

After several intense discussions (and emergency cigar-smoking sessions) with consulting producer Ken Horton, Gordon had the notion of dragging two other story elements—melanin-sucking albino vampires and the notion of xenophobia, or fear of foreigners—off the back burner. Chris Carter happily approved the story line, and Gordon wrote a first draft of the script—which everybody hated. "It was way off the mark," says Gordon. "But Chris stayed calm. He convened a meeting and I got significant notes, then we reconvened with Frank [Spotnitz] and the gang and we completely restructured the story and then I basically wrote it all over again in four days."

The episode hurtled toward production—and one final session of self-flagellation. Gordon says, "I'd just come back from pre-production meetings in Vancouver when Chris said, in front of the whole group, 'Why are we telling this story?' And I said, 'Well, Chris, I don't know. But it's shooting, so I'll have to get back to you on that.'

"And once again," Gordon adds, "Chris was telling me that the episode needed one more rewrite, one more polish, to give it thematic cohesion. And that's when he came up with the notion of 'deceive, inveigle, and obfuscate.' I went through the whole story that day and night with that template, that tonic chord, in mind. And it came out just fine."

It was also Carter's idea, says Gordon, to

equip the melanin-sucking Samuel Aboah with a combination blowpipe and pituitary extractor—and have him carry the lethal instrument in his esophagus. The notion of the Teliko is not entirely fictional—it is the name of a mythological African "spirit of the air," sometimes thought to be an albino. In fact, in certain African cultures, albinos are shunned and reviled. The Teliko's emergence from the West African country of Burkina Faso was suggested by John Shiban, who remembered it from his days programming foreign air-mail rates into electronic postage meters for a computer software company.

The casting process was difficult. "We wanted real African guys," says L.A. casting director Rick Millikan, "but in television you don't have a lot of time. We only had a few days, so we called in every real African person we could find. We brought in an African theater troupe passing through town. We called African consulates, the Olympic committee."

In the end, the American actor Carl Lumbly, well-known for his role as Detective Mark Petrie on the CBS series *Cagney & Lacey*, played the Afro-Caribbean INS official Marcus Duff. Winning the role of Aboah was Willie Amakye, a citizen of Ghana who speaks English well but his first language, Fanti, better. (Director James Charleston remembers that Willie Amakye was "a little green, but extremely adaptive and extremely willing.")

Amakye is a four-time member of the Ghanian Olympic track team (he's run the 800 meters and the 4X400 relay). He was cast in *The X-Files* shortly after returning home from the Atlanta Games—home for the past dozen years being Southern California, where he's made his living acting in commercials and movies like *Congo* and *Amistad*.

Amakye's on-screen transformation from black to white and back again posed a difficult challenge for makeup artist Laverne Basham and her assistant Pearl Louie. "Before he came up here, we looked at photographs of albinos and black people with vitiligo," says Basham.

"But we weren't really prepared for how black Willie's skin was." The answer, she says, was to prepare a base of several layers of Dermablend cover-up cream, topped by several more layers of standard white powder augmented with a touch or two of pink powder for color. Aboah's pink transparent eyeballs were created with contact lenses.

While composing his music for the episode, Mark Snow called up an electronic smorgasbord of African drums, flutes, and chants—and admits sneaking in some samples from "The Bulgarian Women's Chorus," a recording well-known in Southern California as a pledge-drive premium for public radio station KCRW.

"Teliko" marks the debut of the expensive airplane cabin mock-up built specifically for "Tempus Fugit" and "Max" (4X17 and 4X18), but used here before its hydraulic special-effects shaking rig was completed.

"Teliko" is Greek for "end."

Ⓧ

The tagline on this episode was changed to "Deceive, Inveigle, Obfuscate."

Ⓧ

When Mulder checks Samuel Aboah's resident alien card, we see that Aboah's birthday is September 25, the same as Gillian Anderson's daughter, Piper Maru.

Ⓧ

The perils of getting into—and out of— character: Before Willie Amakye's first day of filming in Vancouver, hair stylist Anji Bembem and her assistant Dean Scheck dyed Amakye's hair bright orange—the better to switch it back and forth from black to white. "Back at the hotel, people thought I was the African Dennis Rodman," says Amakye.

Ⓧ

Back in Los Angeles, Amakye adds, a young couple in Malibu he's friendly with watched the episode with their children and when he asked them for their reaction they told him, "Willie, we love you very much, but stay away from the kids for awhile."

Ⓧ

the field where i died

In an effort to prevent a mass suicide at a
fanatical religious cult, Mulder and Scully
interrogate one of the wives of the polygamous
cult leader. Under hypnosis, her accounts of
her past lives—and deaths—are inexplicably
tied to the agents' own.

episode: 4X05

first aired: November 3, 1996

written by: Glen Morgan and James Wong

editor: Heather MacDougall

directed by: Rob Bowman

guest stars:
Mitch Pileggi (AD Walter Skinner)
Kristen Cloke (Melissa Riedel-Ephesian)
Michael Massee (Vernon Ephesian)
Anthony Harrison (FBI Agent Riggins)
Donna White (Therapist)
Doug Abrahams (Harbaugh)
Michael Dobson (BATF Agent)
Les Gallagher (Attorney)
Douglas Roy Dack (Mighty Man)

principal settings:
Apison and Chattanooga,
Tennessee

fox Mulder stands alone in a verdant field, his expression one of profound sadness. We are privy to his thoughts. They are:

> At times I almost dream I too have spent a life the sages' way, and tread once more familiar paths.
> Perchance I perished in an arrogant self-reliance an age ago;
> And in that act, a prayer for one more chance went up so earnest, so . . .

He is gazing at two faded Civil War–era daguerreotypes of a man and a woman. He hesitates, then continues.

> Instinct with better light let in by Death that life was blotted out—not so completely but scattered wrecks enough of it to remain dim memories: as now, when seems once more the goal in sight again.

In search of illegal firearms, a large team of federal agents—including Mulder and Scully—storm the Deep South rural commune of the Temple of the Seven Stars. There is no sign, however, of either the weapons or the cult's leader, Vernon Ephesian.

As the agents tear apart the compound, Mulder is drawn ineffably into a field behind it. He hears faint voices in the distance and walks toward their source. He reaches a wooden trap door, almost undetectable in the weeds and grass. He pulls it open.

In a bunker below him, Ephesian and his six wives, holding glasses of colored liquid, recite Scripture. Mulder knocks the poison from the lips of Melissa Riedel-Ephesian, the youngest. She spits her first mouthful back in his face. None of the other cult members commit suicide; all are arrested.

At a nearby command post, AD Skinner addresses the assembled FBI and Bureau of Alcohol, Tobacco, and Firearms agents. He plays a tape recording of an informant—a raspy-voiced middle-aged man identified only as Sidney—telling the feds about a major arsenal at the compound, child abuse, and plans to do "something crazy."

Skinner tells the agents that without further evidence, they will have to release the cult members within twenty-four hours. He pulls aside Mulder and Scully and explains that they've been drafted into the task force to investigate Ephesian's alleged paranormal abilities.

Scully disagrees with this analysis. "We believe Ephesian is a paranoid charismatic sociopath," she says. "He is obsessed with the Book of Revelation, and he'll use his knowledge of biblical text to get anything he wants from his followers."

Skinner reminds them that Ephesian had six women on the brink of suicide. "My concern is," he says, "if the Temple members are released, any subsequent investigation will ignite Ephesian's paranoia to such a degree that we won't have another Waco on our hands. We'll have Jonestown."

Mulder and Scully interrogate Ephesian, a blue-eyed fanatic who claims to have heard the preaching of the Apostle John Mark in a past life. His lawyer denies that there are any members of his church named Sidney.

Ephesian has a chilling warning for the agents: "For your own souls," he says, "it is vital to understand that soon, very soon, all disbelievers, all beasts—if that means 'me' or this 'Sidney' or 'you'—all will be destroyed by God's Mighty Men."

Mulder and Scully begin their interrogations of Ephesian's wives. "Let's start with her," says Mulder, pointing to a picture of Melissa.

Melissa is a beautiful woman, obviously deeply troubled. She acts the perfect cult member, however, giving blissed-out answers to Scully's questions.

Then Scully asks her whether she's witnessed any child abuse at the Temple. Melissa becomes agitated. She begins

making masculine gestures and speaking in a raspy voice.

"Lookit, I don't know where you two are gettin' that from," she says. "I mean, I saw a couple of things. It coulda been anything, right?"

Scully calls Melissa's name.

"Melissa? I don't know nobody named that."

"Sidney?" Mulder asks.

"What is this, the McCarthy hearings?" says Melissa.

On her notepad Scully writes "multiple personality." Mulder glances at it and writes "past life."

"Sidney, can you tell me who is the president of the United States right now?" Mulder asks.

"Who is the president? What kind of dumb question is that? Harry Truman!"

Mulder and Scully brief Skinner and request permission to take Melissa back to the cultists' compound in hopes that one of her personalities will reveal the whereabouts of the weapons.

After Skinner reluctantly agrees, Scully upbraids Mulder for not revealing what he really believes—that Melissa is being "invaded" by her past lives.

"Because he wouldn't believe it," says Mulder.

Scully says, accusingly, "I don't believe that you feel responsible for those fifty lives, or Melissa Riedel. You're responsible only to yourself."

Revisiting the compound with Mulder and Scully, Melissa gazes sadly at pictures of herself with Ephesian. In the nursery, she briefly assumes the personality of a four-year-old named Lily. When Scully presses Lily about child abuse, Sidney reappears.

"Lookit, leave the kid alone," he says. "I'm sending the kid home."

Mulder tells "Sidney," "You can all go home. You can all be safe. All he—they—need to do is tell him where the weapons are hidden."

At this, Melissa walks slowly out of the compound and into the field where Mulder found her. With a mounting sense of unease, Mulder and Scully follow. Melissa speaks—this time in a strong Southern accent.

"The weapons were placed in the bunker," says Melissa. "Which they had built the night before."

Scully says to Mulder, excitedly, "That's why it wasn't on the ATF report!"

Melissa continues. "The Federals would arrive in the morning before the sun," she says. "Realizing the government's might and number, most believed that they indeed would never again see the light of day—just as they had watched their brothers die days before on Missionary Ridge."

She speaks with bittersweet dignity.

"We had received word of General Cleburn's retreat from the Union Army," she says. "As a nurse, I had been ordered from Hamilton County to meet the troops, but in actuality, I was searching—for him. Knowing he would attempt to remain in Tennessee rather than retreat to Dalton.

"I found him here. Amongst the others who had been lost as General Thomas pushed through the Confederate line. The Federal troops would appear from that direction. Rather than retreat any further, they fought them, hiding us in the bunker. Inside, I could smell the smoke, feel the bodies as they dropped down upon the ground above. Every last one. Twenty-sixth of November, 1863. I was here."

She turns to Mulder. "As were you," she says.

On Mulder's face is an expression of profound loss and longing.

Melissa, gazing at Mulder with sadness and love, says, "This is the field where I watched you die."

Over Scully's strong objections, Mulder arranges for a therapist to perform a past-life regression on Melissa. While under hypnosis, the cult member—speaking in her own voice—recounts a heinous incident of child-beating by Ephesian and his goon squad, the Mighty Men.

Sidney breaks in to say that Ephesian has hidden the guns in some Civil War bunkers, but he doesn't know where they are. Scully suggests to Mulder that they might examine some maps of the Civil War battlefield. Mulder turns to Scully and says, intently

but inexplicably, "You *know* where to find the other bunkers."

Then Mulder addresses the still-hypnotized woman.

"Melissa, it's me," he says. "I want you to go back. Back to the field." She looks at him with agonized longing. The Confederate Army nurse speaks.

"Your eyes may have changed shade," she says to Mulder, longingly, "but it cannot color the soul behind them. We have come together in this life, this time, only to meet in passing. It is so heartbreaking to wait. I miss you."

Scully tells a devastated Mulder that Melissa's voices are a product of mental illness, and besides, there's no way to prove she's telling the truth.

"There's one way," says Mulder firmly.

The therapist hypnotizes Mulder. "I want you to go into your past," she says. "Beyond your life as Fox Mulder. What do you see?"

Eyes closed, Mulder forces out the words.

"Ghetto streets. Shattered glass. I am a woman. A Jewish woman. Poland. My son is with me. He is Samantha. In this life, she is my son. My father is dead in the street. He is Scully. He's gone on now, waiting for us. Souls come back together, different but always together. Again and again. To learn.

"I can't go to my father. The Gestapo standing next to him. An officer. He is Cancer Man. Evil returns as evil. But love—

souls mate. Eternal. My husband is taken away from me. To the camps. He is Melissa. We're always taken away."

Tears run down Mulder's cheek.

"I'm rising now. High above my body. Above the field. My face is bloody. In the bunker. The Federals are gone. My sergeant is also dead. He is Scully. Sarah, hold me. She is sad. She is Melissa. She lives near the battle. Her name is Kavanaugh. My name is Sullivan Biddle."

At the Hamilton County courthouse, Scully examines an antique map of the Civil War battlefield. She turns to a stack of old county registers and finds the names "Kavanaugh, Sarah," and "Biddle, Sullivan" written in longhand. She looks inside a drawer marked "Photographs—People— Civil War" and finds daguerreotypes of Sullivan Biddle, in Confederate gray, and Sarah Kavanaugh, in a prim dress.

They look strikingly like Fox Mulder and Melissa Riedel.

At the command post Mulder gazes at the faded images. Scully tells him that Ephesian—along with Melissa and the other cult members—are about to be released.

"Dana," says Mulder, "what if early in our four years together somebody told you that we'd been friends together—always. Would it have changed the way we look at one another?"

Scully says, tenderly, "Even if I knew for certain, I wouldn't change a day."

She turns to leave, then pauses. "Well, maybe that 'flukeman' thing. I could have lived without that just fine."

In the interrogation room Mulder plays Melissa the tape recording of herself as Sarah Kavanaugh. "I don't believe in it," she says.

She adds, "Those tapes are saying that we chose the lives we lived before we were born. And who we live with. It's a nice idea. It's a beautiful idea. I want to believe. And if I knew it were true I'd want to start over. I'd want to end this pointless life."

Mulder grasps her hand. "Sarah, if it were true, no life would be pointless," he says.

Melissa tears the photographs in half. The door opens and Vernon Ephesian looks in.

"Melissa," he says, his eyes glinting with madness. "It's time to leave."

Scully tells Mulder that the BATF is searching the fields outside the cult compound. Inside the Temple of the Seven Stars, Ephesian greets his followers warmly—but notes the agents in the field with alarm. He looks suspiciously at Melissa.

Mulder warns Skinner that, cornered, Ephesian might endanger the lives of everyone inside. In the compound the Mighty Men order the cultists to listen to Ephesian speak.

"Marvel not, my brethren, if the world may hate you," says Ephesian. "We know that we have passed from death to life—because we love the brethren. You will receive the love of God because he laid down his life for us."

At the command post an agent relays Ephesian's ravings via a parabolic microphone. Skinner, alarmed, orders an armed assault on the Temple.

Inside, Ephesian preaches his doomsday sermon. The Mighty Men pour out glasses of poison. Other cultists fire assault rifles at the agents, wounding several. There is a brief cease-fire, amid which Mulder and Scully arrive. Mulder lays down his gun and walks toward the compound.

"Mulder, no!" shouts Scully. "You're dead!"

Mulder runs into the now-silent compound—where most of the cult members are sprawled lifeless.

Ephesian, poisoned drink in hand, stands

over a sobbing Melissa. "Behold. I am the life forevermore," he says. Melissa takes the cup and gazes out the window and into the fields.

Mulder arrives. He is too late.

Ephesian is dead, and there is only enough time to cradle Melissa, who lies beside him. Her lifeless hands clutch the torn photographs.

Fox Mulder stands alone in a verdant field at dawn, his expression one of profound sadness. We are privy to his thoughts. They are:

> At times I almost dream I too have spent a life the sages' way, and tread once more familiar paths.
> Perchance I perished in an arrogant self-reliance an age ago;
> And in that act, a prayer for one more chance went up so earnest, so . . .

He is gazing at the pictures of Sarah Kavanaugh and Sullivan Biddle. He hesitates, then continues.

> Instinct with better light let in by Death that life was blotted out—not so completely but scattered wrecks enough of it to remain dim memories: as now, when seems once more the goal in sight again.

back story:
Although Shirley MacLaine, David Koresh, and Jim Jones are standing just out of camera range, the real creative godfather of this episode is Ken Burns, the creator of the PBS documentary series *The Civil War*. The wartime romance between Sullivan Biddle and Sarah Kavanaugh—Mulder and Melissa Ephesian in their supposed former lives—was inspired by the touching letters from Major Sullivan Ballou, a Union officer,

and his wife, Sarah, that were a highlight of Burns's documentary.

"That part was a favorite of Glen's," says Kristen Kloke, who should know. Not only is Kloke the principal guest star in the series, she is the consulting producer and cowriter's fiancée. She was also, like many of the leading actors in Morgan and Wong's fourth-season offerings, a star of their former series *Space: Above and Beyond*.

Kristen Cloke did her own research on multiple-personality disorders before filming started, and based each of her several personae on people in her own life. As was evident to even the most casual of viewers, acting the part of such a disturbed woman was an intense process. "All her switching from one personality to another was provoked by sadness," she says. "You have to be incredibly sad to run away from yourself like she did."

Michael Massee, who played Vernon Ephesian, isn't currently in a relationship with anyone from *The X-Files*, but he did have a supporting role in *Playing God*, the feature film starring David Duchovny due out this fall. "I play a kind of quirky FBI agent," he says with a chuckle.

For the role of Ephesian, says Massee, he tried to make the cult leader as normal-looking and nondemonic as possible. "The whole basis of that performance was to be understated—to be the guy next door," he says. "You have to believe that he believes his own rap. When he speaks, he's just

explaining that 'this is the way it is'—and that's when it gets very scary."

A scare of a different sort was experienced when editor Heather MacDougall put together her first cut. At more than an hour long, "The Field Where I Died" set an unofficial *X-Files* record for excess length. In order to make room for the commercials, a full eighteen minutes had to be painfully excised: onto the digital equivalent of the cutting-room floor went two entire personalities of Melissa. Also lost was most of a third—the little girl Lily, who now floats to the surface only briefly.

To create the Waco-like Temple of the Seven Stars, the Vancouver production team made the relatively rare decision to build it all on a soundstage at their home base, North Shore Studios. Art director Gary Allen, for one, thinks it was the most expensive in-studio set the series has ever constructed. To stimulate the proper mood for Melissa's death scene, composer Mark Snow "sampled" a recording of Gregorian chants.

To provide verisimilitude for Scully's county courthouse scenes, props master Ken Hawryliw contacted local officials in the real town of Apison, Tennessee—it's about an hour's drive east of Chattanooga—who sent him an actual citizen's registry from the Civil War period. It was reproduced by the props department with the aid of an expert calligrapher. The photographs of Sullivan and Sarah—which at first, second, and even third glance seem to be daguerreotypes of Duchovny and Kloke—are actually public-domain photographs copied from books of the period. "They're hybrids," says Hawryliw. "We took the clothing from one picture, the face from another, and the hair from still another. It's a very good job of computer melding, and you really can't tell what we've done. The man whose face we used, in particular, looked so much like Mulder it was uncanny."

Events of the present, however, have many other ways of intruding on historical reveries. The fact that the Heaven's Gate tragedy occurred less than six months after the episode aired produced some overheated calls from the press to Chris Carter, who understandably declined to comment.

Another type of question was posed by many fans: Is the fact that Mulder and Scully were always friends, not lovers, in their past lives a way to explain why in their current incarnations their relationship hasn't blossomed into romance?

Adhering strictly to the *X-Files'* Rule of Ambiguity, none of the writer-producers are willing to commit themselves one way or another.

Gillian Anderson, however, has her own preference. "I loved that script," she says. "It made me cry. And the concept of Mulder and Scully meeting in a past life— it's something that, for once, I'd truly love to believe."

Kristen Cloke formerly appeared in *Space: Above and Beyond*, the series produced by writers Glen Morgan and Jim Wong, as Lieutenant Shane Vansen. In one episode from that series, she actually appeared in a scene with David Duchovny, who had a cameo role as a pool-playing android.

ⓧ

The poem in the teaser and at the end is from "Paracelsus," by Robert Browning.

ⓧ

Vernon Ephesian's name combines real-life cult leader David Koresh's real first name, Vernon, and the title of a book of the Bible.

ⓧ

episode: 4X06
first aired: November 11, 1996
written by:
Valerie Mayhew and
Vivien Mayhew
editor: Michael S. Stern
directed by: Kim Manners

sanguinarium

At a busy—and lucrative—cosmetic surgery clinic, doctors are murdering patients with the tools of their trade. Several clues point toward demonic possession.

guest stars:
Richard Beymer (Dr. Jack Franklyn)
O-Lan Jones (Rebecca Waite)
Arlene Mazerolle (Dr. Theresa Shannon)
John Juliani (Dr. Harrison Lloyd)
Gregory Thirloway (Dr. Mitchell Kaplan)
Paul Raskin (Dr. Eric Ilaqua)
Marie Stillin (L.A. Surgeon)
Norman Armour (ER Doctor)
Andrew Airlie (Attorney)
Martin Evans (Dr. Hartman)
Nina Roman (Jill Holwager)
Nancy J. Lilley (Liposuction Patient)
Celine Lockhart (Patient)
Kevin McCrae (ER Surgeon)
Erin Jeffery (ER Nurse)
Leanne Adachi (ER Nurse #2)
Constance Barnes (Nurse)

principal settings:
Chicago and Winnetka, Illinois;
Los Angeles, California

rebecca Waite, a nurse at the Aesthetic Surgery Unit of Greenwood Memorial Hospital, prepares a female patient for liposuction.

"Is it going to hurt?" asks the patient.

"You won't feel a thing," says the nurse.

Waite and an orderly wheel the patient, on a gurney, toward the operating room. "I'm going to give you a tranquilizer now," says the nurse, "and then right before the operation the doctor will give you an injection of saline and anaesthetic. All you have to worry about is buying a new wardrobe."

In the scrub room Waite tells the plastic surgeon, Dr. Harrison Lloyd, that his patient is ready and waiting.

"Fine," says Lloyd. "What else am I scheduled for?'

"You've got a scalp reduction and a blepharoplasty following."

"Are they prepped?"

"Um, no," says Waite, puzzled. "Would you like me to—"

"Get them ready, please," says Lloyd. "I'd like to move right along this morning."

Waite leaves, and Lloyd prepares to operate. The surgeon trembles and perspires; he scrubs his hands so harshly that they bleed into his surgical gloves. He walks into an operating room, stands over an unattended patient, and opens the man's belly with a shaky slash of his scalpel. Lloyd jabs a cannula probe into the wound and suctions out globules of viscous human fat.

Waite completes her work and returns to the liposuction patient, still waiting.

"Is the doctor going to be much longer?" asks the patient. "I think my tranquilizer's starting to wear off."

In the operating room, Lloyd saws his instrument violently through the man's body; the yellow ooze entering the collection chamber turns bloodred.

Nurse Waite, puzzled at Lloyd's absence, leaves her patient, walks into the hallway, and sees Lloyd's horrendous act on a TV monitor outside the operating room. She flings open the door and calls Lloyd's name. The doctor is covered with blood. He looks up with a blank stare. "I think this patient is finished," he says.

Mulder and Scully, called into the case, question Lloyd at his apartment. The distraught surgeon explains that during the murder, he felt completely unable to control his actions—at once inside and outside his own body. Mulder raises the possibility of spirit possession.

"What else do you call it?" says Lloyd.

Scully breaks in to ask if Lloyd had been taking prescription drugs. Lloyd answers that he's been taking an occasional sleeping pill—as well as a prescription antacid. In fact, they learn from his medical records that Lloyd has been taking dangerous levels of a controversial central nervous system depressant. To Scully, that seems a plausible explanation for his bizarre actions.

At the crime scene—Operating Room 3, still splashed with blood—Scully explains to Mulder just what the real problem is.

"This place is a veritable factory, Mulder," she says. "Cosmetic surgery is the boom industry of the medical world, and ASU wards like this are a gold mine."

Mulder looks down at the floor and discovers five circular scorch marks. He dips his finger in blood and connects the circles.

"The shape of a pentagram," he says.

Outside the operating room, they run into Nurse Waite and question her about the patient's death. Waite says she is unable to help them.

"Are you aware that Dr. Lloyd is claiming he was possessed during the incident?" says Mulder.

Nurse Waite says, "I guess it's cheaper than malpractice insurance."

Mulder smiles. Scully looks up at the unit's TV monitors: the four remaining operating rooms are going full blast.

"There's magic going on here, Mulder," says Scully. "Only it's being done with silicone, collagen, and a well-placed scalpel."

In a hospital conference room the unit's remaining plastic surgeons—Drs. Theresa Shannon, Eric Ilacqua, Mitchell Kaplan, and Jack Franklyn—hold an emergency meeting. They discuss the murder and vow to continue business as usual. A maid

into their expensive conference table is a five-pointed star.

Nurse Waite, in Operating Room 2, preps a partially anesthetized female patient for a laser face peel. The patient asks with some anxiety why she cannot feel her feet. Waite soothingly reassures her, all the while removing five large leeches from the woman's stomach.

In Mulder's motel room the agent stares into a mirror and contemplates his nose from several different angles. This investigative procedure is interrupted by Scully's knock.

Mulder pops a tape into a VCR and plays back the fatal operation, pointing out that the five circular marks on the floor were already present.

"Presuming it has anything to do with this," says Scully, "who put them there?"

Mulder replies that he doesn't know, but that a pentagram is a symbol of protection and positive power.

"It makes sense," he adds, "that witchcraft or black magic would find a theater in a place like this—preying on the weak and vainglorious."

Scully protests that there is no further evidence that witchcraft is taking place. Mulder points out that there is: The antacid Lloyd has been taking contains belladonna—an herb used in hexing rituals.

"Well, if it's that simple," says Scully, "why don't you put out an APB for someone riding a broom and wearing a tall black hat?"

In the ASU scrub room Dr. Ilacqua—his face oddly expressionless—prepares to go home. Dr. Shannon arrives to scrub up for her last surgery of the day. It is the face peel in OR2.

Rebecca Waite enters to announce that the patient is prepped and ready. Shannon and Waite walk down the corridor to their operating room, but when Shannon tries to open the door, it is locked. She looks up at the TV monitor.

Inside, Ilacqua is standing over her patient—he is burning a hole through her brain with a hand-held laser. Shannon, frantic, pounds on the door and screams for Ilacqua to open up.

Waite turns and flees the scene.

Mulder and Scully open a new murder file. In OR2 Scully questions an ashen-faced Ilacqua, who says he doesn't remember how he got into the operating room, but realizes exactly what he's done. Scully reaches into the shirt pocket of his scrubs and pulls out a bottle of prescription medicine.

In the ASU consultation room Mulder stares, fascinated, at a computer monitor. On the screen is his own face, viewed head on and in profile. Just a touch of a button gives him a slimmer, trimmer nose. He toggles his proboscis from "before" to "after" several times.

Scully's entrance interrupts his reverie. Mulder pops a tape into the VCR; it shows Ilacqua's atrocity in all its horror. The five leech marks on the patient's stomach, representing the five points of a pentagram, are clearly visible. Scully shows him the prescription pills she took from the surgeon.

"Think it's just a coincidence?" she says skeptically.

At the ASU conference room the remaining doctors hold another damage-control meeting. Mulder and Scully enter unannounced.

"It appears we've interrupted a gathering again," says Mulder.

"A gathering?" says Dr. Franklyn stiffly.

He adds, "Sir, can you imagine this group's concern about what's happened? And our urgency to resolve this—and to finally bring the person responsible to justice."

"Finally?" says Scully.

The other doctors squirm as Franklyn discloses that there were a series of similar deaths in the ASU ten years previously. All were ruled accidental.

"Were any of you here at the time?" asks Mulder.

Several staff members were, says Franklyn, but adds quickly that Rebecca Waite was on the ward during all the earlier incidents. She left the hospital then, he says, and transferred back only six weeks previously. Even more suspiciously, he adds, they have been unable to reach her since she fled.

Rebecca Waite's house is dark, save for candles illuminating a path to a kind of altar. Waite, stripped to the waist and chanting softly in an unknown tongue, kneels in front of it.

She is in a trancelike state. She cuts a lock of her own hair and consigns it to the flame.

Mulder and Scully pull up in front of the darkened house and cautiously step onto the front porch. They spot an old straw broom leaning beside the screen door.

"Probable cause," Mulder deadpans.

A metal pentagram is affixed to the door frame. Guns drawn, they kick open the door and enter. A few of the candles still burn, but the house is deserted.

A Jaguar sedan pulls to a stop and Jack Franklyn walks through the front door of his starkly modern suburban home. It too is dark.

He flips the light switches. Nothing. He cautiously climbs a staircase and enters a second-floor bathroom. On the bathroom wall, in jagged bloodred letters, is scrawled the words:

"VANITAS VANITATUM."

His bathtub is filled to the brink with blood; blood drips from the bathtub faucet.

Franklyn peers down into his own bloody reflection—and a hand shoots up from the bloody basin, grasping at his face.

Another hand, holding a knife, emerges. A blood-covered female form flings itself on Franklyn, knocking him violently to the ground.

Then nothing. The blood-drenched doctor is alone.

He creeps down the stairs, picks up the phone, and dials 911. He gets a recording. Rebecca Waite springs from hiding and attacks him from behind. He grabs the dagger from her hand and, gasping for breath, strikes.

Mulder and Scully arrive on the scene just as Waite, struggling and raving incoherently, is being pulled into an ambulance by a pair of policemen.

"They don't understand! You have to tell them!" she tells Mulder. "I tried to stop him but it's too powerful! Someone has to stop it!"

She tries to explain but retches—then coughs up small, sharp metallic objects. She collapses in pain.

Scully summons the paramedics and orders them to take her to the hospital. Scully leaves with her, and Mulder kneels to examine the considerable pile of straight pins that Waite has left behind.

Inside the house, Dr. Shannon sews up a wicked cut on Franklyn's forehead.

Mulder looks in on the pair. "Nothing that a little plastic surgery won't fix up, huh?" he says.

Franklyn glares at him, annoyed. "I'm sorry," says the surgeon. "This evening has all been a bit much, and I need to get some rest."

Mulder and Shannon leave, and Franklyn lies down on his bed faceup.

A few moments later, his rigid body levitates several feet above the bed surface. Eyes wide open, he smiles with satisfaction.

At the motel Scully tells Mulder that Waite has died on the operating table: "From massive blood loss due to esophageal hemorrhaging, caused by the expulsion of hundreds of straight pins."

Mulder suggests that the real cause of death was allotriophagy: "The spontaneous vomiting or disgorgement of foul or strange objects, usually associated with someone possessed."

He shows Scully a book on witchcraft he took from Rebecca Waite's home. He also shows her a calendar from the witch's house, with hand-drawn pentagrams marking the dates of several major holy days celebrated by practitioners of the occult. Each holiday she marked coincides with one of the plastic surgeons' victims birthdays.

"So you think she was choosing her victims based on their birth dates?" asks Scully.

Mulder replies, "Remember—I said the pentagram was a protective symbol. I think Rebecca Waite was trying to save those patients."

In the ASU scrub room Drs. Kaplan and Franklyn prepare for the day's surgery. Kaplan is worried that Franklyn, after his close call the night before, is in no shape to operate.

"Look at yourself," he says. "You look like hell, Jack."

Kaplan tells Franklyn to go home and declares that he will perform Franklyn's first procedure—a chemical face peel.

In their car on the way to the hospital, Mulder and Scully get a phone call from the hospital records department telling them that the face peel patient has a birthday corresponding to one of the witches' holidays.

Kaplan, in a trance like voice, tells Franklyn's patient that he is taking over her case. Mulder and Scully arrive at the ASU—to the sound of screaming. Kaplan

has poured acid over the patient's face. Her skin burns and bubbles. She has been horribly disfigured.

In the conference room Shannon explains to Mulder and Scully just what is at risk. "The ASU accounts for over 50 percent of this hospital's revenue," she says. "Do you understand what that means?"

Scully replies, "It means that while doctors in other fields have seen their earnings fall because of managed health care, you've all become wealthy."

Shannon bitterly concedes as much. That was why, she says, the hospital succeeded in covering up five mysterious deaths ten years ago.

"There were *five* deaths?" asks Mulder.

Four were patients, says Shannon, and the fifth was a staff surgeon, Dr. Clifford Cox, who overdosed on drugs. Mulder asks for the files on Cox and the four patients.

"Why, Mulder?" asks Scully. "What are you thinking?"

At a computer terminal—the same one where Mulder underwent his virtual nose job—Shannon calls up Clifford Cox's file. His birth date doesn't correspond to any witches' holiday, but Mulder asks Shannon to run Cox's face through the cosmetic surgery program anyway.

"Let's move the eyes further apart and strengthen the forehead," says Mulder.

Shannon says stiffly, "That is beyond our surgical capabilities."

Mulder says, "I know."

With a few clicks of the keyboard, Cox's face morphs into another, familiar-looking visage.

"I don't understand," says a shocked Shannon. "It looks like Jack Franklyn."

Emerging from the darkness inside his

chillingly impersonal mansion, Jack Franklyn perspires, trembles, and breathes heavily. Wielding an ornate dagger, he carves something indecipherable into his black marble floor.

At the hospital Scully tells Mulder that Franklyn hasn't answered his telephone or responded to her pages.

"What are you thinking, Mulder?" she says. "That Dr. Cox murdered these patients ten years ago and then became Dr. Franklyn?"

"No, Scully," he says. "I think he murdered those patients so that he *could* become Dr. Franklyn."

"This kind of transformation is medically impossible," says Scully.

"It's not medicine, Scully. It's blood sacrifice—the most potent offering in black magic. What if this man, having reached the limits of medical miracles, decided to stage a miracle all his own?"

In an empty operating room a haggard Jack Franklyn selects several surgical instruments from a tray. Shannon enters and asks him what he's doing.

"Stay right there," she says, suddenly frightened. She turns to leave. Shannon concentrates briefly on the instruments in his hand. They—plus the other ones on his tray—disappear.

Shannon doubles over in pain. Blood bubbles from her mouth.

Franklyn kisses her on the forehead as he leaves.

"I hope those instruments were properly sterilized," he says.

Mulder and Scully enter Franklyn's empty home. Mulder stands on the stairway landing and looks down. He discovers a large pentagram inscribed on the floor below.

"This one's different," he tells Scully. "It's been inverted. These two upright points represent the goat of lust attacking heaven with its horns."

Scully says, "He's inscribed all the names of the patients who were killed. Including Shannon."

In Greenwood Memorial Hospital's emergency room Shannon lies on a gurney. ER doctors work frantically to save her.

In an empty ASU operating room Jack

Franklyn stands stone-faced. He takes a scalpel and makes a careful incision across the top of his forehead.

Mulder and Scully arrive at the ER and learn of Shannon's condition.

"Don't let them operate, Scully," says Mulder. "Hold them off until you hear from me."

Franklyn stands in a pool of his own blood. He begins peeling the skin away from his face—from the incision down.

Scully enters the room where Shannon is being prepped for surgery. She flashes her badge and demands that the attending surgeons postpone the operation. The doctors look at her incredulously and refuse.

In the now empty ASU operating room, Mulder kneels down and discovers a lifeless mask of flesh—Dr. Franklyn's old face.

He returns to the ER. Shannon's surgery is over. The doctors have removed the surgical instruments from her intestinal tract. Shannon will survive.

"Then he failed," says Mulder softly.

He is somewhat surprised.

An alarm sounds and there is a commotion in the hall outside. Mulder and Scully sprint toward the sound. In another operating room a blood-covered blank-faced surgeon is being restrained.

"I tried to stop him!" cries a nurse. "He just went crazy!"

Other doctors try to revive the crazed doctor's patient.

"What is this patient's birth date?" asks Mulder. Scully snatches a chart from the wall.

"October thirty-first," she says. "Halloween."

A Jaguar sedan pulls into the parking lot of City of Angels Hospital Medical Center.

Inside her office, a middle-aged female

physician is interviewing an attractive, square-faced younger colleague in her office.

"I can't tell you happy we are that you're joining us, Dr. Hartman," she says.

Dr. Hartman receives the compliment handsomely. "I like what I've seen so far," he says. "But the truth is, I've always been drawn to Los Angeles.

"I like to say: 'Whoever God didn't get around to creating in His own image, it's our job to re-create in ours.'"

back story:
Written by Valerie and Vivian Mayhew, the most junior writers on the *X-Files* staff, "Sanguinarium" proceeded with eerie smoothness from beginning to end. The story was conceived, "beaten out," and outlined in one ultra-productive brainstorming session—then immediately approved by Chris Carter, written, and put into production with the bare minimum of script changes. Filming and postproduction went off without a hitch. After viewing the finished version, hardened and cynical Fox Network executives were seen to burst into tears of joy and spontaneous applause. END DREAM SEQUENCE.

In reality, making "Sanguinarium" was a rather bumpy and drawn-out "learning experience." But what else would you expect considering:

1. The gory and touchy subject matter
2. The *X-Files*' high standards and demanding production schedule
3. The fact that the sisters were turning out their very first hour of network television

"It took a while before we got the story right—and 'Sanguinarium' evolved with input from the entire *X-Files* team," says Valerie Mayhew, the younger and more talkative of the pair. "We did have some of our own ideas, but one of the things we did was bounce some of them off of Glen Morgan and James Wong. And they kept saying to us, 'The scariest things are the most everyday things. So—what's scary?' And during one of these conversations, Vivian was paged. She didn't recognize the phone number, but she called it anyway. And we said: 'Isn't that interesting? That could have been *anybody* on the other end of the line. We're *so* accessible via modern technology. You're connected to a completely unknown person who can influence your behavior as soon as you pick up the phone."

She adds, "So—pagers are scary. That was the first idea for the episode. But who uses pagers? Doctors use pagers. We all go to the doctor. We all hate hospitals. And doctors are someone you *don't* want to be influenced; you *don't* want to have them lose control of their faculties. So what would happen if doctors lost control? And why would they lose control? Well, of course, if they were bewitched. But who would bewitch a doctor? And why?"

By that time, says Valerie, the pagers were long gone.

The Mayhews took their idea to Morgan and Wong, who told them to change the sex of their villain from female to male. "They told us: 'Turn it around again. Plastic surgery is about vanity—and you expect vanity from a woman. But not from a man.'"

Shortly thereafter, the Mayhews submitted a first draft of their script. It triggered a restrained response—and several major rewrites by Carter and the other members of the writing staff, working individually and as a whole. Carter is credited with focusing the story more tightly on its twin themes of greed and vanity. Howard Gordon came up with some of the more graphic elements—like the words "Vanitas Vanitatum" scrawled in blood on Dr. Franklyn's bathroom wall.

Vince Gilligan named one of the surgeons after one of his favorite actresses, Shannon

Tweed. As it turned out, the producers ended up choosing Arlene Mazzerolle for the part of Dr. Shannon. Mazzerolle's previous screen experience had primarily been in made-for-TV movies. The role of Franklyn was played by Richard Beymer, well-known to musical comedy fans for his portrayal of Tony, the love-struck gang member, in the 1961 movie version of *West Side Story*. Among the regular cast, though, one guest performance stands out: that of O-Lan Jones, the veteran character actress (*Edward Scissorhands*, *Natural Born Killers*, *Mars Attacks!*) who played Nurse Rebecca Waite. "I loved her. She was really good," recalls Duchovny.

Chris Carter came up with the idea of decorating the plastic surgeons' wooden conference table with a subtly inlaid pentagram—and production designer Graeme Murray took his idea to undreamed-of lengths. In a *tour de force* of suggestive design that registered with most viewers only subliminally, he made the ASU surgical unit a suite of five operating rooms, each one positioned at the point of an imaginary pentagram. The scrub room the doctors use is also five-sided, as are the five stainless-steel scrub sinks themselves.

Opinions of the lead actors regarding "Sanguinarium" are decidedly mixed.

"This was one of the most repulsive scripts that I've done," says Gillian Anderson. "During a couple of scenes—like when the doctor is stabbing his patient—I just had to shut my eyes."

David Duchovny, however, looks back on the bloodbath fondly. "This was a script I didn't get at all, but the show I really liked. This was another case where the script was kind of weak and when it came in it didn't make any sense. But Chris did a quick rewrite and everybody worked really hard and Kim Manners did a great job. It was really fun."

Less of a funfest was working with Fox's Standards and Practices department— which had been lying in wait since the battles over "Home." They were particularly upset with the fat sucking and the face peel, and there were literally frame-by-frame discussions of how much could be left in. Unfortunately for Michael Stern, this was the next episode he did after "Home." In the end, Chris Carter stepped in to get many of the cuts reversed.

Of her long meetings with the censors, Valerie Mayhew recalls: "They were not happy. When (Director of Standards and Practices) Linda Shima-Tsumo came down to talk to us, her first words were: 'And you look like such *normal* girls!'"

No spell or incantation was powerful enough to stop the flood of angry letters and e-mail from supporters of Wicca and ritual magic in the *X-Files* audience. One of the witches prosecuted at Salem was named "Rebecca Nurse," and the most popular Tarot deck is the Rider-Waite deck. Angry practitioners and sympathizers accused the Mayhews of insensitivity, defamation, blasphemy, and worse.

Ⓧ

Actually, say the Mayhews, who are still a bit shell-shocked by the experience, they tried hard to avoid offending anyone—taking care not to mention that either Nurse Waite or Franklyn were members of any particular sect or belief system.

Ⓧ

And Rebecca Waite? "Originally she was Rebecca White—we named her after a friend of ours," sighs Valerie. "But the name didn't clear. There was a nurse in Chicago by that name. So we plucked another name out of the air at the last minute."

Ⓧ

The words written in blood on Dr. Franklin's mirror are "vanitas vanitatum," or "vanity of the vanities."

Ⓧ

Black magician Jack Franklin lives at 1953 Gardner Street. Englishman Gerald Gardner founded the most popular form of modern witchcraft, or wicca, and published his first book on the subject in 1953.

Ⓧ

The dates on which Dr. Franklin's victims are born are significant because they fall on the traditional holidays of the ancient pagan world:

Beltane—May 1
Lammas—August 1
Lughnasadh—June 21
Samhain or Halloween—October 31
Yule—December 21
Imbolc—February 1

Ⓧ

musings of a cigarette-smoking man

The secret biography of a sinister, all-powerful conspirator. Some old mysteries are cleared up—and some new ones created.

episode: 4X07

first aired: November 17, 1996

written by: Glen Morgan

editor: Jim Gross

directed by: James Wong

guest stars:
William B. Davis (Cigarette-Smoking Man)
Chris Owens (Young Cigarette-Smoking Man)
Morgan Weisser (Lee Harvey Oswald)
Donnelly Rhodes (General Francis)
Tom Braidwood (Frohike)
Bruce Harwood (Byers)
Jerry Hardin (Deep Throat)
Peter Hanlon (Aide)
Dean Aylesworth (Young Bill Mulder)
Paul Jarrett (James Earl Ray)
David Fredericks (Director)
Laurie Murdoch (Lydon)
Jude Zachary (Jones)
Tim Bissett (Cook)
Fred Beale (Newsstand Operator)

principal settings:
Washington, D.C.;
Fort Bragg, North Carolina;
Dallas, Texas; Memphis, Tennessee;
Dogway, West Virginia

i n a decaying, rat-infested loft, the Cigarette-Smoking Man sits down, lights up a Morley, and plugs in an electronic eavesdropping device. Through his headphones he hears Mulder and Scully holding a fevered conversation with the Lone Gunmen.

Frohike, ever paranoid, declares that he "won't utter another syllable" until something called a "CSM-25 Countermeasure Filter" is activated. There is a brief burst of static; Cancer Man calmly flips a switch and the intercept comes back loud and clear.

"Now, tell us what you're so close to," says Scully impatiently.

"Not a 'what'—a 'who,'" says Frohike. He adds: "If you find the right starting point, and follow it, not even the secrets of the darkest of men are safe."

The next voice is Mulder's. "Cancer Man?" he says. "What did you find?"

"Possibly *everything*," says Frohike, a slight swagger in his voice. "Maybe his background. Who he is. Who he wants to be."

The subject of their discussion matter-of-factly sets up a tripod-mounted sniper's rifle. He peers through its night sight and aims the crosshairs on a door marked "The Lone Gunmen—Publishers of the Magic Bullet Newsletter."

He sits, calmly smoking and listening, while Frohike spins out his tale. Cancer Man's father, he says, was a convicted Communist spy who died in a Louisiana electric chair before his son could talk. His mother, a smoker, died of lung cancer before her son could walk. A ward of the state, the boy was raised in various Midwest orphanages.

"He didn't make friends," says Frohike. "He spent all his time reading, alone. Then he appears to have vanished—a year and a half after the Bay of Pigs."

Cut to the Center for Special Warfare, Fort Bragg, North Carolina. It is October 30, 1962. A young Army captain lies on his bunk, reading *The Manchurian Candidate*. A buddy comes over and sits on the bed next to his.

"Why don't you just see the movie?" asks his pal.

The intense young officer replies, "I'd rather read the worst novel ever written than see the best movie ever made."

The captain is summoned to a meeting with a General Francis. Before he leaves, his friend shows him a photograph.

"My one-year-old just said his first word," he says.

"What was it?" says the captain.

"JFK," says his friend.

They laugh and the captain turns to leave.

"Catch you later, Mulder," he says.

In the meeting, Francis, a rabidly anti-Communist two-star general is surrounded by several Strangelovian civilian associates. They question the young officer about his background.

They ask him whether he'd participated in several recent clandestine operations— the assassinations of Patrice Lumumba and Rafael Trujillo and the invasion at the Bay of Pigs. He issues stone-faced—but at the same time totally unbelievable— denials.

They ask him about his father. The cap-

tain replies: "My only regret, sir, was that I was too young to throw the switch."

Pleased, the general offers the captain a cigarette. "No thank you, sir," he says. "I never touch 'em."

Cutting to the chase, the general declares himself one of a small number of "extraordinary men"—men who must "identify, comprehend, and ultimately shoulder responsibility for not only their own existence, but their country's—and the world's, as well."

He offers the captain an assignment: "So classified, so compartmentalized, that if you accept you will no longer be an officer of the United States Army, nor will any record exist of your service."

It is: "The assassination of an American civilian, aged forty-six. Former naval PT boat commander. Married. Father of two."

The captain asks: "Is there a cover story?"

"We have found and are setting up a patsy," he is told.

Thirteen months later the ex-captain— now in civilian clothes—meets with Lee Harvey Oswald in Dallas. Oswald calls him "Mr. Hunt."

"Mr. Hunt" advises Oswald to give up smoking.

"I'm reading studies that say they can kill you, Lee," he says.

As the conversation proceeds, it becomes clear that Oswald believes his contact to be

a fellow Communist sympathizer. "Hunt" suggests obliquely to Oswald that they meet again that afternoon at the Texas movie theater.

He gives Oswald a rifle, tells him to hide it on the sixth floor of his workplace—the Texas School Book Depository—and promises to have money and a Cuban visa waiting for him at his apartment afterward.

Obligingly, Oswald hides the rifle at the Depository.

His coconspirator, identical rifle in hand, crawls into a large drainage tunnel that leads to a sewer grate facing Dealey Plaza. He has a good view of the Grassy Knoll. As the presidential motorcade nears his position, a black-suited man on the Knoll opens a black umbrella, signaling him.

He fires.

John F. Kennedy slumps mortally wounded onto his wife's lap.

Dallas policemen rush the Depository. Oswald goes to his apartment to collect his Cuban visa. It isn't there.

Oswald grabs a revolver, bolts outside, and is stopped by a Dallas policeman in a passing cruiser. He shoots the officer.

Oswald enters the Texas theater during the middle of a movie. As he takes a seat near the front, the lights go up. Dallas policemen swarm the auditorium. He is found, captured, and carried out kicking and cursing.

Near the back row of the movie theater sits the man whom Oswald was looking for. Trembling only slightly, he lights up a cigarette and takes his first puff.

April 4, 1967. In his apartment late at night, the Cigarette-Smoking Man taps away on a manual typewriter. A cigarette hangs from his lips; with obvious satisfaction, he finishes the last page of *Take a Chance: A Jack Colquitt Adventure*, by "Raul Bloodworth (nom de plume)." As he types, he mouths its last line: "'I can kill you any time I please . . . but not today.'"

From Cancer Man's table radio comes the unmistakable voice of Martin Luther King. The book complete, he listens intently to the broadcast.

The civil rights leader is giving the famous speech so seldom quoted in high school history textbooks.

"It is a sad fact," says Dr. King, "that because of comfort, complacency, a morbid fear of Communism, and our proneness to adjust to injustice, the Western nations that initiated so much of the revolutionary spirit of the modern world now become the arch antirevolutionaries. This has driven many to feel that only Marxism has the revolutionary spirit."

The Cigarette-Smoking Man listens with real sadness.

"No, no," he says. "Why'd you have to do that?"

At a secret cabal of powerful men—of which the Cancer Man is now a prominent member—the Cancer Man insists that something "intense" must be done.

"I respect King," he says. "He's an 'extraordinary man,' but now he's talking like a Maoist."

On April 3, 1968, the Cigarette-Smoking Man is in Memphis. He stands outside the church where King is speaking to a crowd of striking sanitation workers.

King's voice flows out onto the street. "The nation is sick," he says. "Trouble is in the land, confusion all around. That's a strange statement. But I know, somehow, that only when it is dark enough can you see the stars."

The next day the Cigarette-Smoking Man has a meeting with James Earl Ray in a cheap rooming house.

"Raul! Got the binoculars you sent me out for," says Ray.

As the conversation proceeds it becomes clear that Ray believes "Raul" to be a well-connected fence helping him sell his rifle.

Cancer Man tells Ray to disappear for a few hours while the actual transaction is

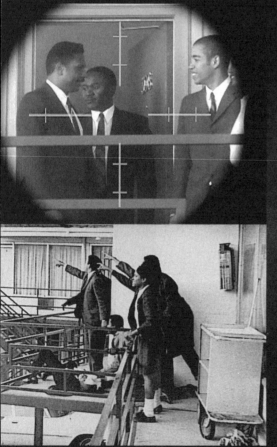

made. He walks into the bushes across from the Lorraine Motel and fixes the sights of Ray's gun on the balcony of King's room, Room 306.

He fires.

King falls, and America's cities burn.

Sitting safely back in his own apartment, "Mr. Bloodworth" reads a rejection letter from a publishing house.

"My advice? Burn it," is one of the editor's milder comments about *Take a Chance*.

On the Cigarette-Smoking Man's black-and-white television screen, Senator Robert F. Kennedy is speaking.

"I would only say that I feel in my own heart the same kind of feeling," says Kennedy. "I had a member of my own family killed. He was killed by a white man. My favorite poet was Aeschylus, and he once wrote: 'Even in our sleep, pain which cannot forget falls drop by drop upon the heart, until in our lonely despair against God's will comes wisdom, through the awful grace of God.'"

As Kennedy says this, the Cigarette-Smoking Man softly repeats RFK's words. He already knows the verse by heart.

Back to the present: The now middle-aged Cancer Man on death watch in the darkened loft. He tries to light another cigarette. He thumbs his lighter once, twice, three times. There is a spark but no flame.

It is Christmas Eve, 1991. A tired-looking Cigarette-Smoking Man—nicotine patch behind his ear—directs his underlings to dispose of the world's problems. The Anita Hill controversy; the Rodney King Trial; Bosnia-Herzegovina; the Buffalo Super Bowl chances—all are effortlessly manipulated by this invisible man.

News of Gorbachev's resignation—and thus the end of the Cold War—briefly piques his interest. So does another matter: "One thing internally, sir," says an assistant. "This 'spooky' kid who talked his way into opening the X-Files. It feels like trouble."

The Cigarette-Smoking Man answers curtly, "It's mine to keep an eye on."

On his way to celebrate a clandestine

Christmas, the Cigarette-Smoking Man pauses briefly at an office door. The sign on it reads: FOX MULDER, SPECIAL AGENT.

In his apartment, Yuletide music tinkling from the radio, the Cigarette-Smoking Man opens a thin envelope from another publishing house. He crumples it and tosses it in the wastebasket. He rolls a sheet of paper into his typewriter.

He writes: "Jack Colquitt sat alone in his apartment at Christmas. He believed in sacrifice. Yes, some nights, he longed for a second chance." He sits back, pleased with himself.

The phone rings. On the other end is the voice of Deep Throat, last seen in "Talitha Cumi" (3X24). "You won't believe," he says, "what we got for Christmas."

At a tightly guarded warehouse in Dogway, West Virginia, Deep Throat tells the Cigarette-Smoking Man that a UFO has crash-landed.

"Occupant?" asks the Cigarette-Smoking Man.

"Critical," says Deep Throat.

The Cancer Man says, "The timing couldn't be worse. That Roswell story we concocted is gaining momentum."

They enter a biologically secure room and gaze at a comatose alien on life support.

"How many historic events have only the two of us witnessed together?" says the Cigarette-Smoking Man. "How often did we make or change history? And our names can never grace any pages of record. No monument can bear our image. And yet once again, tonight, the course of history will be set by two unknown men—standing in the shadows."

Deep Throat takes an automatic pistol from his pocket and extends it silently, butt first, to his colleague. For the first time, the Cigarette-Smoking Man refuses.

"I have a chance to go an entire lifetime," the Cigarette-Smoking Man says, "to go without killing anybody—or anything."

That is, of course, a lie.

They argue, then flip a coin for the task.

Deep Throat loses. He fires a bullet into the alien. His colleague, watching this, rips off his nicotine patch and lights up.

It is March 6, 1992. In an empty Washington conference room, the Cigarette-Smoking Man opens a folder and reads Dana Scully's University of Maryland senior thesis.

In another room nearby Agent Scully meets with Section Chief Blevins from "Deep Throat"(1X01) and is assigned to work with Fox Mulder and the X-Files.

The Cigarette-Smoking Man, a slim wire running from his electronic listening device to his ear, eavesdrops on Mulder and Scully's first meeting.

"Sorry!" says Mulder jauntily—also from "Deep Throat" (1X01)—"nobody down here but the FBI's most unwanted!"

In the decaying loft the Cigarette-Smoking Man resights his rifle on the Lone Gunmen's doorway.

Frohike says: "Henry David Thoreau wrote, 'The mass of men lead lives of quiet desperation.' *His* life has been anything but quiet—yet, I believe, nothing but desperate. He's the most dangerous man alive. Not so much because he believes in his actions, but because he believes those actions are all which life allows him. And

pocket. He reaches for a cigarette—and crumbles the pack in his fist.

At the corner newsstand, he grabs a fresh copy of *Roman à Clef*. He glances at the "men's adventure" mag's tawdry cover and opens it. His elation turns to anger.

"This isn't the ending that I wrote!" he says. "It's all wrong!"

Stunned, his dream shattered by bad editing, the Cigarette-Smoking Man buys a fresh pack of Morleys and slumps down next to a homeless man on a skid row bench. The bum is eating a moldy box of chocolates.

"Life is like a box of chocolates," says the Cigarette-Smoking Man bitterly.

yet, the only person that can never escape him is himself."

In his apartment not too long ago, the Cigarette-Smoking Man opens up yet another thin letter from a publisher. *Second Chance: A Jack Colquitt Story* has been accepted for serialization in a magazine called *Roman à Clef*.

Elated, "Raul Bloodworth" phones his editor. He'll have to "give up some control," he is told, but the first installment will be on the newsstands November 12.

On that fateful morning, the Cigarette-Smoking Man types a letter of resignation, signs it, and places the envelope in his

He adds, "A cheap, thoughtless, perfunctory gift that no one ever asks for. Unreturnable because all you get back is another box of chocolates. So you're stuck with this undefinable whipped mint crap, which you mindlessly wolf down when there's nothing else left. Sure, once in a while there's a peanut butter cup, an English toffee, but it's gone too fast and the taste is too fleeting. You end up with nothing but broken bits and teeth-shattering nuts, which if you're desperate enough to eat, all you've got left is an empty box filled with useless brown paper wrappers."

He tears up his resignation letter and walks away.

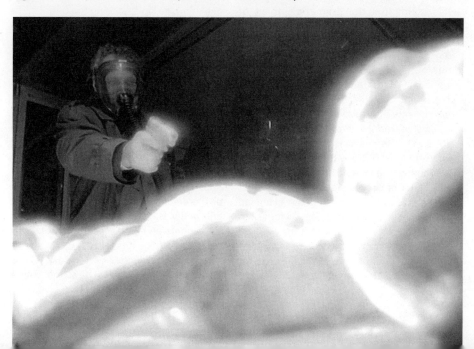

In the loft—at this very moment—the Cigarette-Smoking Man jacks a cartridge into the chamber of his rifle.

Frohike says, "So far, this is based only on a story I read in one of my weekly subscriptions that rang a few bells. I'm going out to check on a private hacker source who's been working on tracking a few leads that can produce definitive proof. And then we'll have him nailed!"

The Cigarette-Smoking Man cocks the hammer of his weapon. Frohike opens the door and walks into the crosshairs.

"I can kill you whenever I please," says the Cigarette-Smoking Man, in the steely voice of Jack Colquitt. Then he lets down the hammer.

"But not today," he says.

back story:

There was some concern before shooting this script that the dramatic impact of the Cigarette-Smoking Man, heretofore a furtive, mysterious figure with virtually no personal history, would be diluted by turning the camera on him for an entire episode. What *nobody* was worried about, apparently, was that many viewers would take its entire premise at face value.

Says coproducer Frank Spotnitz, with a sly smile: "In the closing scene, Frohike tells Mulder and Scully that the whole story was something he read in a crummy magazine. A lot of people didn't pick up on that subtlety. They thought that this was indeed the factual history of the CSM. As far as I'm concerned, it's not. Some of it may indeed be true, and some of it may—well, never mind."

Other outside observers guessed that the whole episode was simply a clever plot to give the lead actors a week off. Wrong again.

"When Glen [Morgan] and Jim [Wong] came back to the show, this was one of the first ideas they had," says Spotnitz, "It just turned out that we could do it without David and Gillian, which was fine with everyone."

Indeed, both Duchovny and Anderson mention this as one of their favorite episodes of the year—with only Duchovny, as to be expected, citing his free week in Los Angeles as a major factor in his favorable review.

Bill Davis was happy to step out of the shadows and get an episode of his own—though at first, like many, he was puzzled at the seeming contradictions in the script. Claiming responsibility for the death of John F. Kennedy and Martin Luther King is one thing, he says; keeping the Buffalo Bills in Super Bowl Hell is another. Finding the fine line between tragedy and comedy proved to be a challenging task.

Says Chris Carter: "I had to speak with Bill several times; I spent hours with him on the telephone talking about the character. He thought it really made his character something that it wasn't. I tried to explain to him, as I think Jim and Glen were trying to express, that even if your mission in life is a destroyer, that you still have some hope in the back of your mind that you can be a creator—and that this all of a sudden, this vanity, is his vanity. And we see that so clearly here and it makes him sort of a silly person."

Davis acknowledges Carter's assistance, and adds, "Jim Wong's direction was a big help, too. A lot of the stage directions point toward farce, but Jim told me to play against that and just let the situation play out. The *Forrest Gump* scene was difficult, too. When I prepared it and did it the first time, I was almost Shakespearean in my approach. Jim made me toss it off more, and it worked out fine."

As usual, Morgan and Wong cast a veteran of *Space: Above and Beyond*—Morgan Weisser, who plays Lee Harvey Oswald—in their episode. Chris Owens, who plays the young Cigarette-Smoking Man, is a Canadian actor (as is Davis) and returned later in the season as the same character in "Demons" (4X23).

Whipping up a sensibly budgeted JFK assassination was an interesting exercise. Producer J. P. Finn coordinated the whole affair, filmed in a downtown Vancouver location doubling for Dealey Plaza. Costume designer Jenni Gullett tracked down her counterpart from the movie *JFK*, borrowed the reproduction of Jackie Kennedy's famous pink suit used in the film, then had her assistant Janice Swayze scour the local stores for the rare pink boucle fabric needed to construct their own pre- and post-blood-spattered copies.

JFK's Lincoln Continental limousine was created by picture vehicle coordinator Nigel Habgood. He located a nonstretched Continental convertible and "customized" it: Within a span of three days, he created the illusion of a limo by (1) removing the rear seats and replacing them with smaller ones, and (2) attaching a pair of milk crates to the floor of the suddenly roomier rear compartment, therefore creating "jump seats" for "Governor and Mrs. Connally."

Sharp-eyed observers might have noticed this—as well as the fact that Chris Owens worked hard to accurately imitate the most important of his character's physical mannerisms.

"He spent a lot of time watching how I smoke," says Bill Davis. "Finally, Jim just said to him: 'When Bill takes a drag on a cigarette, it's just like sex.'"

Can you find the references to Morgan and Wong's former series *Space: Above and Beyond* buried in this episode?

1) the Cigarette-Smoking Man's first novel is called *Take a Chance* (a catch phrase from the series)
2) certain cases are "classified compartmentalized" (a level of secrecy invented by Morgan and Wong for their show)
3) in Cancer Man's novels, his main character is named Jack Colquitt; this was also the name of a soldier in the Space episode "Who Monitors the Birds?"

Ⓧ

Deep Throat cites "UN Resolution 1013" as the resolution requiring the execution of any aliens found on Earth. The number refers to Chris Carter's production company, Ten Thirteen.

Ⓧ

"Walden Roth," the editor who finally buys the Cigarette-Smoking Man's story for a magazine is named for Dana Walden, Twentieth Century Fox's head of drama, and Peter Roth, president of the Entertainment Group for Fox Broadcasting Company. Roth was one of the strongest supporters of *The X-Files* in its early seasons.

Ⓧ

The magazine in which Cancer Man's story appears is called *Roman à Clef*. French for "novel of a key," the term refers to a novel in which the knowing reader is expected to identify, within the light disguise of fiction, actual people or events.

Ⓧ

Very sharp-eyed observers might have noticed that in the penultimate scene, when the Cigarette-Smoking Man goes to the newsstand to pick up his copy of *Roman à Clef* magazine, his eye passes over several magazines aimed at aspiring writers. One of them, *End Credits*, bears the cover lines "Mastering Writer's Block"; "How to Handle Rejection"; and "Where the Hell Is Darin Morgan?"—a reference to Glen Morgan's brother, who left the *X-Files* writing staff before the beginning of the fourth season.

Ⓧ

paper hearts

Prompted by a series of prophetic
dreams, Mulder reopens the case of a
convicted child killer. The murderer
claims to know the circumstances of
Samantha Mulder's abduction.

episode: 4X08

first aired: December 15, 1996

written by: Vince Gilligan

editor: Heather MacDougall

directed by: Rob Bowman

guest stars:
Mitch Pileggi (AD Walter Skinner)
Tom Noonan (John Lee Roche)
Rebecca Toolan (Mrs. Mulder)
Byrne Piven (Frank Sparks)
Vanessa Morley (Samantha Mulder)
Carly McKillip (Caitlin)
Edward Diaz (El Camino Owner)
Jane Perry (Care Operator)
Paul Bittante (Local Cop)

principal settings:
Washington, D.C.; Manassas, Virginia;
Norristown, Pennsylvania; Hollyville,
Delaware; Greenwich, Connecticut;
Forks of Capacon, West Virginia;
Martha's Vineyard, Swampscott,
and Boston, Massachusetts

In the middle of the night, Mulder awakes. A dot of red laser light—seemingly with a mind of its own—darts around the walls of his apartment. He follows the moving light through his doorway, onto the street, and to a suburban park in a place called Bosher's Run.

A white El Camino is parked at the entrance; the dot stops on the side of the car and spells out the words "Mad Hat."

The light moves on quickly; Mulder follows to a clearing in the woods. In the clearing a little girl lies dead. The dot changes into a glowing heart shape on her breast; the body, untouched, sinks slowly into the ground.

Mulder wakes with a start. Apparently, he has been dreaming. He drives to the real Bosher's Run Park in Virginia and retraces his dream route. There is an identical clearing in the woods.

At 5:00 the next morning a forensic excavation of the site is underway. Scully arrives, and Mulder explains his actions by telling her that he's been having a recurring dream—or nightmare.

"You're saying you're out here because there's something you saw in a dream?" says Scully incredulously.

"Sir!" shouts a forensic tech, summoning Mulder.

The agents kneel down besides the clearing. Emerging from the soil is a child's skull.

"Tell me about this dream," says Scully, still confused.

"I've had it three nights in a row," says Mulder. "Last night it went on long enough to lead me right to her."

The forensic techs carefully sift the soil around the burial site. Mulder grabs a trowel and digs impatiently.

"Mulder, if you destroy evidence we may never know what happened here," says Scully.

Mulder replies curtly, "I know what happened." The little girl, he says, was strangled.

"He used eight-gauge electrical cord. He took something from the body postmortem. A trophy. A piece of fabric cut from her clothes, shaped like a heart."

The murderer, he adds, was a man named John Lee Roche—a serial killer who is known to have slain thirteen girls between the ages of eight and ten.

Mulder keeps digging until he reaches the skeletal remains of a little girl. A heart-shaped swatch of fabric has been cut from her clothing.

"This makes fourteen," he says.

In their office at the FBI building, Mulder explains to Scully how he "solved" the crime. Victims of the so-called "Paper Hearts" murderer were buried up and down the East Coast. In 1990, before he took over the X-Files, he was brought into the case because of his insights into the minds of mass murderers.

"I concluded we were looking for a salesman," says Mulder. "Someone who traveled a lot. Someone who could gain people's trust. Someone ordinary."

He was correct, and he cracked the case. Roche turned out to be a door-to-door vacuum-cleaner salesman who buried his victims far from where they were killed.

"What about the trophies he took?" says Scully. "The cloth hearts?"

"We never found them. But we didn't need them to make the case. We had him cold on thirteen counts of murder. He admitted to thirteen. The polygraph said he was telling the truth."

He adds, "But that always bugged me about this case. I always wanted to find those hearts to count them—to see if they really added up to thirteen." He pauses, downcast. "I guess they didn't."

To Scully, this self-criticism is unnecessary. "If nothing else," she says, "I think I can at least help explain your dream. I don't think you ever stopped thinking about this case. I think you may have solved it in your sleep.

"You said it yourself once," she adds. "A dream is an answer to a question we haven't yet learned how to ask."

The next day Scully examines the child's remains. With the help of a missing children's database, she identifies the murdered girl as Addie Sparks, kidnapped in 1975.

"That would mean," says Mulder, "that Roche started way before we thought he did."

This new discrepancy unsettles Mulder even further. The agents travel to Pennsylvania, where Addie's father—her only surviving parent—lives. They have the horrific duty to tell the now middle-aged Frank Sparks that the remains of his daughter have been found.

"How many more people like me are you going to visit today?" the grieving man asks. "Are there other victims you didn't know about?"

Neither of the agents dares to answer.

As the agents leave the Sparks house, Mulder is downcast. He stares at an old car parked on the street, then flashes back to a half-repressed memory.

"Roche's car," he mutters.

Then to Scully, excitedly: "The white El Camino. I saw it in my dreams. The cloth hearts he collected—he would have kept them close."

They track down Roche's old vehicle to its present owner, a teenager who has extensively restored and modified it. On a hunch, Mulder checks the El Camino's discarded camper shell. Inside its fabric headliner is a copy of *Alice in Wonderland.*

"'Mad Hat'—Mad Hatter," says Mulder.

Between the pages of the book are sixteen fabric hearts.

The agents travel to the federal prison where Roche—a banally repellent man in his forties—is serving his life sentence. The agents talk to him while he shoots hoops in an otherwise empty gymnasium. They ask him to explain the remaining two hearts.

"You're in here for life. You've got nothing to lose," says Mulder.

"I got nothing to gain," says Roche.

"You can gain one moment of decency in your life. You can finally let those families put their daughters to rest," says Mulder.

Roche answers, taunting, "I understand you'd take this very personally, Mulder. How about this? Sink one from there and I'll tell you."

Mulder calmly hits a set shot from half court.

Roche is unimpressed.

"You'd trust a child molester?" he says, heading for the gym door.

As he nears the exit, he calls back over his shoulder, "You bring my hearts, give them back to me," he says, "I'll tell you everything you want to know."

Late that night Mulder pores over the swatches of heart-shaped fabric. The red laser light reappears and beckons him out the door and into the family room of his childhood home—last seen in "Little Green Men" (2X01)—circa 1973.

Talking heads discuss Watergate on the TV screen. An eight-year-old girl peers up from a game of Stratego.

"Fox, it's your move," she says.

Mulder—the adult Mulder—stares at her, stunned.

"Samantha," he says.

Annoyed, she replies, "Are you gonna move or not? Do we have to watch this, Fox?"

"*The Magician* comes on at nine," says Mulder, remembering.

"Mom and Dad said I could watch the movie—Buttlunch!" says Samantha.

"They're next door at the Galbrands'. They left me in charge," says her big brother.

The lights go out suddenly.

"No!" shouts Mulder.

The room begins to shake.

"Not again!" he says.

The windows glow with a blinding white light. Mulder reaches for his gun. It's not there. The front doorknob begins to turn.

"Run!" he shouts to Samantha.

Mulder grabs for a steel box atop the breakfront—for his father's gun inside it. The revolver falls to the floor and he scrambles after it. He's too late. There is a terrifying rumbling noise and the front door flies open. John Lee Roche stands there, the bright headlights of his El Camino behind him. He turns his head and—smiling demonically—heads toward Samantha.

"Fox! Fox!" Samantha screams.

"Samantha!" cries Mulder desperately.

He jerks awake at his desk. In his hands are the two unidentified fabric hearts—either one could be from the clothing that Samantha was wearing.

In the prison visiting room the next day Mulder questions Roche. "Yesterday you said something about me taking it personally," he says. "Why did you say that to me?"

Roche smiles enigmatically.

"Where were you in 1973?" demands Mulder "November. The twenty-seventh of November. Do you know what I'm getting at?"

Roche's smirk grows a little larger. He tells Mulder that he was on a sales trip to Martha's Vineyard that year.

"I sold a vacuum cleaner to your dad," he says. "He bought it for your mom. It was either the Electrovac Duchess or the Princess model. Your dad and I talked about it at great length. He had a really hard time choosing."

Mulder, straining for control, says, "What do you know about my sister?"

"You bring me my hearts, and maybe I'll tell you more," Roche says.

Furious, Mulder hauls off and punches Roche—hard—in his face. At the sound of the blow, a male prison guard enters the room.

"I didn't see that," says the guard.

Scully, entering right behind him, says, "I did."

On their way out Scully demands that Mulder get a grip on himself and realize that his dream was only that—a dream. She tells Mulder that Roche could have easily gotten information about him and his sister via the Internet hookup in the prison library.

"He's playing with you, Mulder. He's committing emotional blackmail and you're letting him," Scully says.

Mulder asks Scully if she's ever believed that his sister was abducted by aliens. Her silence is her answer.

There was a table set out unde
and the March Hare and the H
Dormouse was sitting between
other two were using it as a cus
it, and the talking over its head.
Dormouse,' thought Alice; `only,
doesn't mind.'

The table was a large one, but th

"No. So what do you think happened to her?" asks Mulder, a bit angry.

Gently now, Scully asks him what *he* believes happened.

"I don't know," he says softly. "I don't know what to believe. I just know I need to find out."

In his mother's house in Connecticut, Mulder roots determinedly through the garage sale fodder in the basement. Mulder shows a puzzled Mrs. Mulder the two fabric swatches. To his relief, she recognizes neither. Just to be sure, he asks her if his father ever bought her a vacuum cleaner.

"A long time ago," she says. "I don't use it anymore. I think its under the stairs."

He hurries to the dusty storage space and uncovers an old canister-type vacuum cleaner. It is an Electrovac Princess.

The next day, Mulder storms into Skinner's office and asks why he's been denied further access to Roche. Scully enters quietly behind him.

Skinner angrily tells Mulder that his assault on Roche was recorded by a security camera. Scully pleads Mulder's case, saying that his past relationship with Roche will help them clear the final two murders. Reluctantly, Skinner relents.

In the prison visiting room Mulder passes Roche the two hearts and asks him to name the victims.

"I think you know one," says Roche.

Responding to Mulder's challenge, he accurately describes the abduction scene in the Mulders' living room. Teasing, cruelly, he offers to disclose the burial site of one—just one—of the children.

In agony, Mulder selects a cloth heart.

The two agents arrive at a woodlands site. On a boulder is scratched the words "Mad Hat." Mulder begins digging immediately, with his bare hands. Scully begs him to wait for a forensics team.

"Help me, Scully," says Mulder, pleading.

She, too, claws at the earth. In a few moments they reach the skeleton of a small child. A heart-shaped patch has been ripped from its clothing.

At the FBI forensics lab Mulder and Scully determine that the body is not Samantha's. They go back to see Roche, who gives them the name of his fifteenth victim. Mulder hands him the sixteenth and final heart.

"It's your sister," says Roche.

He promises to reveal "the big mystery"—but only if Mulder takes him to the scene of Samantha's abduction. Scully refuses his demand. Mulder's face betrays his doubts and fears.

After a night of soul searching, he phones the prison and arranges to remove Roche temporarily. On the flight to Boston, the handcuffed Roche slips away from Mulder and kneels down beside a young blond girl traveling with her mother.

"Are you having fun? What's your name?" he asks her, smiling.

"Caitlin," she smiles back before Mulder hustles him along.

At FBI headquarters, Skinner is livid. "What the hell do you mean, he checked out Roche?" he says.

Scully explains that she'd left Mulder alone to get some rest. She adds that she has a good idea where he and Roche are going, and she is sure they can catch up.

"I'll be the one to catch up with him," he growls. "Where's he headed?"

Inside the Mulder family's old house on Martha's Vineyard, Roche recalls the night of Samantha's abduction with a kind of sick nostalgia. Eerily, he tells Mulder how he sat outside the house for hours; how he watched their parents leave; how he peered in at young Fox and Samantha through the window, watched their board game, and then cut off the lights at the junction box and pushed in the door.

He accurately describes their board game, the TV program they were watching, and young Mulder's efforts to stop him.

"You tried to get your father's gun—I give you credit for that," says Roche. "But then you sort of froze. I took your sister away from all this. To a happier place."

Mulder eyes him coldly and walks toward the murderer.

"That's exactly how it happened? In this room?"

"Yeah," says Roche.

"Wrong house," says Mulder contemptuously.

He adds—with a kind of triumph—that Bill Mulder bought the house they are standing in six years *after* he divorced his wife. The house where the abduction took place is six miles away.

"You screwed up," he says. "You were never here. You didn't take Samantha."

Roche protests feebly. "Wishful thinking," he says.

Mulder says, "No. But I think I know what happened. Somehow, you got inside my dreams. I got inside your head. You got inside mine. Maybe some nexus or connection was formed between us. You got access to my memories of my sister Samantha, and you used them against me—for this."

Mulder adds, "You must have been a hell of a salesman, Roche. First flight's at six o'clock A.M. Enjoy your last few hours of freedom."

Late that night, Mulder sits in his motel room guarding the sleeping Roche and staring at the final heart.

He hears the faint cries of a child outside his window. He looks out and spots the El Camino in the parking lot. Samantha is locked inside it, calling frantically for him.

He runs outside. The engine of the truck is racing. He pulls a set of keys from his pocket, unlocks the door, and lifts Samantha into his arms. He sees the red laser dot. It briefly forms the word "bye."

Samantha is gone. The El Camino roars away.

Mulder wakes up to a frantic knocking. It is Scully and Skinner, pounding on the motel room door. Roche is gone, and Mulder is shackled with his own handcuffs. The killer took the last cloth heart, plus Mulder's badge and gun.

"A predator is loose because of you," Skinner tells Mulder. "God only knows how many hours' lead he's got. Any idea where he might be headed?"

"Yeah," Mulder says, the awful realization sinking in.

Mulder checks his airline ticket and, identifying himself as an FBI agent, asks for the passenger manifest of yesterday's flight. He's told that Roche—identifying himself as Mulder—called for the same information ten minutes earlier.

The three agents race to Caitlin's day care center and learn that Roche, again using Mulder's badge, has just taken her away.

"It's all my fault," says the day care operator.

Mulder says, "It's not your fault. It's my fault."

The agents desperately try to guess Roche's next move. Scully suggests that he might return to his old apartment in the Boston area. They get the address; it is 9809 Alice Road.

"Alice," says Mulder. "*Alice in Wonderland*. He's the Mad Hatter. That's where he got the idea in the first place. He's there."

They rush to the apartment. It is dirty, run-down, and empty. But the view out the back window is of a weedy field. Mulder has a flash of intuition—of certainty. He runs out into the field, climbs over a steel wall, and enters a vast graveyard for retired electric transit buses. Their trolley poles reach uselessly into the sky. Mulder runs through row after neat row of the rusting vehicles. There is the faint scream of a child in the distance. Mulder stops, listens, and looks up. One of the dozens of trolley poles is jiggling slightly.

Silently and carefully, Mulder pulls open the door of the bus and enters. Caitlin is sitting, terrified, in the next to last row. Roche is in the seat behind her.

The killer speaks with a chilling casualness. "I'm beginning to believe we do share that nexus you spoke of," he says. "You always seem to find me."

Mulder slowly and carefully advances toward the little girl.

"Caitlin, can you do me a favor?" he says gently. "Can you count to twenty? Can you do that? Can you close your eyes and count to twenty out loud? Quietly and slowly?"

Caitlin nods.

Mulder draws his gun and points it at Roche's head. Roche shows Mulder that he has his other gun—and that is aimed through the seat at Caitlin.

"You don't really give me very much choice," says Roche. "I really don't want to go back to prison."

At the front of the bus Scully and Skinner crouch with guns drawn.

"Put the gun down, Roche!" yells Skinner.

Ignoring him, Roche pulls the final heart from his pocket.

"I have one left," he says to Mulder. "How are you going to find her without me? How sure are you that it's not Samantha?"

Mulder's resolve wavers for a split second.

"How do you know?" says Roche.

Mulder glances down and sees Roche's trigger finger tightening. He fires a bullet through Roche's brain. Caitlin screams and runs into Scully's embrace. Roche slumps dead in his seat.

In his office later that day, Mulder sits exhausted—physically and emotionally. Scully tells him that analysis of the dye on the final heart has determined that it was manufactured between 1969 and 1974.

"Beyond that," she says, "there's nothing more they can tell us."

She notes Mulder's despair.

"Mulder, it's not Samantha," she says. "And whoever that little girl really is, we'll find her."

"How?"

"I don't know," says Scully. "But I do know you. Why don't you go on home and get some sleep?"

For a moment Mulder lays his head on Scully's breast. Then he stares at the nameless heart one last time, places it in his desk drawer, and locks it away.

back story:
An episode that might be classified as pseudo-mythological, "Paper Hearts" has elements of both a conventional serial-killer thriller and a quintessential *X-Files* mind-twister. That it all mixes together surprisingly well is the reason why both Anderson and Duchovny, among others, consider it to be one of the best shows of the season.

Coproducer Vince Gilligan—who admits to having "interesting" dreams, but claims that he never lets them affect his writing—says he came up with the idea for "Paper Hearts" while reconsidering one of the series' longest-running story lines. "Mulder's sister's abduction is the very bedrock of the show," he says. "But what if, instead of being attributable to aliens, it's all because of some mundane horror—like a child killer—instead? And wouldn't the best way to convince Mulder quickly of this be through a series of prophetic dreams?"

Wanting to include some kind of "fetishistic" killer but not one who simply mutilated his victim's bodies and dragged home the body parts—"That would be going way too far," says Gilligan—the writer created John Lee Roche and his penchant for heart-shaped fabric souvenirs. Mulder's pre-*X-Files* expertise as a serial-killer stalker was established in the series pilot.

Tom Noonan, who played John Lee Roche, is a well-known New York-based actor, screenwriter, playwright, and director whose independent films, most notably *The Wife* (1995) and *What Happened Was. . . .* (1994), have won awards at film festivals in the United States and abroad. He has also had feature roles in movies like *Heat*, *Robocop 2*, and *F/X*. The role was written specifically for him as Gilligan is a fan of Noonan's work.

The key to playing Roche, says Noonan, was keeping in mind the one-sided friendship—for lack of a better word—between the serial killer and Mulder. "Mulder was Roche's soul mate—a guy he felt he could really connect with," he says. "When he'd say something about Samantha or his other victims and Mulder would get upset, he'd think: 'What are you upset about? This is our life together.'"

The dream-induced laser light that puts Mulder on Roche's trail had its origins during Gilligan's years at New York University, when the then film student made extra money working for a company that made laser-illuminated custom holograms; Gilligan learned all he needed to know about lasers while toiling away in a basement factory "and breathing a lot of xylene fumes." In the final draft of Gilligan's teleplay, Mulder's laser dot is blue, but because of its shorter wavelength, a blue laser is much more expensive and harder to employ than a red one. As the show went into production, the practical choice was made.

How did the laser dot morph into written messages to Mulder? The on-set technique tried by David Gauthier and his special effects crew was to project a slide image along the same light path as the laser beam. This proved unsatisfactory. In the end, the same effect was accomplished by the show's LA-based visual effects experts, who computer-animated the dot in postproduction.

In the real world there is no Bosher's Run Park—but there is a Bosher's Dam in James River Park, a favorite haunt of Gilligan in his native Virginia.

Roche's Chevy El Camino was obtained in the usual manner: vehicle coordinator Nigel Habgood flagged it down on the street and asked its owner if he'd like to rent his baby to *The X-Files*.

The bright red flames on the sides of the truck in its incarnation as a teenage driver's vehicle were actually decals. After filming was completed, the decals were peeled off and claimed by first assistant director Tom "Frohike" Braidwood, who, much to the chagrin of his wife, stuck them onto the front end of his personal Ford Taurus.

The trolley bus graveyard really exists. It is in West Vancouver and was discovered by a locations department staff member on a scouting trip last year. Producer Joseph Patrick Finn sent a set of photos of the place to the production office in Los Angeles, and Vince Gilligan wrote the episode's climactic scene specifically for it.

Composer Mark Snow, nominated for an Emmy Award for his music for "Paper Hearts," was particularly happy with the Tinkerbell-like motifs that mark the presence of the laser beam. "It was a different kind of texture for the show," he says. "Light, magic, nothing terribly threatening." An inspiration for this theme, he adds, was Mendelssohn's "A Midsummer Night's Dream."

Snow reports that he's also gotten many requests for a recording of the "Pete Seeger-like folky type of melody" he composed for the show's closing moments. Unfortunately, he says, the piece was only about thirty seconds long—so don't bother hanging around your local record store.

"Paper Hearts" was the season's eighth episode filmed but the tenth aired. Its completion and airing was postponed in order to free up postproduction resources for "Terma" and "Tunguska." The two-parter had to be finished quickly in order to air during the February sweeps period.

Ⓧ

To answer the most frequently asked question about this episode: a jump-shooting double was *not* hired to replace Duchovny in the shot in the prison gymnasium. In a total of seven takes of that scene, Duchovny (once a backup guard on the Princeton basketball team) swished four 25-footers.

Ⓧ

"Paper Hearts" guest star Tom Noonan had a lead role playing a character named Scully, in the 1989 movie comedy *Collision Course*.

Ⓧ

Mulder finds Roche's trophy cloth hearts inside a copy of Lewis Carroll's *Alice in Wonderland*. Later we learn that Roche lived on Alice Street. The veiled reference here is to Carroll's alleged fascination with prepubescent girls.

Ⓧ

When Scully says to Mulder: "A dream is an answer to a question we haven't yet learned how to ask," she is quoting Mulder back at himself. He originally said this to her in "Aubrey" (2X12).

Ⓧ

episode: 4X09

first aired: November 24, 1996

written by:
Frank Spotnitz and Chris Carter

editor: Michael S. Stern

directed by: Kim Manners

guest stars:
Mitch Pileggi (AD Walter Skinner)
William B. Davis (The Cigarette-Smoking Man)
Nicholas Lea (Alex Krycek)
Laurie Holden (Marita Covarrubias)
John Neville (The Well-Manicured Man)
Brendan Beiser (Agent Pendrell)
Fritz Weaver (Senator Sorenson)
David Bloom (Stress Man)
Malcolm Stewart (Dr. Sacks)
Campbell Lane (Committee Chairman)
Stefan Arngrim (Prisoner)
Brent Stait (Timothy Mayhew)
Dawn Murphy (1st Customs Officer)
Andy Thompson (2nd Customs Officer)
Phillip Heinrich (Assault Agent)
Jano Frandsen (Older Agent)

principal settings:
Washington, D.C.; Honolulu, Hawaii;
New York City, New York; Crystal City, Virginia;
Greenbelt, Maryland;
Charlottesville, Virginia;
Tunguska, Siberia, Russia

tunguska

Diplomatic couriers are bringing a lethal
alien life-form into the United States. Mulder
and Scully's investigation points to a high-
level international conspiracy beyond even
their comprehension.

a t a hearing of the U.S. Senate Select Committee on Intelligence and Terrorism, FBI Special Agent Dana Scully is sworn in and prepares to give her testimony. She reads from a prepared statement.

"'I left behind a career in medicine to become an FBI agent four years ago,'" she says, "'because I believed in this country. Because I wanted to uphold its laws—to punish the guilty and to protect the innocent. I still believe in this country, but I believe there are powerful men in the government who do not, men who have no respect for the law and flout it with impunity. I have come to the conclusion that it is no longer possible—'"

She is cut off by the committee chairman, who insists irritably that she has been summoned before them to answer questions, not make speeches.

"Agent Scully," says another senator named Sorenson, "do you or do you not know the whereabouts of Agent Mulder?"

Scully replies, "I respectfully decline to answer that question, sir, because I believe answering that question could endanger Agent Mulder's life."

The chairman is incredulous. "You don't seem to understand," he says. "Your response is not optional. You're an agent of the FBI."

"Well, then," says Scully, nervous but determined, "if I may please finish my statement?

"'That it is no longer possible for me to carry out my duties—'"

Senator Sorenson interrupts. "Are you tendering your resignation, Agent Scully? Is that what you're trying to say?"

"No, sir," says Scully. "What I *am* saying is that there is a culture of lawlessness that has prevented me from doing my job."

She adds: "The real target of this committee's investigations should be the men who are beyond prosecution and punishment. The men whose secret policies are behind the crimes that you are investigating."

Sorenson leans forward and fixes Scully with a withering gaze. "Either you tell us what you know about Agent Mulder's whereabouts," he says, "or you will be held in contempt of Congress."

Scully says nothing more. She stares back at the senator, defiant.

Ten days earlier, a nervous-looking man carrying only a briefcase reaches the head of the Customs line at Honolulu Airport. He tells the customs agent that he's inbound from the Republic of Georgia on government business.

She asks him to step aside for a random check. Protesting vehemently that he has diplomatic immunity, the man refuses.

In response, he is subjected to a strip- and body-cavity search. Another Customs officer breaks open his locked briefcase and pulls out two metal canisters.

"Can you tell me what material you're transporting in these, sir?" he asks.

"Those are filled with biohazardous materials," he says.

"Then where's the paperwork? Why aren't the containers marked?"

To the courier's mounting alarm, the agent opens one of them, and accidentally drops its interior glass canister to the floor.

The glass shatters, and a substance that looks like black dirt spills out. The dirt starts to move, forming what appear to be dozens of black, oily worms.

The worms crawl up the Customs agent's shoe and under his pants leg. In complete panic, the courier pounds on the door of the inspection room, screaming to be let out.

"Somebody open this door! Somebody let me out of here!" he shouts.

The Customs officer says, "What the hell is this?"

He stamps his feet and spasms wildly.

"Oh, my God! Let me out of here!" howls the courier in total terror.

The Customs agent—still standing rigidly upright—lapses into a kind of blank, staring paralysis. The whites of his eyes become clouded, then black—invaded by the relentlessly marauding organisms.

In a seedy industrial area near Shea Stadium in New York City, Mulder and Scully are part of large force of armed federal agents. They are on the trail of domestic terrorists.

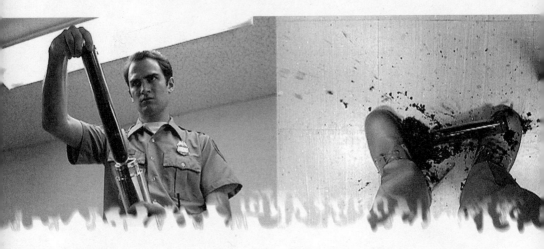

Mulder explains to Scully that someone has been anonymously sending him receipts for bomb-making materials, a warehouse storage space nearby, and a two-ton rental truck.

"We could be looking at the next Oklahoma City," he says.

The rental truck rolls into view. It stops, and the agents make their move. In the midst of a brief, fierce firefight, the truck's driver makes a run for it, but Mulder causes the truck to crash by shooting out its tires. Its driver is dead, but a passenger is still alive. Hands raised, he exits the vehicle.

It is the turncoat agent Alex Krycek—the murderer of Mulder's father and an accessory in the death of Scully's sister.

"You son of a bitch!" shouts Mulder.

High on adrenaline and rage, he knees Krycek—last seen locked in an abandoned missile silo in "Apocrypha" (3X16)—in the gut. He aims his rifle at the fallen man.

"Mulder!" yells Scully, afraid of what her partner plans to do next.

"I handed you this bust, Mulder!" says Krycek, protesting. "Who do you think sent you those receipts?"

As the other militiamen are rounded up, Krycek tells the agents that the terrorists— "pathetic revolutionaries who'd kill innocent Americans in the name of boneheaded ideologies"—rescued him from the silo on a salvage hunt.

"You're full of crap, Krycek," says Mulder. "You're an invertebrate scum-sucker whose moral dipstick is about two drops short of bone-dry."

Krycek says, still defiant, "I love this country."

Mulder hits him again, nearly knocking him off his feet.

Scully says, "What do you want, Krycek?"

"The same thing you do," says Krycek. "To find the man who tried to kill me."

He turns to Mulder: "The same man who's responsible for your father's death."

He turns to Scully: "And your sister's."

Closely guarded by Mulder and Scully, Krycek leads the agents to an international terminal at Dulles Airport outside Washington. He tells them to intercept a passenger on a flight from Russia.

"He'll be carrying a diplomatic pouch," Krycek says.

He points out a man emerging from the Customs area—who flees at the sight of them. The agents give chase. They lose him when he runs through a jetway and onto the airport tarmac, but they recover the pouch—which the courier has jettisoned. They return to their starting point and show it to Krycek, whom they've handcuffed to a railing.

"Is this some kind of joke?" says Scully, opening the pouch.

Inside it is a single, coal-black rock.

"What did you get for Halloween, Charlie Brown?" says Mulder to Krycek, dripping contempt.

Mulder and Scully take Krycek to the

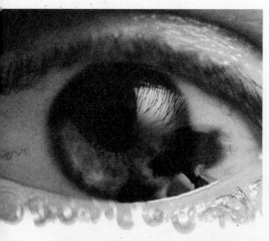

high-rise apartment building where Skinner lives. They ask their supervisor to provide a safe house for their informant.

"Relatively safe," says Skinner.

He delivers a vicious punch to Krycek's stomach, handcuffs the ex-agent to his outside balcony, and—despite Krycek's loud protests that the weather is freezing—leaves him chained there for the night.

The next morning, Mulder and Scully take the rock to NASA's Goddard Space Flight Center in Maryland. An exobiologist, Dr. Sacks, tells them that the rock resem-bles meteorite fragments found recently in Antarctica. In fact, says Sacks, the rock might very well have originated on Mars—and may contain fossilized evidence of alien bacterial matter.

With barely contained excitement, he asks permission to take a core sample.

The Cigarette-Smoking Man intercepts Skinner outside his apartment building. He brings up the intercepted diplomatic pouch.

"I'm afraid it's created a problem in foreign policy circles. Quite a problem, actually."

Skinner says—truthfully—that he knows nothing about the pouch. The Cigarette-Smoking Man's tone turns menacing.

"I need that pouch, Mr. Skinner. And I need to know who gave them the order to intercept it."

Skinner says acidly, "I'll get back to you."

The Cigarette-Smoking Man replies, "Wars have broken out over far less, Mr. Skinner. Far, far less."

At Skinner's apartment, Krycek is still cuffed to the balcony. The escaped courier from the previous night enters, rifles Skinner's desk, and hears a noise outside. He investigates. Krycek, clinging unseen to the outside of the balcony railing, surprises

him. He grabs the courier by the neck and flips him to his death below.

In his office, Mulder tells Scully that he's talked to his sources in the State Department and learned about the courier detained in Honolulu with a "toxic soil sample."

"Which leads me to believe," says Mulder, "that what's in this rock we intercepted are answers beyond the existence of extraterrestrial life—even beyond the conspiracy to cover up that existence."

He adds that Krycek has given them "a pivotal piece of an even larger plot."

Scully, however, is skeptical. She says, "What he's given us is a rock. And Alex Krycek is a liar and a murderer."

"Who now wants to expose the same men we do," says Mulder. "And who will go to any length to succeed."

Scully says, "What I worry about is you, Mulder. How far you'll go. And how far I can follow you."

At the NASA laboratory, Dr. Sacks—wearing full biological anticontamination garb—lowers a drill bit into the rock sample. A thin mist of black liquid sprays onto his face shield. He wipes it off with his fingers—and watches the black worms begin to crawl over him.

He screams, spasms, and goes rigid.

Mulder, on his way to Goddard with Scully, receives a call from Skinner. From a phone booth near his apartment, he tells Mulder of the dead man lying at the base

of his building. Mulder jumps out to grab a cab.

At the entrance to the apartment building, a police detective questions Skinner, who tells the cop that (1) he lives on the seventeenth floor, (2) he didn't see the man fall, and (3) he's an assistant director of the FBI.

"Oh, my apologies," says the detective. "I got some bad information from my lieutenant—that there was a man hanging from your balcony."

Mulder storms into Skinner's apartment, hauls Krycek back over the railing, uncuffs him, and barks that they're going to walk out of the building together as if nothing had happened.

"I've got no problem with that, Mulder," says Krycek sarcastically. "You put me up here, I'm looking forward to seeing how you get me out."

Mulder grabs Krycek by the lapels and gives him a vigorous, gratuitous shaking.

"Stupid-ass haircut," he snarls.

Having seen the black rock's effects on Dr. Sacks, a badly shocked Scully phones Mulder from Goddard.

"Dr. Sacks. . . . He's . . . I don't know, Mulder," she says. "I've never seen this before. I don't know if he's dead or alive."

Mulder says simply, "I think you'd better find out. I want you to get me an address in New York. You're going to have to go through the Bureau to get that."

In Manhattan late that night, Mulder

knocks on the door of Marita Covarrubias's apartment. The mysterious woman—her attraction to Mulder still undefined but obvious—lets him in.

Mulder asks the UN official to help him trace the diplomatic pouch from Russia. He dozes, exhausted, on her couch. She makes several phone inquiries and, appearing somewhat alarmed by what she's learned, wakes him.

She tells him that the pouch originated in Krasnoyarsk, Russia.

"Just north of Tunguska," says Mulder.

"Tunguska?" says Covarrubias.

The diplomat adds that it is no place she has ever heard of. She volunteers, however, to arrange a diplomatic passport and visa, with cover credentials, for Mulder.

"Why?" says Mulder. "Why are you helping me?"

"Because I can," says Covarrubias. "Because there are those of us who believe in your search for the truth."

At 3:15 that morning, Mulder leaves Covarrubias's apartment and returns to his car. Krycek, handcuffed inside, asks if he's being kept in the dark about their travel arrangements.

"Yeah," says Mulder, adding a right cross to the jaw for punctuation.

At Goddard, Scully suits up with Agent Pendrell and examines Sacks,

still in his suit. As she watches him, he spasms, leading her to believe that he is still alive, albeit in a deep coma state.

At JFK Airport, Mulder parks his car—in the long-term lot—and exits, quite willing to leave Krycek, still cuffed to the car, to the fates. As he walks away, Krycek yells at him. The traitor's curses are in a foreign language.

Mulder walks back to the vehicle. "You speak Russian, Krycek?" he says through the car window.

"What's it to you?" the still-insolent Krycek tells Mulder.

At a plush horse farm in Virginia, the Well-Manicured Man, watching an attractive woman ease her mount around the show jumping ring, smiles. The Cigarette-Smoking Man arrives and tells his colleague that their courier is dead.

"Can this expose us?" asks the Well-Manicured Man.

"No, of course not," says Cancer Man. "Our necessary and plausible denial is intact."

He adds that he's learned from CIA intercepts that a man holding UN credentials is heading toward Krasnoyarsk. The man fits the description of Fox Mulder.

"You fool! Stupid fool!" says the Well-Manicured Man. "This must be corrected! This must be handled!"

The Cigarette-Smoking Man replies defensively, "It can be. You know my capabilities in a crisis."

The Well-Manicured Man is furious. "I don't think you realize what's at stake here," he says. "What levels this must be carried to. This will take more than a good aim."

In Skinner's office, the AD tells Scully that they've been subpoenaed to testify before the Senate committee by Senator Sorenson. The full weight of their predicament is only beginning to sink in.

In the Siberian forest near Tunguska, Mulder and Krycek climb down from a truck. Its Russian driver gives directions to Krycek.

Krycek translates for Mulder, "He says its about five kilometers through those woods."

They set off and come to a barbed-wire fence. As they dig their way under, Mulder finally tells Krycek what they're looking for.

Mulder explains that in 1908, Tunguska was the site of the largest cosmic event in history. A huge fireball—possibly a comet or an asteroid, maybe even a piece of anti-matter—smashed into Earth with the force of 2,000 Hiroshima-sized bombs.

"No real evidence was ever found to provide a satisfactory explanation of what it was," says Mulder. "I think somebody found that evidence. And the explanation was something nobody dreamed of."

Past the fence, lying flat on a bluff, Mulder and Krycek see a huge gravel pit. It is filled with toiling workers. What at first seems like a mining camp is a slave labor camp; men on horseback flail at the workers with bullwhips.

As this realization hits them, they hear the sound of horse's hooves. They scatter and run, but are hunted down like cattle. A bullwhip sweeps Mulder's legs from under him. He gazes up at the sky, dazed.

Mulder awakes, filthy and alone, on the floor of a dark cell. His face is bleeding; whispered messages from another, unseen prisoner echo around him.

"I don't speak Russian," he says.

"Then no one has told you," says the whisperer, eyeing him through a crack in the wall.

"Told me what?" says Mulder.

"That you've been brought here to die. To wish you were dead."

"I wasn't brought here," says Mulder. "I came here. Looking for something."

"The only thing you will find here is death. Death and suffering."

"What is this place?" says Mulder.

"The gulag," says the whisperer. "Where the guilty rule the innocent."

The door of the cell is opened and Krycek, cursing in Russian at his jailers, is flung in.

"We've got to get out of here," says Krycek. "They're going to torture us."

He tells Mulder that the jailers accused him of being a spy and tried to get him to confess.

"What did you tell them?" shouts Mulder, slamming Krycek against the wall.

"That we were stupid Americans, lost in the woods," says Krycek.

Mulder releases him.

"Hey, Mulder," says Krycek menacingly. "You're going to need me in here. Don't touch me again."

A dangerous power shift has occurred.

At the Senate Executive Office Building in Washington, the oily Senator Sorenson welcomes Skinner and Scully to his office. His false solicitude wears off quickly, however.

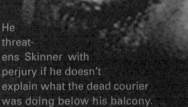

He threat- ens Skinner with perjury if he doesn't explain what the dead courier was doing below his balcony.

"And then there's Agent Mulder," says Sorenson. "Can you explain to me why he declined my invitation to be here today?"

Scully says, "Agent Mulder is in the field, getting answers to the questions you are asking."

Sorenson counters, "And where is he seeking those answers?"

In Mulder and Krycek's gulag cell, a guard shoves two bowls of disgusting, bug-infested liquid through the door. Mulder drinks, but Krycek throws down his food and curses loudly in Russian.

The door opens and a guard appears. Krycek speaks to him loudly and forcefully. Krycek and the guard exit.

The whisperer tells Mulder, "That man is not your friend. He speaks differently to the guards. In formal language. As if to an equal. You are deceived."

"Who are you?" asks Mulder.

"A prisoner. Like you. But I have committed no crime."

"Then why are you here?"

"To do the work. Like the others. Like them, I will die in an experiment, when there is no longer any use for me."

"What kind of experiment?" asks Mulder.

Before the whisperer can answer him, Mulder's cell door bursts open. A neatly dressed man wearing glasses barks at the guards to seize Mulder. He injects a large syringe into the desperately struggling Mulder's arm.

Mulder awakens in a place of horror. He is naked, suspended on a wooden frame between two sheets of chicken wire in a dark room full of men immobilized in the same way.

A plastic pipe runs at a tilted angle along the ceil- ing above him, coming to an end above his face. There is a sound like that of a gate being lifted. The human guinea pigs begin screaming.

Black liquid spills out of the pipe. The oil splatters on Mulder's cheek, and the worms begin to move into Mulder's nose, eyes, and mouth. As he lapses into rigor, the worms slowly cloud the whites of his eyes.

To be continued . . .

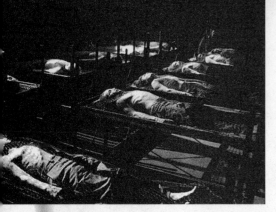

back story:

On August 7, 1996, the National Aeronautics and Space Administration convened a news conference at its offices in Washington, D.C. It announced:

"A research team of scientists at the Johnson Space Center [JSC], Houston, Texas, and at Stanford University, Palo Alto, California, has found evidence that strongly suggests primitive life may have existed on Mars more than 3.6 billion years ago. The NASA-funded team found the first organic molecules thought to be of Martian origin; several mineral features characteristic of biological activity; and possible microscopic fossils of primitive, bacteria-like organisms inside of an ancient Martian rock that fell to Earth as a meteorite."

This startling and still-controversial finding was broadcast around the world—and came to rest inside the collective mind of the *X-Files* writing staff, which used it as the seed pearl of the "Tunguska"/"Terma" two-parter.

"Oh, yeah," says coproducer Frank Spotnitz. "The idea of putting the alien oil in the rock was because of the Mars rock stories. After the news broke, I came in the next morning and said: 'Well, *X-Files!*'"

This ripped-from-the-headlines plot device—which harkened back at least subliminally to the black liquid alien substance featured in last season's "Piper Maru" (3X15)/"Apocrypha"(3X16) serial—was melded with two other previously discussed story lines: a healthy serving of just desserts for the evil Krycek, and a peek inside the Russian security services' counterpart to the FBI's X-Files.

Chris Carter says: "Krycek was now a character who had no political alliances, which left us an opening. We'd been wanting to expand the conspiracy globally, and we had done that as early as 'Talitha Cumi,' the finale of Season Three, when we'd brought in a sort of global perspective, this is a further escalation of that, and you'll see that the Russian thing plays out through the next season and into the movie."

Also, says Carter, the description of the alien life-form as "black cancer" works well as a subtle, almost subconscious precursor to the cancer theme introduced a few weeks later in "Leonard Betts" (4X14).

The two-parter's Russian prison scenes owe a large debt to the works of Aleksandr Solzhenitsyn, particularly *The Gulag Archipelago* and *One Day in the Life of Ivan Denisovich*. The sequences involving Krycek were energized by the obvious enthusiasm of actor Nicholas Lea—who, when informed by Chris Carter that his character was going to have his arm torn off, reportedly shouted out in delight at the dramatic possibilities this presented.

To flesh out the cast for 4X09/4X10, an even more eclectic than usual collection of actors was recruited. Fritz Weaver, who played Senator Sorenson, is a well-known American actor (he's played at least two other senators in the last decade or so) whose career goes back to starring roles in two episodes, "The Obsolete Man" and "Third from the Sun" of the original *Twilight Zone* series. That was his voice you heard on those schmaltzy CBS promos for the Winter Olympics.

Jan Rubes (pronounced Yan RU-bish) is one of Canada's best-known performers. A refugee from communist Czechoslovakia, he has starred in major films like *Witness* and was an internationally known opera singer who for many years hosted his own music program on CBC Radio. Stefan Arngrim, who played the whispering prisoner, is a former child actor who played the character Barry Lockridge ("I was that kid with the dog," says Arngrim) in the late-sixties ABC series *Land of the Giants*.

In the midst of all of this, series regulars

William B. Davis and John Neville, as the Cigarette-Smoking Man and his colleague, the Well-Manicured Man, were happy to have some of their meatiest dialogue of the season—although not quite as much of it as they would have liked. Because of time pressure, a couple of contentious scenes between the two were cut from the final edit.

For her part, Gillian Anderson recalls with pride the way her character stood up to the congressional committee—and the realistic strength with which she played those scenes. She also, she says, had a sort of semi-mystical experience during the late-night filming of the scenes in which she, as Scully, is sitting in jail for contempt.

"I don't know exactly what it was," says Anderson. "I just remember working on that scene and feeling some aspects of Scully that I hadn't felt before or since. I don't know if that actually came across, but it was just, well, *different*. I remember walking away feeling very odd."

David Duchovny remembers 4X09 and 4X10 as being action-heavy and "lots of fun," even though he spent considerable time standing around in the snow and rain and getting chased around a gravel pit by men on horseback. "My dad was visiting and he got to see what it was all about," he says.

The actors' behind-the-scenes colleagues describe "Tunguska" and "Terma" somewhat differently. *They* remember them as two of the most expensive, complicated, and stubbornly trouble-plagued *X-Files* filmed to date.

Malcolm Stewart, who plays Dr. Stays, previously appeared in "Avatar" (3X21) as Agent Bonnecaze. This is his fourth *X-Files* appearance: He also appeared in the pilot episode and "3" (2X07).

Ⓧ

In the closed captioning for this episode, viewers saw Mulder pull a cockroach out of a tin of food and say, "Bambi?" This is, of course, a reference to "War of the Coprophages" (3X12) and the memorable entomologist Dr. Bambi Berenbaum.

Ⓧ

to be

Stranded in the gulag, Mulder discovers the effects of the alien toxin—firsthand. In Washington, Scully battles a corrupt U.S. senator to keep their investigation alive.

episode: 4X10
first aired: December 1, 1996
written by:
Frank Spotnitz and Chris Carter
editor: Jim Gross
directed by: Rob Bowman

terma

continued...

guest stars:
Mitch Pileggi (AD Walter Skinner)
William B. Davis (The Cigarette-Smoking Man)
Nicholas Lea (Alex Krycek)
John Neville (The Well-Manicured Man)
Stefan Arngrim (Prisoner)
Jan Rubes (Vassily Peskow)
Fritz Weaver (Senator Sorenson)
Brent Stait (Timothy Mayhew)
Malcolm Stewart (Dr. Sacks)
Campbell Lane (Committee Chairman)
Robin Mossley (Dr. Kingsley Looker)
Brenda McDonald (Aunt Janet)
Pamela MacDonald (Nurse)
Eileen Pedde (Angie)
Jessica Schreier (Dr. Bonita Charne-Sayre)
Oleksiy Shostak (Bundled Man)
Denis Krasnogolov (One-Armed Leader)
Anatol Rezmeritsa (Glasses Man)
John Hainsworth (Gaunt Man)

principal settings:
Boca Raton, Florida;
St. Petersburg, Russia;
Tunguska, Siberia, Russia;
Greenbelt, Maryland;
Richmond, Virginia;
Charlottesville, Virginia;
Washington, D.C.

In the middle of the night at the Harrow Convalescent Home in south Florida, a woman in her late thirties—her name is Angie—shines her flashlight in the faces of several sick, elderly patients. She finds the person she's looking for.

"It's time, Auntie Janet," says Angie softly. The two women leave the facility and enter a van parked outside. In the van is a thin middle-aged man; he hooks up the IV tubes of a simple but lethal "suicide machine." Auntie Janet embraces her niece.

"Don't you cry for me, dear. I'm tired of the pain. You're my angel of mercy," she says.

She turns a switch and starts the flow of drugs. She gasps and falls silent.

Small black, oily worms are crawling out of the dead woman's nose, mouth, and eyes.

"Something's wrong here!" says the thin man.

Her niece's screams echo through the silent streets.

In a neat but threadbare apartment in the Russian city of St. Petersburg, an old man named Vassily Peskow sits drinking tea. A heavily bundled-up man, a messenger, arrives with an urgent communiqué from one Comrade Arntzen in Krasnoyarsk.

Peskow protests that he is retired.

"Comrade Arntzen anticipated this response," says the messenger, handing Peskow an envelope. "He wants you to know the Cold War isn't over."

In his prison cell in Tunguska—in the Russian district of Krasnoyarsk—Mulder recovers slowly from his exposure (in 4X09) to the black worms.

"Hey, prisoner!" whispers the English-speaking inmate in the next cell. "I thought maybe you were dead."

Mulder asks him how long he's been unconscious.

"Hours. I don't know. The first time is bad. Very bad. It becomes easier each time. Until it kills you."

The whisperer tells Mulder that they are both part of a secret Russian experiment.

They've been exposed to "the black cancer—the cancer that lives in the rock."

Hundreds of fellow human guinea pigs have already died.

"I'm not going to die," says Mulder. "I have to live long enough to kill that man Krycek."

Partly impressed by this, partly amused, the whisperer passes Mulder a homemade knife.

"I made it to kill myself," he says. "It took me nearly two weeks. By then I had lost the desire."

Mulder says, "You'd rather suffer the torture?"

The prisoner replies, "It is wonderful, the persistence of life. That rock we found so deep in the earth; that anything could survive down there against all reason. No. They will have to kill me themselves."

At NASA's Goddard lab, Scully and a scientist named Dr. Kingsley Looker examine Dr. Sacks's comatose body for clues. They get nowhere until Looker, probing Sacks's body with a fiber optic rod, examines the base of his pineal gland. Wriggling creatures cluster tightly around the tiny organ.

"It looks like a nest, some kind of black vermiform organism," says Scully.

At a bus stop in Richmond, Virginia, a gray-haired man in a dark overcoat waits patiently. It is Vassily Peskow; he gets on a bus whose destination sign reads CHARLOTTESVILLE.

In a darkened paddock, an attractive blond horsewoman—it is the Well-Manicured Man's protégée from "Tunguska" (4X09)—checks her horses to see what is spooking them.

Vassily Peskow steps out from the shadows. He introduces himself and gives one of the horses a friendly pat. The woman, however, is alarmed.

"You're going to have to leave here," she says. "I'm going to call a cab. Do you know where you're going?"

"Going? I was coming here to see you, Dr. Charne-Sayre."

Dr. Charne-Sayre says, "Do I know you?"

"No," says Peskow evenly. "I don't know how you could."

With his huge hand, the Russian applies a vicelike grip to Charne-Sayre's carotid artery, killing her quickly and silently.

Waiting at the front door of Scully's apartment, AD Skinner intercepts his subordinate on her way inside. He explains to her—forcefully—that the missing diplomatic pouch, the murder on his balcony, and the upcoming Senate investigation have placed them in deep trouble. He demands that Scully tell him exactly what is going on.

Scully tells him what she can: the diplomatic pouch contained the biohazardous material that is now being quarantined inside Goddard.

Skinner says, "That pouch you intercepted—do you know what its intended destination was?"

"No, sir," says Scully.

"Well, I do, Agent Scully. Because I bent some rules this morning when I couldn't find you. To find out who was to receive it."

"Who was it?"

"Dr. Bonita Charne-Sayre. Are you familiar with that name?"

Scully answers immediately, a bit puzzled. "Yes, sir. She's a well-known physician, a virologist who's looked in on presidents. She's also an authority on variola viruses. Smallpox."

Skinner says, "Well, she was killed tonight. A horse stepped on her throat in a riding accident in Virginia."

A guard enters Mulder's cell and delivers a vicious kick to his ribs. The agent is herded outside and onto to a long gray line of inmates shuffling slowly forward to another nightmare of some kind.

"Prisoner—is that your friend?" says the man standing behind Mulder.

It is the familiar voice of the whispering prisoner.

On a raised platform stands Krycek, dry and warm, embracing the bespectacled man who had injected Mulder in "Tunguska."

"You have but one chance," says the whisperer.

They shuffle forward a few more yards.

Mulder breaks ranks and—brandishing the homemade knife—sprints to the plat-

form. He knocks out Krycek, tosses him into the flatbed of an idling truck, and races off. Mulder guns the truck down a dirt road. Krycek revives and scrabbles at him through a wire-mesh rear window.

The guards regroup and pursue Mulder on horseback. The truck's brakes fail, and it careens downhill through the forest. At a sharp curve, Krycek throws himself clear. The truck crashes off the road, flies down a rock-filled ravine, and tumbles onto its side. There is no sign of movement from the cab.

At the horse farm in Charlottesville, the Cigarette-Smoking Man visits the Well-Manicured Man. They discuss the murder of Dr. Charne-Sayre—the Well-Manicured Man's "personal physician"—and the Cigarette-Smoking Man gloats over his associate's loss.

"Were you sleeping with her?" he asks.

The Well-Manicured Man doesn't answer.

"Surely you wouldn't be so foolish as to put the project at risk for the sake of your personal pleasures."

"Find her killer," says the Well-Manicured Man with a grimace.

"Call off this congressional investigation," says the Cigarette-Smoking Man urgently.

"I can't," says the Well-Manicured Man.

Then, with heavy irony: "But Senator Sorenson is an honorable man. They are *all* honorable, these honorable men."

The Well-Manicured Man turns to leave, but the Cigarette-Smoking Man has more news. "I heard Mulder was captured in Tunguska," he says. "I hear now he has escaped."

The Well-Manicured Man betrays a small jolt of surprise—an opening for one more taunt.

"Wake the Russian Bear," says the Cigarette-Smoking Man to his fellow conspirator, "and it may find we've stolen its honey."

In the Siberian forest, Krycek staggers away from the truck wreck. He comes upon a group of ragged men—all of them missing their left arms. Speaking in Russian, he tells them that he is an American, falsely accused of spying, who has just escaped from the prison camp.

"Then your enemy is mine," says the group's leader. "We can protect you."

That night the gulag guards search the forest on horseback. Their flashlight beams probe through the trees. As they pass Mulder, he peers from his hiding place beneath a thick carpet of fallen leaves.

At a hearing of the U.S. Senate Select Committee on Intelligence and Terrorism, FBI Special Agent Dana Scully is sworn in and prepares to give her testimony. She reads from a prepared statement.

"'I left behind a career in medicine to become an FBI agent four years ago,'" she says, "'because I believed in this country. Because I wanted to uphold its laws—to punish the guilty and to protect the innocent. I still believe in this country, but I believe there are powerful men in the government who do not, men who have no respect for the law, and who flout it with impunity. I have come to the conclusion that it is no longer possible—'"

She is cut off by the committee chairman—who insists irritably that she has been summoned before them to answer questions, not make speeches.

"Agent Scully," says another senator named Sorenson, "do you or do you not know the whereabouts of Agent Mulder?"

Scully replies, "I respectfully decline to answer that question, sir, because I believe answering that question could endanger Agent Mulder's life."

The chairman is incredulous. "You don't seem to understand," he says. "Your response is not optional. You're an agent of the FBI."

"Well, then," says Scully, nervous but determined. "If I may please finish my statement?

"'That it is no longer possible for me to carry out my duties—'"

Senator Sorenson interrupts. "Are you tendering your resignation, Agent Scully? Is that what you're trying to say?"

"No, sir," says Scully. "What I *am* saying is that there is a culture of lawlessness that has prevented me from doing my job."

She adds: "The real target of this committee's investigations should be the men who are beyond prosecution and punishment. The men whose secret policies are behind the crimes that you are investigating."

Sorenson leans forward and fixes Scully with a withering gaze. "Either you tell us what you know about Agent Mulder's whereabouts," he says, "or you will be held in contempt of Congress."

Scully says nothing more. She stares back at the senator, defiant.

In the forest, a burly bearded Russian—the owner of the truck Mulder stole—

reaches down into the pile of leaves and angrily yanks the agent to his feat.

He shoves Mulder through the door of his cabin. His wife takes pity on Mulder and gives him a drink.

"No Russian," says Mulder.

She nods and rolls up his left sleeve—uncovering the angry mark from his recent injection.

"The test!" she says in heavily accented English. "They kill everybody for the test."

She and her husband have been spared, she says, because the prison overseers needed him and his truck to make deliveries. But now, no more truck, no more safety.

"We have to go now," insists Mulder. "They'll come looking for me. They'll come looking for you."

The Russian woman shakes her head. "There are other ways," she says.

A small boy with his left arm missing stands in the doorway.

"No arm. No test," the woman says.

Realizing what she is suggesting, Mulder pleads with her. "You don't understand," he says. "These tests—the smallpox scar on your arm is some kind of identification. You have to help me escape. I'll help you escape. You have to help me get to St. Petersburg."

Mulder turns in his seat. The truck driver has reentered. He is carrying a large carving knife.

In the forest, the band of one-armed partisans sits gathered around a small campfire. They seize the sleeping Krycek, tie him down, and rip off his left shirtsleeve. Their leader grabs a red hot knife from the fire and advances on him. As Krycek screams in agony, he saws away.

In her jail cell, Scully reads a book by Dr. Bonita Charne-Sayre. It is a treatise on smallpox.

Skinner visits her. She explains to him why she persists in her defiance of the Senate Committee: Because they choose to ignore her information about the intercepted diplomatic pouch, the alien toxin, and the several murders attached to it while persisting in prying loose the whereabouts of Fox Mulder.

"You mean it's the wrong question," says Skinner.

Scully nods. "Several of the men on this committee are lawyers," she says. "It is my experience that lawyers ask the wrong question only when they don't want the right answer."

At the NASA lab late that night, Pescow enters the isolation area where Dr. Sacks is being treated. The Russian injects a large syringe of amber fluid through Sacks's contamination suit and into his body. Sacks dies; we know this because the black worms crawl out of his body.

In Charlottesville, the Cigarette-Smoking Man identifies Pescow—"a KGB Line X stringer working out of Moscow Center"—for the Well-Manicured Man.

"But how could this be?" says the Well-Manicured Man. "How could the Russians have known we were working on our own inoculation? Six of us knew."

The Cigarette-Smoking Man, his voice dripping with innuendo, says simply, "Dr. Charne-Sayre?"

"She was trusted!" insists the Well-Manicured Man.

"Then I don't know," says the Cigarette-Smoking Man softly.

Swallowing his humiliation, the Well-Manicured Man insists that Vassily Pescow be found.

"If my intelligence sources are right," replies Cancer Man, "I think there's someone who might save us the trouble."

In the Senate hearing room, the standoff continues. Sorenson and the chairman persist in asking Scully about Mulder, and she forcefully brings up the dead courier, the lethal toxin, and the death of Dr. Charne-Sayre. Sorenson loses his composure.

"Answer the question, Ms. Scully!" he shouts.

A man in the back of the room answers him. "What is the question?" he says.

It is Mulder, bruised and disheveled but alive. He sits behind Scully in the gallery.

Buoyed by his presence, Scully redoubles her efforts to redirect the focus of the committee. "Sir, if I may, I would like to continue making my point," she says.

"What is your point, Miss Scully?" says the chairman.

"That the death of Dr. Charne-Sayre, given her field of expertise, strongly suggests that she knew something about the toxin—about its origins. And that knowledge may be directly linked to the murder of the man in Assistant Director Skinner's apartment building."

Skinner arrives and whispers in her ear. Scully announces the death of Dr. Sacks to the committee. She has finally managed to at least partially convince the committee chairman of the gravity of the situation. He adjourns the hearing for one day, or "until this new matter can be explained. So that we may them begin moving in a forward direction."

Scully and Mulder embrace.

"It feels good to put my arms around you, Scully. Both of them," says Mulder.

Scully explains to Mulder that she's traced the toxin to Florida. Dr. Bonita Charne-Sayre was a board member and chief physician for a nationwide chain of elder-care hospitals.

"Guess what one of her patients died of in Boca Raton?" says Scully.

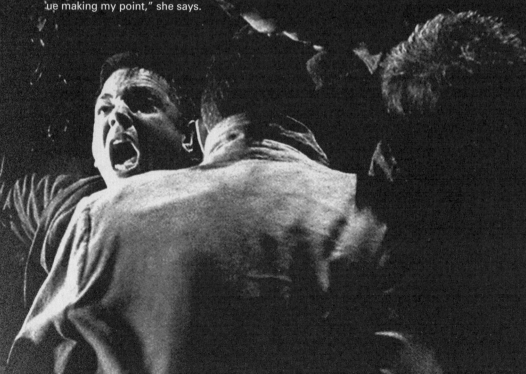

At the Harrow Convalescent Home, the Russian agent Peskow enters a medicine closet and switches a large bottle of gray capsules with one of his own.

Later that evening, Mulder and Scully arrive. Brushing past the duty nurse, they check the bedridden patients—last looked at, says the frightened nurse, four hours ago.

"This man's dead," says Scully.

In fact, all the patients are dead. Mulder bends down over an old woman. Black worms have crawled out of her nose.

"These people are test subjects," says Mulder to the horrified nurse. "I think they've been poisoned."

The agents rush off to seal the building's exits. A patient throws off his blanket and walks away. It is Peskow.

At the Federal Correctional Facility in New York, Mulder and Scully are escorted toward the jail cell of Terry Edward Mayhew—the head of the right-wing militia unit that Alex Krycek betrayed in "Tunguska" (4X09).

"I still don't understand what it is you hope to learn here," says Scully.

Mulder says, "Everything that's happened—every death we've seen—can be traced back to one man."

Scully says, "But according to you, that man's in Russia. Or possibly dead."

Mulder says, "Then he's not working alone."

Mayhew and the agents have "a little off-the-record chat." The terrorist tells them that Krycek—or Arntzen, as he called himself then—wasn't rescued from the missile silo. Instead, he approached the militiamen himself, offering them "building materials" and plans with which to build two "devices."

"Did he ever mention 'black cancer'?" says Mulder.

"Oh, yeah," smirks Mayhew. "Developed by the Soviets. Saddam used it in the Gulf. That's why they made those servicemen take all them pills. U.S. government knew about the black cancer. They lied. Didn't have no cure. No inoculation.

"I think I'll quit right there. I got nothing more to say."

Mayhew refuses to reveal where Krycek's second bomb is hidden. But a little friendly persuasion by Mulder—he grabs Mayhew in a headlock and squeezes—loosens his tongue.

The bomb, says Mayhew, is inside a stolen truck in Terma, North Dakota.

As they leave, Mulder asks Scully to trace the license numbers of all stolen two-ton trucks in that area. "Call Canadian border authorities and have them stop any vehicle fitting that description. Tell them they're looking for a bomb."

He adds, "This has been a big setup from the beginning, almost perfectly executed. Someone used Krycek, then Krycek used us. Someone who didn't want that rock in American hands."

"But what's in Canada?" asks Scully.

"Where would you put this rock if you didn't want it to be found?" says Mulder.

"Back in the ground," says Scully.

They begin their search.

At a rural Canadian border crossing, Vassily Peskow opens the back of his two-ton truck and shows a Customs agent the bags of ammonium nitrate fertilizer inside. "For my hothouse tomatoes," he explains.

Under angry-looking clouds, Mulder and Scully's helicopter skims the Canadian forest, flies over an oil refinery, and lands in a gravel pit—in which sits the truck they've been looking for. Scully rides the chopper back to the refinery.

Mulder examines the truck. It's doors are locked; there is no one in the cab. Behind the truck is an oil wellhead and, next to it, what looks like a ventilation shaft.

The chopper sets Scully down. She scales a fence to enter the refinery. Peskow spots her from a catwalk above. She hears the clanging of a door—marked "Valve Room"—behind her.

Mulder reaches down into the ventilation shaft—some kind of container seems to be suspended in it. Before he can fish the object out, the wellhead next to him erupts, spewing oil high into the air. Within seconds, he is covered with the black fluid.

Reaching down into the ventilator shaft, Mulder pries at the container with a metal

Pescow turns and walks away. Scully races across the gravel pit to Mulder's fallen body. The erupting oil well is still burning. She pulls her partner away from the inferno.

In the Senate hearing room several days later, Scully once again prepares to testify.

"What evidence are you presenting us today?" says the chairman.

"Documents and interviews," says Scully, "in support of a wide-ranging conspiracy to control a lethal biotoxin that is in fact extraterrestrial."

Senator Sorenson laughs in her face. "Are we, what? Talking about little green men here?"

Mulder has seen enough. He rises from his seat in the gallery and addresses the committee angrily.

"Why is this so hard to believe?" he says. "When the accepted discovery of life off this planet is on the front page of every newspaper around the world? When the most conservative scientists and science journals are calling for exploration of Mars and Jupiter—with every reason to believe that life and persistence of it are thriving outside our terrestrial sphere? If you cannot get past this, then I suggest this whole committee be held in contempt—for ignoring evidence that cannot be refuted."

Nonplussed—or perhaps just confused—the chairman quickly adjourns the hearing "until the evidence can be properly evaluated."

At the back of the committee room, the Cigarette-Smoking Man rises and quickly exits.

In St. Petersburg, Vassily Peskow enters his apartment. A man is waiting for him inside.

"Please," says Peskow in Russian. "If you are here to ask another favor, I am retired—Comrade Krycek."

Krycek says, replying in kind, "I am only here, Comrade, to congratulate you on a job well done."

The double agent slowly dips a tea bag with his new prosthetic hand.

In Washington, the Cigarette-Smoking Man sits with Senator Sorenson in his

tool. Something inside the truck begins emitting a high-pitched beeping noise. Mulder takes a precious split second to figure out what is happening, then runs for his life.

The truck explodes in a massive fireball.

Scully stares in horror at the explosion from the refinery catwalk. Pescow grabs her from behind, yanks her gun out of its holster, and sticks it in her face.

"I would just as soon kill you," he says. "But please don't make me. My work is done."

office. They are reading the evidence Agent Dana Scully has submitted.

The Cancer Man glances down at the senator's wastebasket. Many of Scully's FBI file folders already fill it to the brim.

back story:

Because of the complicated nature of the enterprise and the perfectionist leanings of its creator and staffers, *The X-Files* has had more than its share of last-minute scrapes, scrambles, and desperate makeovers. But the show that Chris Carter and his producers have signed off on has *always* gotten onto the air.

Until "Tunguska."

"It was a nightmare situation," recalls Frank Spotnitz.

In retrospect, the trouble began when the show's original visual effects wizard, Mat Beck, left the show (to work on feature projects, including *Volcano* and *The X-Files Movie*) after the third season. An independent special-effects production company was hired for the fourth season, and it was charged with the task of digitally animating the oozing black alien organisms for 4X09 and 4X10.

"They just never got those worms right," says Spotnitz, shaking his head. There were some shots we didn't see until Wednesday, and the show was airing Sunday. And on Wednesday we gave them lots of notes on how we'd like to see them redone. Finally, on Friday, they show up and say, 'Sorry, this is the best we can do.' And it wasn't what we wanted, *and* we're actually missing two shots that are in the show. They were not done at all.

"And we said, 'Wait a minute—you don't understand. This cannot happen.'"

At this thirteenth hour, says Spotnitz, he, coproducer Paul Rabwin, and associate producer Lori Nemhauser made frantic calls to nearly every special-effects house and video artist in Los Angeles. Several of these outside companies worked to produce the effects closer to the producers' vision. Along with editor Michael Stern, the trio pulled a Friday-Saturday all-nighter to slam the new and improved worm scenes into the show.

Finally, as things came together on Sunday, they fed three different—and progressively better—versions of the episode up to a waiting satellite. The first version went to two television stations

in the Midwest that needed an early feed; the second to Canada; and the third to the rest of the United States.

"That means different people saw different versions of the show," says Spotnitz. "That's my biggest regret in terms of visual effects since I started work on the series."

Shortly after this, says Spotnitz, Laurie Kallsen-George was hired to take over the job as visual effects supervisor.

Fortunately, he adds, the other *X-Files* departments met their challenges successfully. The bulk of the "Russian" scenes—of the prison camp and Siberian forest—were shot in Stanley Park, adjacent to downtown Vancouver, and the Seymour Demonstration Forest, just a short drive north of the city.

"We chose our camera angles carefully and trucked in a lot of mud," says locations manager Todd Pittston. "It was pretty straightforward, actually, but it worked well and looked really great."

To get that extra *frisson* of verisimilitude, production designer Graeme Murray—whose chilling chicken-wire restraints in the final scene of "Tunguska" was only vaguely hinted at in the original script—directed that real rocks, not fake prop ones, were to be used in the prison camp mining scenes. Art director Gary Allen went to a nearby quarry, picked out boulders in a pouring rain, and had them delivered by forklift to the location.

A considerable number of horses and their handlers were needed for the two episodes; the animals and their handlers were employed not only in the make-believe tundra forest but at a rented horse farm in South Surrey that served as the Well-Manicured Man's home base. A less fragrant requirement was that Alex Krycek speak Russian with the proper syntax and accent: a Russian-speaking dialogue coach was hired to work with him during the filming.

The U.S. Senate hearing room was actually an elaborate set constructed on North Shore Studio's Stage One. "Terma's" climactic oil refinery scenes were shot at what is actually a thermal energy plant, near Port Moody, B.C. Rainy weather plagued the production during the filming of the sequences, but the spectacular set-piece scene—the explosion and fire at the oil wellhead—went off perfectly.

"At first they wanted to blow up the entire refinery," recalls special effects supervisor David Gauthier, "but I told them it would be very difficult and there would be a huge bill. Then I suggested: 'Why not do the oil fires of Kuwait?'"

Gautier and his crew rigged their dummy wellhead with pipes and nozzles and then used a high velocity pump to spew 35,000 gallons of oil-colored water into the air. The same wellhead was equipped to shoot a mixture of burning kerosene and gasoline—and when the time was right, 2,000 gallons of liquid propane pressurized to 250 psi.

"We had a remote control valve," says Gauthier, "so we could switch from one nozzle to another. So we essentially switched from liquid oil to burning oil, blew up the van directly in front of the oil well, and away we went."

The tagline was changed to "E Pur Si Muove" or "Still, it moves," a phrase attributed to Galileo as he defiantly refuted the Inquisition, which forced him to recant his theory that the Earth revolved around the sun. Of course, the phrase also evokes the movement of the "black cancer" within the episode.

ⓧ

In Tibetan Buddhism, a "terma" is a hidden text. In Russian, the word means "prison." In Latin it means "death."

ⓧ

el mundo gira

episode: 4X11
first aired: January 12, 1997
written by: John Shiban
editor: Heather MacDougall
directed by: Tucker Gates

Fear, jealousy, superstition, and prejudice
converge when a young female migrant worker
is killed by a mysterious yellow rain.

guest stars:
Mitch Pileggi (AD Walter Skinner)
Ruben Blades (Conrad Lozano)
Raymond Cruz (Eladio Buente)
Jose Yenque (Soledad Buente)
Simi (Gabrielle Buente)
Lillian Hurst (Flakita)
Susan Bain (County Coroner)
Robert Thurston (Dr. Larry Steen)
Michael Kopsa (Rick Culver)
Markus Hondro (The Barber)
Janeth Munoz (Village Woman)
Pamela Diaz (Maria Dorantes)
Fabricio Santin (Migrant Worker)
Jose Vargas (INS Worker)
Tito Mata (INS Guard)
Tony Dean Smith (Store Clerk)

principal settings:
San Joaquin Valley, California;
Fresno, California

In a squalid shantytown in California's Central Valley, a middle-aged Hispanic woman, Flakita, stands in the center of a candlelit shack. She is speaking to an audience of chattering women.

"Quiet! Quiet! Listen to me!" says the storyteller.

She says, "It was a terrible thing. You're not going to believe me, even when I tell you. Some say it's a story, a fairy tale. But I saw it. I saw it with my own eyes."

This is the story she tells:

On a bleak workday morning, an Anglo foreman drives his pickup truck down a dirt road and into the middle of the camp. Hispanic men gather around him, calling out to him for work.

One of the lucky ones is a young man named Soledad Buente; he kisses his beautiful girlfriend good-bye before climbing onto the truck bed. As soon as Soledad walks away, his handsome brother, Eladio Buente, approaches the young woman—Maria Dorantes—and flirts openly with her.

"I missed you last night, my love," says Eladio.

Firmly but good-naturedly, Maria insists that she's not his girlfriend—and that if Soledad sees them talking to each other, he will think that she is cheating on him.

It is too late, however. Soledad sees them. As the pickup pulls away, there is pain and budding rage in his eyes.

"Maria!" shouts Flakita.

Absorbed in her conversation with Eladio, the young woman has forgotten to close the gate of her goat pen. Three of the scrawny animals are scrambling over a nearby hill. Maria chases them, followed by Eladio.

"Two brothers. One woman. Trouble," says Flakita.

There is a loud clap of thunder—or, at least, a loud noise—followed by a flash of lightning and a sudden torrential downpour. The rain runs down from the rooftops in sulfurous yellow streams. The women of the camp note this with puzzlement and fear.

Large yellow puddles form on the ground. The rain stops as suddenly as it started. Two of the goats clamber back over the hill.

"Maria!" shouts Flakita once more.

The women of the camp run—with a great deal of fear—toward Maria. She is lying dead on the ground, as is the third goat. Both woman and animal have had their eyeballs eaten away; their lips and noses are partially gone.

Eladio Buente is nowhere to be seen.

Three days later, Mulder and Scully stand at the same spot, staring down at the decomposing goat carcass.

Scully, a handkerchief pressed to her mouth, asks her partner just what they're doing there. Mulder explains that the death they're investigating was preceded by a "Fortean event": an unusual or highly infrequent meteorological phenomenon. The hot yellow rain that witnesses reported, he adds, is called a "liquid fall" by Fortean researchers.

"Black and red rains are the most common," says Mulder, "but there have been reported cases of blue, purple, and green rains."

"Purple rain?" says Scully.

"Yeah," says Mulder. "Great album. Deeply flawed movie, though."

Scully asks Mulder what the examination of Maria's body has revealed. There has been no examination, he says.

"Nobody cares, Scully. The victim and many of the witnesses are illegal immigrants. Migrant farm workers."

They walk off toward the center of camp.

"I thought it might be important to talk to them," says Mulder, "before they migrated."

Scully and Mulder's arrival causes a panic: They are mistaken for agents of the U.S. Immigration and Naturalization Service. The migrants flee their shacks and run for safety.

"La Migra! La Migra!" shouts Flakita.

"No La Migra! No La Migra!" shout Mulder and Scully.

Flakita reappears and asks them warily what they're looking for. They want, says Mulder, to find out what happened to Maria Dorantes.

"El Chupacabra," says Flakita. "That's what happened to Maria Dorantes."

Scully is baffled, but not Mulder.

"A Mexican folk tale," he tells her. "El Chupacabra, the goat-sucker. It's a small gray creature with a big head and big black bulging eyes."

Flakita's suspicious look fades—Mulder is a kindred soul.

"Si! Si!" she says. "Light. Then rain. Then La Chupacabra. He comes and eats away at Maria's eyes and face."

The migrant workers stand awestruck—all except Soledad Buente, who pushes his way toward the agents.

"This woman is a liar! There is no Chupacabra. The Chupacabra is nothing but a story told to children. I know the killer of Maria Dorantes."

Scully looks at Soledad with interest. "Who would that be, sir?" she says.

"It's my brother, Eladio Buente," says Soledad. "He killed Maria because she loved only me."

Mulder says, "How do you explain the yellow rain and the dead goat over there?"

"It's a trick," he says. "For fools who believe in fools' superstitions."

His explanation hits home with Scully. "Thank you, Mr. Buente," she says. "You've been very helpful."

At the federal office building in Fresno, Mulder calls on Conrad Lozano, a Mexican-American INS agent. He asks whether Eladio Buente could now be in his agency's custody.

"He might," says Lozano, checking a long list.

"Let's see. Okay! We have a Jose Feliciano. We have Juan Valdez, we have Cesar Chavez, we have Placido Domingo."

Mulder takes the subtle hint: Nobody arrested by La Migra ever gives their real name. But Lozano, it turns out, has heard about Maria Dorantes's murder.

"Oh, man," he says disgustedly. "La Chupacabra?"

"You don't believe in it," says Mulder.

"No. I believe these people," says Lozano. "But their lives are small. So they have to make up these fantasies just to keep on going—to feel alive. Because they are strangers here. They feel hated, unwanted. Whenever their passions are inflamed, they resort to violence."

He adds, "And because they cannot turn to the law, they make up these fantastic tales. Call it anything you want, but this is an age-old story."

At the Fresno County Coroner's office, Scully tells the physician in charge that she's investigating the death of a migrant worker.

"Juan or Juanita?" says the coroner nonchalantly.

The name Maria Dorantes is "vaguely familiar," she adds, but only with much prodding will she put her Anglo autopsy aside to help Scully. They finally locate Maria—in a back room in a body bag.

Scully unzips her, and the coroner gasps. Maria's body is completely covered by a frightening thick green fungal growth.

In the bowels of the INS building, Lozano and Mulder find Eladio Buente. He is sitting alone, disconsolate, in a holding cell. He has been segregated from the other prisoners, who have refused to go near him.

"They think he's the Chupacabra," says Mulder.

"That may be," says Lozano, scanning Buente's booking sheet. "But I will tell you with a tremendous degree of certainty this guy is not Erik Estrada."

With Lozano translating, Mulder asks Eladio whether he killed Maria. Lozano

116

translates Eladio's answer—which he delivers with all the passion and fervor of a Mexican soap opera actor.

The migrant worker denies killing Maria. He insists histrionically that after the yellow rain fell, he regained consciousness just in time to see Maria die in his arms.

"This guy is *better* than Erik Estrada," cracks the INS agent.

Mulder and Lozano watch as Eladio is loaded into a van for deportation—up front with the driver, because the other prisoners refuse to sit next to him.

Mulder asks Lozano to delay Eladio's departure for Mexico until after Maria's murderer can be found. Lozano looks at him with something like disdain.

"I gotta believe the FBI's got something better to do," he says.

Mulder holds his ground.

"File your paperwork," says Lozano, shrugging him off. "By the time they process it, he'll probably be back here anyway."

Scully arrives in the rental car to pick up her partner. As she and Mulder drive away, she tells her partner that Eladio didn't murder Maria. The woman was killed by a massive fungal growth—*Aspergillus*, a commonplace mold usually harmless to humans. Tests have also found high levels of pesticide residue in her blood. Scully hypothesizes that Maria's immune system was compromised.

"But that still doesn't explain the flash of light or the yellow rain," says Mulder. "Or *El Chupacabra*."

Scully replies, "Mulder, I know you don't want to hear this, but I think the aliens in this story are not the villains. They're the victims."

She stops the car behind a crashed vehi-cle just ahead: the INS van. It has crashed into a guard rail; its back door is wide open, and the last of the detainees are running from the scene as fast as they can. The agents cautiously open the front door.

The INS driver/guard is dead. The skin on his face, which is flaking away in chunks, is covered with a multicolored fungal growth.

Eladio Buente has vanished again.

Lozano arrives at the scene a few minutes later. The agents split up—Scully to look into the epidemiological basis of the fungus, and Mulder and Lozano to find *El Chupacabra*.

At a local barbershop, the proprietor—also the local *coyote*, or illegal immigrant smuggler—watches a steamy Mexican soap opera on his TV. He is a Spanish-speaking Anglo; cruelty and bigotry ooze from his every pore.

Eladio Buente, noticeably ill, enters his shop. He begs to be driven back to Mexico in *El Barbero's* truck.

Says the barber: "We haul *mucho basura* in that truck. What makes you think we haul it back?"

After much desperate pleading, the man agrees to take Eladio home—for *mucho dinero*, deliverable that evening. Eladio hurries off.

At an illegal curbside labor exchange nearby, a group of aliens clamor for the attention of Rick Culver, a construction foreman in search of two day laborers. He selects a pair of men. However, they—as well as all their *compadres*—leave quickly at the sight of Eladio, crouched shivering in the bed of the truck.

Culver grabs Eladio by the shirt and tries to throw him out—then realizes that Eladio is the only cheap help he'll get that day.

"You'll have to do," he says disgustedly.

At the state university in Fresno, Scully consults with Dr. Larry Steen, a mycologist. Steen has identified the second deadly fungus. It is *dermatophytosis*—commonly known as athlete's foot, "the most ubiquitous fungal spore known to mankind."

From Scully's samples of both deadly fungi, Steen has also isolated an enzyme— a liquid looking very much like the yellow rain. He tells Scully that the enzyme works to accelerate the growth of the fungi, enabling them to overwhelm any normal organism's natural defenses.

To demonstrate, he places a tiny drop of the stuff on a petri dish filled with black stem rust, a local crop blight. The fungus grows so fast it bubbles over the side of the dish.

"I must say," says Steen, "that if this were to get out into the environment, *dermatophytosis* might give the cockroach a run for its money."

At the spot where Eladio was hired, Mulder stares at some graffiti on a cement wall.

"*El Chupacabra Vive!*" it reads.

Lozano questions the laborers and learns that Eladio has left with Culver.

"Story's out," says Mulder, pointing to the wall.

"Oh, yeah," says Lozano. "These people love their stories. It's the one thing that keeps them from going mad when they're out there standing on the street corner waiting for work."

"So they really don't think he's the *Chupacabra*?"

"No," says Lozano. "They're certain of it."

Mulder asks Lozano if he's told them about the fungal infection.

"Yeah, they wouldn't listen. They're only interested in what will become of Eladio Buente."

"What *will* become of Eladio Buente?" asks Mulder.

Lozano states what to him has become perfectly obvious: When Soledad, his jealous brother, finds Eladio, he will kill him.

"So we gotta find him first," says Mulder, moving to his car.

Lozano reaches out to stop him. "My mother warned me," he says, "that blood must be left to cleanse itself. That God curses the man who stands between two brothers."

Mulder disagrees. "In this case," he says, "he's going to curse the man who doesn't."

At the Culver construction site, Eladio toils away alone. He calls for his boss, but there is no answer. He wipes some sweat from his face with his T-shirt. It leaves a yellowish stain.

"Eladio Buente!" yells a Hispanic man.

It is Soledad, carrying an iron pipe as a crude weapon. But Eladio has disappeared. Soledad searches for him. He stands in front of a portable toilet, yelling angrily in Spanish.

"Come out of there!" he says. "Come out like a man so I can split open your face, bastard!"

Soledad yanks open the door. Rick Culver is inside, dead and covered with mold. Soledad falls back, horrified.

Eladio roars past in Culver's truck. Soledad recovers from his fright and screams at his departing brother: "*Assesino!*"

In one of Fresno's upper-middle-class neighborhoods, Eladio staggers to the rear entrance of the house that Gabrielle Buente is cleaning.

He tells his young cousin that he is innocent of the crime of which Soledad has accused him. He begs her to go with him to Mexico. But Gabrielle is very frightened.

"They say that you are the *Chupacabra*, and that you killed Maria Dorantes and many more," she says.

Once again, Eladio passionately proclaims his innocence. He asks Gabrielle for money. Gabrielle tells him that she will have some money that evening, when she is paid at the supermarket where she works.

"Gabrielle, I can't wait," he sobs.

As his cousin cries for him to stop, he climbs a fence and is gone.

At the state college, Scully phones Mulder—who is at the Culver death site with Lozano—and warns him not to come in direct contact with the fungus.

Mulder tells Scully he's been thinking the matter over. He lays out his thesis.

"These Fortean transients that the woman described," he says, "could have been caused by an object falling at a high rate of speed through the atmosphere, causing a sonic boom and a flash of light.

"What astronomers call a bolide. Created by a meteorite or a piece of extraplanetary material—of which two thousand tons falls to Earth every day. Now, this yellow rain. Space debris could have fallen into a nearby lake, superheating the water and sending it skyward. Which means it's alien."

Scully listens with as much patience as she can muster—then tells Mulder she'll keep working the fungus angle while he keeps looking for Eladio. Conrad Lozano has overheard Mulder's end of the conversation.

"So. You've got your own 'stories' too, huh?" he says.

Mulder smiles and nods sheepishly.

A Cadillac pulls up to where they're standing. Inside is *El Barbero*.

"Hey, Lozano," he says. "I hear you're looking for the *Chupacabra*. For a modest fee, I can tell you where he might be found."

At a rural truck stop later that day, Mulder spots Eladio, coughing convulsively. Mulder and Lozano chase him among the parked trucks, causing a panic among a group of newly arrived illegal immigrants.

Eladio dives under a moving semi—and disappears. The agents throw up their hands in frustration. Eladio has escaped hiding in the middle of a truckload of live goats.

At a roadblock on Highway 99 that evening, Mulder and Scully examine the truck Eladio hid in. It is now full of dead and rotting goats. Mulder asks Lozano how one poor man can keep eluding them.

Lozano says, "These people are invisible. You look at them and don't see them. Just workers, cheap labor, to pick crops and clean houses. To most people they're aliens in the true sense of the word."

A police car brings Flakita to the scene. She tells the agents of Eladio's visit to Gabrielle—and that Soledad is seeking out his brother to kill him.

At Gabrielle's tiny apartment, the agents ask her if she's seen Eladio or Soledad. "*Si*. But I am afraid," she says. "Because of what they say about Eladio. About *El Chupacabra*."

Scully says, "There is no *El Chupacabra*, Gabrielle. But Eladio is a very sick man. If he comes here you must not let him in. If he comes to this door you must call the police."

As the agents enter Lozano's vehicle, Mulder asks them to linger at the scene for a few minutes.

"Something's going on here," he says.

A deathly ill and hungry Eladio enters the upscale supermarket where Gabrielle works. He staggers down the aisles and scoops up some cashews from a bin.

"Hey, Jose!" shouts an Anglo supermarket clerk angrily. "This ain't no restaurant! You have to pay for all that!"

Eladio gasps and falls, pulling a whole display down on him. He scrambles away from the angry clerk, who stops, stares, and picks up a cashew Eladio has touched. It is covered with a green, furry mold.

Outside Gabrielle's apartment, the agents watch Soledad leave the building and drive away. They follow him. Eladio gets a call at a phone booth near the supermarket. It is Gabrielle.

In despair, he asks her why she hasn't shown up for work.

"Listen to me, Eladio!" says Gabrielle. "Soledad—I could only lie to him so long."

But Eladio has already fled; he'd spotted his brother's car entering the parking lot.

Soledad enters the supermarket and searches the aisles. Eladio is long gone, but the three agents are now there—and they order him to halt. Soledad draws a cheap pistol and points it at the agents. The dangerous standoff lasts a few seconds, until Soledad, sobbing vengeance against his brother, breaks down into tears.

"Quiet, *loco*!" says Lozano.

"He's been here," says Mulder softly.

The Anglo clerk lies in the aisle, completely covered with green fungus. The body is at the center of a massive infestation—it has spread completely over the food spilled around it.

Gabrielle Buente opens her apartment door and recoils in horror. It is Eladio.

"What are you afraid of?" he asks.

Gabrielle says, "Look! Look at yourself!"

In the mirror, Eladio sees the monster he is becoming.

"You are what they say you are," says his terrified cousin. "You killed Maria Dorantes! You are *El Chupacabra*."

"No!" screams Eladio.

Later that night, the agents kick in the door of Gabrielle's apartment. They call for Eladio to show himself.

"He's not here. He's gone," sobs Gabrielle.

"Gone where?" asks Scully.

"To Mexico. Where he can hide his terrible face."

Now the young woman is hysterical.

"How's he going to get to Mexico?" asks Mulder.

"I gave him all my money! Yes! Because I was afraid. Afraid that *El Chupacabra* would kill me, too!"

Lozano sighs and shakes his head. Mulder turns to him.

"How're we going to find this man?" he asks.

The INS agent is strangely withdrawn. He mutters something about paperwork and walks away. In their car, Mulder and Scully discuss their next move.

"Mulder, he could be anywhere right now," says Scully. "If he were to enter a metropolitan area with what he's carrying . . ."

"He won't," says Mulder distractedly.

Scully says, "If he's going to Mexico . . ."

"She's lying," says Mulder.

The pieces are beginning to fit. "If this man really thinks he killed Maria Dorantes, he won't be going to Mexico," he says.

"Then where's he going?" asks Scully.

"The same place Agent Lozano and Eladio's brother are going. He's going to face his brother."

Mulder's voice softens. "'God curses the man who stands between two brothers,'" he says.

Then, sharply, to Scully: "Get on your cell phone and have a haz-mat team assembled."

At the migrants' camp, Flakita peers out of her shack and sees Lozano.

"Eladio Buente!" he shouts. "Come on out! Be a man and face your brother!"

Eladio emerges from the shadows, running away. Lozano chases him out of Flakita's sight. A handcuffed Soledad pursues him, also.

There is a gunshot.

A terrified Flakita forces herself to see what has happened. Around the corner, she sees Lozano lying dead on the ground, his nose and mouth already eaten away.

A brilliant light envelops her. From over the hill, coming from the light, walk three—no four—faceless alien figures. Flakita flees.

She is back in her candlelit shack, finishing the story for her audience.

"They came from the sky," she says. "More *Chupacabras*! Coming to save Eladio. I slammed the door and prayed that they would not come to kill me, too!"

One of her neighbors, transfixed, asks, "What will happen to Soledad?"

"He was taken up by a *Chupacabra*," she says. "He will suffer for his treachery. He is made to suck the blood of only the sick and dying goats when the *Chupacabra* come to feed."

Another villager in the audience disputes this. "That is not what Gabrielle says," she says. "Gabrielle says she lied to *La FBI*, so that her cousin Eladio could live. But *La Migra* Lozano knew that Soledad could not live with vengeance in his heart."

This is Gabrielle's version of the incident:

In pursuit of Eladio through the shantytown, with Soledad at his heels, Conrad Lozano fires a warning shot.

"*Alto!* Turn around and face the man whose love you killed!" shouts the agent.

Soledad shouts, "You killed Maria! Because she wouldn't love you! Because her heart belongs to only one man!"

He grabs Lozano's revolver.

"Don't make me shoot you in the back, Eladio!" says Soledad. "Turn around like a man."

Eladio turns to face his brother. He is now a horrible gray creature with a huge head and black bulging eyes.

"I am not a man! I am the *Chupacabra*!" he says.

Now Gabrielle herself, speaking to a circle of awestruck laborers at the graffiti-strewn wall, picks up the narrative.

"'Shoot! Shoot!' *La Migra* shouted," says Gabrielle, "but Soledad began to cry.

"'No! No!' Soledad cried. 'I cannot shoot my brother. He is my brother! My flesh, my blood.'

"'Shoot him! He's *El Chupacabra*!' shouted *La Migra*. 'He is the goat-sucker and he must be killed!'"

Gabrielle continues, "But Soledad could not kill Eladio, because he knew I would never forgive him. *La Migra* Lozano tried to pull the gun from Soledad's hand, calling him a coward.

"'No!' cried Soledad. 'He is my brother!'

"And the gun went off," says Gabrielle. "*Bang! Bang!* And *La Migra* Lozano fell dead."

The illegal aliens nod happily at this ending.

"*Pero no!*" says Gabrielle, frowning and shaking her head. This is not the end.

Gabrielle says, "*La Migra* Lozano brought Soledad to kill Eladio so he would not be cursed. So God cursed Soledad for his treachery and turned him into *El Chupacabra*—like his brother.

"Together, they run. To Mexico."

In his office in Washington, AD Skinner takes all of this in. "Frankly," he says, "I'm confused by this story."

Mulder says, "I don't blame you."

"We can't really explain it ourselves, sir," says Scully.

The agents give it a try. They tell Skinner that they arrived at the spot where Lozano's body lay immediately after the members of the haz-mat team—who, in their protective suits and backlit by spotlights, look a lot like faceless aliens.

The fungus was contained within the camp. Lozano's revolver was found ten miles away, next to the fungus-covered body of the man known as "The Barber."

Scully hypothesizes that Soledad, like his bother, is a carrier of the enzyme and partially immune to the fungus.

"And this enzyme came from where?" says Skinner.

"Outer space, sir," says Mulder.

Skinner sighs, irritated. "So this is the story you want me to report?" he says.

He adds, "You would think with the resources we have we'd be able to find these men. I'm not hearing a good explanation of why this hasn't happened."

"Well, sir," says Scully, shifting uneasily. "These people have a way of being almost invisible."

Alongside a busy rural road, automobile headlights shine on Eladio Buente and his brother. They have both indeed become *Chupacabras.*

They have their thumbs out, hitchhiking. Nobody stops.

"The truth is," adds Mulder, "nobody cares."

back story:

"El Mundo Gira" (translation: "The World Turns") had its genesis several years ago during the not-so-golden era when story editor John Shiban, still an aspiring television writer, was working as a computer programmer for a company based in Ventura County, a semi-rural area north of Los Angeles.

"I'd look out my window and see the long lines of migrant workers in the strawberry fields alongside the freeway," says Shiban. "It's a shame, but just about everybody, including myself, passed them every day on the way to work without noticing them at all."

Shiban adds, "Chris actually pointed this out to me when I was pitching the story. He said to me, 'These people are invisible. We see them, but we don't see them. They move through our world—they clean our homes and tend our gardens and pick our food—but we just don't think of them as

people like us.' And that actually became one of the central themes of the episode."

The migrant workers were the final ingredient to a contagious fungus story line that Shiban—"My first idea was that it was being spread by a schoolkid; then I suggested an interstate trucker"—had been kicking around for months. Chris Carter was attracted to the over-the-top, Mexican soap opera–like aspects of the plot, and to prevent the episode from becoming too solemn or self-important, emphasized those elements during story conferences and rewrites.

To research the episode Shiban spent several days observing illegal aliens being processed at an INS facility in San Pedro, California. ("Yeah, the detainees do give the officers false names," says Shiban, "but they usually use something like Juan Gonzales. We embellished that a little.")

As for *El Chupacabra*, it is a folk myth that still circulates powerfully throughout the Spanish-speaking world. "A year ago," says Shiban, "I saw an article in the *L.A. Times* about a *Chupacabra* sighting in Northern California. Somebody had claimed that one of them kidnapped a baby. So I started looking into it. I discovered there was even a song about *El Chupacabra* that played on Spanish radio stations."

Spanish-language music fans certainly noted the presence of Ruben Blades. The Panamanian artist was one of the hottest stars of *salsa* in the late seventies and early eighties, and his eclectically themed albums still sell briskly today. A political activist who ran for president of Panama after the U.S. invasion of his country in 1989, he has accomplished all this while appearing in films like *The Milagro Beanfield War*, *The Two Jakes*, and *Dead Man Out*. Somewhere along the line, he made the acquaintance of a longtime fan, Chris Carter, who had been looking to place him in his show for quite a while.

The other guest stars, reports L.A. casting director Rick Milliken, were just as easy to find, mainly because there are many more talented young Latino actors in Los Angeles than there are good roles being written for them. Raymond Cruz, who played Eladio Buente, had just had a successful run starring in *Blade To the Heat*, a controversial play at the Mark Taper Forum. Gabrielle Buente, who played Simi, starred in HBO's *Grand Avenue*. The couple were living together at the time—a fact that the producers found out only after production had started. They plan to be married in March of 1998.

Although not noticeably heavy in exotic locales or special effects, the episode had its share of production problems. The migrant workers' camp was built from scratch in the middle of a large waste ground near Vancouver's Boundary Bay Airport. (This uninviting area also served as the site of the plane crash in "Tempus Fugit.")

Unfortunately, a freakish storm dumped several inches of snow onto the sunbaked "San Joaquin Valley" the night before filming was to start. Several panicky calls between Shiban, first-time director Tucker Gates, and executive producer Robert Goodwin produced Plan B: Crew members scurried ahead of each camera setup, melting the snow with hot water and blow dryers.

The art department's hardest task was finding an old-fashioned revolving "Gas" sign to put on the scratch-built truck stop. Assistant art director Vivian Nishi was in charge of the search; one was finally found in a local junkyard. Before it was finally approved, the correct look of the single fungus-covered cashew held up in the supermarket was the subject of a lengthy and highly charged debate between the producers and the visual special-effects department.

"El Mundo Gira" was a milestone of sorts for Mark Snow—it was the only

episode in his memory during which Chris Carter asked him to throw out his entire score and start again.

"Well, when Chris saw it [with my music] he said, 'Listen, it's just too serious. You have to put in a little Spanish flavor, blah blah blah.' So I went for it—rewriting the whole thing in one day. When I was finished, there was no non-Spanish music in the whole piece. I put in some flamenco guitar and did this whole tango thing when the migrant workers run away. And it worked!"

The fungoid special-effects makeup for "El Mundo Gira" was provided by Toby Lindala—but the stamp of approval was provided by Gillian Anderson's daughter Piper. The little girl, her mother recalls, was fascinated by many of the strange fuzzy individuals on the set that week.

"Piper calls them 'yucky guys,'" says Anderson. "These are the people who are covered with blood or fungus or have an eyeball hanging down or whatever. Sometimes in our own lives we'll pass a dark place and she'll get very excited. She'll ask me, 'Is there a yucky guy in there?'" "Anyway," she adds, "in one of the scenes in that episode the yucky guy was actually a mannequin. He obviously wasn't feeling very well, so Piper went up to it and said, 'You okay? You okay?' He didn't answer, so she started singing 'Itsy-bitsy Spider' to him. It was hysterical. We got some wonderful video of her."

Ⓧ

kaddish

episode: 4X12
first aired: February 16, 1997
written by: Howard Gordon
editor: Michael S. Stern
directed by: Kim Manners

Someone—or something— is killing the
members of an anti-Semitic gang. To find
the truth, Mulder and Scully delve into the
ancient canons of Jewish mysticism.

guest stars:
Justine Miceli (Ariel Luria)
David Groh (Jacob Weiss)
David Wohl (Kenneth Ungar)
Channon Roe (Derek Banks)
Harrison Coe (Isaac Luria)
Jonathon Whittaker (Curt Brunjes)
Jabin Litwiniec (Clinton Macguire)
George Gordon (Detective)
Timur Karabilgin (Tony Oliver)
Murrey Rabinovitch (Hasidic Man)
David Freedman (Rabbi)

principal setting:
Brooklyn, New York

At Ben Zion Cemetery in Brooklyn, a gathering of Hasidic Jews surrounds the open grave of a young man, Isaac Luria. They recite the Kaddish, the mourners' prayer, in Hebrew. As is traditional, each of the mourners drops a handful of earth onto the coffin.

Watching with quiet grief is Ariel Luria, Isaac's wife. She flashes back to the day of her husband's death: He was a storekeeper, knocked to the floor by three marauding punks.

Supported by her father, Jacob Weiss, Ariel is the last to stand before the grave. She grips her handful of dirt tightly, unable to let go. In her mind's eye, one of the punks stands over Isaac—and fires his cheap handgun into her husband's head.

Lightning flashes; a peal of thunder booms over the cemetery. Jacob gently helps his daughter unclench her hand. The service ends.

That night, in the middle of a driving rainstorm, a pair of bare hands sculpt the wet earth near Isaac's grave. The mound of mud takes the rough shape of a man. The interloper retreats, and there is another clap of thunder.

The crude earthen figure begins to move.

At FBI headquarters several days later Scully shows Mulder Isaac Luria's driver's license. Luria lived in the Williamsburg section of Brooklyn, she says—home to his Hasidic religious sect since the nineteenth century.

"An area also known for its history of racial tension and hate crimes," says Mulder. "Tawana Brawley, Yankel Rosenbaum. . . ."

"And now Isaac Luria," says Scully.

But solving that crime, she says, is not their responsibility. In fact, the police know who killed Isaac Luria. A videotape from the store's security system—showing the murder—was found in the VCR of a sixteen-year-old named Tony Oliver.

"Has he been arrested?" asks Mulder.

"No," says Scully. "Because he's dead. Apparently he'd been watching the tape when he was strangled."

"Very Old Testament," says Mulder.

"Yeah," says Scully. "But with a new twist."

Brooklyn homicide detectives, reports Scully, contacted the FBI's civil rights branch after finding a set of fingerprints on Tony Oliver's body.

The fingerprints belonged to Isaac Luria: a man who was already dead.

At Ariel Luria's Williamsburg apartment, Mulder and Scully show up as she is sitting *shiva*, the seven-day Jewish period of mourning.

Jacob Weiss answers the door. In his sixties, but quite robust, he strongly objects to their interviewing Ariel. Weiss is even more adamant when they request that Isaac's body be exhumed for a fingerprint check. When he learns that they are trying to solve the murder of his son-in-law's killer, he explodes.

"He's an animal!" says Weiss of Tony Oliver. "A monster! Just like the others who killed Isaac—whose grave you're asking us to desecrate so you can now protect them."

Ariel, who has been standing quietly behind her father, tries in vain to calm him.

"But where were *you*," says Weiss, "when *Isaac* needed your protection? When we called them, the police, they said we were paranoid. That there was nothing to worry about. They always say that whenever someone threatens the Jews."

Mulder says, "Then there was a specific threat of violence?"

Weiss says, "The threat is *always* there."

Weiss shows Mulder an anti-Semitic pamphlet. On its cover is a crude hook-nosed caricature and the title, "How AIDS Was Created by the Jew." Weiss tells them that it had been slipped under their door that morning.

"And now you've come here," he says. "Not to help us, but to ask our help. So you can impose your justice on the only man who has taken justice into his own hands."

Scully tells the older man that, if necessary, they can get a court order for the exhumation. The tense standoff is escalating. Ariel steps in to end it.

"Do what you feel is necessary," she says. "Just leave us alone. Let us mourn in peace."

In their car, Scully tells Mulder that she thinks Jacob Weiss knows the identity of Tony Oliver's killer.

"Maybe," says Mulder, handing Scully the pamphlet. "But it's hard to fault his attitude when you see something like that."

At a small local print shop, Mulder and Scully question the proprietor, a bespectacled, outwardly normal-looking man named Brunjes. He tells them that yes, he certainly knew Isaac Luria, whose store was across the street from his, although he doesn't know who killed him.

"But I'd be lying if I said I was surprised it happened," he adds, smirking. "You know how they are—always trying to find a way to make a dollar off honest folks who work for a living."

The agents struggle to hide their disgust. Mulder asks him if he knew anyone who had a grudge against Isaac.

"I can't think of anyone who didn't," sneers the bigot.

"Did you?" says Mulder.

Brunjes snaps to attention and becomes extremely defensive. He says he cannot identify photographs of Derek Banks and Clinton Macguire, the other two boys in the videotape. When Mulder asks if he's familiar with the anti-Semitic pamphlet, his paranoia hits high gear.

"You work for them, too, don't you?" says Brunjes.

"Who?"

"You know who," he says to Mulder. "You look like you might be one yourself."

Dropping all pretense of respect for their interview subject—and ignoring several more bursts of racist tripe—the agents tell him that Tony Oliver was murdered and that his accomplices in the Luria murder are in danger.

They also tell Brunjes that there have been rumors that Isaac Luria rose from the grave to kill the youth.

"What kind of Jew trick is this?" says Brunjes.

"We're just relating the evidence, sir," says Scully. "You can draw your own conclusions."

Hiding in the print shop's back room, Derek Banks watches the interview on a TV monitor. Out front, the agents are glad to be finished with Brunjes.

"Bless you," says Mulder beatifically as he leaves.

The printer goes into the back room and calls for Derek, but he is gone.

That night at the Jewish cemetery, Derek Banks and Clinton Macguire dig frantically—and fearfully—into Isaac Luria's grave.

"You sure about this?" says Clinton.

"I heard them, man," says Derek. "I'm not waitin' around to find out if it's true."

Someone is watching them work. The watcher's hand—it has several Hebrew letters written on it—rests on a nearby tombstone.

The vandals dig down to Isaac's plain pine coffin and scrape away the last layer of dirt. The lid is nailed tightly shut. Clinton curses, then goes to his car to find some tools. He rummages around in the trunk.

A shadow falls over him. He looks up in horror.

At the grave site, Derek breaks through the coffin lid with his shovel. He calls to his friend to come see what he's uncovered. There is only silence.

He calls again, tremulously. He climbs up out of the grave and looks out, quaking, over the edge. Clinton's body is nearly buried in a mound of mud. Only the shallow crown of his head—and one grasping hand—are visible.

Later that night, a coroner wheels away Clinton's body. The ligature marks on his neck, Scully tells Mulder, are consistent with the vigilante's prior MO.

It's her theory that Macguire and Banks were desecrating Isaac's corpse in revenge for the death of their cohort.

"That seems pretty redundant, doesn't it?" says Mulder. "Messing up someone you've already killed?"

He adds, "I'm thinking that they came here because they were afraid—afraid that the man they hated enough to kill wasn't really dead."

The agents stand in the grave, pull away a temporary plastic covering, and—recoiling at the stench—uncover Isaac's partially decomposed face. Isaac's hands are still there—negating one theory of how his fingerprints got onto Tony Oliver—and there are partially smudged Hebrew letters on the back of one of them. Resting underneath Isaac's head is a leather-bound book.

"A little bedtime reading?" says Mulder.

He pulls the book out and opens it. It bursts into flame. Reflexively, Mulder drops it onto the ground. It continues to burn brightly.

The next morning, Brunjes enters his print shop. Derek emerges from a dark corner. His face is shiny with dirt, sweat, and fear.

"You owe me for two weeks," sneers the youth.

"Where have you been?" asks Brunjes.

From Derek's defiant silence he guesses the answer.

"Is it true?" he asks. "That you and your friends killed the Jew?"

"I just want my money," says Derek.

Brunjes ignores this. "What the hell were you thinking?" he says. "I never told you to kill anyone. I never told you to do that!"

Derek looks at his role model with disdain. "No? What did you expect me to do? Hide back here like you did? Calling them names?"

"We're working to spread the truth!" replies Brunjes.

"The truth?" says Derek scornfully. "Man, you're as pathetic as they are."

"We're exposing their lies!" whines Brunjes.

"That's all just words," says Derek. "You think they killed my friends with just words?"

There is another flash of fear on Brunjes's face.

"Yeah, that's right," Derek tells him. "Clinton's dead, too."

He looks at the older man menacingly. "Now—I'd like my money."

At the Judaica Archives in Manhattan, Mulder and Scully consult with Kenneth Ungar, a thirtyish scholar. Ungar easily identifies the remains of the burned book.

"It's called the *Sefar Yezirah*—the Book of Creation," he says. "It's the earliest known Hebrew text on man's mystical communion with the divine."

To the agents' queries, Ungar replies that no, the *Sefar Yezirah* is never buried with the dead, it is not printed on special paper or with special ink, and—this with a chuckle—it has never been known to self-combust.

"It's a book on mysticism—not mysticism itself," says Ungar.

Scully broaches a scientific theory that

HOW AIDS WAS CREATED BY THE JEW

the book could have been contaminated by gas-filled groundwater leaching into the coffin. Both men look at her bemusedly, then move on.

"Is there anything," asks Mulder, "that distinguishes this particular *Sefar Yezirah* from other such books?"

"Yes," says Ungar, "but it's barely legible because of the burning. It's a name engraved in the leather. A Hebrew name. 'Veiss.' 'Ya-cob Veiss.'"

At Ariel Luria's apartment, the agents tell the young widow that they need to speak to her father.

"We found evidence linking him to the crime scene," says Scully. "This is escalating into something else, Ariel. Something that has to stop."

Ariel turns away, shudders, and finally confides in Mulder and Scully.

"My marriage to Isaac—you have to understand what it would have meant to my father."

"What do you mean 'would have meant'?" says Mulder.

"We got our marriage license a few weeks ago," says Ariel. "But the wedding wasn't until today."

The agents melt into silence at the utter sadness of her words. Ariel accepts their sympathy, then smiles. "I'd like to show you something," she says.

She leads them into the living room. On the mantelpiece is a miniature castle, smaller than a matchbook, with remarkably intricate filigree and metalwork. It sits atop a thick steel band, displayed in a delicate glass case.

"It was a communal wedding ring made in Kolin, a village near Prague," says Ariel. "My father apprenticed to the man who designed it."

"It's beautiful," says Scully, gazing at the precious object.

"Yes. Every woman who got married in the synagogue wore this ring. As a symbol that she was a queen, her husband a king, and the home they made a castle, not only on their wedding day but for the rest of their lives together."

Ariel's voice becomes solemn, muted.

"But most of those lives ended one day in the spring of 1943. Nine thousand Jews were massacred after digging their own graves."

Ariel explains that her father survived because he was ten years old and a jewelers' apprentice. The Germans needed children's fingers to make bullets in their munitions factories.

"And through all this," says Scully, "he hid the ring?"

"Even after the war he hid it. Even from my mother. To him, it was a dead relic from a forgotten place. Until the day that I told him I was getting married.

"For the first time in fifty years, he took out this ring. He said he felt like his village was born again. He knew how much I loved Isaac."

"Ariel, tell us where your father is," says Scully.

Ariel says, "I know my father. He would never kill anyone."

Scully asks gently, "What if you're wrong?"

Scully and Mulder enter the Park Street Synagogue and stand at the rear of the sanctuary. Facing away from them, toward the ark of the covenant, several dozen Hasidic men recite their prayers. The worshipers become aware of the agents' presence. They fall silent, turn around, and face the interlopers.

"Who are you?" asks one of the Hasids brusquely.

Scully flashes her shield. "We're with the FBI. We're looking for Jacob Weiss."

"Why?"

Mulder spots Jacob Weiss among the congregation. Weiss realizes this and begins to move away. Mulder and Scully shoulder their way through the silent crowd in pursuit of him, past the ark and up a flight of dimly lit stairs. In a dark dusty attic, Derek Banks's body hangs from a rafter.

A fast-moving figure slides past a beam of light at the far end of the room, reentering the shadows. Guns and flashlights drawn, the agents peer into the gloom. A dark figure strikes Mulder, knocking him to the ground. Another figure flashes past Scully, knocking her down. She fires into the blackness.

"Don't move! Federal agents!" shouts Scully.

The second figure freezes and stands still, chest heaving. Scully places Jacob Weiss under arrest.

Mulder senses something, turns around, but sees nothing. In a dark corner, resting on one of the beams, is the back of a hand we've seen before.

In the holding area of the local precinct house, Ariel Luria begs Scully to let her talk to her father. Scully tells her that she'll have to wait—that Weiss has been arrested on suspicion of murder; that her father is close to confessing; and that Ariel should seriously consider hiring a lawyer. The shy young woman tries to absorb this new tragedy.

"Ariel, I'm sorry," says Scully.

In an interrogation room, Weiss readily—perhaps too readily—admits to Mulder that he killed Derek Banks.

"Our synagogue has been vandalized thirteen times in the last year," he says. "I heard a noise in the attic, I went up to see what it was, and he attacked me. It was self-defense."

"Hanging a man in self-defense?" says Mulder incredulously.

"Is it any worse than they did to Isaac?" asks Weiss.

"Is it any better?"

Mulder tells Weiss that his *Sefar Yezirah* was found in Isaac's coffin. Weiss stiffens noticeably and becomes even more insistent about implicating himself.

Mulder tells Weiss that he suspects there was someone else with him in the attic. Jacob stares searchingly into Mulder's eyes, then turns away. Mulder reaches across to Weiss's coat sleeve and rubs at a small clump of dried mud.

Afterward Mulder tells Scully that he believes Weiss's entire confession is bogus and that there was a second person in the attic.

"Weiss knows it, too," he says, "and he's protecting whoever it is."

"His daughter?" says Scully.

"No. Someone big and strong enough to knock me to the ground."

The agents look through a one-way mirror into the interrogation room. They see Ariel and Jacob in a tearful embrace. Mulder turns to leave.

"Where are you going?" asks Scully.

"To see a man about a burning book," he says.

In the back room of the print shop that evening, Curt Brunjes runs off a new batch of anti-Semitic pamphlets. A Nazi flag hangs on the wall. He hears a noise, looks up, and returns to his printing press. Another noise sends him to a metal cabinet—from which he pulls out a revolver.

Hands shaking, he tries to load it. Before he can finish, he is slammed against the cabinet, pinned by a powerful hand, on the back of which three Hebrew letters are visible. The fingers tighten around Brunjes's neck, strangling him.

At the Judaica Archives, Mulder looms over the table where Kenneth Ungar is reading. The agent places a familiar-looking volume in front of him.

"There's something you didn't tell me about the contents of this *Sefar Yezirah*," Mulder says. "I want to know about the myth of the Golem."

Ungar is surprised that a gentile—an FBI agent, no less—is interested in such information. But he readily tells Mulder that the Kabbalists—early Jewish mystics—believed that a righteous man could actually create a living creature formed of mud or clay.

"But this creature could only be brought to life by the power of the word," says Ungar. "In practical terms, by a correct application of certain secret letter combinations."

Mulder listens intently while the scholar thumbs through the Hebrew text. "These pages," says Ungar, "are basically instructions for animating the inanimate. This passage here talks about inscribing a single word on the Golem itself."

"On the back of his hand?" asks Mulder.

"I'm impressed," says Ungar, surprised again.

Ungar tells him that the three letters—

aleph, mem, and tov—form the Hebrew word *Emet.*

"*Emet* means 'truth,'" Ungar adds. "But you see, Mr. Mulder, therein lies the paradox. Because the danger of the truth is contained in the word 'Golem' itself, which means matter without form, body without soul."

"So the Golem is an imperfect creation?"

Ungar nods. "A kind of monster, really. Unable to speak or to feel any of the most primitive emotions. In the legends, it runs amok and has to be destroyed by its creator."

"Destroyed how?"

"By erasing the first letter. Thus, *Emet* becomes *met*—which means 'dead.' Again, Mr. Mulder, the power of letters. Not just to create—but to kill."

Mulder's cell phone chirps. He raises it to his ear.

"Mulder, it's me," says Scully. "There's been another homicide."

At the print shop—now a crime scene—Brunjes lies on the floor. Mulder crumples one of his pamphlets.

"A man on a mission," he says disgustedly. "Look at all the energy he spent spreading his hatred."

Scully shows him Brunjes's mailing list. It contains hundreds of names—including the three young murder victims. The agents agree that Jacob Weiss—in jail during the fourth killing—can now be released.

An NYPD detective calls them over. He has been scanning the tape from the store security camera. On the monitor, a tall Hasidic man enters the store.

"Oh, my God!" says Scully. "It's Isaac Luria. He's still alive!"

"I'm not so sure about that," says Mulder, staring at the flickering image.

Mulder and Scully rush to Ariel's apartment. The front door is unlocked.

"She's not here, Scully," says Mulder. He looks at the empty glass case on the mantelpiece. "It's her wedding day."

At the darkened and empty synagogue, lit eerily with candles, Jacob Weiss walks through the sanctuary. He climbs the steps to the attic. A hand touches his shoulder from behind.

It is Ariel, wearing her wedding dress.

"Please go," she begs her father.

"Not without you," he says. "I'm not leaving without you."

"I want to see him," says Ariel.

"He's dead," says Jacob, his voice breaking with grief. "Isaac is dead.

"The boys who killed him—their hate took him from you. You tried bringing him back with your love. But what you brought back—you have to understand, Ariel, it isn't him. It's an abomination. It has no place among the living."

Ariel embraces her father and recalls the last time she spoke to Isaac.

"We were talking on the phone, about the wedding," she says. "He said he had to go, a customer needed his help, and he'd call me back. But when I heard the phone ring, something told me not to pick it up. A woman's voice was on the line, but I wasn't listening. I didn't have to. I knew Isaac wasn't calling me back."

She softens. "That's all I wanted," she says. "To say good-bye. It was just a wish. They were just . . . words."

A lumbering creak is heard. Jacob commands her daughter to stay where she is, then moves off in its direction.

Scully and Mulder enter the sanctuary. Jacob Weiss, still struggling, is hanging from a wooden beam.

Working frantically, Scully lifts his body to slacken the rope while Mulder takes out his penknife and cuts him down. Scully tends to the unconscious man while Mulder searches for Ariel. He finds her in the attic, slumped in a dark corner. He tells her that her father is alive.

"I know about Isaac," he says. "Where is he?"

"I don't know," says Ariel in despair.

Mulder helps her to her feet. She spots something over his shoulder.

"Isaac?" she says.

Mulder whirls and draws his gun.

"Stop! Or I'll fire!" he says.

He looses several shots into the advancing figure. The bullets hit but have no effect. The Golem knocks Mulder down and places its huge foot on the agent's throat. Mulder gasps for air, only a few seconds of life left.

"Isaac!" says Ariel. Her face suggests she is consumed as much by love as by fear.

Ariel's outstretched arm beckons the Golem toward her. The elaborate wedding ring is visible in her upturned palm.

Isaac removes his foot from Mulder's neck. His expression blank, he walks over to Ariel and takes the ring. Ariel recites the ancient Hebrew wedding vow:

"*Ani le-dodee, ve-dodee lee*—I am to my beloved as my beloved is to me."

Isaac slips the ring onto her finger.

Crying, Ariel rubs the first Hebrew letter off the back of his hand. Tenderly, she kisses it. The Golem turns back to earth and dissolves before her eyes.

Scully rushes up the stairs to check on Mulder, who is not hurt badly. She did not arrive in time to see the transformation.

Kneeling over the lifeless mound—the rough shape of a man—Ariel recites the mourner's Kaddish. She takes a handful of soil, grips it tightly, then lets it slip through her fingers.

back story:
With its virtually seamless integration of character development, social commentary, *and* the supernatural, "Kaddish" is generally considered to be one of the best nonmythological episodes of the fourth season. This is despite the fact that the show's basic premise had been lying lifeless on the writing room floor for years. "Probably every Jewish writer who's passed through here has pitched a Golem episode," says executive producer Howard Gordon, who finally got a green light in his fourth—and last—year on the show. The key to getting the Golem on its feet, he says, was connecting the monster to the heartbreaking relationship between Ariel and her dead husband.

"In the end," adds Gordon, "we know that this was something created not out of revenge or the notion of 'an eye for an eye'—which, granted, is an obvious bit of wish fulfillment for millions of Jews who have endured persecution—but out of love."

To serve as a thematic contrast Gordon played up the element of anti-Semitism and intolerance, but decided early on not to mirror the actual situation in Brooklyn, which involves tension, sometimes erupting into violence, between Orthodox Jews and their African-American neighbors. "On my first stab at this I made the protagonists black," he says, "but then I realized that black anti-Semitism is a very subtle and difficult subject and not what I needed in my dramatic structure. I needed straw dogs—characters whose bigotry was unbridled

and excuseless. This was also what the network wanted, and I didn't put up much of fight, because I think they were right."

To research the current state of American bigotry, Gordon contacted the Anti-Defamation League, which sent him the hate literature that was reproduced—with only minor alterations—to serve as the products of Curt Brunjes's print shop. A twelfth-century communal wedding ring was used by the rabbi, a survivor of the Holocaust, who married two of Gordon's good friends in Detroit last year.

To play Jacob Weiss, the producers went after Ron (*Kaz*) Leibman, but when he was not available the role went to David Groh, best known as Valerie Harper's husband on *Rhoda*. Groh caused a minor crisis when (due to a communications mix-up) he shaved off his natural beard before leaving for Vancouver.

To play Ariel Luria the producers chose Justine Miceli, a young actress best known for portraying Detective Adrianne Lesniak from 1994 to 1996 on ABC's *NYPD Blue*. Miceli is not Jewish, but one of her best friends, who is, was recently married to an Orthodox Jewish man. "About a month before I was cast in the part, I was at Holly's house in Buffalo while they were celebrating the Jewish holiday of Sukkoth," says Miceli. "We went over to their rabbi's house and the rabbi told me, 'Maybe one day you'll play a Jew. You've got the soul for it.' "

To capture Ariel's sorrowful demeanor and mental state, Justine used the memory of the death of her father, who passed away from lung cancer. Upon winning the part she phoned her friend's rabbi in Buffalo, who taught her the absolutely cor-rect Hebrew pronunciation of the Jewish prayers she was to recite. Unfortunately, this was *not* the absolutely correct pronunciation taught to her by an on-set expert hired in Vancouver. "It was a little confusing," says Miceli. "Things changed throughout the week until we came up with the version we wanted. Still, many of the my Jewish friends who've seen it told me my accent wasn't bad for an Italian broad."

Actually, director Kim Manners says, "Kaddish" had yet another technical advisor: A Hasidic rabbi who was an avid fan of the show, but who, for cultural and religious reasons, didn't exactly want news of this addiction to get around. "When you called him at the Hasidic Center," says Manners, "you had to leave a message for Rabbi So-and-So without saying you were from *The X-Files*. Then he'd call us back—until somehow the cat got out of the bag and everybody found out what he was doing. Then he didn't help us anymore."

Manners thought that "Kaddish" was "very moving—a great love story." However, shooting it proved sporadically frustrating. For much the same reasons that Rabbi So-and-So went into hiding, no Jewish congregation in Vancouver would rent out their synagogue for filming. Instead, an empty Protestant church was rented, and production designer Graeme Murray designed a new interior that was literally built and dressed overnight. (So were dozens of extras in the synagogue scenes.

During a shopping expedition to stores frequented by Vancouver's sizable Hasidic community, assistant costume designer Janice Swayze was so taken by the round black hats worn by some Orthodox men that she bought one for her own wardrobe.)

An interesting snafu occurred, says art director Gary Allen, when a Hebrew translation of the Ten Commandments was needed to hang above the fake

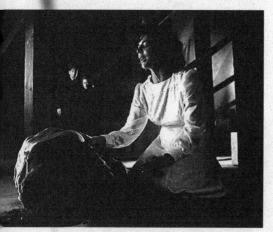

synagogue's altar. The show's Hebrew translator was unavailable to help them—she had the day off because it was a Jewish holiday. "We ended up faking it," says Allen.

Even more frustrating was the absolute refusal, during Mulder and Scully's graveyard scene, of the mystical Jewish book to burst into flames on cue—and when it finally did, to burn with a sudden flame so huge that David Duchovny had to fling the specially rigged book to the ground and dash out of camera range. Duchovny and Gillian Anderson literally spent hours working with the second unit on that one brief scene; their adventures eventually became a highlight of the show's Christmas gag reel.

Mark Snow, who is Jewish, says he enjoyed composing several clarinet, violin, and cello solos for the show's score. He borrowed J.S. Bach's "Little" Fugue in G Minor for one of the synagogue scenes. "The aim was to wind up somewhere between a Klezmer band and *Schindler's List*," he says.

Although this was the twelfth episode of the fourth season filmed, it was the fifteenth aired. The reason: when "Leonard Betts" (4X14) was slotted for the twelfth week—crucial post–Super Bowl time slot— it meant that Scully's cancer would be revealed. Her uncharacteristic behavior in "Never Again" (4X13) and "Memento Mori" (4X15) can be attributed to that fact, so those two episodes had to run immediately afterward.

A card placed before the closing titles of "Kaddish" states that the episode is dedicated to Lillian Katz. She was Howard Gordon's maternal grandmother, a wife and mother who worked in New York City as a newspaper clipper for Warner Brothers.

"I never met her because she died at age 43, before I was born," says Gordon. "But my mother tells me that she loved show business, was an avid reader of the movie trade newspapers, and took her kids—my mother and my uncle—to the movies or to a Broadway play whenever she got the chance. In that respect nobody else in my family was even remotely like her. My mother always tells me that it's to my grandmother that I owe my genetic predisposition towards Hollywood. The night that 'Kaddish' aired would have been her eighty-ninth birthday."

According to several historical accounts, the myth of the Golem inspired Mary Shelley when she wrote *Frankenstein*.

ⓧ

"Isaac Luria," the murder victim, is named for the famous rabbi Isaac Luria. Luria is credited as the father of Jewish mysticism, and a major contributor to the body of mystical knowledge known as the Kabbalah.

ⓧ

A "kaddish" is a Jewish prayer for the dead recited in daily synagogue services by relatives of the deceased.

ⓧ

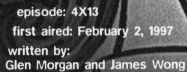

episode: 4X13

first aired: February 2, 1997

written by:
Glen Morgan and James Wong

editor: Jim Gross

directed by: Robert Bowman

On a solo assignment out of town,
a lonely Scully meets Mr. Wrong—
a single guy who thinks his new tattoo
is talking to him.

never again

guest stars:

Rodney Rowland (Ed Jerse)
Jodie Foster (The Voice of "Betty")
Bill Croft (Comrade Svo)
Jay Donohue (Detective Gouveia)
B. J. Harrison (Jehovah's Witness)
Igor Morozov (Vsevlod Pudovkin)
Jillian Fargey (Kaye Schilling)
Jan Bailey Mattia (Ms. Hadden)
Ian Robison (Detective Smith)
Barry "Bear" Hortin (Bartender)
Marilyn Chin (Mrs. Shima-Tsuno)
Rita Bozi (Ms. Vansen)
Natasha Vasiluk (Russian Store Owner)
Peter Nadler (Ed's Lawyer)
Jenn Forgie (Ed's Ex-Wife)
Sean Pritchard (Ed's Ex-Wife's Lawyer)
Carla Stewart (Judge)
Doug Devlin (Young Man)

principal settings:

Philadelphia, Pennsylvania;
Washington, D.C.;
Memphis, Tennessee

In a family law courtroom in Philadelphia, a man named Ed Jerse—in his early thirties and fairly good-looking—watches helplessly as the judge bangs down the gavel on his marriage. It's obvious that the settlement is in his now ex-wife's favor: She happily celebrates with her attorney while Jerse grimly signs his life away.

That night Jerse drinks himself into a near stupor at a low-life bar called the Hard Eight Lounge. He pulls out a snapshot of himself and his two children, then drunkenly burns a hole in it—erasing his own smiling face with the tip of a lit cigarette.

Jerse lurches off his barstool and wobbles outside into the rain; the gaudy neon of a tattoo parlor across the street catches his eye. He stares boozily at one particular tattoo in the window: a saucy 1940's ingenue—think of the legendary pinup icon Bettie Page—winking alluringly over her shoulder.

Afterward, Ed staggers drunkenly into his pathetic apartment, strips off his shirt, and peels the bandage off his new tattoo. It is, of course, the girl in the window. Now she winks out from his right biceps, over the words "NEVER AGAIN." Completely spent, he passes out on the floor.

Both of the tattooed girl's eyes are now wide open.

At the Vietnam Veteran's Memorial in Washington, Mulder and Scully conduct a clandestine, middle-of-the-night interview with a Russian emigré named Pudovkin. In the thickest accent imaginable, Pudovkin tells of a UFO sighting at a secret space research center in the former Soviet Union.

Pudovkin says: "On route home. Me. Others. Valk on ze mine field near base. Long black car drive up. No door handle. No vindow. No persons drive. We runs. Mines explosion. But! No sound! Nothing. Silent."

Mulder asks several follow-up questions, but Scully, plainly tired and bored, drifts away toward the Wall. She kneels down next to a small shrine to a fallen soldier—a model of a seventies muscle car, surrounded by rose petals. Plainly more interested in it than the interview, she lifts up one of the petals and gazes at it sadly.

In Ed Jerse's cubicle the next morning—he is a telephone boiler room stock salesman—the burnt snapshot rests against his computer monitor. The hungover man grimly makes the coldest of cold calls; he reads his scripted pitch to a harried housewife who keeps losing track of Jerse's spiel when she yells loudly at her kids. Sweat begins to bead up on Ed's face.

"Loser!" says a mocking female voice from the next cubicle.

"What?" says Jerse, thrown even further off stride.

The same voice giggles and cackles at him from somewhere nearby. Jerse rips off his headphones and stalks through the office. Two women in an adjoining cubicle are conversing.

"Say it to my face!" he shouts at them.

They look up, uncomprehending.

"Right to my face. Now that I'm in front of you, call me a loser to my face!"

"Calm down," says one of the women.

"Trash her desk!" says the Voice.

Jerse sweeps the contents of the desktop to the floor. Other workers, attracted by the commotion, eye him warily. A female supervisor arrives and addresses him with forceful calm.

"Why don't you go home, Ed?' she says. "We'll discuss this later."

In the X-Files office in the basement of the FBI building, Scully leans back in Mulder's chair, idly taking in the windowless room's eccentric collection of posters, photos, and other wall hangings. She turns over her partner's name plate in her hands.

Mulder, casually dressed, bustles in and makes a startling announcement: He is going on vacation.

"I made a last-ditch effort to get out of it," he says, "but the Bureau is holding fast to this federal employees vacation policy. I haven't taken a day off in four years, so either I take a week's vacation now or they start not paying me for eight weeks vacation time. I don't like it, but I gotta do it. I gotta pay the rent. I gotta eat."

The hyperactive Mulder bounces around the office, stuffing X-files into his duffel bag.

In contrast, Scully is a model of stillness and calm. Or, perhaps, low-grade depression. She looks up at her partner with mild curiosity—as if seeing him for the first time—and says nothing.

"Part of me can't help thinking," adds Mulder, "this is just another way to get me out of here. But it's only a week and you can keep an eye on things for me.

"So here's a few things you can keep an eye on when I'm gone."

Mulder plops a pile of folders in front of his partner. She doesn't look at them.

"Why don't I have a desk?" she says.

Caught off guard, Mulder stops and looks at her. "What do you mean?" he says.

Scully flashes the name plate at him. He points vaguely to the far corner of the office.

"I always assumed that was your area," he says.

"Back there," says Scully, sadly, peering into the abyss.

"Okay," says Mulder. "So we'll have them send down another desk, and there won't be any room to move around here, but we can put them really close together, face-to-face. Maybe we can play some Battleship?"

Mulder's little joke flops.

"So," says Scully, testily. "What is it you want me to keep an eye on?"

They proceed to have a long overdue argument about the nature of their working relationship. Mulder criticizes Scully for abandoning him during the Pudovkin interview; Scully expresses her doubts about Pudovkin's bona fides—in fact, she tells

him that Pudovkin's doorless-limousine-and-silent-explosion story uncannily parallels the plot line of an old episode of *Rocky and Bullwinkle*.

In conclusion, she refuses to spend Mulder's vacation week trailing the ex-Soviet spaceman through the Little Russia section of Philadelphia.

"So you're refusing an assignment based on the adventures of Moose and Squirrel?" says Mulder.

"'Refusing an assignment?'" says Scully. "You make it sound like you're my superior."

Mulder blows up. "Do what you want," he says. "Don't go to Philadelphia. But let me remind you that I worked my ass off to get these files reopened. You were just assigned. This work is my life."

Scully replies, quite unhappily, "And it's become mine."

The mood changes. More in sadness than in anger, Scully tells Mulder that she feels she's lost her way in the maze of ambiguities they've been pursuing together.

"I wish I could say we were going in circles," she says, "but we're not. We're going in an endless line—two steps forward and three steps back—while my own life does nothing but stand still."

Mulder doesn't really understand this, but his anger cools. "Maybe it's good to get away from each other for a while," he says.

He declines to tell Scully exactly where he's going.

"Ironically, it's personal," says Mulder solemnly. "A place I always wanted to go. What I anticipate to be a spiritual journey. I hope to discover something about myself. Maybe you should do the same."

In Philadelphia, Ed Jerse phones his supervisor from his apartment and begs for his job: "I just would like another chance. . . . I *need* another chance. . . . I know. . . right. . . I understand. . . . Thank you for your time. Good-bye."

He slams the telephone onto the table.

"'*Thank you for your time,*'" says the mocking Voice. "*If you were any kinda man you would have told her to kiss your ass. But no. Another woman sticks it to ya. Ain't that right, Eddie?*"

Frantic to pinpoint the source of the sound, Ed presses his ear to the heating ducts along the floor. Concluding that the Voice is coming from the apartment below him, he pounds the metal ducts.

"Hey! I can hear you down there! Stop it!" he yells.

In the apartment beneath him, a young woman, Kaye Schilling, looks up in confusion and turns up her stereo to drown out the pounding. The sounds of some Partridge Family impersonators—singing "Doesn't Somebody Want to Be Wanted"—waft back up to Ed's flat.

"You hear that?" says the Voice. *"It's you, Ed. It's all about you."*

There is a knock on Jerse's door. He opens it to face a pair of Jehovah's Witnesses.

"Do you hear that?" he tells them. "Downstairs. She's trying to drive me crazy. Somehow she knows what I'm thinking."

One of the Witnesses tells him that they've just met his downstairs neighbor and she seemed like a nice person. This whizzes right past Jerse.

"I don't want to feel it," he says, raving. "But they *know*—like psychics or an implant thing trying to drive crazy. They've even programmed the TV to criticize me. Do you hear it? There!"

"We'll come back some other time," says the Witness, eyeing him warily.

As she leaves, she hands him a copy of *Faith Today* magazine. He reads the cover line: "Are You a Failure?"

"You see?" says the Voice triumphantly. *"Even the Jehovah Witness babe won't waste her time on you. No woman would. And you just sit and take it—take it like a man."*

Kaye Schilling sits on her couch, reading and angrily ignoring the pounding on her door. Ed bursts through. Despite her protests—then her screams—he attacks her, kills her, and, as the seventies bubble gum music slowly fades out, drags her downstairs in a bloodstained carton to the incinerator room.

He feeds her to the leaping yellow flames.

"Atta boy, lover! From now on I'm your right-hand gal. You and me. As long as I'm with you, no one will ever hurt you. Never again."

Ed looks down at his tattoo, finally realizing the awful truth.

On a deserted mountain road, Mulder does a kind of weird dance around his parked car, trying to wiggle his way into a stronger cell-phone signal. He rings Scully's FBI number and gets her voice mail.

"Just calling to see how you're doing," he says. "Give me a call on my cell when you get a chance. Let me know where you're at."

In Philadelphia, Scully sits in her parked car and conducts surveillance on Pudovkin. She shadows him into a small Russian-owned grocery and peeks into the back room, where Pudovkin, speaking Russian, is unmistakably shaking down the proprietor for protection money. Pudovkin leaves, crosses the street, and disappears into the tattoo parlor.

Still tailing Pudovkin, Scully drifts inside the parlor—where Ed Jerse is pointing to his tattoo and demanding that the tattoo artist, whose name is Comrade Svo, cover it up.

"Why you want to cover it?" says Comrade Svo.

"Listen, friend," Svo adds, "everyone gets tattoo they deserve."

Scully gazes nonchalantly around the parlor. Her eyes settle on an interesting flash—a snake eating its own tail. Jerse, sounding desperate, asks the tattooist to merely cover the tattoo's eyes and mouth; Svo answers that even if her were to do it, he'd have to wait for the skin to heal.

Comrade Svo notices Scully and calls her over.

"Miss. Miss. You!" he says. "You like this? On his arm?"

She takes a look at the winking lady on Ed's biceps.

"Ed-die," says the Voice, warning him to be careful.

"Well . . ." says Scully.

"Eddie!"

"The color, the red on the lips, is extraordinary," Scully says.

Comrade Svo folds his arms in triumph. He tells Scully and Ed that he learned to make the special color in a Soviet prison and that it's ground from a special rye grass.

"And besides—everyone gets tattoo they deserve."

"I thought I was your girl," says the Voice to Ed, angrily. *"You'd break my heart over a cheap redhead? You talk to her, and I'm gonna be bad."*

The door to the parlor's back room opens and Pudovkin beckons to Svo. This makes the artist a bit nervous, but he leaves.

Ed strikes up a conversation with Scully, telling her he realizes now that getting his tattoo was too impulsive a decision.

"Sometimes I wish I were that impulsive," says Scully.

"Careful what you wish for," says Ed.

Ed asks Scully what brought her to Comrade Svo's parlor. Her instant cover story is that she's been "visiting an aunt in the neighborhood."

Flirting just a little bit, Scully asks him what brought *him* there. Ed truthfully recounts the previous night's adventure—complete with his drinkathon at the Hard Eight.

"So," says Scully, with a tolerant smile. "It wasn't so much 'impulsive' as it was 'hammered'?"

Ed takes what may have been a hint and invites Scully to dinner that night.

"I'd like that," says Scully, looking pleased—until something unspecified stops her.

She quickly adds that she has to leave town that night. Ed takes it pretty well; he writes his phone number on his business card.

"That's my home number," he says. "I work there, mainly."

In her hotel room early that evening,

Scully types up her case notes. Mulder phones her from his "special place": a room in Elvis's Graceland mansion, done up in impeccable *Blue Hawaii* style.

"How did you know where I was?" says Scully.

"I checked where we always stay in Philadelphia," he says. "I knew you wouldn't abandon me. How's the case going?"

Scully tells him that she's handed the case over to the FBI's Philadelphia Bureau. This is no X-file, she insists—Pudovkin is merely a con man connected to the Russian Mafia.

Annoyed, Mulder asks her how she knows all this.

Scully bristles. "What do you mean how do I know? You *assigned* me the background check. I did as I was told, as always."

As their renewed argument escalates, Mulder asks Scully to let him take over the case from her. Scully refuses.

"It's over," says Scully. "Done. Pudovkin is out of our hands. Look, Mulder, I've got to go."

"What, have you got a date or something?" says Mulder facetiously.

Scully ends the call quickly, then looks at Ed Jerse's business card propped against her laptop.

Back in his apartment, Jerse sits in a depressed stupor, smoking a cigarette.

"Isn't it better this way, baby?" says the Voice. *"Me and you—alone. Women are so petty. Jealous. Controlling. That bitch today would have been just like all the others."*

His phone rings.

It's Scully, who fibs that her flight has been delayed by a storm. Ed perks up instantly, and—because his car is "in the shop"—they arrange for Scully to pick him up at his place.

"Go ahead," says the Voice, dripping venom. *"This girl is a real doll. But beauty is only skin deep, baby. I go all the way to the bone."*

Jerse looks at the tattoo, picks up his lighted cigarette, and presses the burning end into his tormentor's face.

In Jerse's building, the two Jehovah's Witnesses—looking worried—knock on Kaye Schilling's door and call her name.

There's no answer. Scully notices this as she walk pasts them, heading for her date.

Jerse welcomes her into his apartment. There's some awkwardness at first: Jerse's tattoo starts to bleed; his burnt-out family photo is in plain sight on his desk, but it's obvious they're making some sort of connection. Jerse talks mournfully about his divorce; Scully admits that she doesn't go out very much.

"The last time I went on a date," she says, "I saw *Glengarry Glen Ross* and the characters in the movie had a better time than I did."

The meagerly furnished apartment seems to radiate loneliness. Outside, the storm rages.

"Ed, the crummy bar you told me about," says Scully. "Take me there."

At the Hard Eight Lounge, the couple quickly drink their way to inebriation, but also into a kind of intimacy: Over their second or third round, Scully launches into a boozy dissection of her life and loves.

"I've always gone around in this, uh, circle," she says, slurring her words slightly. "It usually starts when an authoritative or controlling figure comes into my life. And part of me likes it, needs it, wants the approval—and then at a certain point along the way I just, you know, um. . . .

"Okay. My father was a Navy captain. I worshiped—I *worship* the sea he sailed on. And when I was thirteen or so, I went through this. . . *thing* where I would sneak out of my parents' house and smoke my mother's cigarettes. And I did it because I knew if he found out he would kill me. And then, along the way, there are—other fathers."

Jerse, seemingly on the same confessional wavelength, nods.

"It looks like your time has come around again," he says.

Scully playfully asks to look at Ed's tattoo again. In the same spirit, Jerse resists.

"If you're so curious," he says. "Get your own."

At the handy tattoo parlor across the street, Ed watches as Scully—her face registering a mixture of pain and arousal—has the circular snake symbol, the *ouroboros*, tattooed onto her back.

"She wants the same red—like mine," says Jerse.

Using his electric needle, Comrade Svo applies the colors to her skin.

In the apartment afterward, Jerse peers out into the storm and suggests that Scully stay there that night.

"I'm not up to anything," he says, "I just want you to be safe. I'll take the couch. That tattoo hurt at all?"

"Yeah," says Scully, now more tired and

vulnerable than drunk. "It feels weird. I can't see it. I feel different, it's like. . . . I don't know how I feel about that."

Jerse moves close to her and peels the bandage from her back. "It looks all right," he says.

Scully notices that his arm is bleeding again. She strips off his coat and shirt and sees the tattoo's burnt face.

"Get her hands off me!" shouts the Voice.

Jerse takes Scully in his arms.

"Those are bad thoughts you're having, baby. You kiss her—and she's dead."

Ed kisses Scully just the same.

In his office at FBI headquarters the next morning, Mulder calls Scully at her hotel. There's no answer, of course.

Jerse, who's been sleeping on the couch in his apartment, awakens. He writes a note for Scully and leaves.

Scully is awakened by the sound of loud knocking. It is two Philadelphia detectives, Gouveia and Smith, asking about Jerse's whereabouts. She tells them that he isn't in and that she doesn't know where he went.

"Were you here the night before last?" asks Gouveia.

"No," says Scully groggily. "I'm with the Bureau. Could I help you with something?"

The detectives exchange skeptical glances—perhaps because the only thing Scully is wearing is Jerse's shirt. She shows them her shield.

They tell her, albeit a bit reluctantly, that Kaye Schilling was reported missing—and that blood other than her own was found inside her apartment. The intruder's

blood, they add, contained an unusual chemical substance.

Scully copies the complicated formula from one of the detectives' notebook. They leave with a warning: If Jerse doesn't contact him when he returns, they will.

Scully, rattled and looking more than a bit ill, uses Jerse's laptop to dial up the FBI forensics lab. She types out the chemical formula and hits ENTER.

A report filled with alarming phrases—"ergot," "rye and related grasses," "Psychotomimetic Drug," "auditory," "psychotic"—pops up on the screen. The eye of Scully's tattooed snake glows a bright red.

She picks up the phone, dials the FBI's main number, and asks to be connected to Fox Mulder. Mulder is in his office, but Scully hangs up just as he picks up at his end.

Jerse lets himself in, bearing breakfast for two.

"Sit down," says Scully.

She faces Jerse across the table and talks to him carefully and dispassionately. "Some detectives were here," she says. "The woman in the apartment downstairs was reported missing. They found some blood in her apartment—and I believe circumstantially it may be yours."

"I was helping her move in," says Jerse. "I cut myself."

"You need to tell that to the detectives," says Scully.

Her tone becomes more urgent, more personal.

"But what I'm also afraid of—and this concerns both of us—is that an ergot alkaloid was found in the blood, which is why I think it might have been yours.

"Now, ergot is a parasite that lives off of rye and other grasses. Svo said he used

rye, somehow, in his ink. Now, if this is true, we may be subject to hallucinogenic ergotism. Aural, visual hallucinogens, and dangerous . . . unlikely behavior. We need to go to the hospital to be tested."

Jerse sinks his head in his hands. "I don't need to be tested," he says with a sob.

He looks up at Scully with a crazed expression we've seen before. "It's such a relief to be able to tell someone. I hear it, Dana. In my *head*. Only deeper. It's more than just some chemical reaction."

His crazed eyes dart to the burned tattoo. "She talks to me. She hates women. My wife. My boss. You. She's so jealous, Dana. She makes me do things I don't want to. But she controls me. But I believe you made her go away."

Scully speaks very calmly. "We need to get help."

She tells him to wait for her as she gets dressed in the other room, then picks up her FBI shield and leaves.

"Mmm-hmm. Who'd she call? Who'd she call—Eddie? C'mon! Aren't ya just dyin' to know?"

The burns are gone from the tattooed demon's face. Both her eyes are wide again. Ed goes to the phone and hits the redial button.

"Federal Bureau of Investigation," says the operator.

"Dana Scully, please," says the Voice.

"Dana Scully, please," says Ed.

Scully reenters, fully dressed.

Jerse assaults her, screaming incoherently. Scully punches him in the stomach, escapes from his grasp, runs into the bathroom, and locks the door behind her. She searches for a weapon and finds a pair of scissors. Jerse bursts in and throws her into the wall, stunning her. He lurches into the bedroom and pulls the sheets off the bed.

"Another woman in my bed? Burn the sheets, lover. Burn her! Burn her!!"

The Voice ricocheting inside his bed, Jerse wraps Scully in the sheet and drags her down to the incinerator room. He opens the furnace door and stares into the leaping flames. Scully partially revives.

"C'mon, baby!" whispers the Voice. *"C'mon, baby! Do it for me!"*

Scully leaps up and stabs Ed in the biceps with the scissors. "This isn't you, Ed!" she says.

"Go on, Eddie."

"Get control of yourself!" says Scully.

"Ah, but it's good to lose control."

"Take control!"

"You better not listen to her. For me, Eddie! Do it!"

Ed clasps his ears, trying to stop the cacophony in his head. He clenches his fist and plunges his right arm deep into the center of the flames.

"No!" says Scully, running toward him.

Screaming in agony, Jerse pushes her away before collapsing onto the floor. The skin on his arm is horribly blackened and seared.

In their FBI office a week later, Mulder matter-of-factly welcomes his partner back from the hospital. "Congratulations for making a personal appearance in the X-Files for a second time—a world's record," he says.

He tells her that Jerse is in custody at a hospital burn center in Philadelphia. Traces of ergot *were* found in his blood, as they were in Scully's—but not enough in her case to cause hallucinations. Comrade Svo has been shut down, and the X-file on Pudovkin closed.

"Which is really a shame," cracks Mulder, "because I was thinking of getting an 'NY' tattoo on my ass to commemorate the Yankees' World Series victory. Better late than never, huh?"

The joke falls flat.

Silently, Scully fingers the dried rose petal from the Vietnam Memorial, which she's kept all this time.

A bit ashamed of himself, Mulder turns away. He babbles a bit about a new case, then sits down and takes a long look at Scully.

"All this because I didn't get you a desk?" he says.

Scully stares at him, but not like she is seeing him for the first time. "Not everything is about you, Mulder," she says. "This is my life."

"Yes, but it's. . . " says Mulder.

He lapses into silence. Scully does not speak either. Whatever it is he meant to say, neither he nor she can bear to say it.

back story:

The aptly numbered 4X13 is perhaps the most talked-about—and certainly the most idiosyncratic—episode of the fourth season. Critics and viewers alike commented on how many iron-clad TV rules were broken in "Never Again."

In which other network drama series, they wondered, had they ever seen:

1. The two yin-and-yang, joined-at-the-hip lead characters nonforcibly sepa rated for most of the episode
2. A thrilling climax in which neither rode to the rescue of the other
3. A scene in which the two heroes sit down and matter-of-factly *discuss* the secret unspoken conflicts, tensions, and inadequacies that underlie and drive the relationship between them

And when has a prime-time heroine ever exposed her basic needs and neuroses so openly—and, yes, embarrassingly?

"I thought it was a great idea," says Gillian Anderson. "I personally was going through a dark period at the time, and I wanted to explore Scully's dark side.

"For some reason, Glen and Jim were on the same wavelength that week. Afterward, a lot of people told me on that episode I was so 'unlike' Scully or that 'it showed my range.' I told them I thought they were wrong.

"On TV shows," she adds, "You get to see such a small percentage of somebody's personality, because that's what the audience wants to see—the norm, that something that they can rely on from week to week to week. But we all have many sides of our personalities, all of us have secrets. All of us have parts of ourselves that we don't show to other people. All of us can go home and be depressed at night—and be smiling during the day. All of us can go home and binge and purge in the middle of the night and nobody would know.

"I don't think that what I did here was out of character for Scully. The only thing different is that the audience hadn't seen it before."

Anderson admits to being a bit disappointed that, in order to move "Leonard Betts" (4X14)—which features Mulder and Scully in the series' customary ratio—into the post–Super Bowl time slot, the air dates of 4X13 and 4X14 were reversed.

"If I'd known that Scully knew she had cancer when we were filming 'Never Again,' I would have played the part differently," she says.

Anderson also cautions that it should not be inferred from this episode that she and Scully have the same needs and desires. She found Scully's erotic fascination with tattooing, for instance, a little hard to understand, which is perhaps why she volunteered to actually have the *ouroboros* tattooed onto her back during filming.

"They told me it would have taken too long. It wouldn't have been practical," says Anderson with a sad smile of regret.

In reality, the tattoos in the show were decals—designed by art department staffer Kristina Lyne, manufactured by an L.A.-based company called Real Creations, then applied, touched up, and altered (for instance, when Bettie opens her other eye) by makeup artist Laverne Basham.

The demonic lady on Ed Jerse's bicep was inspired by the work of an old-style tattoo artist named "Brooklyn Joe" Lieber, who practiced his trade in the San Francisco Bay Area, but that's another story.

Of all the music that Mark Snow composed for the episode—"There was a real *film noir* quality to it. So I thought, What a great time to use a lot of jazz-type stuff. And a lot of saxophone"—he was most jazzed by the wild, discordant riffs that accompany Ed Jerse as he drags the stunned Scully downstairs. It was, he says, a strange combination of a dance rhythm track combined with "oddball samples of alternative rock" that did the trick.

The Partridge Family tunes floating up from the unfortunate Kaye Schilling's apartment were actually performed by a Partridge Family soundalike band.

However, the Jodie Foster who's credited as the voice of Bettie is actually *the* Jodie Foster. The Oscar-winning actress, a close friend of Fox Television casting chief Randy Stone, is a longtime fan of *The X-Files*—and, in fact, was Stone's original role model for casting the role of Scully in 1993.

When Stone phoned and asked her to play the part, Foster agreed immediately. Working with a somewhat awed Morgan and Wong, she nailed her lines in the recording studio in less than an hour—then went off to work with Robert Zemeckis on *Contact*.

The only problem, says Stone, was that his friend was thus unavailable to record her lines for any of the foreign-language versions of the episode. "She speaks French fluently," says Stone. "She would have been great."

Social notes from the cutting edge:

When Gillian Anderson was told about the groundbreaking storyline of "Never Again," she made the unusual request to participate in the choice of guest star. "I said, 'Is it possible that I can just have a sneak preview of the man you're thinking about casting for this character who's supposed to have his tongue down my throat'?" says Anderson.

Adds Anderson, "They said, 'Uh, sure.' So they sent me a head shot of the person they had in mind, and I said 'Oh, I don't know. This doesn't feel right. Can I look at some more people? Can you show me some tape on this guy?' Whatever. And we go back and forth; it ends up the show was really written for him; and that's who they chose, and he was perfect. He really pulled it off on many levels.

"And the fact is," says the actress, smiling, "we've been dating for six months now."

At press time Anderson and Rodney Rowland—the former star of, you guessed it, *Space: Above and Beyond*—were still an item.

The basement incinerator that Ed uses to dispose of his victims is actually, notes art director Garry Allen, the third incinerator that has been designed and built for the series. The first two were for "F. Emasculata" (2X22) and "Hell Money" (3X19). Yet another incinerator, a big industrial unit, will appear later in the season in "Zero Sum."

Ⓧ

Ed Jerse's favorite bar is named Hard Eight for Morgan and Wong's production company.

Ⓧ

The camera angles and long tracking shot backward down the stairs are a conscious homage to a similar shot in Alfred Hitchcock's *Frenzy*.

Ⓧ

episode: 4X14

first aired: January 26, 1997

written by:
Vince Gilligan, John Shiban,
and Frank Spotnitz

editor: Heather MacDougall

directed by: Kim Manners

A headless corpse escapes from a hospital
morgue. Mulder and Scully investigate; what
they find leads them to the jagged dividing
line between life and death.

guest stars:
Paul McCrane (Leonard Betts)
Jennifer Clement (Michele Wilkes)
Marjorie Lovett (Elaine Tanner)
Bill Dow (Dr. Charles Burks)
Sean Campbell (Local Cop)
David Hurtubise (Pathologist)
Peter Bryant (Uniformed Cop)
Laara Sadiq (Female EMT)
J. Douglas Stewart (Male EMT)
Don Ackerman (Night Attendant)
Brad Loree (Security Guard)
Ken Jones (Bearded Man)
Greg Neumayer (New Partner)
Lucia Walters (EMT)

principal settings:
Pittsburgh, Pennsylvania;
College Park, Maryland

leonard betts

a speeding ambulance, carrying two Emergency Medical Technicians and an apparent heart attack victim, races toward Monongahela Medical Center in Pittsburgh. In front, Michele Wilkes—a young woman in her twenties—handles the driving and the radio. In back, Leonard Betts—a young, albeit bald, man in his thirties—tends to the patient.

The elderly black man goes into cardiac arrest. Betts jabs a large-bore needle through his chest, and the heart monitor begins to beep steadily, showing a return to normal function.

"What'd you do?" asks Wilkes.

"Aspirated his chest," says Betts. "He had a tension pneumothorax pressing on his heart. It just looked like a cardiac."

"Nice catch! How did you know?" asks Wilkes.

"Because he's dying of cancer. It's already eaten through one lung."

Amazed at Betts's diagnostic skill, Wilkes turns to compliment him. At that moment, a speeding flatbed truck runs a red light and plows into the side of the ambulance.

The two wrecked vehicles slide to a halt. Wilkes, dazed but relatively unhurt, climbs from the cab and calls her partner's name. She finds Leonard behind the truck, lying in the street. His body lies in one spot. His severed head lies in another.

In the hospital morgue that evening, an attendant closes the door on Leonard's body, lying in its own refrigerated compartment. Later that evening the attendant hears a noise, looks up from his reading, and investigates.

The door of Leonard's temporary resting place yawns open. A lumpy sheet lies on the floor in front of it. The attendant kneels down and lifts the sheet. Leonard's severed head is underneath.

From out of the darkness someone swings a shiny metal bar, knocking down the attendant from behind. A pair of naked legs walk slowly out of the morgue. In the reflection of the metal bar there is another view of the departing assailant. Seen from the back, he is absolutely uninjured—except for the fact that has no head.

At the morgue the next day, Mulder and Scully examine Betts's now empty blood-stained compartment.

"Pretty cozy," muses Mulder. "Who'd ever want to leave?"

He tells Scully that Betts was an exemplary EMT, there was no sign of a break-in, and someone stole the morgue attendant's clothing.

"Mulder, what are we doing here?" asks Scully, exasperated.

Mulder says, "Did I mention that Mr. Betts had no head?"

The obvious explanation, Scully replies, is *not* that a headless body kicked its way out of its compartment. It's that they're looking at a bizarre example of body snatching for profit.

Mulder is unconvinced. Why, he asks, would anyone looking for a hot cadaver steal a headless, hence incomplete, corpse?

A hospital security guard brings them some video stills from the ER surveillance camera. They show a man dressed in the attendant's stolen clothes leaving the hospital at 4:13 A.M. Unfortunately, a thick band of lens flare obscures the suspect's head. The picture is clear enough, however, to see that the man was not carrying the corpse.

"Where could he hide an adult body where it wouldn't be found?" asks Mulder.

"I'll show you," says Scully confidently.

In an obscure corner of the hospital, Scully shows Mulder the biohazard/medical waste disposal facility: the large bin where the byproducts of surgery—"amputations, excised tumors," she says authoritatively—are saved before they're ground up, zapped with microwaves, and turned into a sterile soot used for road fill.

"Are you sure about this?" asks Mulder squeamishly. "Because if you're not sure, I don't see there's a reason to disturb all this stuff just to . . . "

"Mulder, I think I'm going to need your help here," says Scully. "Your arms are longer."

With whatever is the absolute opposite of relish, Mulder sticks his rubber-gloved hands into the flesh pile.

"I think I got the toy surprise," he says, pulling out a pink, smooth, roundish object.

"Leonard Betts," says Scully.

"That's his head," says Mulder. "Where's his body?"

Neither of the agents has even a good guess, but Mulder suggests that Scully autopsy the head while he examines Betts's apartment.

"We know how he died," he says. "I want to see how he lives."

"*Lived*," says Scully.

"Lived," agrees Mulder halfheartedly.

In an autopsy room, Scully places Betts's head on a scale. It weighs 10.9 pounds. The remains show no sign of rigor mortis or lividity. Neither are Leonard's corneas clouded, as is usual after death. She picks up her scalpel and starts her first incision.

"Oh, my God!" she says.

Leonard Betts's eyes and mouth open slowly, seemingly of their own volition. She pulls away her scalpel. They slowly close again.

Mulder enters Leonard Betts's clean, sparse apartment, where nothing much seems out of the ordinary until Mulder enters the bathroom. The bathtub is filled with an opaque, dark reddish fluid. He checks the cabinet underneath the sink and finds several bottles of Povidone-Iodine antiseptic solution. Clothing lies crumpled on the floor, there are what appear to be bloodstains around the toilet bowl, and there are brown stains on the windowsill.

Scully phones to tell her partner that the PET scans of Leonard's head have come out completely clouded—like the security footage—and that the only explanation is that the remains are emitting some form of radiation. As for the rest of the autopsy, Scully admits that she still hasn't performed it.

"Why not?" asks Mulder.

"Well, because I experienced an unusual degree of postmortem galvanic response," says Scully.

"The head moved," says Mulder with a tinge of excitement.

Scully knows where he's going and tries to stop him.

"It blinked at me. But I know exactly what it is—residual electricity stored chemically in the dead cells. It's, uh . . . "

"Blinked or winked?" asks Mulder, enjoying this. "You're afraid to cut into it. Scully, you're not saying that it's alive, are you?"

"No! I am certainly not saying that at all."

"But has it crossed your mind that it's not quite dead, either?"

He adds, "I'm standing here in Leonard Betts's apartment. Whoever we saw on

those video grabs—his clothes are strewn all over the floor. He made himself at home. Maybe he was home."

"Leonard Betts? Without his head?" says Scully skeptically.

"Yeah," says Mulder a bit sheepishly.

Scully tells him that she doesn't even know how to reply to such a theory. Nevertheless, says Mulder, he'll have the local police place the apartment under surveillance.

He pockets his phone and leaves.

After he exits, several bubbles float to the top of the liquid in the bathtub. A bald head slowly breaks the surface. It is glistening—with no hair or eyebrows—and strangely alien, unformed. But it is, unmistakably, Leonard Betts.

In the parking lot at Monongahela Medical Center, Michele Wilkes heads back to an ambulance to work with a new partner.

Mulder intercepts her and asks about Leonard Betts. Wilkes is cooperative but unable to explain the theft of Betts's body. He had no family and few close friends, she says. He was in perfect health, and about the only thing that was special about him was his uncanny ability to diagnose illnesses—especially cancer.

"I always told him he should be an oncologist or something," says Wilkes. "He used to volunteer weekends at the cancer ward. Read to patients, stuff like that."

Inside the hospital Mulder watches as his partner oversees another examination of Leonard's head—this one involving a procedure called biopolymerization.

"It's basically a high-tech mummification process," says Scully. "The remains are dipped in epoxy, and once it's cured, the specimen can be sliced for observation."

"Or, you've got yourself a nice paperweight," says Mulder.

A pathologist examines a cross-section of Leonard's frontal lobe. He peers into his microscope.

"This is certainly strange," he says. It turns out that Betts's head and brain are a solid mass of cancer. Every single cell has been affected.

"Could you live in this condition?" asks Mulder.

"Live?" says the pathologist. "This man would have been long dead before reaching such an extreme metastatic state."

"Then how do you explain it?"

"Maybe the polymerization process distorted the sample somehow," says the doctor. "Maybe we're not really seeing what we think we're seeing."

"Hmm," says Mulder. "Maybe we're just seeing it clearly for the first time."

Scully asks, "What are you suggesting?"

"Let's get a slice to go."

In her new ambulance with her new partner, Michele Wilkes answers an emergency call. On her radio she hears a familiar voice crackling out advice to another team facing a tricky medical problem.

"Leonard?" she says, turning up the volume.

At the lab of Dr. Charles Burks, a gnome-like true believer—last seen in "The Calusari" (2X21)—Mulder explains to Scully that the University of Maryland researcher did some pioneering work in Kirlian photography.

"Although I prefer the umbrella term 'aura-photography,'" says Burks.

As Scully looks on skeptically, Burks places the slice from Leonard's head into a device designed to measure the coronal discharge of an object.

"The life force. The Chinese call it 'Chi,'" explains Mulder. "It's an accepted fact in most Eastern cultures."

Coronal discharge, he adds, could explain why the video grab was blurred and the PET scan fogged.

Burks chimes in with the news that he's been able to photograph phantom images of the missing parts of leaves torn in half—or even a lizard's tail after it's been cut off.

"Which you have to admit," says the scientist, "is pretty cool."

When the Kirlian negative of Leonard's tissue is developed, the aura around it glows brightly. Burks sighs with pleasure.

"Oh, yeah. There's definitely some kind of energy happening here," he says.

Mulder says, "Chuck, would you believe this man's head had been decapitated?"

"Aw, c'mon. No way," says Burks, excitedly.

"Way," says Mulder.

It is obvious that he has made his friend's month.

In the corridor afterward, an excited Mulder lays out his theory for Scully: What if, he proposes, the coronal evidence proves that Leonard Betts is still alive? What if the cancer wasn't evidence of his death—but of his life?

"What is cancer," he says, "but normal cells growing rapidly out of control, usually

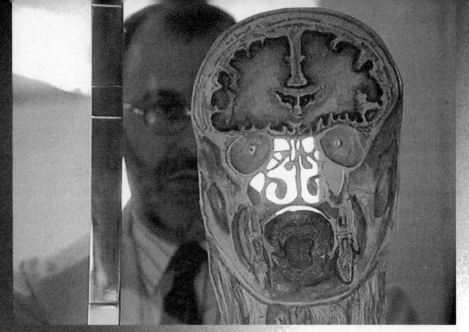

caused by some damage to their DNA? What if there was a case where the cancer was not caused by damaged DNA—where the cancer was not a destructive or even an aggressive factor, but rather a normal state of being?"

"Well, even if that were possible," says Scully, "he's been *decapitated*."

Mulder is undeterred. "What if this man's life force—his 'Chi,' whatever you want to call it—somehow retained a blueprint of the actual man itself. Guiding rapid growth not as cancer, but as regeneration."

"You think that Leonard Betts regrew his head?"

Mulder tells the flabbergasted Scully that Povidone, the liquid in Betts's bathtub, is often used by researchers to help reptiles and amphibians regrow missing limbs.

Scully states the indisputable fact that Leonard was not a salamander. In the middle of this discussion Scully's cell phone rings. She listens briefly, then relays the message to Mulder. An FBI records check turned up the interesting fact that Betts and a man named Albert Tanner had identical fingerprints. And that Tanner's mother is alive and living in Pittsburgh.

At the absolutely ordinary house of Elaine Tanner—a pleasant, grandmotherly woman—the agents notice a snapshot of her son Albert. It shows that Albert is an absolute dead ringer for Leonard Betts.

Mrs. Tanner, however, says she's never heard of Leonard and that Albert died in an auto accident six years earlier.

"Confused yet?" says Mulder to Scully.

That night, in the parking lot of Allegheny Catholic Hospital, Michele Wilkes asks a fellow EMT where she can find the driver of unit 208.

"The new guy?" says her colleague. "Yeah, 208's over there. He just went off shift, but you just might catch him."

Michele spots a lone figure at the far end of the lot. As she approaches, he walks away. She finally catches up with him in a secluded area underneath a tree.

"Leonard . . . ?" she says.

The man who emerges from the shadows is indeed Leonard Betts.

"Oh, my God!" she says. "How can it be? Leonard—is it you?"

Leonard walks forward, calls her name softly, and embraces her. "It's okay," he says, quietly. "I just wish you hadn't found me."

"What are you talking about?" says the stunned woman.

Leonard grabs Michele's neck with his left hand. A large autoinjector syringe appears in his right. He jabs her with it between the shoulder blades.

"I'm sorry. I'm sorry," he says.

She convulses and dies. He lowers her gently to the ground. A flashlight beam hits Leonard's face. A security guard chases Betts through the parked cars—to Leonard's own—and catches up with him as he's trying to unlock it. The guard clouts him with his flashlight. Then he pats him down, pockets Betts's car keys, and handcuffs him to the door handle.

"Stay there, you son of a bitch!" he shouts.

The rent-a-cop growls into his radio and leaves to get help. As soon as the guard is out of sight, Betts places his right hand in his left. Grimacing in pain, he pulls. When the guard returns, the handcuffs are empty.

Betts is gone. His right thumb, severed, lies on the ground.

At the crime scene the next morning, Mulder examines the bloody handcuffs. Scully reports that Michele was killed with a lethal dose of potassium chloride, a substance normally undetected by coroners.

"Betts was here, Scully," says Mulder. "She must have discovered that—and then he had to kill her to protect his secret."

Scully nods and tells him that the security guard ID'd Betts as a rookie EMT named Truelove. For Mulder—if not for his partner— the picture becomes clearer.

"You know how this man escaped?" he says. "He tore off his thumb. Because he knew he could regrow another one."

Scully says, "Mulder, it just doesn't work that way."

"But is it unimaginable?" says Mulder. "Is Betts's ability to regenerate any greater a leap forward than our ancestors' ability to communicate or walk upright?"

Scully protests that evolution is a gradual process. Mulder argues that recent evolutionary theorists now hold that sudden leaps are possible.

"But what you're describing is someone so radically evolved that

you wouldn't even call him human," says Scully.

Mulder shrugs and nods toward Betts's car. "On the other hand," he says, "how evolved can a man be who drives a Dodge Dart?"

Mulder opens the trunk. Inside is a picnic cooler filled with plastic bags of surgical waste.

"Oh, my God!" says Scully, reading the labels. "Myeloid sarcoma. Epithelial carcinoma. These are all cancerous tumors."

Mulder takes another leap. "Scully," he says, "there's a great possibility that Leonard Betts not only *is* cancer . . .

"But that he needs it for survival? Then this is . . . "

"Snack food," says Mulder.

He adds, "Wouldn't it make sense that evolution or natural selection would incorporate cancer—the greatest health threat to our species—as part of our genetic makeup?"

"Why do I think," says Scully, "Charles Darwin is rolling in his grave right now?"

A Pittsburgh cop arrives and tells them that the Dart is registered to an Elaine Tanner. The agents, armed with a search warrant and accompanied by a platoon of policeman, arrive at Mrs. Tanner's house.

She seems genuinely shocked by their arrival, but refuses to discuss her son. Scully warns her that she could be charged as an accessory to Michele's murder. Mulder finds a large bottle of Povidone and asks her whether she's had a lot of cuts. Finally, she speaks to the agents.

"When my son was eight years old," she says, "there were two boys who picked on him—because he was different. He just ignored them. He knew he was better than they were. One day they cornered him walking home and beat him up. He didn't even try to fight back. Just lay there, taking the blows. So I don't believe you when you tell me he killed someone. But if he did, he had his reasons."

"What reasons, Mrs. Tanner?" says Scully.

"God put him here for a purpose. God means for him to stay—even if people don't understand. And that's all I've got to say."

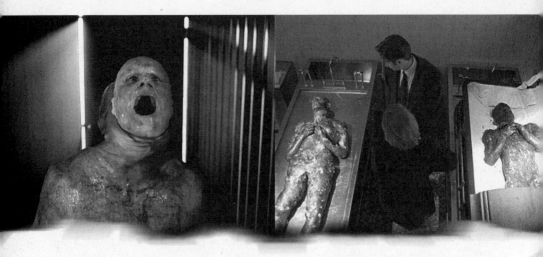

In a low-life bar nearby, a burly bearded man gulps his drink, takes a deep drag on an unfiltered cigarette, and lets loose a hacking smoker's cough. Leonard Betts—a bruise on his forehead, his right thumb now a small unformed bud—watches him from across the room. The bearded man settles up and heads back to the parking lot. Leonard follows him. In his good hand he palms a scalpel.

Betts's prey stands with his key in his car door.

"Excuse me," says Leonard. "I'm sorry. But you've got something I need."

At Mrs. Tanner's house, the agents locate a receipt and a key for a rental storage room—#112. In that stark room Leonard Betts stands naked, silhouetted by a beam of light. Blood is spattered on his lips. His skin is wet with perspiration, his eyes wide-open. He is obviously suffering extreme pain.

Betts lowers his head, struggling with something deep inside him. The top of his skull begins to expand; his skin and muscles stretch and his bones crack. He raises his head. His mouth opens impossibly wide and his neck bulges.

The face of a second Leonard Betts—embryonic, unformed—forces itself into view. It pushes upward and outward, straining to get free. The new man, reborn, screams in agony.

Mulder and Scully arrive at to the storage facility. A puddle of blood is oozing from

inside #112. The agents draw their guns and lift the roll-up metal door. The body of the bearded man tumbles out and falls at their feet.

A split second later, Leonard Betts, at the wheel of his victim's old Camaro, roars out of the storage room, sending Mulder and Scully sprawling. They struggle to their feet and shoot at the fleeing car. It explodes in a huge ball of bright yellow fire.

In the hospital pathology lab, Scully examines the body of the bearded man. He died, she says, from massive blood loss—created by the skillful removal of his left lung.

Mulder says, "This man's medical records will show he had lung cancer. And Leonard Betts was in need of what he had."

Later, working in the same room, they crack open Tanner's exhumed casket. Inside is another corpse of Leonard Betts; after six years in the ground, it is eerily identical to the one they pulled from the burning car.

In Mrs. Tanner's house, the elderly woman kneels next to the bathtub. Immersed in the tub is Leonard Betts. She gently sponges Povidone over her pink, still smooth, and hairless son.

"I'm scared, honey," she says. "The FBI! They seem to know all about you. They dug up the coffin. They found your. . . friend. I don't think they're ever going to leave you alone. And you're weak. You have to

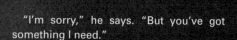

conserve your strength. You know what you have to do.

"I'm your mother. And it's a mother's duty to provide."

Later that night, Mulder and Scully stake out the Tanner house. An ambulance, lights flashing and siren sounding, rolls up. It stops in front of them. Is it Leonard?

Mulder and Scully leap out of their car, guns drawn, and yell for the occupants of the ambulance to freeze. But neither of the EMTs is Betts.

"We got a call. Elderly woman with massive blood loss and chest trauma," explains one of the frightened paramedics.

The agents kick open the front door and cautiously search the house. Scully finds Mrs. Tanner lying unconscious and bleeding on her bed.

"She has an open wound. A surgical cut," says Scully.

"Three guesses what was removed," says Mulder. "He did this to her and then he called an ambulance."

"Judging by the response time, he might still be here," Scully whispers.

Mrs. Tanner is loaded onto the ambulance. Scully climbs into the back to accompany her to the hospital. Mulder calls the Pittsburgh police to tell them to search the area for Leonard.

The ambulance arrives at Allegheny Catholic. Mrs. Tanner is carried into the emergency room; Scully phones Mulder and tells her that the woman's condition has taken a downturn.

Mulder lays out his plans for a massive manhunt. As he speaks, Scully reaches up and touches her hair. Her fingers are wet with a watery red liquid. She looks up. Blood is dripping from the roof of the ambulance.

"Mulder, get out here right now," she whispers into her cell phone.

She draws her gun and climbs up the side of the ambulance. Leonard Betts, who had been hiding below the vehicle, grabs her legs and pulls her violently to the ground. Betts looms over her, scalpel in hand.

"I'm sorry," he says. "But you've got something I need."

For a heartbeat, Scully stares—wondering—into his eyes. Then she fends off his scalpel thrust.

There is a short but brutal hand-to-hand fight—which Leonard gets the better of. Betts readies his scalpel again. Scully reaches desperately for the portable defibrillator in the ambulance.

Betts lunges at her. She presses the paddles to his head and shocks him with a massive jolt of electricity. He flies backward through the ambulance doors and drops, twitching, to the ground.

Exhausted, Scully looks down at him in fear and horror. Mulder arrives not long afterward.

"They pronounced Betts ten minutes ago," he says.

"He's dead?" says Scully.

"As near as anyone can tell. His mom's alive, though."

He tells his partner that Mrs. Tanner, as suspected, was suffering from cancer.

"You did a good job, Scully," he adds. "You should be proud."

Scully's thoughts, however, are elsewhere.

"I want to go home," she says dully.

Mulder closes her car door for her. He gets in his own vehicle and drives away.

A bedside clock glows 2:08. Scully coughs in her sleep, wakes, and rolls over to see several bloodstains on her bed linen.

Her hand reaches out, touching the red circles. She looks at the blood on her fingertips—and stares into the darkness, thinking the unthinkable.

back story:

The TV broadcast of the Super Bowl is rotated annually between the three over-the-air networks that carry NFL football; every couple of years or so, one of them tries to boost the fortunes of one of its fledgling series (remember *The A Team*? *MacGruder & Loud*? *Davis Rules*?) by scheduling it directly after the championship game. In 1997 the honchos at Fox managed to resist this temptation—and won an audience for its highest-rated series nearly twice as large as usual. Close to 30 million Americans watched a quintessential—and pivotal—*X-Files* episode.

"It was like a good first season–style show," says story editor John Shiban. "There was humor; there was some Mulder-and-Scully back-and-forth; there

were some cool special effects; it was scary—and there was even some real science behind it."

It was also the show in which the producers "gave" Scully cancer: a decision that would seriously affect the course of the rest of the fourth season. From 4X14 on, every episode—even if it was designed to take viewers' minds off Scully's condition—would have to deal with that single factor.

"It was an idea that I'd suggested the summer before—but we'd sort of tabled the discussion," explains coproducer Frank Spotnitz. The idea stayed tabled, he adds, until with the fourth season well under way, he and Shiban—"We're good friends and had worked a lot together last season"—decided to collaborate on an episode.

The seed for "Leonard Betts" had been planted a short time before. John Shiban, Spotnitz explains, had read an article in a New Age–type magazine on the quasi-scientific concept of "edglings": humans who have taken an evolutionary leap past their fellow men, therefore acquiring strange powers and abilities that would be useful in the future but are bizarre and frightening today.

"So," adds Spotnitz, "together we worked our way through this concept: Well, we thought, what's the greatest threat to us right now? Cancer. And so a great leap forward for evolution would be someone who not only was immune to cancer, but fed on it."

It was Shiban who realized that the still-embryonic story line would be the "perfect entree" to Scully's cancer arc. "At that moment," says the story editor, "I realized that we'd better go see Chris. And he was all for it—he told me that it was the moment he was waiting for."

"Actually," says Chris Carter, "I knew this was a great opportunity to tweak the audience—to get them thinking. But I honestly thought it might pass some people by. That they wouldn't get it. But they got it in a big, big way."

Vince Gilligan, the third member of the "Leonard Betts" writing troika, is credited with fleshing out the character of Leonard himself, making him more of a sympathetic character who killed not out of vengeance or anger, but for survival.

To play this tricky part, the producers chose Paul McCrane, a former teenage actor who has successfully made the transition to adult character roles in projects like *Robocop* ("I was the guy who wound up in the vat of toxic waste," he says) and the well-reviewed 1996 CBS crime drama *Under Suspicion.*

To turn himself into a thin, bald emergency medical technician, McCrane had to do practically nothing. Playing the rest of the role, though, was a different matter.

In preparation for his transformation scenes, he had to spend several hours in makeup having his plastic appendages installed. To portray his own severed head in the autopsy scene, he had to wrench himself through a hole in Scully's autopsy table, then hold perfectly still.

The pale, babylike eyes in his "new" head were created with contact lenses—which at one point during the shoot were accidentally installed, quite painfully, backward. During his bathtub scenes, he had to remain motionless for long minutes underwater—his body covered with barrier cream so that the colored glop standing in for antiseptic wouldn't dye his skin for the rest of the shooting week.

The Academy of Television Arts and Sciences nominated Toby Lindala and Laverne Basham for an Emmy award for their work in this episode. It was Lindala, of course, who created the special effect illusion of Leonard's new head emerging from his old one.

Pulling all of this off was even dicier than he realized at the time. In the finished sequence, brief shots of McCrane, fully outfitted with glistening prosthetic makeup, are intercut with a from-the-waist-up puppet of the actor equipped with motor-driven mouth and eyes. When Lindala attempted to extrude Leonard's new head out of the puppet's mouth, he found that none of the foam and urethane materials he'd used before would do the trick.

"So we tried this new stuff from a company called Circle K Silicone," says Lindala.

"They called it their 'XP' series."

The new material worked fine. But about a week into the project, says Lindala, he found out what "XP" stands for.

"It stands for 'experimental,'" says Lindala.

In other words, the manufacturer still hadn't fine-tuned the formula and really didn't know what, if anything, the substance would do.

"They were still doing R&D with their catalysts and plasticizers," says Lindala, his eyes widening at that scary thought.

"Every few days they'd send us new batches mixed slightly differently. Then they'd say: 'Hey, after you try it out, give us a call and let us know what happened.'"

Despite Scully's calm explanation that laminating dead bodies and turning them into something resembling prosciutto are accepted forensic tools, the organ-slicing machine that the pathologist uses on Betts's severed head was conceived, designed, and built by props master Ken Hawryliw. His department also whipped up all of Dr. Charles Burks's cool Kirlian X Rays.

Ⓧ

The faculty of the prestigious Berklee School of Music in Boston was so impressed with Mark Snow's work on "Leonard Betts" that this year, when he agreed to give a guest lecture on film scoring techniques, they asked him to concentrate on the seemingly seamless changes of mood and tempo he pulled off in the episode's opening scene.

Ⓧ

Bill Dow played Dr. Burks in an earlier episode, "The Calusari" (2X21), where his photo analysis of Charlie Holvey revealed a spectral twin.

Ⓧ

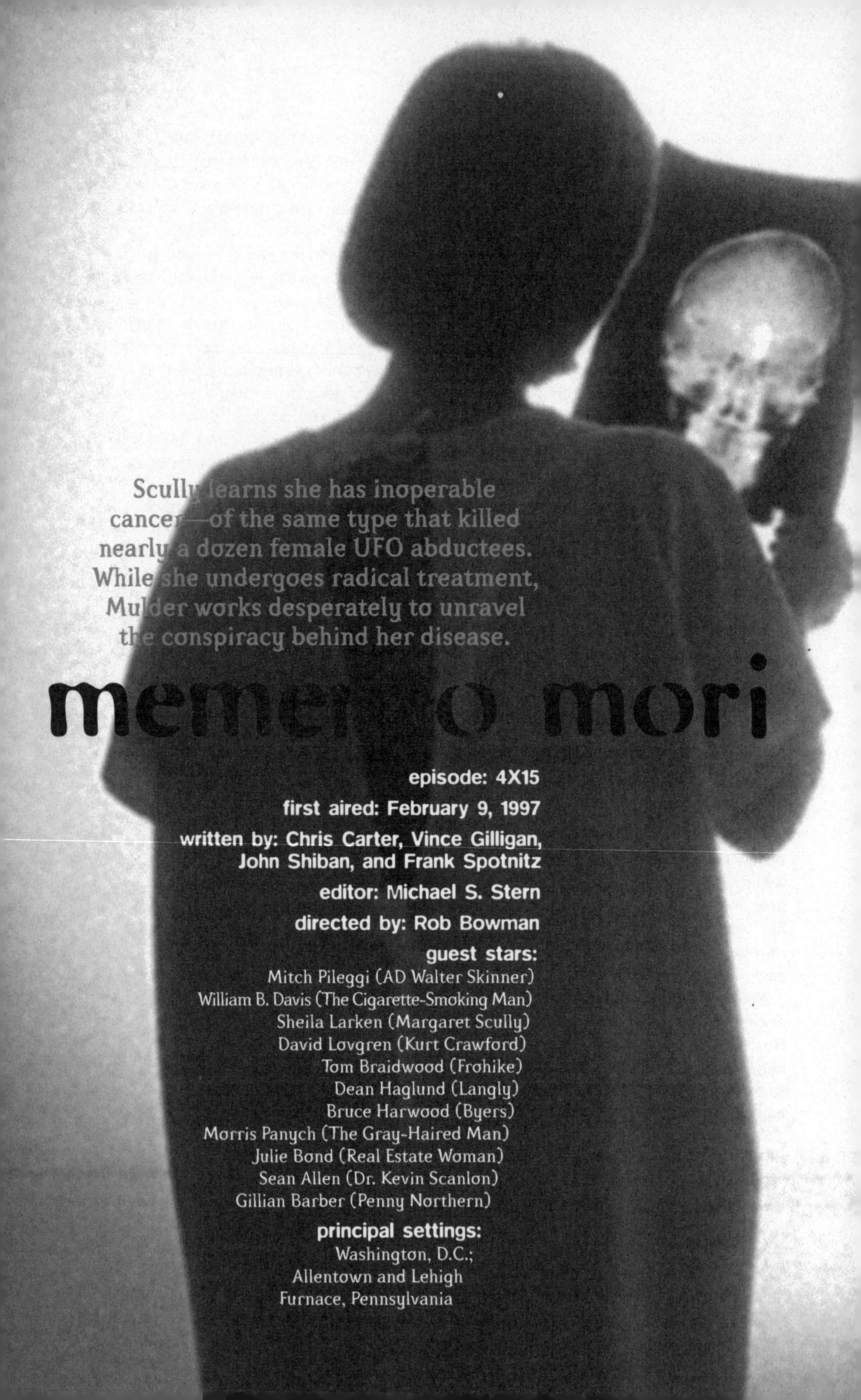

Scully learns she has inoperable
cancer—of the same type that killed
nearly a dozen female UFO abductees.
While she undergoes radical treatment,
Mulder works desperately to unravel
the conspiracy behind her disease.

memento mori

episode: 4X15

first aired: February 9, 1997

**written by: Chris Carter, Vince Gilligan,
John Shiban, and Frank Spotnitz**

editor: Michael S. Stern

directed by: Rob Bowman

guest stars:
Mitch Pileggi (AD Walter Skinner)
William B. Davis (The Cigarette-Smoking Man)
Sheila Larken (Margaret Scully)
David Lovgren (Kurt Crawford)
Tom Braidwood (Frohike)
Dean Haglund (Langly)
Bruce Harwood (Byers)
Morris Panych (The Gray-Haired Man)
Julie Bond (Real Estate Woman)
Sean Allen (Dr. Kevin Scanlon)
Gillian Barber (Penny Northern)

principal settings:
Washington, D.C.;
Allentown and Lehigh
Furnace, Pennsylvania

We are at one end of a long tunnel; at the other is a small rectangle of light. Its glow is soft and diffuse—the now classic image of a near-death experience. We hear the voice of Dana Scully. She says:

For the first time, I feel time like a heartbeat, the seconds pumping in my breast like a reckoning; the numinous mysteries that once seemed so distant and unreal threatening clarity in the presence of a truth entertained not in youth, but only in its passage. I feel these words as if their meaning were weight being lifted from me, knowing that you will read them and share my burden as I have come to trust no other. That you should know my heart, look into it, finding there the memory and experience that belong to you, that are you, is a comfort to me now as I feel the tethers loose and the prospects darken for the continuance of a journey that began not long ago, and which began again with a faith shaken and strengthened by your convictions. If not for which I might never have been so strong now as I cross to face you and look at you incomplete, hoping that you will forgive me for not making the rest of the journey with you.

As we get closer, the bright light becomes a large lighted wall, the kind on which MRI films are studied. Scully, dressed in a hospital gown, holds one in her hand. It is of a human skull. A small dark mass is clearly visible above the nasal cavity.

A short time later, Fox Mulder enters the oncology unit of Holy Cross Memorial Hospital in Washington. He meets his partner—now fully dressed—in front of the same wall we'd seen previously. Mulder hands her a bouquet of flowers.

"I stole these from some guy with a broken leg down the hall," he says, smiling. "He won't be able to catch me."

He drops his forced pose of nonchalance. "How are you doing?" he asks.

"I guess that's the question," says Scully. "Actually, I feel fine."

She tells Mulder that the dark area is a nasopharyngeal mass—a small growth in the wall between the superior concha and the sphenoidal sinus.

"A growth?" says Mulder.

"A tumor," says Scully. "You're the only one I called."

With as much clinical detachment as she can muster, Scully tells Mulder that the tumor is inoperable. All other forms of treatment are problematical.

"The truth is," she says, "the type and placement of the tumor make it difficult. To the extreme."

"I refuse to believe that," says Mulder, stunned.

Scully smiles ruefully. "For all the times I've said that to you," says Scully, "I am as certain about this as you have ever been. I have cancer. It is a mass on the wall between my sinus and cerebrum. If it pushes into my brain, statistically there is about zero chance of survival."

"I don't accept that," says Mulder. "There must be some people who've received treatment for this. We can. . ."

His voice trails off.

"Yes. There are," says Scully, smiling sadly.

Staring into the pain and uncertainty now facing her, she pulls her MRI from the wall and tucks it away.

At FBI headquarters, she hands her medical report to Skinner. "This news comes as the worst kind of surprise, Agent Scully," says the assistant director, obviously greatly distressed. "I'm sorry. Very sorry."

Scully thanks him, then asks that her condition be kept confidential. She also requests that she be allowed to stay on the job until she and Mulder have exhausted a "possible avenue of investigation."

"Investigation?" asks Skinner.

Mulder, standing behind Scully, answers him.

"Last year," he says, "Agent Scully and I pursued a case in which a number of women, purported abductees, experienced similar symptoms after having implants removed from the base of their necks. A woman in Allentown, Pennsylvania, named

Betsy Hagopian was being treated for a nasopharyngeal tumor. We just haven't been able to contact her."

Not particularly encouraged by this, Skinner offers to put all of the medical resources of the Bureau at Scully's disposal. Scully nods her appreciation but briskly turns him down. She says she will pursue treatment on her own.

The agents arrive at Betsy Hagopian's house in Allentown. Someone is scraping a MUFON—Mutual UFO Network—sticker off the front window. The woman who answers the door tells them they're too early for the garage sale.

"We're not here for the garage sale," says Scully. "We're looking for Betsy Hagopian. No one's returning our messages."

"Sorry," says the woman, her expression softening. "Betsy's passed away—just two and a half weeks ago. Are you a relation?"

The news hits Scully with terrible force. She struggles to remain in control.

Mulder flashes his ID and asks the real estate agent if they can look around. They enter the living room. Scully flashes back to her meeting at Betsy Hagopian's house—from "Nisei" (3X09)—with the MUFON group. As the women's faces float before her, she unconsciously touches the back of her neck.

"Hey, Scully, listen to this," says Mulder, jolting her out of her sad reverie. He hands her the telephone; she hears the high-pitched screech of an electronic transmission. He'd noticed, he says, that one of the house's two phone lines is in use.

"Somebody's sending a fax or using a computer modem," says Scully.

They race downstairs to a makeshift basement office. MUFON paraphernalia decorates the walls; a desktop computer monitor indicates a remote data download in progress. A phone trace determines its source: the nearby apartment of someone named Kurt Crawford.

At Crawford's building, there's no answer to his intercom buzzer. Mulder investigates around the back of the building. A rear door bursts open and a young blond man sprints down the alley. Scully has his escape route covered, however, and after a brief chase, Mulder knocks him down. Gun in hand, Scully runs toward the arrest.

"Is your name Kurt Crawford?" she asks. She is breathing heavily from the exertion.

"Yes," says the blond man, resigned to his capture.

Mulder signals discreetly to his partner. A small trail of blood is leaking from her nose. She wipes it away.

"I'm fine, Mulder," she says defensively. "Quit staring at me. I'm fine."

In Crawford's apartment, Scully rinses the blood—still dripping stubbornly from her nose—into the bathroom sink.

When she emerges, Mulder is talking to Crawford, whose handcuffs he's already removed. Mulder tells Scully that Crawford

is part of the MUFON network; he was downloading Betsy's data for safe-keeping.

Out of Crawford's hearing, Scully says, "Then why did he run?"

"He thinks his life's in danger," says Mulder. "He thinks there's a government conspiracy to suppress the information gathered in those files."

"Do you think he's credible?" says Scully.

"He seems to know an awful lot about what happened to Betsy—and about the other women from the MUFON group you met at her house."

"Well, that will have to be cross-checked," says Scully.

"We can't," says Mulder.

He cannot bear to explain any further. Scully stares at him until the obvious explanation sinks in. She turns to Crawford. He confirms her worst fears.

He tells her that eleven MUFON members—all women who claimed to have been abducted by UFOs—have died of brain cancer in the past year. Of the woman Scully met in the Betsy Hagopian's house, only one, Penny Northern, is still alive. And she is in the hospital, gravely ill.

"What makes you think that this is a conspiracy?" says Scully. "That the government's involved?"

"What makes you think there isn't?" says Crawford.

Bitterly, he recaps the chilling confluence of the women's near-identical experiences and illnesses.

Unconvinced, Scully turns away. Mulder grabs her and urgently tells her to face the one fact she's denying: where her cancer came from.

"Mulder, it doesn't matter," she protests.

"It *does* matter. If what you have is the result of your abduction—if that abduction is something that the government knows about—then these are facts that should be brought to light."

Scully flares into anger. *"I don't know what happened to me,"* she says. "I have no clear recollection, and I don't think these abductions are even abductions."

"These women are dead," says Mulder gently.

"No, they are not!" says Scully, near tears. "One woman isn't—this Peggy Northern."

"If you won't listen to me," says Mulder, "then you should talk to this Penny Northern."

"About what?" says Scully, furious again. "What it feels like to be dying of cancer? What it's like to know that there's nothing you can do about it?"

Mulder stiffens, refusing to give in to her—or to his emotions. He speaks softly but forcefully. "If that's too hard for you," he says, "then I think you should go as an investigator. You have one remaining witness, Agent Scully. I'd think you'd want to know what her story is."

At Allentown-Bethlehem Medical Center, a gaunt, terribly sick woman lies in a hospital bed. A turban-style dressing covers her skull. Scully enters her room.

"Dana, hello!" says Penny Northern, obviously happy to see her again.

She explains that she recognizes her from their visit last year—and from the time they spent together in the aliens' custody.

Scully winces. "I'm sorry," she says. "I don't mean to be insensitive, but I don't share those memories."

"That's all right," says Penny, smiling gently.

Scully tells her that she's come to ask a few questions.

"About Dr. Scanlon?" asks Penny.

"No. Who's Dr. Scanlon?" says Scully.

Penny explains that Scanlon is the physician who's been treating her cancer.

"He treated Betsy, too," she says. "He thinks he might have isolated the cause. And that if he'd caught it earlier, he might have been able to do more for her—or me."

Scully listens to this, transfixed by fear and hope. The rest of her questions are forgotten.

"I made some phone calls and tried to get some information, but nobody's talking," he says.

"Mulder, I need you to come up here," says Scully.

"Why? Did you find something there?"

Scully asks her partner to bring him her overnight bag. And to ask her mother to bring her the rest of her things.

There is a moment of silence.

"Mulder," says Scully finally, "whatever you've found, and whatever you might find, I think that we both know that, right now, the truth is in me. And that's where I need to pursue it."

Mulder tells her that he'll be right over. He hangs up the phone, slams a desk drawer in frustration, and heads into the night.

As his car pulls away, another one rolls to a stop behind him. The Gray-Haired Man gets out. In his hand is a familiar weapon—the stiletto.

Crawford hears a noise.

"Agent Mulder?" he says.

The Gray-Haired Man enters.

Crawford knows he's in grave danger. He scrambles back awkwardly, falling over the file boxes. His assailant advances inexorably, does his work efficiently, and leaves.

What used to be Crawford lies sprawled on the floor, his body melting into green ooze.

At Allegheny Medical the next day, Scully is already checked in and sleeping in her hospital bed. Dr. Kevin Scanlon—a smooth-looking man of about forty—steps through the pool of bright light falling through her open door, waking her. He tells her that his experimental treatment involves high doses of drugs and radiation.

"You're going to feel like dying," he adds with a sad smile.

Margaret Scully arrives, carrying a suitcase. After Scanlon leaves, and before they reconcile in a tearful embrace, she attacks her daughter fiercely.

"I don't know why you didn't tell me immediately!" she says.

Her daughter replies quietly, "I wanted to get all the answers first."

In the basement of the Hagopian house, Mulder and Crawford comb through the MUFON files. Mulder's phone rings; it is Scully, calling from the hospital.

Mulder quickly tells her that he is on to something: that all of the women abductees—including Penny and Betsy—were childless and had been treated at a fertility clinic nearby.

"Mulder, that's—" says Scully.

He is too excited to let her speak.

"And you've found them here?" asks Mrs. Scully.

Scully says, "I have found some clarity. And maybe a way to fight back."

In the oncology treatment room the next morning, Scully is strapped into a linear accelerator. Technicians operate the machinery. We hear, in Scully's voice, the diary entry she will make later that day. She says:

In med school, I learned that cancer arrives in the body unannounced—a dark stranger who takes up residence, turning its new home against itself. This is the evil of cancer—that it starts as an invader, but soon becomes one with the invaded; forcing you to destroy it, but only at the risk of destroying yourself.

Scully's head is clamped into place. A form-fitting plastic mask is put over her face. A beam of radiation is aimed at her.

It is science's demon possession; my treatments, science's attempt at exorcism. Mulder, I hope that in these terms you might know it and know me, and accept this stranger so many recognize but cannot ever completely cast out.

The high-tech instrument of torture begins to do its work. Scully's eyes are wide open.

And if the darkness should have swallowed me as you read this, you must never think there was the possibility of some secret intervention, something you might have done. And though we've traveled far together, this last distance must necessarily be traveled alone.

At the Center for Reproductive Medicine in Lehigh Furnace, Pennsylvania, a man enters surreptitiously in the middle of the night. It is Mulder; he shines his flashlight past racks of medical files and sits at a computer keyboard. He types the names of Peggy Northern and Betsy Hagopian. "Access Denied/Password Req'd," flashes on the screen. He hears a noise behind him and hides behind a receptionist's desk.

A dark figure opens a door and enters.

"I've got a gun pointed at your head," says Mulder, rising. "Turn around very slowly."

He shines his flashlight in the intruder's face. It is Kurt Crawford.

Mulder accuses Crawford of betraying him, of failing to return his calls after he'd stolen some files from the Hagopian house. Crawford explains that he's been too busy trying to hack into the clinic's computer system—and that he's been unable to find the password. Mulder sheaths his weapon and picks up a snow globe next to the monitor.

"Vegreville," says Mulder, reading the legend printed on it.

Crawford types the strange word. The computer program unlocks.

"We're in," says Crawford triumphantly.

Back in her hospital room, Scully awakens, drained and nauseated, from a nightmare. Penny Northern sits at her bedside.

"I had a bad dream," Scully tells her fellow cancer patient. "Someone—someone was returning something back to me. You were there. I could hear your voice."

"They let me come to you during the procedures," explains Penny. "I don't know why. Human compassion is something they don't have."

Scully sighs and turns away. "I'm sorry, Penny, but I can't hear this right now," she says.

Her friend continues. "You've got to try to make sense of this, Dana," she says. "It'll help you through the pain. To understand why this is happening to you."

Mulder is sitting in Walter Skinner's office when the assistant director arrives for work the next day. Skinner seems less than thrilled to see him.

"I need you to set up a meeting," says Mulder.

He shows Skinner a computer diskette. He tells him that Scully's name is on it. It is part of a file directory at the federal fertility clinic, even though he's sure—"pretty damn sure"—that she's never been treated for infertility.

"So you want to set up a meeting. With whom?" says Skinner.

"Cigarette Man. I've no doubt in my mind he's behind this."

Skinner grimaces—and turns Mulder down flat.

"Find another way," says Skinner. "You deal with that man—you offer him anything—and he'll own you forever."

"He knows what they did to Agent Scully!" shouts Mulder. "He may very well know how to save her!"

"If he knows, you can know, too. But you can't ask the truth of a man who trades in lies. I won't let you."

"We are talking about Agent Scully's life," says Mulder adamantly.

"Find another way," says Skinner.

At the Lone Gunmen's office, Frohike, Byers, and Langly sit with Mulder watching bursts of gibberish scroll down a computer screen.

"The Lombard system is a dedicated mainframe," says Frohike. "Impossible to hack—or so they say."

"Then how'd you guys get in?" asks Mulder.

"A modified Clipper chip we cannibalized from a government surplus army field encoder," says Byers.

Frohike adds, "We bought it back from the Chinese. But for all the work it took to get in, what we got in Agent Scully's file—we don't know how much help it's gonna be."

They tell Mulder that the file contains a gene code they've seen before—the code detected in Scully's blood after her abduction. It might be, they say, what made her sick.

"Somebody might be working to find a cause," says Langly.

"Or a cure," says Mulder.

He contemplates this for a moment and adds: "You guys ever been to the Lombard Research facility? Wear something black and sexy, and prepare to do some fancy poaching."

In the basement of the FBI building, Walter Skinner enters Fox Mulder's office. Sitting in the agent's chair is the Cigarette-Smoking Man. He asks about Agent Scully's health.

"Is it terminal? The cancer?" asks the Cancer Man breezily.

Skinner can barely contain his fury and revulsion. He asks his adversary what he wants in exchange for a cure for Scully's illness.

"Well!" smirks the Cigarette-Smoking Man, "you think a lot more of me than you let on, Mr. Skinner."

"What'll it take?"

"For Agent Scully's life? What will you offer?"

"What'll it take?"

"Well, I'll have to get back to you on that," says the Cigarette-Smoking Man coolly.

A pulling tool and an equipment bag are dropped down a storm drain at the Lombard Research Facility. Frohike and Langly descend the dark tube and hook up their laptop to some communication lines. They're in radio contact with Mulder and Byers, waiting on a nearby hillside.

"We got to go," says Mulder impatiently.

Mulder and Byers enter the front door of the building—just as Langly manages to bypass its alarm system and redirect the security cameras' output to his computer screen. The two intruders hustle down a long corridor, but are held up by a Plexiglas internal security door. While Langly hacks his way past this obstacle, Mulder peers into a nearby office. There is a signboard that reads "Doctors on Call." One name leaps off it: Dr. Kevin Scanlon.

"Boys, we've got a problem," radios Mulder. "The doctor who's treating Scully is on staff here."

"More mysteries await," says Langly. "Bypass is complete."

Mulder barks an order to a nervous Byers, already on adrenaline overload. "Look," he says. "I need someone to get to

cully and get her to stop treatment. Right ow, you're the only one who can do that."

Mulder runs through the open doorway. yers can only swallow hard and watch m go.

In her room at Allentown-Bethlehem, an nervated Scully lies in her bed making ntries in her diary. She writes:

I have not written to you in the last twenty-four hours because the treatment has weakened my spirit as well as my body. Mulder, it's difficult to describe to you the fear of facing an enemy which I can neither conquer nor escape. Penny Northern has taken a downturn. I now look at her with a respect that can only come from one who is about to walk the same dark path. Seeing her, I can't help but see myself in a month or a year. I pray that I have the courage to face this journey.

Mulder moves down a wide hallway cauously and carefully.

Mulder, I feel you close, though I know you are pursuing your own path. For that I am grateful—more than I could ever express. I need to know you're out there if I am ever to see through this.

"Langly, where the hell am I going?" houts Mulder into his radio.

The Gunmen's control of the security ystem breaks down; Mulder loses communication with the hackers. Byers, on his wn now, spots a police car pulling up to he building's front door.

Mulder's path is blocked by a locked oor, and he pounds on it in frustration. It opened from the inside by a man in a hite lab coat—Kurt Crawford.

Standing nearby, scattered throughout e large laboratory, are several other Kurt rawfords. They are identical copies of ach other.

"You're hybrids," says Mulder.

"Please come in so that we might xplain," says Crawford.

The lab is filled with large liquid-filled ass tanks reminiscent of those in "The lenmeyer Flask" (1X24).

"You've been using me," says Mulder.

"Not at all," says Crawford. "Your arrival was only coincident with the execution of our objective."

"What objective?"

Another clone answers Mulder. "To subvert the project," he says. "The project that created us."

Mulder wipes the condensation from the outside of one of the tanks, revealing the face of a blond boy—the one he saw in "Herrenvolk" (4X01).

"These boys are you," says Mulder.

"We're among the end results," says Kurt #1.

SCULLY, Dana
0000121336540-009
10/29/94

"And you want to destroy them?" says Mulder.

"No," says Kurt #2. "What we want is the same thing that you want."

Kurt #1 escorts Mulder into a large narrow room lined with hundreds of stainless steel drawers. They contain human ova, says Crawford.

"Taken from whom?" says Mulder.

Crawford points to a drawer. The label on it reads: "SCULLY, DANA. 0000121336540-009 10/29/94."

Mulder opens it.

Inside, under refrigeration, are several slim glass tubes filled with clear fluid.

"Harvested during her abduction," explains Crawford. "Through a high-amplification radiation procedure that caused superovulation."

"Why?"

"For fertilization. They constitute one-half of the necessary raw materials."

Mulder begins to understand.

"For genetic hybridization. For reproduction. These are your birth mothers."

"Barren now," adds Crawford. "From the same procedure that caused their cancer. Now they're left to die—their conditions hastened by the men running the project."

Mulder asks, "And you're trying to save them."

Crawford answers simply, "They're our mothers."

Mulder pockets the tube. He exits the lab and—his voice link to Langly working again—learns that another intruder has entered the building.

Byers ducks into a doorway to avoid a posse of policemen. The Gray-Haired Man enters the now deserted laboratory.

By radio, Langly steers Mulder toward the building exit: through one Plexiglas door and into a locked metal one, which the Gunmen struggle to open. At the other end of Mulder's corridor, the Gray-Haired Man strides into view.

Mulder has nowhere to go. The Gray-Haired Man raises his pistol and blasts the Plexiglas. He fires one clip, reloads, and fires another. The glass shatters. A hole—big enough to stick a gun barrel through—is formed.

"Get me out of here!" shouts Mulder to the hackers.

They finally override the building's systems.

"Go!" says Frohike as the Gray-Haired Man aims through the hole.

Mulder beats the killer's bullet through the door.

At Scully's hospital, he races to her room and finds it empty. He bends down to read the diary at her bedside. He races out, grabs the duty nurse, and demands to know where Scully is. The nurse is alarmed that Scully is missing.

"Mulder!" shouts Byers from the other end of the corridor. "I got to her."

Scully is in Penny Northern's room, kneeling beside the bed and talking to the dying woman.

"Dr. Scanlon—is not coming back?" says Penny, barely audible.

"No. I don't think so, Penny," says Scully, stroking her cheek.

"Dana. I want you to get well. You've been such a comfort. You've got to be the one. You can't give up hope."

"I haven't," Scully whispers. "I won't."

Mulder waits outside, slumped with fatigue and sorrow. Scully, her face as drawn and strained as we've ever seen it, leaves Penny's room.

"Is she gone?" asks Mulder.

Scully, crying, can only nod.

Mulder tells Scully that he's glad to see her—that he was frightened when he saw her empty bed—and that he has read the diary.

Scully tries to pull herself together. "I didn't want you to read that," she says. "I'd decided to throw it out. I decided tonight that I wasn't going to let this beat me, Mulder. I came into this hospital able to work. And that's how I'm leaving."

Mulder nods. He tells her that Scanlon may have killed the other MUFON women and they will prove that when they find him.

"If we find him," says Scully.

"When we find him," says Mulder.

He leans toward Scully and speaks—underneath several layers of logic, obsession, and control—with great emotion.

"Scully, something was done to you," he says. "Something you're just beginning to remember. You can't quite figure it out, but it can be explained, and it will be explained.

"And no matter what you think as a scientist, or a doctor—if there's a way, you will find it. To save yourself."

Scully looks into her partner's eyes.

"Mulder, I can't kid myself. People live with cancer. They carry on—and so will I. You know, I've got things to finish. To prove to myself, to my family. But for my own reasons."

Even while crying, she smiles. Mulder takes her in his arms.

"The truth will save you, Scully," says Mulder. I think it will save both of us."

He kisses her gently on her forehead.

It is 5:30 in the morning. While Scully prepares to leave the hospital, Mulder phones Skinner—expecting to get his voice mail, but reaching the AD himself.

Mulder tells Skinner that Scully is feeling well and that she will return to work soon. He adds: "I was calling to thank you for your advice—about our chain-smoking friend. I think you were right. We have to know what he knows. We'll simply have to find another way."

"There's always another way," says Skinner.

"Yes, I believe there is," says the Cigarette-Smoking Man, sitting opposite Skinner. "If you're willing to pay the price."

end of the long passage; the coming and the going, and all that.

"Also, the whole cancer theme leads us very strongly into Season Five. It helps us tie together so many things in the two-parter that begins the season. It's all going to really play out interestingly."

It was realized immediately, adds Carter, that Scully's disease would cause she and Mulder to fall back on their very different belief systems in their search for answers—thus straining their relationship to the breaking point. This was considered good. The realization was also made that Scully's dread disease would enable the writers to milk the situation and the audience's relationship with the characters for sympathy, allowing the characters to collapse gooily in each other's arms. This was considered very bad.

"I do *not* write gooily," says Carter with a brief laugh. "I've already had people say, 'You've got to give the audience that moment, they're expecting it,' but I try to keep away from it as long as I can. I mean, look at what happens in 'Memento Mori'— Scully writes to Mulder in her diary, but when he actually visits the hospital, they don't really talk about it. I think their relationship is defined not by what's said but by what's being withheld."

Carter adds: "But it's absolutely plain that they love each other—in their own way. And it's the best kind of love. It's unconditional. It's not based on a physical attraction, but on a shared passion for life and for their quest. These are romantic heroes, romantic heroes in the literary tradition."

The lead actors, long attuned to Carter's sensibilities and how they translate into their respective characters, didn't need much coaching to hew to the proper dramatic line.

"Sure, Scully is scared by the disease," says Gillian Anderson. "But fear is not a good emotion to play on a constant basis. There's only so much of that I can do before it gets ridiculous. And in one sense that's useful, because it informs me that Scully is trying to avoid it in some way. She

back story:

A good argument can be made that "Memento Mori"—which was submitted to the television academy to represent *The X-Files* in this year's Emmy competition—is the finest episode of the fourth season. An even better case can be presented that 4X15 is a nearly pure expression of the qualities that set the show apart from its peers.

Case opened:

"We decided early in Season Four to give Scully cancer," says Chris Carter. "I had talked about it with Gillian the previous year, when we were discussing having her mother contracting it. We were playing around with all of this because cancer provides an interesting platform on which to discuss many different things: faith, science, health care, and also a certain element of the paranormal—the light at the doesn't want to deal with it until it rears its ugly head. Sure, sometimes she's scared. Sometimes she's overwhelmed. Sometimes I have to think of the things that I will lose, but I have to focus on what's right in front of me, making choices in my life so that if I *have* to go, I'll feel that while I've been here I have accomplished something."

David Duchovny says, "When this script first came up I thought we had a chance to bring in a new dimension, one that wasn't symbolic or typical of an ideal relationship. I said, 'I don't want Mulder to play the "you're a brave little soldier," beat.' The actual truth of the matter is that when you do that you're hurting yourself, you're hurting everyone.

"I also wanted to get beyond 'You should really get home and rest,' which is soap operatic, and get into some true semblance of a human relationship—which includes that people get angry with each other even when they're dying. *Especially* when they're dying. So I said to the writers: 'If there's anything I can do here, please let me be totally unsympathetic and be an asshole to her, because this is what people do. They go against their better instincts. They're not always princes in this situation.'"

Ambitious as it was, in many other respects "Memento Mori" was typical of nearly every other *X-Files* episode in that the many people involved in making it alternated frequently between brief moments of inspiration and long periods of struggle and frustration. Before deciding what type of cancer Scully should have, cowriter Frank Spotnitz consulted with his brother Seth Spotnitz, a neurologist, and determined that a nasal-pharyngeal tumor, though inoperable and virtually untreatable, would not affect Scully's strength or appearance until its terminal stage.

The first draft of the script, written mostly by Spotnitz, Vince Gilligan, and John Shiban, was extensively rewritten by Chris Carter. The first cut of the film was long—so long that an emotional performance by actor Pat Skipper, playing Scully's brother Bill Scully, Jr., was completely excised. (Skipper appears again for the first time,

however, in "Gethsemane," the final episode of the season.)

To create the Orwellian ovum depository that plays such a prominent part in 4X15, art director Graeme Murray went way beyond the bounds of conventional TV-series set design. For instance, the refrigeration units are not painted plywood; they are custom-made cabinets constructed of stainless steel and machined aluminum. The entire art department worked fanatically on designing the most minute details of the drawers and handles.

"It was total overkill. Insane!" says another member of the production crew—who asked to remain anonymous—admiringly.

For their efforts, Murray, art director Gary Allen, and set decorator Shirley Inget shared this year's Emmy Award for Best Art Direction, Series.

Case closed.

Mulder uses the word *Vegreville* as the password to enter computer records in a doctor's office; the real Vegreville in Alberta, Canada, hosts a tourist attraction in keeping with the theme of the episode: a giant Easter egg.

Ⓧ

The date on the drawer holding Scully's ova is November 29, 1994—the date she was returned to the hospital in "One Breath" (2X08).

Ⓧ

episode: 4X16
first aired: February 23, 1997
story by: Howard Gordon
written by:
Howard Gordon and Chris Carter
editor: Jim Gross
directed by: Michael Lange

unrequited

A Marine Corps prisoner of war, abandoned
in Vietnam by his superiors, returns to the
United States with a vengeance—and a special
talent for hiding in plain sight.

guest stars:
Mitch Pileggi (AD Walter Skinner)
Peter Lacroix (Nathaniel Teager)
Scott Hylands (General Benjamin Bloch)
Don McWilliams (Private First Class Gus Burkholder)
Bill Agnew (General Peter MacDougal)
Larry Musser (Denny Markham)
Lesley Ewen (Renee Davenport)
William Nunn (General Jon Steffan)
Ryan Michael (Agent Cameron Hill)
Mark Holden (Agent Eugene Chandler)
Allan Franz (Dr. Ben Keyser)
D. Harlan Cutshall (Adjutant)
Jen Jasey (Female Private)

principal settings:
Washington, D.C.; Fort Evanston,
Maryland; Demeter, Virginia

near the Vietnam Veterans Memorial in Washington, D.C., a large crowd is gathered: The monument is being rededicated.

Marine Corps Major General Benjamin Bloch addresses the throng; standing behind him on the platform is AD Walter Skinner (a Vietnam vet himself) coordinating security. Mulder, Scully, and Agent Cameron Hill are in the crowd, connected to Skinner by earwig radios. They seem to be on the lookout for one man.

"He's here. I feel him," says Mulder.

"Then where is he?" asks Skinner impatiently.

Scully spots him first. He's a gaunt, bearded man in an old field jacket, and he moves quickly through the crowd and out of her field of vision. Next, Hill picks him up and then loses him. The target veers back toward Scully, who catches another glimpse before losing visual contact. Responding to Skinner's frantic queries, the agents herd their quarry toward the speaker's platform and Mulder.

"I got him," says Mulder.

He scans the cheering crowd again—and loses him.

"Pick him up, Mulder! He's right in front of you!" shouts Skinner.

Mulder sees him. The man pulls something from his pocket.

"He's got a gun!" shouts Mulder, drawing his own.

Skinner throws his body in front of the general. The crowd shrieks with panic. Mulder aims his weapon at the gunman—who shimmers, fades, and vanishes into thin air.

Twelve hours earlier, a three-star army general named Peter MacDougal arrives by helicopter at Fort Evanston in Maryland. He salutes his driver, PFC Burkholder, and enters his waiting limousine. As they drive away, the privacy partition rises and the doors lock mechanically. MacDougal opens his briefcase and pulls out some files. He notices something on the floor.

It's a playing card, the King of Hearts. On the reverse is a crude graphic: a leering skull floating above two crossed swords dripping blood.

Looking up again, MacDougal sees the gaunt, bearded man.

"Who the hell are you? How did you get in here?" he asks.

The intruder pulls an automatic pistol from his pocket. From inside the car, a single shot rings out.

At FBI headquarters two hours later, Skinner chairs a hastily assembled FBI task force—which includes the late-arriving Mulder and Scully. General Bloch sits next to Skinner; the AD tells the agents that Private Burkholder, who has ties to a radical paramilitary group called the Right Hand, is the prime suspect. He adds that a chemical test indicated that Burkholder did not fire the murder weapon, but with dozens of other top military leaders converging on Washington for the ceremony, the FBI is taking no chances.

Mulder speaks up. "What if Private Burkholder's telling the truth—that he's innocent?" he asks.

"Until we can find another suspect," says Skinner, "the FBI will pursue the Right Hand and their leader—an ex-Marine named Denny Markham—in a preemptive strategy to put a stop to any other plans they have made."

The meeting breaks up and the agents get their assignments. Scully and Mulder approach Skinner.

"Was that for the benefit of the general," Scully asks, "or have you been able to develop a real strategy?"

"Right now I'm flying by the seat of my pants," confesses Skinner.

Mulder says wryly, "You mean there's no procedure outlined for an invisible assassin?"

Scully tells her supervisor that she convinced Burkholder to take a lie detector test. He passed.

"You heard his story, Mulder?" asks Skinner.

"Yeah. I found his story compelling, personally," he says. "But then again, I believe in the Warren Commission."

Scully asks Skinner to allow her and Mulder to question Denny Markham. Skinner reluctantly agrees.

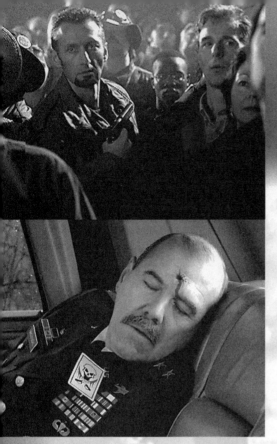

"And Private First Class Gus Burkholder."

Markham denies any knowledge of the murder or of Burkholder. He refuses further cooperation. His rottweilers pick up a scent and move toward the tree line, where a task force of FBI agents—in camouflage gear and carrying assault rifles—is moving toward them.

"There goes the neighborhood," says Mulder.

Markham takes in this scene as if he'd been expecting it.

"The Right Hand," he says contemptuously, "believes in empowering the individual over a corrupt and corrupting federal government. We're prepared for the time when armed resistance will be necessary—when lives will have to be sacrificed—but that day has not yet come."

"Would you take a polygraph, sir?" asks Scully.

"My word's good enough," growls Markham.

Mulder says, "What's your word on this?" He holds up a copy of the King of Hearts death card.

"Where'd that come from?" asks Markham surprised.

"I'd like to ask you that," says Mulder.

The militia leader stares at Mulder with narrowed eyes. He speaks in a low voice, anger mixed with menace and alarm.

"More men," he says, "are gonna die."

As the federal agents catalog and confiscate the Right Hand's illegal arsenal, a handcuffed Markham directs Mulder to pull a photograph from his files. The photo shows the gaunt veteran standing next to Markham.

"His name's Nathaniel Teager," says Markham. "Twenty-six confirmed solo enemy kills. A veritable killing machine, left for dead by the government that created him."

According to Markham, Teager was a member of Green Beret Detachment B11—a squad known as the "Bloody Sabers." Declared missing in action in 1971, Teager was liberated by the Right Hand from a Vietnamese prison camp in December 1995—twenty-three years after the U.S.

In rural Virginia, the agents approach the Right Hand's primitive-looking gated compound. Mulder identifies himself as an FBI agent over the intercom. Denny Markham replies immediately.

"Gate's unlocked," he says sourly.

Mulder and Scully push the gate open and walk forward. A pack of fierce rottweilers is loosed from the back of a nearby pickup truck; the agents just manage to beat them back to the front entrance. They slam the chain-link fence in the snouts of the attack dogs.

Denny Markham, a bearded middle-aged man wearing jeans and a flight jacket, emerges from a double-wide at the center of the settlement. He calls off his dogs. Swaggering slightly, he approaches the fence.

"Now, you wanted to see me about...?" he says

"The murder of General Peter MacDougal," says Scully.

"Am I under suspicion?" asks Markham.

"No, but your group is," says Scully.

government declared that all American POW's had left North Vietnam. The U.S. military, adds Markham, tried to capture Teager when the militiamen brought him back to the States.

"The government kidnapped a U.S. prisoner of war?" says Scully skeptically.

"I said they tried," says Markham. He adds: "They had their commandos board our plane in San Diego. When they broke into the cargo hold where we hid him, he was already gone. I never did figure out how."

At the Vietnam Memorial, an African-American woman lays a spray of flowers at the base of the black granite. The name "Nathaniel Teager" is visible.

"Mrs. Davenport? Renee Davenport?" says a man standing behind her.

She turns to face him. It is the gaunt man, Nathaniel Teager.

"Yes?" she says.

"Wife of Lance Corporal Gary Davenport of the Special Forces?"

"Yes," she answers. "I'm sorry, do I know you?"

"No, ma'am," says Teager. "I have come back in his behalf—for the reason that Gary remains a prisoner of war."

"Gary's dead," says Mrs. Davenport.

"No, ma'am," says Teager solemnly. "May you forgive me as you forgive him, as a man and a soldier, for restoring the honor of the B One-One."

Teager hands her a set of metal dog tags. They are her husband's.

"Where did you get these?" asks Mrs. Davenport, shocked.

Teager says nothing. The woman, trembling and crying, stares at the dog tags—and her husband's name—again.

"Who gave you these?" she says.

She looks up again. Nathaniel Teager has vanished.

Elsewhere near the Wall, preparations for the rededication ceremony are under way. At the Wall, Skinner tells Scully and Mulder that Renee Davenport has identified Teager from an old photograph. He can't declare Teager his only suspect, though, because the Army Forensics Lab reports that Nathaniel Teager's remains have been recovered.

Scully suggests that Markham and his organization staged the entire incident.

"Why go to all that trouble?" asks Mulder.

"To create a decoy," says Scully. "To divert our attention—which seems to be working."

Skinner says, "Well, this woman saw someone. I want to know who."

Renee Davenport, still badly shaken, is shown Markham's photograph of Teager. She is positive that that was the man she saw. She is also certain that Teager vanished into thin air.

"It was so strange," she says. "One minute he was standing right in front of me. Then he was gone."

She breaks down in tears. "Oh, God!" she says. "What if he was telling the truth? What if Gary is alive? I've tried to get on with my life. I've remarried. What do I tell my husband now? What am I supposed to do?"

Scully leans forward. She points out to Mrs. Davenport that her eye is bleeding—a capillary has burst. Mulder tells Scully to arrange an eye exam for their witness.

"An eye exam? For what?" says Scully.

Mulder says, "By all reports the man we're looking for—the man we saw—has a knack for vanishing in plain sight. Maybe there's a connection."

"Mulder," says Scully, "what she has is a simple subconjunctival hemorrhage. It's probably brought on by her emotional state."

"And how did she reach that emotional state?" says Mulder.

He turns to leave. "I'm going to see if we're really chasing a dead man," he says.

At the Army Central Identification Lab, a doctor named Keyser shows Mulder the supposed remains of Nathaniel Teager—three teeth, two bicuspids and a molar. He cannot tell whether the teeth were removed pre- or postmortem. In fact, the partially destroyed report on Teager's death is marked "inconclusive."

"Whoever signed off on this death," says Mulder, "chose to ignore the facts, huh?"

Keyser agrees, but adds that because much of the record has been lost, there's no sure way to know who was responsible.

"Is there any other way to tell?" asks Mulder.

"Well," says Keyser, "based on the records, and the reports filed at the same time, we can make a pretty good guess."

In the backseat of a limousine heading toward the Pentagon, a U.S. army general named Jon Steffan gets a phone call. It's from Mulder. The agent tells him that his life is in danger—that he might be the next target for General MacDougal's assassin.

"Based on what information?" says Steffan.

"Based on a death certificate that you may have put your signature on. The death certificate for Sergeant Nathaniel Teager," says Mulder.

"I don't know anything about that," says Steffan unconvincingly.

Steffan nervously agrees to rendezvous with two FBI agents that Mulder has dispatched. He strides through the public area of the Pentagon flanked by Agent Hill and a second agent. They all pass through a metal detector.

A few seconds later, Teager passes through the same security point. He sets

off the machine's alarm, but when the security officer looks up at the sound, the intruder is gone.

The FBI agents survey Steffan's office. Satisfied that nothing is amiss, they step outside. The general walks to his desk. On his desktop is a Bloody Sabers' death card. On the reverse: the King of Diamonds.

As he enters the Pentagon, Mulder gets a call from Scully at the Georgetown Medical Center. She tells him that the ophthalmologist examining Renee Davenport has discovered a transient scotoma: a floating blind spot.

According to the medical literature, she says, a scotoma can be caused by such conditions as diabetes, glaucoma, or macular degeneration—none of which Mrs. Davenport is suffering from.

"Well, don't you think it's odd, Scully, that she'd have a blind spot that she wouldn't have noticed before?"

"Not necessarily. The processes of the brain fill in, and the visual cortex compensates conceptually."

"That might account for Teager's vanishing," says Mulder.

"I asked the doctor that," says Scully, "and he laughed at me."

Another caller beeps in to Mulder's line. It is General Steffan, sitting alone in his office.

"I found something on my desk," says the general. "Something—very troubling."

Mulder tells Steffan urgently to get the two FBI agents into his office. Distraught, the general shouts into his phone.

"Who put this here?" he demands.

Teager is now standing behind Steffan's

right shoulder. Over the phone, there is the sound of a gun being cocked.

"Listen to me very carefully, okay?" says Mulder. "I'm on my way over there, and—"

There is the sound of a gunshot.

"General Steffan?" says Mulder.

He breaks into a run. By the time he reaches the general's office, the other two agents are standing over Steffan—who is sprawled dead on the floor, shot through the forehead.

Mulder kneels down to examine the body; the death card lies on its chest. Teager stands behind Mulder's left shoulder. The agent spots the killer out of the corner of his eye. He swivels his head.

Nothing.

At the crime scene, Scully and a crew of forensic techs examine the body. There is no evidence, she says, to explain the death scenario as described by Mulder.

Skinner arrives, very agitated, and shows Mulder and Scully a surveillance videotape of Teager walking through the security checkpoint. He demands an explanation.

"I think that Teager has an ability," says Mulder. "The ability to effectively erase himself from the visual field."

"If he's invisible," says Skinner, "then why is he on this video, clear as day?"

Mulder replies, "I think that he can hide himself from human sight by manipulating something that Scully has described as naturally occurring: a blind spot."

"That is conjecture, sir," says Scully.

"Isn't it true that U.S. soldiers reported the unexplained disappearance of VC guerrillas? I've read the dispatches myself," Mulder says.

He adds, "Maybe Teager learned something from his captors in twenty-five years of isolation."

Completely exasperated, Skinner says that if Mulder's thesis is correct, he has absolutely no way to guard the thirty-one top military men gathered for the ceremony—and a parade to the site beforehand.

"Call it off," says Scully flatly.

Mulder disagrees. "Parade or no parade," he says, "those men are going to be vulnerable. The only way to stop this killer is to stop him."

"How do we do that?" asks Skinner.

"By finding his next victim before he does."

At the Army Detention Center in Fort Evanston, General Bloch enters the jail cell of Denny Markham. Markham smirks.

"He did it again, didn't he?" says the militia leader. "I told them he would."

Bloch asks Markham to tell them why the authorities can't find Teager.

"Same reason you can't," says Markham. "Which I imagine is the same reason you're here right now."

Bloch bristles. "I am here because people are dying," he says self-righteously. "Soldiers who dedicated their lives to the defense of this country!"

Markham says, disgusted, "I guess that's one way of looking at it."

Bloch changes tactics. He threatens to charge Markham and his followers with conspiracy and treason. Then he offers Markham a deal: If he'll help them find Teager, they'll reduce or even eliminate the charges against him.

"I just need to know what he wants," says the general.

"You know what he wants," says Markham. "And we both know you can't give it to him—not without dragging that nice clean uniform through the mud."

Bloch grabs Markham by the shirt front, lifts him out of his chair, and slams him against the wall. Markham is unfazed.

"Whatever you do to me won't change his mind, General," he says. "He's sending a message. And making damn sure everyone hears it loud and clear."

At the parade staging area, a military band marches in place. A line of military vehicles prepares to get under way. A cheering crowd lines the boulevard; in its front rank stands Nathaniel Teager.

On the steps of the Lincoln Memorial, a woman is waiting for Mulder. It is Marita Covarrubias. She has no information about Teager, but she does know about Steffan and MacDougal.

"They have a connection," she says. "A recent news story extremely embarrassing to the U.S. military. About the disposing of South Vietnamese soldiers."

Mulder nods; he's familiar with the scandal. He says, "Men employed by our government as spies and commandos. Left behind enemy lines to certain capture or death. The operation was disavowed and their lives erased from the records."

Covarrubias adds: "By a secret three-man commission. Who may now be facing charges. Whose testimony might be used in the calculation of reparations."

"Are you saying that our government wants these officers dead?" asks Mulder.

Covarrubias says nothing.

"Then why would they ask us to protect them?" says Mulder.

Covarrubias says, "Because they know you can't."

Mulder is staggered. It takes a second or two for the information to fully sink in.

"Well, who's the third man?" he asks.

Again, Covarrubias is silent. She begins to walk away.

Mulder calls after her. "I need a name!" he shouts.

She does not reply.

At the beginning of the parade route, the marchers begin to move out. Scully and Skinner run toward General Bloch's Jeep, tell him that his life is in danger, and ask him to leave the parade. Scully scans the crowd. She spots Nathaniel Teager.

"Shooter! Get down!" she yells, drawing her weapon.

The crowd scatters in panic. Scully tries to locate the man she'd glimpsed just a second ago, but Teager is gone.

As darkness falls at the Vietnam Memorial, participants and spectators prepare for the start of the ceremony. Backstage, Scully tells Mulder about her baffling encounter with Teager. Mulder tells Scully that Bloch is Teager's next target and that the masterminds behind the plot are betting that the FBI will not be able to protect him.

Scully refuses to believe this. "Mulder," she says, "the government is not about to sacrifice the lives of ranking military officers just to discredit us."

"Discrediting us in this case is only secondary," says Mulder, "to maintaining their secret policy of denial about POWs—which required silencing the men who made that policy."

Mulder approaches Bloch and challenges him to refute his theory. But the general, unnerved, insists he has a speech to give—immediately. Skinner urges Bloch to reconsider giving the keynote address.

"He won't reconsider," says Mulder. "Not going out there would be an admission of guilt."

Bloch turns and walks toward the stage.

As the preliminary speakers are introduced, Teager shoulders his way through the spectators. Another vet, also wearing an old fatigue jacket, spots him.

"Teager!" he shouts. "Hey, man, is that you?"

The vet, surprised but pleased to see his old buddy, shoulders his way through the crowd—just barely managing to keep Teager in sight. He follows him to a deserted area behind the grandstands. But Teager is gone.

The veteran doesn't give up.

"Teager? Hey, Teager!" he shouts. "It's me, Leo Danziger. Saw you, man. Where are you?"

"Behind you," says Teager quietly.

Startled, Danziger turns to face him.

"I-I thought you were dead. That's what they told us," he says.

"Because that's what they wanted you to believe," says Teager.

"I don't understand."

"You will. After tonight."

"What are you talking about?"

"I waited for them, Leo," says Teager. "I waited for them to come. They never came."

"Maybe they didn't know," says Danziger.

"They knew," says Teager. "They just figured letting me die off was easier than admitting the truth."

Danziger says, "It's all over now, Teager. It's been over for a long time now."

Teager says, "Not for me. Not for the others."

"You're telling me there's more?" asks Danziger.

Teager nods and hands Danziger a piece of tattered paper. On it, written in neat handwriting, are dozens of names. Danziger looks up. Teager has disappeared.

Bloch is introduced to the crowd. Standing ramrod straight, he strides onstage. On his podium is a death card—the Ace of Clubs.

Mulder, Scully, and Hill are in the crowd, connected to Skinner by earwig radios.

"He's here. I feel him," says Mulder.

"Then where is he?" asks Skinner impatiently.

Scully spots Teager first. He moves quickly through the crowd and out of her field of vision. Hill picks him up next—then loses him. The target veers back toward Scully, who catches another glimpse

before losing visual contact. Responding to Skinner's frantic queries, the agents herd Teager toward the speaker's platform and Mulder.

"I got him," says Mulder.

He scans the cheering crowd again—and loses him.

"Pick him up, Mulder! He's right in front of you!" shouts Skinner.

Mulder sees him. Teager pulls something from his pocket.

"He's got a gun!" shouts Mulder, drawing his own.

Skinner throws his body in front of the general. The crowd shrieks with panic. Mulder aims his weapon at the gunman—who shimmers, fades, and vanishes into thin air.

Mulder frantically scans the crowd. Scully stops him.

"Mulder, he's gone," she says. "He's gone."

"Where's General Bloch?" says Mulder. "We've got to stop him."

"What's going on?" asks Scully.

"He can only hide himself in somebody's direct line of sight," says Mulder. "That's why he killed General MacDougal and Steffan at close quarters. MacDougal in his car, Steffan in his office."

They rush behind the grandstand, where Skinner is hustling Bloch into his limousine.

"He's in the car! Teager's in the car!" shouts Mulder.

A shot rings out. The shooter is in the backseat of the limo.

Skinner knocks Bloch to the ground, covering him. Mulder calls for Teager to surrender. The limousine starts and the vehicle moves forward. Mulder dives out of its way.

Agent Hill stands in the limousine's path. He fires several shots through the windshield. The limo swerves and slides to a halt. The driver's door swings open, and Teager—critically wounded—tumbles to the ground. Scully kneels over him. His skin is pale and there is a froth of blood on his lips. Forcing the words out painfully, his voice becoming fainter and fainter, he speaks: "Teager, Nathaniel J., Sergeant,

Green Beret Detachment B One-One. Service number 82278. Date of birth— March 7, 1954."

Again.

"Teager, Nathaniel J., Sergeant, Green Beret Detachment B One-One. Service number 82278. Date of birth—March 7, 1954."

Again.

"Teager, Nathaniel J. . . ."

At the Vietnam Memorial the next day, Skinner stands somberly facing the Wall. Mulder arrives to bring him up to date.

Mulder says, "The Pentagon is claiming that the man who was killed was a Thomas Lynch. He's a vet who's been in and out of VA psychiatric hospitals for the last fifteen years."

"And a sometimes member of the Right Hand," says Skinner. "He was on Markham's mailing list. Markham made a positive ID."

Mulder snorts with disgust. "They must have gotten to him," he says.

Skinner adds that the army forensics unit claims to have multiple confirmations of the murderer's identity. Mulder flares into anger.

"You *heard* him," he says. "We *both* did. It's happening all over again! They're covering the lies with more lies, trying to make him invisible."

Mulder demands that they reopen the investigation.

"I can't do that, Agent Mulder!" growls Skinner.

He tells Mulder that the investigation has been turned over to the army intelligence service.

"Don't let them do this!" pleads Mulder.

"Let it go, Agent Mulder," says Skinner, his voice lowered. "You did your job."

"So did Nathaniel Teager," says Mulder.

"You found the man you were looking for," says Mulder. "But now he's dead. It's over."

"Is that what you believe?" asks Mulder. "Is that what you really believe?"

Skinner says nothing.

"They're not just denying this man's life," says Mulder. "They're denying his

death. And with all due respect, sir, he could be you."

back story:
For the last quarter century or so, a sizable ice floe of suspicion—based on the belief that U.S. servicemen remain imprisoned in Vietnam—has floated along the surface of the American psyche. Last year, CBS's *60 Minutes* aired a segment reporting that in the 1960s and 1970s the Central Intelligence Agency had cruelly abandoned and declared dead hundreds of South Vietnamese secret agents it knew to have been captured by the North Vietnamese.

This so intrigued and inspired executive producer Howard Gordon that even though he wasn't scheduled to write his next episode until 4X19, he ended up writing "Unrequited" during the show's Christmas break.

"There was a bit of a mix-up, a last-minute scramble," says Gordon. "So the day before Chris's vacation, Frank and Chris and I sat down and beat out the story. Then I wrote a draft of the script and I felt it was just not right. So I went back to Chris and I was honest with him. I said, 'I need your help, and I think it's right that I share the credit with you.' And that's why his name is on the script as well as mine. It was a difficult birth, as usual, but I think it came out fine."

Gordon explains that his theme of a human being becoming invisible—politically and metaphorically—had been kicking around for some time.

"The problem was," he says, "how can a human being become *physically* invisible? Last year I was talking to my brother [a practicing ophthalmologist] about this, and he told me that we all have blind spots—nonworking portions of our retinas and optic nerves that normally don't affect us because of our brains' compensatory apparatus."

He adds: "As far as creating a 'disgruntled vet' was concerned, as writers, we're always looking for disenfranchised people, characters on the fringe of society that we can sink our teeth into. Then, too, I felt that this was the last Vietnam vet story I'd ever be able to write, because they're beginning to age as a population and, just like the Holocaust survivors in 'Kaddish,' die off."

Gordon also explains that he is always happy to write a substantial part for Mitch Pileggi; it was easy to do in this case, because Walter Skinner had been established as a Vietnam veteran in "One Breath" (2X08).

The entire show was cast in Vancouver—which explains why several of the U.S. military men speak with pronounced Canadian accents. The re-creation of the Vietnam Memorial, which had begun with four panels for Mulder and Scully's rendezvous with Pudovkin in "Never Again" (4X13) was completed with the construction of two seven-foot-tall sections, one sixty feet long and the other thirty-six, built out of Plexiglas spray-painted from the rear to look like granite.

Whose names are silk-screened on the face of the fake monument? Mostly nobody's. For legal reasons, the actual names could not be used. Art assistant Kristina Lyne asked her sister, who runs a typing service, to sit at her keyboard and make up 2,000 imaginary names. It took her twenty hours, imagining and typing nonstop.

For daytime filming, the monument was set up in Vancouver's Jericho Park. Night shooting in the park is not allowed, however, and no soundstage at North Shore Studios was large enough to accommodate, so the set was moved to Ballantyne Pier, a semi-enclosed (and definitively drafty) cruise ship dock that sits unused for most of the Pacific Northwest winter.

The teeming crowd in the rededication scene consisted of 450 strategically placed extras augmented by the 50 lucky winners of a "get a walk-on part on *The X-Files*" contest sponsored by Fox and run through local U.S. radio stations. Also pitching in to help was Laurie Kallsen-George and her visual effects crew, which electronically doubled the crowd when necessary.

Of any unique acting requirements for this episode, only Gillian Anderson had anything much to say. "The challenge there," she says, "was to comprehend physically how we were actually seeing this guy—to wrap our mind around the fact that we were only seeing him through our peripheral vision. Besides that, I just remember that this was one of those episodes where we really had to run around. A *lot*."

"General Peter McDougal" was named for series editor Heather MacDougall.

When Nathaniel Teager confronts Mrs. Davenport in front of the Vietnam Memorial, two of the names visible on the wall behind her are Jesse R. Ellison and Harlan L. Hahn. Harlan Ellison is a famous science fiction writer and fan of the show, while Jessica Hahn is well-known for the scandal involving her and Rev. Jim Baker.

A former UFO abductee is killed in a
catastrophic plane crash. Mulder
suspects a conspiracy—and a cover-up.

episode: 4X17
first aired: March 16, 1997
written by:
Chris Carter and Frank Spotnitz
editor: Heather MacDougall
directed by: Rob Bowman

guest stars:
Joe Spano (Mike Millar)
Tom O'Brien (Sergeant Louis Frish)
Scott Bellis (Max Fenig)
Chilton Crane (Sharon Graffia)
Brendan Beiser (Agent Pendrell)
Greg Michaels (Scott Garrett)
Robert Moloney (Bruce Bearfeld)
Felicia Shulman (Motel Manager)
Rick Dobran (Sergeant Armando Gonzales)
Jerry Schram (Larold Rebhun)
David Palffy (Dark Man)
Mark Wilson (Pilot)
Marek Wiedman (Investigator)
Jon Raitt (Father)
Kathy Rollheiser (Mother)
Maria Lusia Cianni (Teenager)
Peter Taraviras (Go Team Member)
Mark Schooley (Go Team Member #2)

principal settings:
Washington, D.C.; upstate New York

tempus
fugit

Somewhere over northern New York State, a Boeing 737 knifes smoothly through the night sky. It carries a nearly full load of bored, weary passengers.

In seat 13D sits Larold Rebhun, a businessman. Rebhun has had one scotch and soda too many.

In 13F, the window seat adjacent to him, sits Max Fenig—who we've seen in "Fallen Angel" (1X09). Fenig, red-bearded and bespectacled, looks very frightened. He's clutching a knapsack tightly in his lap; his face appears to have been recently burned.

Unsolicited, the well-lubricated Rebhun addresses his seatmate. "I used to be just like you," he says. "Used to hate flying. I mean, the moment I got on the plane I'd be grippin' those armrests like my teeth were being drilled. Truth is, statistically, you could fly every day for the next 26,000 years before you'd have an accident. Ya believe that?"

Fenig doesn't reply. He cranes his neck and peers apprehensively at a dark-complected man several rows in front of him. The man leaves his seat and enters a lavatory.

Inside the washroom, the Dark Man removes a pen from his pocket, disassembles it, and, combining it with some other unidentifiable parts, constructs what appears to be a plastic handgun.

As he does this, the plane begins to shimmy and shake—and then vibrate far more violently than any normal turbulence can explain.

In the cockpit, alarm bells sound and warning lights glow.

"What the hell is this!?" says the pilot.

In the passenger compartment, the shaking gets much worse. The cabin lights go off. The passengers scream.

A blast of extremely bright light shines through the forward windows, then moves aft, as if searching for something. The light nears Fenig's row. He is frozen in his seat.

The light beam reaches an emergency exit door not far from Fenig. Impossibly, the light appears to grab the door, pulling it outward from the fuselage. Light begins to show around the seams of the exit. The metal stresses and buckles as the gaps between the door and the rest of the plane begin to grow.

The light intensifies, and the plane dissolves into a white blankness.

At the Headless Woman Pub, an agreeably downscale drinking establishment in Washington, Scully and Mulder sip afterwork drinks. A trio of waiters—their leader carrying a pink Hostess Snowball topped with a glowing sparkler—advance on their table and sing "Happy Birthday" to Scully.

"Mulder, you have never remembered my birthday in the four years I have known you," says Scully.

"That's the way I like to celebrate—every four years," says Mulder. "It's like dog years."

"Dog years. Thank you," repeats Scully with all the gratitude that his simile deserves.

Undeterred, Mulder reaches down for a small, nicely wrapped gift box. "It's just something that reminded me of you," says Mulder.

"What? An alien implant?"

"Two, actually," says Mulder. "I had them made into earrings."

Inside the box is an *Apollo 11* commemorative key ring. As Scully contemplates this thoughtful but slightly bizarre gift, an attractive young blond woman kneels down beside the agents' table.

"Excuse me," says the woman. "Are you Scully? And Mulder?"

Scully rolls her eyes. "Promise me," she says to Mulder, "that this isn't leading to something embarrassing."

Mulder shakes his head in honest confusion.

"My name is Sharon Graffia," she says. "I'm sorry to approach you like this. But I followed you. I was asked to find you if something happened."

"Excuse me?" says Scully.

"You have no good reason to believe me," says Graffia, "but my brother, who I believe you know—he said you'd understand what to do."

"About what?" asks Mulder.

"If he didn't make it."

Scully says, "What are you talking about?"

"Max. Max Fenig," says his sister.

She adds, "He was on his way here, to deliver something that made him fear for his life. Something he said the government would kill for. But his plane went down two hours ago."

At a large conference room in Washington, the two dozen or so members of a National Transportation and Safety Board "Go Team"—an NTSB investigative unit on alert for major air crashes—assembles. In charge of the team is Mike Millar, a capable-looking fortyish man.

Millar announces that Flight 549 crashed several hours ago in a wooded area near Albany and that local law enforcement reports no survivors among the 134 aboard.

He plays a tape recording of the plane's last radio transmission:

"Copy, Tower," says the pilot. "Please advise. Do you see a need to adjust?"

"Negative, 549. Steady airspeed at two-niner-six knots. Maintain heading one zero zero and two niner thousand feet. Go ahead 549."

"What the hell is this?"

"549? Do you read?"

"There's something . . . an intercept . . . . My God! My God! . . . Mayday! Mayday!"

"And that's all she wrote," says Millar.

He wraps up the meeting, announcing that the team will meet next at the crash site.

Mulder, who's been standing with Scully at the back of the room, interrupts. "Excuse me, sir," he says. "I'm Special Agent Mulder, FBI. Is there any indication or suspicion that Flight 549 might have been forced down?"

"Forced down?" says Millar.

"You can clearly hear the pilot say 'intercept' on the recording," says Mulder.

Millar tells him that there was no indication of any other aircraft in the area—unless Mulder has other information.

"No," says Mulder. "But there was a passenger on that plane who was well-known to our government as an alien abductee."

The conference room breaks out into scattered guffaws and nervous chuckles.

"An alien abductee?" says Millar.

"A man named Max Fenig," says Mulder. "A multiple abduction victim. What's known as a Repeater. He predicted the accident. And from the sound of the tape, the plane may have been forced down."

The laughter and snide comments rise in volume.

"Forced down by whom? Or what?" says Millar.

"I'd hesitate to speculate," says Mulder.

Millar takes a long hard look at Mulder.

"Mulder? You're name's Mulder? Mulder, I've been doing this for eighteen years, and I thought I'd heard everything."

A Go Team member looks at a flight manifest and says that Max Fenig is not listed as a passenger. Mulder replies that someone may be covering up the evidence.

"Agent Mulder—is this an official FBI position?" says Millar.

"No, sir," he says.

"Because what you're suggesting trivializes this tragedy and casts these fine people and the work they have to do in a light I think you'd be well advised to avoid."

"I think we all share the same goal here, sir," says Mulder. "And that is to find out what caused that plane to crash."

Millar says, "If any of the capable people in this room find Dr. Spock's phaser or any green alien goo, we'll be sure to give you all the credit."

Mulder does not reply.

The crash site is a scene of utter devastation. Little of the smoking wreckage is even identifiable as being from an airplane: small red flags mark the spot where bodies and body parts have been found. Some victims have already been placed in yellow body bags—a long row of them stretch along the side of an adjacent road. Dozens of NTSB workers, many wearing face masks, go about their work somberly but efficiently.

Scully and Mulder, obviously affected by the horror they're witnessing, survey the scene. Scully tells Mulder that the crash is being initially attributed to rapid decompression caused by a vortex of wind coming over the Adirondacks.

"But not to Max Fenig," says Mulder.

Scully grimaces. She protests that even if Fenig were on the flight, he'd be in pieces so small that identification would be impossible.

"He was on this flight, Scully. I'm sure of that," says Mulder.

"But say we do find him," says Scully. "What's that going to prove?"

"I don't know. But maybe that one man's life was worth sacrificing for 133 others."

Elsewhere at the crash site two investigators—one, whose name is Garrett, we've seen at the Go Team meeting—locate a body below a piece of wreckage.

It is the Dark Man. Garrett pulls the plastic handgun out of the dead man's pocket. His companion sprays something on the corpse's fingertips and burned face.

The sprayed flesh begins to bubble and melt.

In another quadrant, Scully finds a charred arm with a wristwatch on it protruding from the wreckage. Close by,

Mulder finds another wristwatch and picks it up. Mulder joins Scully. Both watches read 8:01.

"What are they saying was the time of the crash?" says Mulder.

"Seven fifty-two P.M.," says Scully.

"That's nine minutes difference," says Mulder. "Nine minutes, Scully. Do you remember the last time you were missing nine minutes?"

Scully protests that the official crash time is just an estimate.

"You know, something just occurred to me," says Mulder. "We're not going to find Max Fenig after all."

Scully says, "Just a few minutes ago you were absolutely certain he was on this flight."

"Yeah. But I'm beginning to doubt that he finished this flight with the rest of the passengers."

Behind them an investigator calls out urgently for a doctor. Scully runs over. On the ground is Rebhun, the drunken passenger—still alive, but barely. His face now bears the same burn scars as the Dark Man.

At a small private airport nearby, Scully awaits the nighttime arrival of a chartered Cessna. Sharon Graffia is its only passenger; she emerges with several suitcases filled with every letter her brother Max has ever written to her. Scully tells her that several passengers on Flight 549 were suffering from severe radiation burns. She warns Graffia that withholding information—especially about what Fenig might have been carrying on the flight—could have severe consequences.

Inside a large hangar, the crash investigators are reassembling the pieces of the 737. Mulder runs a Geiger counter over two burned and twisted airplane seats. There is a spike of sound each time he passes them over. Scully, newly arrived, joins him.

Mulder says that Larold Rebhun—and his seat number—have been identified.

"My guess," he says, "is that Max Fenig was in 13F. The window seat. But the manifest has the passenger in that seat as a—"

"Paul Gidney," says Scully. "It's one of many aliases used in his letters when he went underground."

Scully adds that under another alias Fenig got a job at the Rocky Flats Environmental Energy sit in Colorado—where they handle weapons-grade uranium and plutonium. He wrote thousands of letters; beginning in January, there were many vague references to a theft—of something he knew was very dangerous.

"If he was carrying fissile plutonium," says Scully, "and it became exposed in the cabin inadvertently, it could conceivably have caused the crash."

Mulder, his Geiger counter still chirping, is unconvinced.

"You want to know what I think, Scully?" he says. "I'll tell you. I think Max was abducted—sucked right out of this door at 29,000 feet, and the burns we're seeing are a result of that abduction."

Scully tries to break in. Mulder won't let her.

"I think all the evidence will point to this conclusion," he says. "But it will be dismissed because of its improbability, its unthinkability—"

"Mulder!"

"—and the crash of Fight 549 will go unsolved, unless we find a way to prove it. And when Max is returned, he's going to tell us exactly the same story—unless someone gets to him first."

Scully finally gets a word in edgewise.

"Mulder. Max *has* returned," she says. "I found out a few minutes ago. They found his body a short way from the wreckage earlier today. Traveling under the name Paul Gidney. Seat 13F."

In her room at a local motel, Sharon Graffia sits sifting through her brother's letters. Bright lights suddenly sweep through the windows around her, terrifying her. The room begins to shake. A wind from no source starts to ruffle the papers lying about. Now an invisible vacuum begins to suck everything toward the front door. The room dissolves into whiteness.

At a makeshift morgue filled with scores of body bags and distraught, grieving relatives, Mulder examines the body of "Paul Gidney." Max Fenig's face is indeed badly burned. In the dead man's pocket is a bloodstained FBI business card—Mulder's.

The agent agonizes over this for a few minutes. He zips closed Fenig's body bag and checks several other bodies, seemingly at random.

At the reassembly hangar, a small knot of Go Team members are conferring. Scully monitors their conversation.

When Mulder strides past, she tells him that the NTSB, while acknowledging problems with the emergency exit and the presence of radiation burns, aren't ready to attribute them as a direct cause of the crash.

"They're not able to or they're not willing to?" asks Mulder contemptuously.

Scully says, "Mulder, why can't you just accept the facts?"

"There *are* no facts, Scully. What they're telling you, what they're going to report—they're the opposite of the facts. They're a claim of ignorance of the facts. Claimed steadfastly, ignorance becomes as acceptable as the truth."

"What would you like them to report?" asks Scully.

"That there is not one wristwatch on any of those bagged bodies," says Mulder. "All the wristwatches have been stolen."

He adds that the crash investigators, hardworking experts though they may be, are not seeing the real picture. Mulder motions toward the wrecked plane.

"They're trained to reconstruct those parts and the past to arrive at the present," he says. "But someone has stolen the past from them. Nine minutes of it. Nine minutes that became a lifetime for those passengers, and now for their families.

"Somehow, someone has to figure out what went on in those nine minutes. Somehow, we've got to get that back."

At an Air Force Reserve airfield along Flight 549's flight path, Scully and Mulder question Sergeant Louis Frish, one of two air traffic controllers on duty in the control tower the night of the crash.

Frish tells the agents what he's already told the NTSB investigators: They saw Flight 549 disappear from their radar screens and, since it was a civilian plane, they had no radio contact with it. When Scully and Mulder drive away, another sergeant—Armando Gonzales—emerges from the control tower.

"What did you tell them?" asks Gonzales.

"What I was supposed to say," says Frish.

Gonzales says worriedly, "Somebody's gonna figure out what's goin' on."

"I don't ask. I don't know. I don't want to know," says Frish bitterly.

Gonzales, panicking, complains that when the truth comes out they'll take the heat. He declares that if the investigators come back, he'll tell them the truth.

This angers Frish. He grabs his partner by the lapels.

"Then you make *me* the liar," he says, and stalks away.

At Sharon Graffia's motel the manager complains to Scully and Mulder—whose name is on the registration—that Sharon has trashed her room and disappeared.

"Look at this!" says the manager. "I don't know what kinda games she was playing in here. She blew the door right outta the jamb. I doubt insurance will cover it."

Mulder says, deadpan, "Does your policy cover the acts of extraterrestrials?"

Mike Millar arrives. He surveys the room—including the empty door frame. Some of his former disdain for Mulder is gone.

"I've come to tell you we've found some evidence. Good evidence," he says.

"About what caused the crash?" asks Scully.

"Quite possibly. But I'm not ready to make an announcement."

"Why not?" says Mulder.

"I'm afraid I'd sound as crazy as you."

Millar shows the agents X-ray pictures of the jetliner's emergency exit door. Jagged stress cracks—never seen in new aircraft, as was Flight 549—run across it.

"The way these cracks radiate from a central point," says Millar, "it looks like the door's been shaken and blown outward—straight off its frame and right off the plane. If it hadn't been for you, we wouldn't have known what to look for."

"Sounds like what you're describing," says Scully, "is physically impossible."

"In normal operation it could never happen, not this way," says Millar.

Mulder says, "But it did."

At the Air Force Reserve control tower, Louis Frish arrives for his evening shift. Armando Gonzales is sitting at the console, his back to his partner.

Frish apologizes for his outburst of the night before.

"I was way outta line," he says. "I was just lettin' this thing get to me, I guess."

Gonzales does not respond. Frish spins his chair around—the sergeant is holding an automatic pistol in his hand. There is a bullet hole through the center of his forehead. Frish is terrified; through the window, he spots a line of headlights coming toward the tower.

Garrett and a squad of commandos enter the base of the tower. They search for Frish in vain. The sergeant is crouched out of sight, nauseous with fear, on the roof of the control tower cab.

In his motel room, Mulder listens, eyes closed, to the audiotape of Flight 549's last moments. Something clicks, and he picks up the phone to dial Scully's room.

"Hey, Scully, it's me," he says. "I just realized something. The voice of the air traffic controller. I've heard it before."

"Mulder, we've been up for thirty-six hours."

"I know, I know, I know, I know. I just need you to come over here and listen to this right now, okay?"

Scully pulls on her overcoat and walks down the outside corridor to Mulder's room. A hand reaches out, grabs her from behind, and covers her mouth. A man steps from the shadows. It is Louis Frish.

"Don't scream. Just listen to me!" he says in an anguished whisper. "I'm the one responsible. I caused that plane crash."

At the reassembly hangar, Scully and Mulder introduce Frish—as the real final controller of Flight 549—to Millar.

"I was asked to lie," says Frish. "I was ordered to lie about what happened to Flight 549."

"By whom?" says Millar.

"By my CO," says Frish. "Flight 549 appeared on my radar at nineteen hundred hours when we were asked to give its coordinates at fifteen-second intervals. About two minutes past thirty degrees north, we saw a second aircraft enter 549's airspace in an intercept pattern. It shadowed 549 for another ten minutes before we were asked for another set of coordinates.

"A few seconds later, there was an explosion and 549 disappeared from my screen."

Millar is unwilling to accept this scenario—or the level of official deception needed to carry it off. He insists that there is no forensic evidence to support Frish's account.

"The military is working to cover up that evidence," insists Mulder.

Millar replies, "The sergeant's story makes no sense."

Mulder says, "Unless the aircraft that was fired on didn't appear on his radar screen. A third, unidentified aircraft that engaged the civilian jet—which the sergeant never saw."

"A stealth aircraft?" says Millar.

Mulder nods.

"Shot down by the intercept aircraft," he says, "which in turn might have caused the crash of Flight 549. Which means that the cause of the crash is not in this hangar—it's out there somewhere at a second crash site."

Scully protests that someone would have spotted a second crash.

No, replies Mulder, because nobody except the military plotters knew to look for it.

"Which means this man's life is in danger," he says, indicating Frish. "Because he can put the pieces together."

"Then somebody has to get him someplace safe," says Scully, finally on board.

"If there's a second crash site," says Millar, at long last bending just a little, "let's find it."

The agents and Frish leave the hangar and get into their rental car. As they pull away, they notice bright headlights in their rearview. The are being followed.

Mulder guns the engine and leads a high-speed chase around the airport's runways and taxiways. Mulder shakes off his pursuers by driving directly toward—and underneath—a jet accelerating to flying speed on its takeoff run. Then they drive off into the night.

At the dark and deserted crash site, Mike Millar leaves his car and stares at the horizon. In the distance, a strange, triangular-shaped craft is hovering. A beam of light from its underbelly stabs into the ground.

Millar runs toward this vision. As he gets closer to the alien ship, its light snaps off—and it vanishes completely.

The light snaps on again—directly at Millar, blinding him. The spaceship is overhead, freezing the lone man in its beam.

The impossibly bright light snaps off. Faster than is possible, the craft zips off into the night and disappears.

"Somebody help me! Please!"

A woman's voice, hysterical, is coming from somewhere close to Millar. He stumbles across the field and finds Sharon Graffia. She has seen something very frightening, and her face is covered with tears. He takes her into his arms.

"Please don't let them take me again!" she says. She breaks down into wrenching sobs.

At the private airport, Scully bundles Frish into a small plane; she will accompany him on the flight to Washington. As the plane's engine warms up, Mulder and Frish examine a map to figure out potential crash sites for a second aircraft. They agree that nearby Great Sacandaga Lake is a good possibility—if only because a crash onto water would leave little evidence.

That night Mulder drives to a fishing lodge located at the edge of the lake. He rouses the proprietor, a man named Bruce Bearfeld. Mulder identifies himself as an FBI agent.

"You got anything to do with what's going on out there?" asks Bearfeld.

"What's going on out there?" says Mulder.

"Some kind of search-and-rescue operation or some damn thing."

"Where?"

"Out over Democrat Point. Some kind of hovering lights. There and then gone."

This gets Mulder's undivided attention. His head snaps around toward the fishing guide.

"Can you show me?" he asks.

Bearfeld points toward the center of the lake.

"No," says Mulder. "I need you to take me."

Scully and Frish enter the FBI agent's Washington apartment. Scully promises to set up a protective arrangement for the air traffic controller; she will then arrange for him to be interviewed by "the right people."

"Do you think I'll be prosecuted?" asks Frish.

"For what?" says Scully, startled.

Frish confesses his guilt at being involved in the death of 134 passengers—plus his friend Sergeant Gonzales. The memory of the jetliner dropping off his radar screen still haunts him. And, he says, he also regrets that he initially lied to and misled the crash investigators.

Scully tries to assure him that he is not to blame. "It wasn't your fault, Louis," she says.

She adds, "Look, I can't tell you how to feel. But I can tell you that I will do everything I can to make sure you tell your story to somebody who will do the right thing."

Frish asks permission to call his girlfriend and tell her that he's safe. Sympathetically, Scully agrees.

On a small powerboat in the middle of Great Sacandaga Lake, Mulder—in full scuba gear—probes the surface of the water with a searchlight.

"How deep is it here?" asks Mulder.

"Fifty or sixty, maybe," says Bearfeld. "You worked at this depth before?"

Mulder lowers his face mask and perches on the boat's gunwale. "Not exactly," he says.

"What exactly is your experience?" asks Bearfeld

"Once," says Mulder, "I got a quarter off the deep end at the Y pool."

He tumbles backward into the black depths.

"Last call, folks!" says the bartender at the Headless Woman Pub.

Scully escorts Frish to a table, then goes to the bar to get him a drink. Sitting at the bar is Agent Pendrell, who is feeling no pain.

"Hey, birthday girl!" says Pendrell.

The FBI man, his inhibitions lowered, offers to buy Scully a drink. He swallows his disappointment when Scully tells him she is "with someone."

"Then lemme buy him a drink, too!" he says.

Scully walks back to the table. Pendrell waits for the drinks, then walks toward where Scully and Frish are sitting. From her seat, Scully spots Scott Garrett at the other end of the room. He is aiming his handgun at Frish.

"Get down!" shouts Scully.

Frish ducks under the table. Scully draws her weapon.

Still carrying the drinks, Pendrell walks right into the line of fire. Garrett's shot hits Pendrell in the torso. Scully returns fire, hitting Garrett in the leg. The panicked crowd shields him from Scully's view.

She kneels over Pendrell, who is seriously wounded.

"You're going to keep breathing, Pendrell!" she says. "Do you hear me?"

In the dark murky water, Mulder swims downward, his flashlight aimed at the lake bottom. He approaches a piece of unidentifiable wreckage, from which a dim glow of light emits. It becomes a trail of wreckage, which he follows slowly to its source. His flashlight beam falls on a gray alien face.

He recoils.

An impossibly intense light source from the surface stabs downward, finding Mulder. The lone swimmer turns toward it, frozen in its beam.

To be continued . . .

back story:

At one point during the past couple of years, Scott Bellis auditioned for a small part as an FBI agent on *The X-Files*. No dice. "Chris took one look at me and said no," says the thirty-one-year old Vancouver-based actor. "He said that people's memories of my other role were too strong."

His "other" role, of course, was Max Fenig, the UFO-obsessed fanatic whom he played during the first season's "Fallen Angel" (1X09). After that

episode, Carter submitted Bellis for a guest actor Emmy nomination. In the years that followed, Bellis—a husband and father of two young daughters who specializes in playing gentle eccentrics—kept running into David Duchovny at his gym; having encouraging conversations with his fellow actor; and hearing enticing rumors that Max would eventually resurface.

This being *The X-Files*, the rumors were correct. In November of 1996, the producers notified Bellis's agent that they wanted him to guest star as Max—and in a two-part episode, no less. Then—again true to form—they told him nothing more until February, approximately one week before "Tempus Fugit" was to begin filming.

Explains coproducer Frank Spotnitz, the episodes' cowriter: "At the beginning of the fourth season, Chris had the idea of bringing Max back in the plane crash episode. I liked that—I knew it would add to Mulder's emotional involvement in the crash to have someone he knew aboard. But I didn't want to bring him back in a way that milked his character or revisited something we'd already done. But then I thought: What a bold choice to bring him back—and kill him immediately! That's why by the first act you know he's dead."

Once ensconced on the set (and surrounded by many of the people with whom he'd worked on "Fallen Angel"), Bellis found little in his original conception of Max that needed changing. "On 'Fallen Angel' my instructions were that ultimately they wanted the audience to like the character," he says. "I made him neurotic, but not in an aggressive way that made him seem dangerous and dark."

For "Tempus Fugit" and "Max," adds Bellis, he made the choice—due to the dire nature of the conspiracy Max was involved in—to make the character slightly more serious. He spent much of his time working with the second unit on his posthumous videotape; he improvised the odd giggles and vocal mannerisms on the spot.

For his airplane abduction scenes, Bellis was rigged up in a harness, then yanked out by a crane through an opening in the cabin mockup. "Then," he adds, "they did the same thing with a stunt man—they yanked him a *lot* harder."

For his efforts on the two-parter, says Bellis, he received a fine credit for his résumé, some good scenes for his demo reel, occasional recognition on the street, and a few scattered fan letters—most asking about the mechanics of how Max was levitated into oblivion.

Fenigian typecasting doesn't bother him, he says. "I usually play characters where it's not really clear that the producers don't know what they're looking for," says Bellis (who notes here that he once portrayed "a mute street urchin who witnessed a murder" on *MacGyver*). "I fill in the gap."

As for Max Fenig, Bellis says he still hasn't quite crossed him out of his future plans. "Somebody told me once that the whole scene on the airplane was just Mulder's *theory* of what happened," says the actor. "So you never really know. Or do you?"

The wife of Scott Bellis—actress Sandra Ferens—played a murder victim during the first season of *Millennium*.

Ⓧ

For their work on "Tempus Fugit" twelve members of the *X-Files* post-production crew—Thierry J. Couturier, Stuart Calderon, Ira Leslie, Maciek Malish, Debby Ruby-Winsburg, Chris Fradkin, Jay Levine, Chris Reeves, Susan Welsh, Jeff Charbonneau, Gary Marullo, Mike Salvetta—won the Emmy Award for Best Sound Editing, Series.

Ⓧ

Character Larold Rebhun, the sole survivor of the crash, who sat next to Max and witnessed his abduction, is named for *X-Files* mix meister Larold Rebhun.

Ⓧ

max

Mulder and Scully get close to proving
alien involvement in the crash of
Flight 549. As they do so, they trigger
a massive military disinformation
campaign—and the deaths of several
friends and colleagues.

episode: 4X18

first aired: March 23, 1997

written by:
Chris Carter and Frank Spotnitz

editor: Michael S. Stern

Directed by: Kim Manners

guest stars:
Mitch Pileggi (AD Walter Skinner)
Joe Spano (Mike Millar)
Tom O'Brien (Sergeant Louis Frish)
Scott Bellis (Max Fenig)
Chilton Crane (Sharon Graffia)
Brendan Beiser (Agent Pendrell)
Greg Michaels (Scott Garrett)
John Destrey (Mr. Ballard)
Rick Dobran (Sergeant Armando Gonzales)
David Palffy (Dark Man)
Jerry Schram (Larold Rebhun)
Stewart Laine (MP)
Stacy Fair (Flight Attendant)
Vladimir Stefoff (Bartender)
Brayden Kayce (Airport Security Officer)
Jaclynn Grad (Stewardess)
Dave Hannay (Waiter #1)
Michael Short (Waiter #2)
Regy Sayhay (Waiter #3)

principal settings:
Washington, D.C.;
upstate New York

Sixty feet below the surface of Great Sacandaga Lake—and several feet above a crashed alien craft from "Tempus Fugit" (4X17)— Mulder stares into a bright light shining down from above. A second beam hits him. Then there is movement.

Two frogmen enter the water and kick downward toward Mulder. Mulder sheds his scuba tank and regulator and swims away from them, surfacing several hundred feet from his entry point. He looks back to where his small boat is anchored. A much larger, sleeker powerboat is anchored next to it.

Mulder swims toward shore. Another craft pursues him; its spotlight finds him as he staggers onto a beach and kicks off his flippers. A Humvee roars out of the darkness and chases him across the sand. A squad of black-clad commandos knock him down and aim their assault rifles at his head. He lies on the ground, gasping for breath.

At the Headless Woman Pub in Washington, Scully ministers to the wounded Pendrell.

"We've got paramedics on the way," says Scully forcefully. "You're going to the hospital. You're going to be okay."

The expression on a bystander's face indicates otherwise.

Scully says, desperately feigning a lack of concern, "We still haven't celebrated my birthday, Pendrell. I'm not going to let you off the hook like this."

Pendrell is carried off to an ambulance. Scott Garrett, the shooter, has escaped; a trail of blood leads out the front door. Scully's nose begins to bleed (see "Memento Mori" [4X15]).

Louis Frish—the air traffic controller involved in the cover-up of the crash of Flight 549—looks on with heightened concern. He tells Scully that he hasn't told anyone that he is in Washington. She concludes that the military conspirators have an informant inside the Bureau.

Skinner arrives at the scene. "What happened to Sean Pendrell?" he says.

"I don't know," says Scully bleakly.

The assistant director is not pleased with her answer. "I got a call about a federal witness being transferred," he says.

"Sergeant Louis Frish," says Scully. "He was the intended target. There was supposed to be a federal marshall here to put the sergeant into protective custody."

"That order was countermanded," says Skinner.

"By whom?" says Scully angrily.

Skinner tells Scully that Frish is being put under military arrest for providing false testimony in a federal investigation. The arrest order came directly from the Joint Chiefs of Staff.

Mulder has also been put under military arrest. The charge against him is "interfering with the military investigation of the crash of a civilian airliner."

Scully is outraged. "Sir, the military is *responsible* for the downing of that plane."

"They are admitting as much," says Skinner. "But Sergeant Frish's story is not the one they're telling."

"What is their story?" asks Scully.

At the Air Force Reserve base near the crash site in upstate New York, Mulder is released from military custody just as Scully arrives to meet him.

"You springin' me from the joint?" says Mulder.

"I came to talk to you," says Scully.

"About what?" says Mulder sarcastically. "A 'big ol' misunderstanding'?"

"According to the military," says Scully, "there was no misunderstanding."

To a highly skeptical Mulder, she repeats the military's new explanation: Frish and Gonzales mistakenly vectored an Air Force F-15 Eagle fighter toward the civilian airliner, which was not visible on their radar screen until it was too late. The jets collided, a distraught Gonzales committed suicide, and Frish lied again to Scully and Mulder—concocting a false scenario to deflect criticism from himself.

"That's why they pursued him," says Scully, clearly struggling to believe this explanation. "So they could bring him to justice."

"Then they could conveniently lay the blame on a dead man," says Mulder.

"Yes," says Scully unhappily.

"Do you believe that story, Scully?" asks Mulder.

Scully says, "I don't know what to believe."

Mulder shows Scully a radiation burn on his forehead. He explains it by describing his underwater encounter with the crashed UFO. The "second plane," he says, was actually the alien craft—shot down by the military, taking the passenger plane with it.

Scully protests that there is absolutely no physical evidence supporting the theory that Flight 549 was involved in a collision.

"According to who?" says Mulder.

"Mike Millar, the IIC," says Scully. "The man running the crash investigation."

"How do you know he's not lying?"

"I don't. Except he seems to be the one man who truly wants to figure out who downed that plane. And who came to me with information he had no reason to have."

Scully describes Millar's strange encounter at the crash site with Sharon Graffia.

"Max Fenig's sister?" says Mulder.

"That's another thing, Mulder," says Scully. "She's not his sister."

Scully tells him that Sharon Graffia is actually an unemployed aeronautical engineer who's spent time in and out of mental institutions—which is where she met Fenig. She also tells him that Agent Pendrell is dead—and how he died. Mulder is genuinely shocked. Scully is near tears.

"What are these people dying for?" she says. "Is it for the truth? Or for the lies?"

"It's got to be for the truth," says Mulder. "If we owe them anything, it's to make sure of that."

At a rather scraggly looking trailer park elsewhere in New York State, the agents search Max Fenig's home—a cramped Airstream trailer whose interior walls are almost completely covered with pictures, clippings, and miscellaneous notes to himself.

"You've got to admit," says Mulder, poker-faced, "the man had an enduring sense of style."

Scully replies, "Only Max Fenig and you would appreciate living like this."

Scully runs her finger across Fenig's dust-layered stereo system, then clicks the

PLAY button on his tape machine. Soul Coughing's "Unmarked Helicopters" blasts forth. After a few seconds, she clicks the music off.

"I think you were actually kindred spirits in some deep, strange way," says Scully.

"How do you mean?" asks Mulder.

"Men with Spartan lives. Simple in their creature comforts, if only to allow for the complexity of their passions."

Mulder's passions are indeed inflamed by a can of food he finds on Max's kitchen counter.

"Mmm. Beans and weenies!" he says.

Scully asks her partner what they're searching for.

"Something to explain what Max was doing on that plane. What he was coming to show me, or tell me."

"What makes you think that Max was coming to see you?"

Mulder shows her the bloodstained business card he found on Max's body.

"Max is the key to all this," says Mulder. "He knew that flight was imperiled even before it entered military airspace, before it even took off."

"How would he know that? And what would be worth taking that risk?"

Mulder rummages around Fenig's desk and finds a videocassette. He pops it into a VCR. Max—standing outside the trailer—appears on the screen.

Someone else is holding the video camera, somewhat shakily. As the tape rolls, the agents watch the red-bearded, mid-thirtyish eccentric deliver his spiel. Max says:

"Hi. Max here—but of course. This is, uh, well, quite obviously my story since I'm telling it. Heh heh. Anyway, for those of you who know me already, this is gonna be ancient history. But for the rest of you, this is, well, what can I say, the story of my life. Actually, all I ever wanted in life was to be left alone. Hah! Don't we all. Uh, so it's just my luck that I'd eventually become an alien abductee! Now I'm never alone. Any minute, when I'm least expecting it—and the worst part is, no one

believes you! Well, almost no one. Heh heh. So I've devoted my life to providing all you disbelievers out there with proof. Proof that there are extraterrestrial, biological entities, right now as we speak, visiting our planet in alien ships, for purposes of a rather troubling agenda known only to certain members of the government, the FBI, and certain high-ranking members of the military-industrial community—"

At the lakeside crash recovery site, platoons of black-clad military men, working under a large tent, are laying out pieces of UFO wreckage. Several filled body bags are laid out on the ground. A grayish alien body is zipped into another.

Inside the Airstream, Max rambles on:

"—who have recovered some of these very craft. Not that they would ever admit to it publicly, of course. Nor would they admit that they have salvaged some of this alien technology and are using it in military applications. No, that would be un-American! And they won't admit it until someone confronts them with irrefutable, undeniable proof. Someone like me. And, uh, I should probably mention that I do this at great risk to my own health and safety, But hey! Hah! When every day's just another day when you might get kidnapped by a bunch of little gray dudes from outer space, what's a few CIA spooks to worry about?"

At the recovery site, a military diver, retching and covered with radiation burns, is helped by other soldiers into the tent. A frogman in even worse shape is carried in on a stretcher. A mustachioed man, bleeding slightly through his pants leg, stands over the dying men.

"We found it," says Scott Garrett.

In the airport hangar where the pieces of the jetliner have been reassembled, Mike Millar gathers the members of his investigative team around him and tells them, sadly, that the evidence they've gathered can neither prove nor disprove the Air Force's explanation. He thanks them for their hard work and sends them home.

Scully and Mulder arrive for one last meeting with Millar. They share their suspicions that the Air Force explanation is a cover-up.

"Of what?" asks Millar.

Mulder says, "Agent Scully and I agree on some of the motives, but not exactly on the facts."

"Do you have facts that I don't?" asks Millar.

"No," says Mulder, "but I do have a story, if you want to hear it. Feel free to tell me it's bull, as Agent Scully has, but I think it's as believable as any story I've heard floated. At least it's the only one that can't be refuted by the facts."

Millar looks around to see the last of his investigators leaving the building. "All right," he says reluctantly.

Mulder tells his story to Millar. This is his theory of the crash:

"There was one man who knew what brought this plane down. And he knew it even before he got on the plane. But he got on anyway. He sat right here in this seat, 13F. His name was Max Fenig. There are a number of possibilities for Max's suspicions, but I believe Max had been followed for some time before he boarded Flight 549. And I believe he was followed onto this plane, by someone who wanted whatever it is Max had carried on board with him—the object that ultimately brought down this plane. The cause which has eluded you."

Intrigued despite himself, Millar follows Mulder as he walks through the wreckage.

"What was this object?" asks the investigator.

Mulder says, "Physical proof of the existence of extraterrestrial life and intelligence."

He continues:

"The person who followed Max on the plane may have been prepared to kill to obtain this object. Its value greater than one human life. Greater than the lives of the 134 people on that plane. Whether that plan was executed we may never know. Because Flight 549 was intercepted by a second aircraft. An aircraft which did not appear on the military's or anyone else's radar screen. Max Fenig knew immediately what this craft was—and that he would not be completing the rest of the flight as scheduled. Max would have recognized immediately all the signs of a classic abduction scenario: The craft taking control of the plane and all its systems—and preparing to take Max. But something happened. Something went terribly wrong. Something unimaginable. A third aircraft, probably an F-15 Eagle, was given the coordinates for Flight 549."

Inside the Air Force Reserve base control tower—in flashback—Sergeants Gonzales and Frish see the blip representing Flight 549 crawl across their radar screen.

"Heading one zero zero and two niner thousand feet," radios Frish.

Mulder again:

"The flight controllers watched the fighter enter Flight 549's airspace on an intercept pattern. Not knowing what they had set in motion. No way of knowing there was a third craft which was not on their screen. Not knowing for the next nine minutes time would stand still on Flight 549."

Somewhere over upstate New York, Flight 549—again, in flashback—is nearing its conclusion. When the light beam reaches Max Fenig's row, the violent shaking stops and a deadly calm falls over the passengers. Max, clutching his knapsack tightly to his chest, goes into a seizure. He is lifted from his seat chest first—drawn by the force of the beam.

The Dark Man pulls out his plastic handgun and aims it at Max. He pulls the trigger, but it does not fire.

Max is slowly pulled through the open emergency exit. He disappears into the intense glow.

Mulder:

"If not for factors unforeseen, I believe Max Fenig would have been abducted and returned to Flight 549. Without any loss of life. Without a trace. *But flight 549 and the alien craft which had taken control of it were intercepted. By the military fighter which had been given a specific set of orders—to take down the UFO. The missing nine minutes aboard Flight 549—nine minutes which would have been erased form the memories of the 134 passengers on board—would prove to be the final minutes of their lives."*

On Frish and Gonzales's radar screen, the blips of the jetliner and the fighter plane converge.

Inside the jetliner, the passengers are in a trancelike state. Max floats back through the hatch and toward his seat. He never reaches it. There is a muffled explosion, and the light beam goes out.

Fenig is sucked out through the door, and the plane, in the throes of a catastrophic decompression, goes into a violent, turbulent descent.

Everything not bolted down—magazines, newspapers, human beings—fly out into the stratosphere. Standing passengers are swept into the aisle. Seated passengers suck desperately at their emergency air masks. Friends, couples, and strangers—knowing death is imminent—link hands across the aisle.

On the Air Force radar screen, Flight 549's altitude readout blinks to triple zero.

The action of "Max" (4X18) resumes: In the reassembly hangar, Mike Millar takes a long, hard look at Mulder and speaks slowly and carefully.

"You're saying, in effect," he says, "that Flight 549 was in the grip of a sort of UFO tractor beam."

"That's a Hollywood term," says Mulder. "But yes."

"And the Air Force shot down the UFO, thereby sending 549 out of control when the beam went off?"

"Yes."

Millar thinks, blinks, and reaches a decision. "Well, where I come from," he says, "that's what we call a whopper."

He adds, "Even if it were true, I couldn't in a million years sell that to Washington. And neither could you."

Mulder concedes as much.

"Not without the object that Max Fenig was carrying," he says.

Scully tells Millar that she agrees with his conclusion—except that nobody can explain the traces of radioactivity on the plane's seats and door.

"You found nothing in the wreckage?" she asks. "No source of any emitter?"

Millar blinks again. "I did find something," he says. "I think you should look at it."

He walks the agents over to his car and opens the trunk. He lifts out a small knapsack. It is Max Fenig's, and it is empty.

Millar leaves.

Scully tells her partner that his story is shaky and that they may never find out what Max was carrying.

"Then we may never know who killed Agent Pendrell," says Mulder. "And if we don't find out, what meaning do their deaths have? Or their lives? Max Fenig will be remembered as a disappointing rummage sale, or some kook on a home video."

He suggests they resume their quest by interviewing Sharon Graffia.

Scully grimaces. "She's a disturbed person, Mulder," she says. "She isn't even who she claimed to be."

She also tells Mulder that the woman is currently in a mental institution. Strangely—or perhaps not—this doesn't register with Mulder as bad news.

"I'd go with you," he says breezily, "but I'm afraid they'd lock me up."

"Me too," says Scully resignedly.

Mulder revisits Max's Airstream. "Unmarked Helicopters" booms out of the stereo speakers; Max's video plays on the TV. The place has obviously been ransacked. The trailer park's manager, a Mr. Ballard, enters. Mulder identifies himself as an FBI agent and tells him that Max Fenig is dead.

Ballard is shocked by the news. He says he genuinely liked his eccentric tenant.

"Have you any idea of who's going to be taking care of his estate?" says Ballard. "Where should I forward his mail?"

"He has mail?"

"Yeah. A small stack of it."

Ballard leaves to empty Max's mailbox. Mulder carefully freeze-frames Max's video and sees the reflection of the camera person in the trailer window. It is Sharon Graffia.

Ballard returns and hands Mulder a stack of letters. The first piece of correspondence is from "Paul Gidney"—Max's alias. Mulder opens it. Inside is a luggage claim ticket.

At a mental institution in Georgetown, Scully visits Sharon Graffia. The young woman, despondent, sits in a dark room. She confesses sadly that's she's not Max Fenig's sister.

"I know," says Scully. "I'm not quite sure why you lied to us, Sharon. Or what else you might be lying about."

"It doesn't matter anymore," says Sharon,

"Yes, it does," says Scully. "If you know anything about what Max was doing, what he was carrying on that plane, it could mean a lot."

"To who?"

"To Max."

Sharon's eyes well up and she turns away. Scully snaps on a nearby table lamp. The woman's face is red and blistered.

"Max had those same blisters," she says. "You both were exposed to something. What was it?"

"It was something I stole," says Sharon.

"From whom?"

Sharon admits that when she was working as an aeronautical engineer, she stole something from her employer. Something radioactive.

"Only because I believed in Max," she says. "Max said it was alien technology. It was three interlocking parts. We divided it into sections. I had one part, Max had another on board that flight."

"There was a third part," says Scully. "What happened to it?"

At Hancock International Airport in Syracuse, New York, Mulder hands in the claim check to a security guard. Mulder turns around; several black-suited men are obviously following him. The officer gives him a small knapsack identical to the one Millar gave him. He turns again. The men are still there.

He flashes his FBI credentials.

"I'm a federal officer," he says. "I need a security entrance to the terminal."

He is escorted through the baggage claim area. The black-suited men follow him. His phone rings. It is Scully.

"Mulder, what you're carrying was stolen from a military contractor—Cummins Aerospace," she says.

"What is it?" he says.

"I don't know," says Scully.

"Well," says Mulder, "I'll let you know in a minute."

He starts to open the knapsack. For some reason there is interference on their phone connection.

"Mulder, it is extremely important that you do not take it out of its container."

"What's that? I'm having trouble hearing you on the phone here."

"Mulder, did you hear what I said?"

"No. Hold on a second. I'm going to tell you what it looks like."

"No, no, no! Mulder—do not handle it. Whatever it is, it is highly radioactive."

"Hold on a second," says Mulder.

As Scully sweats bullets, Mulder places the knapsack—unopened—onto the conveyor belt of an airport security machine.

"It looks like a small superstructure with three circular pieces inside. It's hard to tell on an X ray."

Scully breathes again.

She tells Mulder that they've encountered a case of high-tech industrial espionage. Mulder asks Scully to meet his flight in Washington.

He boards the plane, his only baggage the knapsack. Already seated in the cabin is Scott Garrett, Pendrell's killer.

The plane is well on its way when Garrett approaches Mulder's seat. "Excuse me," he says. "You look like you've got some room here. You mind?"

"Go ahead," says Mulder sleepily.

Garrett sits in the aisle seat; Mulder has the window. He tries to make small talk. But Mulder—who notices blood seeping through the man's pants leg—has him made.

"You live in D.C.?" asks Garrett.

"I've got this weapon pointed at you right now," whispers Mulder. "At this range, I'm pretty sure that it wouldn't just hit you in the leg. If you so much as raise your arms off the armrests, I'm going to test that theory."

"What if you miss?" asks Garrett.

"I won't."

Garrett describes to Mulder the catastrophic results of a bullet hole in the fuselage—and the subsequent catastrophic depressurization. He says he's equipped with a lightweight parachute for just such an event. He's prepared to grab the knapsack and jump.

"What if the pilot can't keep control of the plane?" says Mulder.

Garrett says, "A man, if he's any man at

all, knows he must be ready to sacrifice himself to that which is greater than he."

Mulder looks at him with contempt. "I'm sure that the other passengers on the plane would appreciate dying for your noble philosophy," he says.

Garrett says, "Look out your window, Agent Mulder. You see the lights? Now imagine if one of those lights flickered off. You'd hardly notice, would you? A dozen, two dozen lights extinguished—is it worth sacrificing the future, the lives of millions? To keep a few lights on?"

Mulder's eyes flick toward the knapsack. "What is this?" he asks.

"Stolen property."

"It's an alien energy source, isn't it?" says Mulder. "What is it? Cold fusion? Over-unity energy? What could be worth killing all those passengers on Flight 549?"

Garrett says, "The cause of that crash has been determined as human error."

"And I'm going to see you pay for that error," says Mulder. "Along with your employer and the government who finances its contracts."

Mulder orders Garrett to leave his seat, herds him up the aisle to a lavatory, and barricades its door with a food service cart. He lifts the in-flight phone and calls Scully. He tells her that he's captured Pendrell's killer and needs reinforcements at her end.

Then he glances at his wrist. "Hey, Scully," he says. "My watch just stopped."

Mulder drops the phone and runs down the aisle to the flight attendant. He tells her that their plane is about to be intercepted, engaged, and boarded—and that the pilot should initiate evasive maneuvers immediately.

The woman looks at Mulder as if he is dangerously insane.

"Put the bag down!" shouts Garrett. "Put it down on the floor!"

He has escaped from the lavatory and, standing at the head of aisle, has his plastic gun aimed at Mulder.

The passengers scream. Mulder puts down the knapsack. The plane begins to shimmy and shake, far more violently than can be accounted for by any turbulence.

Garrett is knocked off balance. The passengers scream again—for a different reason this time. A brilliant light streams through the windows and works its way rearward. Garrett fights his way to the knapsack and picks it up. He hugs it to his chest, still aiming the gun at Mulder.

"Drop the bag!" shouts Mulder. "Drop the bag! Drop it!"

The light reaches the emergency exit.

"Let it go! Let it go!"

The light appears to grab the door, pulling it outward from the fuselage. Light begins to show around the seams of the exit. The metal stresses and buckles as the gaps between the door and the rest of the plane begin to grow. The light intensifies—and the plane dissolves into a white blankness.

At National Airport in Washington, Mulder's airliner taxis to its gate. Scully, Skinner, and several other agents race down the jetway and onto the aircraft.

On board the plane, everything is completely normal. Passengers rise, stretch, grope through their overhead compartments, and shuffle off. The agents look around them, baffled.

Mulder sits calmly in his window seat. Alone.

"Mulder, where is he?" asks Scully.

"He's not here," says her partner.

"What do you mean? You said you had him on this plane. You said you had what Max Fenig had. The stolen part."

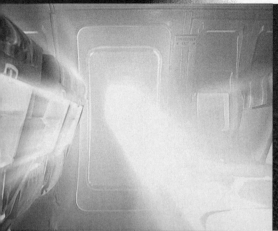

Mulder looks at his watch.

"What time do you have?" he asks.

"Ten fifty-six," says Skinner.

Mulder looks at his watch again. It reads 10:47. He shows it to Scully.

Skinner says, "Would you like to tell me what's going on here, Agent Mulder?"

Scully says wearily, "I don't think you'd want to hear the answer."

She leaves. Skinner faces Mulder.

"Is this man on the plane?" he asks.

Mulder says, "He got the connecting flight."

In Max Fenig's trailer, his posthumous video is playing. Max rambles on, talking as usual about superconductors, antigravity discs, and government conspiracies.

Sharon Graffia watches her old friend fondly. She turns to Mulder and Scully, standing nearby, and smiles.

"These tapes," she says. "You don't mind if I keep them?"

"No," says Mulder. "I think you should consider yourself the sole curator of the Max Fenig rolling multimedia library and archive, and you should probably get tax exempt status as soon as you can. This stuff could be worth something someday."

Sharon Graffia thanks the agents for their help.

"Max would have wanted it that way," says Scully. "You lost someone very close to you."

"So did you," says Sharon.

Scully leaves the trailer and gazes up at the night sky. Mulder joins her.

"Thinking about Pendrell?" asks Mulder.

"I realized," says Scully sadly, "that I didn't even know his first name."

She pauses. "Actually," she says, "I was thinking about this gift you gave me for my birthday."

She takes her *Apollo 11* key chain out of her pocket.

"You never got to tell me why you gave it to me. Or what it means. But I think I know.

"I think you know that there are extraordinary men and women, and extraordinary moments when history leaps forward on the backs of these individuals. That what can be imagined, can be achieved. That you must dare to dream, but that there's no substitute for perseverance and hard work. And teamwork. Because no one can get there alone. And that while we commemorate the greatness of these events and the individuals who achieve them, we cannot forget the sacrifice of those who make these achievement and leaps possible."

Mulder edges toward her, not quite making fun of her sentiments, but smiling.

"I just thought it was a pretty cool key chain," he says.

He leads her away. High above the trailer, Orion aims his arrow through the night sky.

back story:

While not, perhaps, the most dramatically or emotionally gripping episodes of the season, "Tempus Fugit" and "Max" showcase the *X-Files'* behind-the-scenes personnel at the peak of their creative powers. "These two episodes were huge—and we probably spent as much money on them as any we've done," says Gillian Anderson.

David Duchovny says, "The episodes were fun to watch. They're full of big—well, big production numbers. It's like Vegas; you bring all the show girls out, and all the hardware. Then you light 'em good, and you get some real entertainment."

Advance preparation for 4X17 and 4X18 began during the third season, when Chris Carter decided that a future episode would be centered around a Boeing 737 that rocked, shook violently, and ultimately crashed. "Beyond that," says Frank Spotnitz, "we didn't know what the story was." This was not considered to be an especially important problem.

This was, however: There were no transportable airplane cabin interiors for rent, either in Los Angeles or Canada, that would simulate the effects of a violent decompression *and* swing open along its length to let in cameras and other equipment.

Design and construction of a full-scale, completely rockable, shakable, and camera-accessible 737—a joint project of the art, construction, and special-effects departments—began immediately. The final result was a full-scale cabin mock-up sitting atop a twenty-foot-high custom-built hydraulic gimbal unit that split open every six feet but could be reassembled seamlessly for filming at any point and from any angle.

"Oh, man! That airplane was a really violent ride," recalls Kim Manners, the director of "Max." "I mean, that thing traveled four feet in each direction and then rolled twenty-two degrees from side to side. You mix those elements together and you're really shaking. You're rocking and rolling."

Manners adds, "I have never before worked with a crew where I had to put helmets on my camera operators. And I had eighty extras working on that scene. They *made* that show. Lisa Ratke, our extras casting girl, really pulled out all the stops on that one. She brought me some of the best talent ever. I mean, imagine saying to people, 'All right, now here's what we're gonna do. We're gonna put you on this airplane for three days, we're gonna shake the s— out of you, and I mean violently.'

"And oh, yeah. We had little kids in there, too. I had four-year-old kids in that scene. And nobody ever complained. Nobody even got airsick—they just got a little queasy every once in a while. Then Chris said, 'Oh, we got to have babies. We gotta have some babies onboard.' I said, 'Chris, we can't put little babies on this thing.'

"He saw my point. We ended up going with dolls instead of babies."

While all this was going on, another type of discomfort was being generated. A real airplane crash investigator was brought in as a technical advisor. With the crash of TWA Flight 800 still fresh in everyone's mind, a piece of waste ground near Vancouver's Boundary Bay airport was singed with blowtorches and scattered with wreckage, luggage, small forensic flags, and "dead" bodies and body parts.

The largest piece of wreckage was a Boeing 707 tail section from an airplane junkyard in North Carolina. After Val Arntzen of the set-decorating department tracked it down, she ordered it loaded onto a truck, driven cross-country nonstop (it took five days and nights), and lowered onto the location for the few seconds of filming that would make it into the final cut.

Greensman Frank Haddad supervised the draping of dozens of pieces of victims' clothing—and a severed hand, a brief shot of which was excised from "Tempus Fugit" by the network's Standards and Practices department—onto newly planted leafless trees.

"I think the plane crash site was the only location I've seen where the crew was actually disturbed by the scenery," says art director Gary Allen.

Perhaps the hardest job of all was undertaken by sound mixer Michael Williams, who had the nearly impossible task of recording the voices of Duchovny and Tom O'Brien (Luis Frisch) as they talked to each other—in an otherwise innocuous night scene—next to the roaring engine of their waiting Cessna.

"It was a night of hell," says Williamson, who declares that scene by far the most challenging of his four full years on the series.

By comparison, the underwater scenes—filmed, as is the show's usual procedure, in the nearby indoor tank of a Vancouver-based diving equipment manufacture called CanDive—went smoothly. The UFO that shined its light down onto crash investigator Mike Millar (ex-*Hill Street Blues* star Joe Spano) was created in postproduction by visual effects supervisor Laurie Kallsen-George. The brilliant light that shines down onto Mulder near the underwater wreckage was actually a spotlight borrowed from a Canadian Coast Guard rescue helicopter.

The light came complete with two Canadian Coast Guard helicopter crewmen, who operated it during the filming of the scene. "They were big fans of the show," says production manager George Chapman. "I think in their minds, at least, this assignment rated as a real adventure."

The song playing in MAX's trailer is "Unmarked Helicopters," by Soul Coughing, which appears on the *X-Files*-inspired song compilation CD *Songs in the Key of X*.

Ⓧ

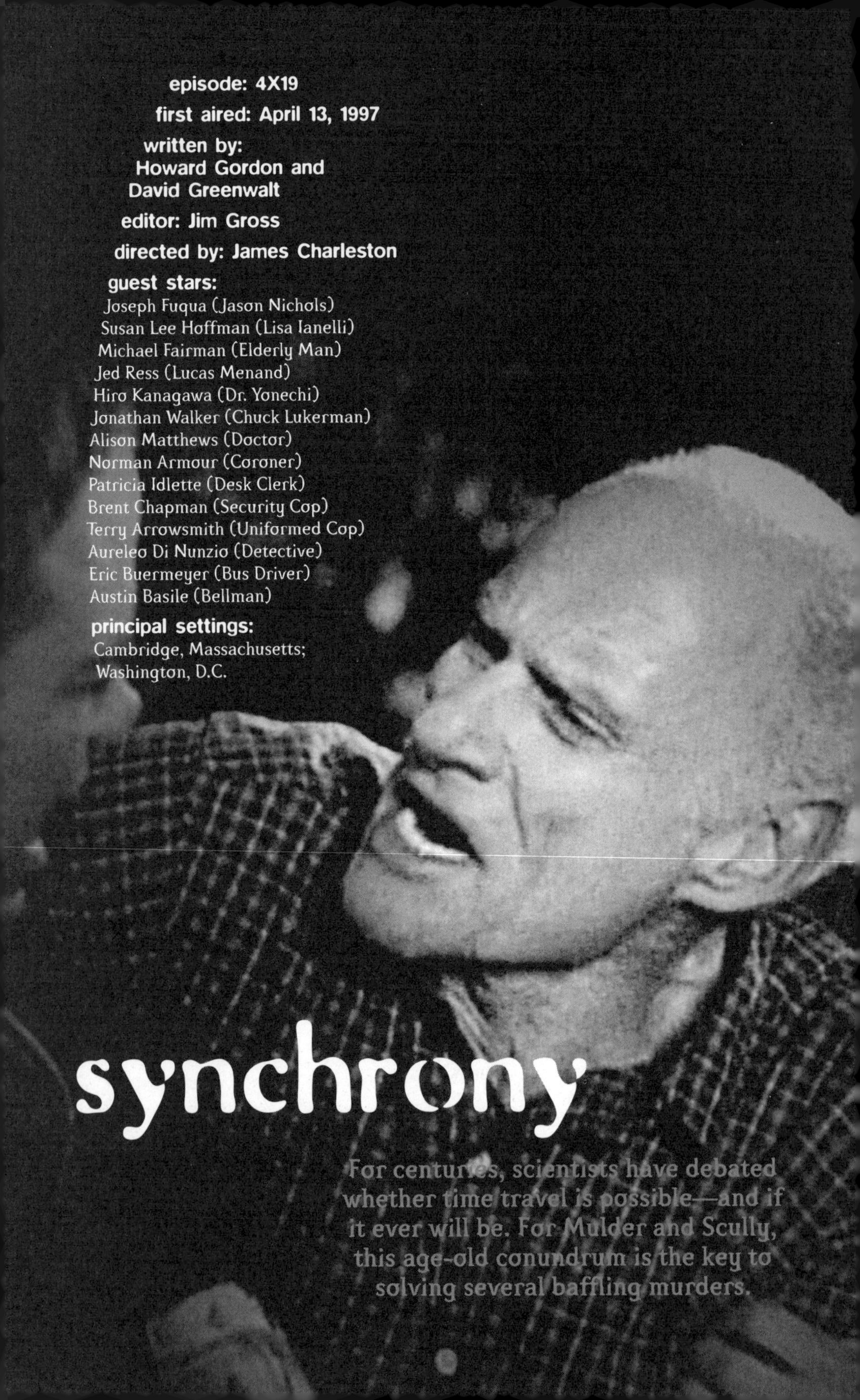

episode: 4X19

first aired: April 13, 1997

written by:
Howard Gordon and
David Greenwalt

editor: Jim Gross

directed by: James Charleston

guest stars:
Joseph Fuqua (Jason Nichols)
Susan Lee Hoffman (Lisa Ianelli)
Michael Fairman (Elderly Man)
Jed Ress (Lucas Menand)
Hiro Kanagawa (Dr. Yonechi)
Jonathan Walker (Chuck Lukerman)
Alison Matthews (Doctor)
Norman Armour (Coroner)
Patricia Idlette (Desk Clerk)
Brent Chapman (Security Cop)
Terry Arrowsmith (Uniformed Cop)
Aureleo Di Nunzio (Detective)
Eric Buermeyer (Bus Driver)
Austin Basile (Bellman)

principal settings:
Cambridge, Massachusetts;
Washington, D.C.

synchrony

For centuries, scientists have debated
whether time travel is possible—and if
it ever will be. For Mulder and Scully,
this age-old conundrum is the key to
solving several baffling murders.

a t 11:15 P.M. on the campus of the Massachusetts Institute of Technology, a rumpled old man runs, gasping, toward two young MIT researchers: Jason Nichols and Lucas Menand.

Nichols and Menand are in the middle of a heated argument. The old man steps in front of them and addresses Menand in a tone of frantic desperation.

"I need to talk to you," he says. "This street is dangerous."

The students look at him as they would any other harmless crank and renew their argument.

"I've traveled a long way!" shouts the old man. "Listen to me! I'm trying to save your life!"

He grabs hold of Menand, who angrily yells for him to let go. Nichols, feeling sorry for the man, pulls him off Menand and tries to soothe him.

"He's going to die!" says the old man to Nichols. "At exactly eleven twenty-one! The bus—"

A campus security guard, drawn to the commotion, arrives.

"He's going to die. At exactly eleven twenty-one! The bus—"

"We're all gonna die, Pop," says the campus cop. "Let's go sleep it off."

He wrestles the old man toward his squad car.

"No! Jason! Don't let him cross the street! His papers! He won't see the bus! Stop him!"

The raving man is bundled into the backseat. Nichols looks at him curiously.

"How did he know my name?" he says.

"How the hell should I know?" says Menand.

Menand strides off angrily—and alone—down the dark street.

Nichols walks off in the opposite direction. Something catches his attention: It's a bus, empty except for its driver, rounding the corner and heading toward Menand.

He checks his wristwatch. It reads 11:20. He looks at Menand. He has dropped a sheaf of papers—right into the path of the hurtling bus.

"Lucas!" shouts Nichols.

He runs toward Menand, who is too preoccupied with his papers to see that he is about to be hit by the bus.

"No!" shouts Nichols.

The bus slams into Menand, hitting him with great force. He lies still, bleeding heavily, on the asphalt. The bus driver, panicked, gets out and looks at Menand's twisted, bleeding figure. Then he see Nichols.

"What'd you do to him?" says the driver.

Nichols, in shock, says nothing.

"You pushed him! You pushed him right in front of me! You killed him! What the hell did you do?"

Nichols is still too shocked to speak. Standing next to the corpse, he looks at his watch. It reads 11:21.

At FBI headquarters, Mulder and Scully sift through the facts of the case. Menand, says Mulder, was a brilliant scientist, a postdoctoral fellow at MIT. Jason Nichols, an associate professor of biology, was Menand's academic subordinate. He has refused to disclose to the police what the two were arguing about.

"Hmm. Sounds like a motive, doesn't it?" says Mulder.

"Then why am I looking at this?" asks Scully.

Mulder says, "Would you like to hear his alibi?"

Mulder plays a videotape of Nichols's interrogation. On it, the scientist protests that he was just trying to keep the old man's prediction from coming true. ·

"That's his alibi?" says Scully skeptically.

"Well, he goes on to tell a pretty convincing narrative," says Mulder, "and give a rather detailed description of the old man."

"What was we wearing—a long black robe, and carrying a scythe?"

"Not when campus security picked him up," says Mulder.

"Has anybody talked to him?" asks Scully. "Has anybody talked to the campus security officer?"

"Can't," says Mulder.

"Why not?"

"He's dead."

"Of what?" says Scully, puzzled.

At the Boston medical examiner's office, a coroner leads Mulder and Scully to the body of the security guard.

"I haven't been able to make a definitive determination as to cause or time of death," he says sheepishly. "There's been some internal disagreement over how to proceed."

"You mean with the autopsy?" says Scully.

"Yes," he replies. "But mostly whether to cut or to saw."

He uncovers the body. It is frozen solid.

Scully notes that something seems to have been inserted in the victim's ear.

"Something has," says the coroner.

He hands Scully an infrared thermometer and tells her that when he placed it in the victim's ear, he got a reading of 15° Fahrenheit. The coroner says he was found in his crashed patrol car, an empty bottle of gin under the driver's seat.

Scully takes a reading herself. The body's temperature is now 8°.

"What's your medical opinion, Scully?" says Mulder.

"My best guess would be that he's been exposed to some chemical refrigerant. Like liquid nitrogen—possibly he even ingested it."

Mulder says, "You see what happens when you drink and drive?"

He suggests they ask Jason Nichols if he can come up with an explanation.

"What if he can't?" says Scully.

Mulder shrugs. "We'll just hope," he says, "that he keeps until Thanksgiving."

At a police station near the MIT campus, Mulder peers through an interrogation room window at Jason Nichols. Nichols is talking intently to a young woman in her mid-twenties. As Mulder enters, the woman leaves.

"That your girlfriend?" asks Mulder.

"Yeah," he replies sullenly.

The scientist asks Mulder if they are searching for the old man in his alibi. Mulder assures him that they are.

"I'm sure you know," says Mulder, "that the man who allegedly detained the man you described is now dead."

Nichols reacts sourly.

"So," he says, "are they going to try and blame me for that one, too?"

"Not unless you're capable of killing a man by flash freezing him," says Mulder.

Nichols becomes agitated and upset by this "accusation." Mulder sees an opening.

"Does this have anything to do with you and Lucas Menand?"

Nichols's indignation grows. He blurts out that Menand threatened his academic reputation by threatening to go public with an accusation that Nichols had falsified data on a research paper.

"Had you?" says Mulder.

"No," says Nichols. "The theory was sound. If my interpretation of certain data was a little lax, it's because I've been under pressure to achieve results. My NSA grant is up for renewal. And Lucas knew how damaging his accusations would be."

"Was Lucas Menand up for the same grant?" asks Mulder.

Nichols nods.

"What research would this grant have funded?"

"Cryobiology," says Nichols grimly, realizing how bad this sounds. "I

studied the effects of freezing temperatures on biological systems."

Mulder's cell phone rings. It is Scully, telling him that Nichols's fingerprint have been found in the patrol car and on the body of the security guard.

"I think," she adds, "the old man in this story is going to be Jason Nichols—serving twenty-five to life in a federal prison."

At a downtown Boston hotel, a Japanese man named Yonechi is trying to check in. To his dismay, the desk clerk has no record of his reservation.

"Dr. Yonechi?" says a voice behind him. It is the old man from the first scene.

He tells Yonechi that there has been a mix-up, that his assistant made a reservation at the hotel, but there is indeed another room available here.

Yonechi is confused. "You are not Dr. Nichols?" he says.

"He apologizes," says the old man. "He was not able to be here to meet you himself. So he asked me to come in his place."

"Excuse me, but who are you?" says Yonechi.

"A great admirer of your work," replies the old man.

Looking somewhat ill, the old man escorts Yonechi to his room. He asks for a glass of a water, then lingers. He has a confession to make: The mix-up with the reservation was actually his fault.

"Your fault?" says Yonechi.

"But I owe you so much," muses the old man.

"For what?" asks Yonechi.

"Your contributions to my work. Vitrification. You were the one who solved the problem."

"Me?" says Yonechi. "No, not yet. No one has solved vitrification."

"Oh yes, Yonni. You found a way to substitute water with a sugar—trehalose. Your paper changed everything."

Unnerved by what he has heard, Yonechi stares at the glass of water in his hand. The old man stabs him in the palm of his hand with a sharp instrument. Yonechi screams in pain as he turns white with frost, then freezes solid.

In Yonechi's hotel room, Scully examines the body of the Japanese scientist, congealed into a picture of pure agony. Mulder learns from the hotel staff that Yonechi had been accompanied by the elderly man.

"Sounds like Jason Nichols has an accomplice," says Scully. "More than that, Mulder, it makes sense. Science is a high-stakes game. Jason Nichols is trying to eliminate his competitors, and he's succeeding."

"Yeah," says Mulder, "but what if he's being set up?"

"He's a cryobiologist, Mulder. He freezes things for a living. How many people could do that?"

Mulder says, "Just about anybody who's up for that grant money could."

Scully shows Mulder a nuclear magnetic resonance chart: a molecular breakdown of an unknown chemical substance found in Yonechi's blood and in the security guard's, as well.

"A lethal injection?" asks Mulder.

"I think you should be asking Jason Nichols," says Scully.

"No," says Mulder. "There's somebody I want to talk to first."

At the MIT biomedical research laboratory, Mulder and Scully interview Lisa

Ianelli—Nichols's girlfriend. She is also a scientist who works closely with Nichols. Scully shows her the tracing of the unknown compound. Ianelli is startled.

"Where'd you get this?" she asks.

"You recognize it?" says Scully.

Ianelli says nothing.

"Lisa," says Scully, "you can tell us now or we can subpoena your testimony in court. Either way, we'll find out what you know about this."

Ianelli reluctantly tells the agents that the substance is a catalyst, a rapid freezing agent that Nichols had been working on. According to Nichols's theory, she adds, individuals who are subjected to its effects can be successfully thawed and revived. She shows the agents a virtual model of the substance, displayed on her computer screen.

"This compound—has Jason actually tested it yet?" says Scully.

"He hasn't tested it yet—because it doesn't exist."

"Is it possible that he could have synthesized the compound without you knowing about it?" asks Scully.

"Not even remotely," says Ianelli. "The technology to engineer something like that is still five, ten years away—minimum."

Mulder says, "Not anymore, apparently."

In a frostbite bay at the cryobiology lab, Lisa Ianelli, surrounded by several doctors and paramedics, attempts to thaw out Yonechi's body. He lies in a bath of warm fluid; when his core temperature reaches 97°, she instructs the doctors to revive him.

They place defibrillator paddles on his chest. Yonechi's heart is jolted into life. The scientist breathes on his own for a few seconds—then goes into a series of violent seizures. His temperature climbs quickly past normal and reaches 106°. The doctors hold him down and monitor his worsening condition helplessly. A few seconds later, he bursts into flames.

Smoke alarms go off. Firemen pour into the lab to extinguish the blaze.

Afterward, Ianelli is at a loss to explain what has happened. "All I can think," she says, "is that the compound used to freeze him must be unstable."

Mulder says, "I think the real question is how someone could have had access to a compound that doesn't exist."

Lisa leaves abruptly, declaring that she has to talk to Nichols. She boards a city bus, then notices that someone is following her. It is the old man. She gets off the bus and

walks quickly through downtown Boston, but the old man—walking as fast as he can—manages to keep up.

Lisa enters a large public library and confronts him in an empty corridor. "You're the man Jason saw, aren't you?" she says. "You killed Lucas Menand and Dr. Yonechi."

He reaches out and grabs Lisa's wrist. "And I can kill you," he says.

"Let go of me!"

The old man pulls the sharp instrument out of his pocket. Lisa gasps.

"I came here to kill you!" he says.

"Who are you?" she says.

The old man says nothing. He turns and walks quickly away.

On a park bench outside the library, Ianelli looks at a police artist's drawing of the old man, then relays a bare-bones account of the incident to Mulder and Scully.

Scully says, "Lisa, if you're leaving anything out, if you're hedging the truth, you could be held accountable if Jason committed a crime."

Lisa agonizes for a moment.

"It wasn't Jason," she says. "It was me. I falsified the data to get the grant. Jason's covering for me. He's sitting in jail because of me."

Mulder asks, "That's why he can't tell anyone?"

Lisa nods.

"But there are people who could have figured it out," says Scully. "Lucas Menand. Dr. Yonechi. If these people were not dead."

The implication of this comment startles Lisa. "It's not what you think," she protests.

Scully and Mulder confer. Scully hypothesizes that the old man is part of a conspiracy to protect the secret of the falsified data.

"This doesn't really make sense, Scully," says Mulder. "Why would he threaten her if she's the one who's protecting the secret?"

Scully says, "Because it's not just her secret, it's Jason's secret, too. And the old man is protecting Jason."

"With a medical instrument?"

Scully sighs. "I suppose it is an unlikely choice as a murder weapon," she says.

Mulder says, "But what if it's not a murder weapon? I'm just speculating, but what if it was designed for another purpose?"

A local cop interrupts them to say that a person matching the old man's description has been spotted at a nearby hotel. The FBI agents leave Lisa under the cop's protection; she stares searchingly at the police drawing.

The hotel is only a level or two above a flophouse. In the old man's room, a notepad on the dresser has Yonechi's flight information. In the nightstand Mulder finds a photograph: It shows Jason Nichols, Lisa Ianelli, and Dr. Yonechi raising a champagne toast.

"A celebration," says Scully. "But of what?"

"Something that never happened," says Mulder.

"What?" she says. "Mulder, this is a photograph. It is a documented moment in time."

"In a future," says Mulder, "that somebody is trying like hell to prevent from happening."

He adds, "Think about it, Scully. If Lucas Menand never gets hit by that bus, his complaint gets heard before the grant committee. Jason Nichols loses his funding, and he never gets to collaborate on his research with Dr. Yonechi. Therefore, this photograph never gets taken because this celebration never happens."

Scully is incredulous. "And if your sister is your aunt," she says, "and your mother

marries your uncle, you'd be your own grandpa."

Mulder ignores this. "The old man couldn't save Menand," he says, "so he had to kill Dr. Yonechi."

"Okay," says Scully, exasperated. "This photo that was never taken—*when* was it never taken?"

"At least five years in the future. When they first synthesized the compound successfully."

Scully protests that the compound already exists—that they have physical evidence of its existence.

"Only because the old man brought it back with him," says Mulder.

"Back from where?"

"Back from *when*, maybe, is the real question."

Mulder contends that the old man has arrived from the future—it is the only way, he says, that he could have predicted Menand's death, known that Jason's fingerprints were inside the patrol car, and been privy to Lisa Ianelli's guilty secret.

"So what you're saying here is," says Scully, "the old man is. . . "

"Jason Nichols," says Mulder.

Mulder adds, quoting, "'Though common sense might rule out the possibilities of time travel, the laws of quantum physics certainly do not.'

"In case you've forgotten, that was from your graduate thesis. You were a lot more open when you were younger."

In his room at the Lighthouse, the old man, looking very ill and perspiring heavily, struggles to prick himself with the medical stylus. He finally does so; a drop of blood oozes out of his wrist and he sighs with relief.

"Jason . . . ?" says a voice behind him. It is Lisa Ianelli.

He does not turn to identify the voice. He doesn't have to.

"I don't understand," says Lisa. "How is this possible?"

"Because you made it possible," he says. "It was you."

At last, the old man turns to face her.

He says, "Thirty years ago—ten years from now—you'll be at a conference in Zurich. You'll meet a man named McGuane, who's just discovered the first evidence of tachyons, subatomic particles that can travel faster than the speed of light—and go back in time, but only for a few seconds and only at a temperature of absolute zero. But from that, and from your correspondence with McGuane, you'll have an idea. A revelation!"

"What revelation?" whispers Lisa.

"One so remarkable," says Nichols, "it would change the course of history."

"Then why did you—you said you came back to kill me," says Lisa.

"I couldn't do it," he says.

The old man stretches out his hand.

"You're cold, Jason," says Lisa, embracing him.

The old man moves toward the young woman he loved—and jabs her with the stylus. She gasps, shudders, and freezes solid. Clearly in agony, the old man lowers her gently to the ground.

At the Boston police station, Mulder bails out Jason Nichols and tells him that something has happened to Lisa.

"Was it the old man?" says Nichols.

"Yes," says Mulder.

"Look, Jason," he adds, "I don't expect you to get your mind around this completely right now, but the man we're looking for—the old man—he's you."

Nichols is indeed too overwhelmed to believe him. As they drive toward the university, Mulder shows him the old man's photograph and tells him that since the old man needs to stop the celebration depicted from happening, the odds favor his being his next target.

"Puts a whole new spin on being your own worst enemy, huh?" says Mulder.

Nichols continues to resist. Mulder continues buttressing his argument.

"Physicists like Stephen Hawking," he says, "have hypothesized the existence of wormhole and closed time loops—actual portals through which matter can travel backward through time. Although phenomena like extreme heat and gravity would render the trip lethal for any organism."

"So you're saying the properties of my compound will make it possible?" says Nichols.

"Eventually, yes. That's what I'm saying."

"But why stop time travel?" asks Nichols.

"That's what I'm hoping the old man will tell us."

At the entrance to the biomedical research facility, Nichols places his hand in an identification scanner. The door opens, but a security guard, sitting at a computer terminal, calls out to him.

"Are you Dr. Jason Nichols?"

"That's right."

"Then something's wrong," he says. "It says that you're already in the building."

Mulder dispatches Nichols to tell Scully—in the frostbite bay with Lisa—that the old man is near. In the bay the doctors

shock Lisa's heart into activity. As her temperature rises, they plunge her into a cold tub. Her temperature hits 107°—rising.

At the entrance to the cryogenics lab, Mulder asks a research assistant whether the old man has entered. The student says that he hasn't. Mulder asks him to access Jason Nichols's computer files.

Scully phones Mulder to tell him that the cold bath has brought Lisa's body temperature under control—and that Jason Nichols has not shown up at the lab. The research assistant interrupts to tell Mulder that Jason Nichols's data has been erased from the computer mainframe.

In the mainframe room, Jason Nichols confronts the old man.

"I knew I'd find you here," says Nichols. "I figured this is where I'd go to stop myself."

"I don't have much time," pleads the old man. "Please—let me finish."

"Let you finish destroying my work?" says Nichols angrily.

"It's my work, too," says the old man sadly.

"I want her back," says Nichols.

"I know," says the old man.

"Tell me how to go back—so I can save her. Please."

The old man looks at Nichols in sorrow. "I don't expect you to understand," he says. "What she created. What you—what we helped her create. A world without history. Without hope. Where everyone can know everything that will ever happen."

He pauses, turning inward toward the truly horrific implications of this. "I've seen that world," he says.

Mulder runs down the corridor toward the mainframe room. Through a locked tempered glass Plexiglas door, he sees Nichols assaulting the old man.

"Jason!" shouts Mulder. "She's alive! Lisa's alive! Don't hurt him! If you hurt him, we'll never know the truth."

Nichols turns away from the old man to face Mulder. The old man runs toward Nichols and jabs him in the wrist.

"It's better that we never were," he says.

Mulder pounds at the glass with a fire extinguisher, but he is helpless. Nichols bursts into flames. The young scientist is

consumed by the fire—as is the old man, who clings tightly to him.

Lisa Ianelli, lying on a gurney, is wheeled from the cryogenics lab to a waiting ambulance. Scully tells her that the theory of the freezing compound's instability was correct—she proved it herself.

Lisa struggles to speak. "He said he was Jason," she whispers.

"The old man?" says Scully.

Lisa nods weakly.

"Look," says Scully. "There's been some incongruous evidence I've had difficulty explaining myself."

"Agent Scully," says Lisa. "It *was* Jason."

"Lisa, Jason's dead. There was fire in the mainframe room. I'm sorry. I'll see you in the hospital."

The ambulance pulls away. Mulder joins Scully and tells her that a second corpse was not found in the mainframe room.

"And I'm not holding out much hope that they will, either," he adds.

Scully says, "We should put out an APB for the old man."

"We won't find him. I know what I saw, Scully, and I know what I believe happened."

"Even if it could never be proven?"

"Never? Never is a very long time, Scully. You said that yourself: 'Although multidimensionality suggests infinite outcomes in an infinite number of universes, each universe can produce only one outcome.'"

Scully says, "I was twenty-three when I wrote that."

"Yeah, but I take it to mean that you were suggesting that the future can't be altered. Which means that the elder Jason Nichols's attempts to stop his own research will fail. That eventually his compound, and time travel, will be discovered."

Mulder moves away and walks toward his car. Scully remains for a moment, thoughtful.

Some time later, in the MIT cryogenics lab, a scientist taps away at a computer keyboard. It is Lisa Ianelli. On her monitor is a 3-D diagram of the freezing compound molecule. The image is reflected eerily in her glasses.

The scientist pauses and stares, thinking.

back story:

Some tongue-in-cheek advice from Howard Gordon to screenwriters everywhere: Avoid like the plague the twin topics of disgruntled Vietnam veterans and time travel.

"They're the two great taboos," laughs Gordon, recalling the gyrations involved in turning out his next-to-last *X-Files* script.

Gordon coauthored this episode immediately after completing ("with much bloodletting, as usual") his work on "Unrequited." Chris Carter teamed him up for the task with David Greenwalt, a new co-executive producer (previous shows: *Profitt* and *Buffy the Vampire Slayer*) who spent several months on *The X-Files* beginning in midseason.

"David lives in Santa Barbara, and I live in Los Angeles, so one rainy weekend we met halfway, in Simi Valley, to come up with an idea for a script that was due two or three weeks hence. Well, we went to a lot of bookstores and sat around in four different Starbucks, and I got to know David, who's a great guy, really well. But just about the only other thing we accomplished was realizing just how difficult it was to come up with a good *X-Files* idea."

Their wet weekend stretched into a damp four days. After a long detour working on an idea concerning a prisoner escaping from jail by switching bodies with a free man—"It felt too much like other episodes I'd done," says Gordon—the pair agreed to adjourn and meet again the next morning, each bringing three fresh ideas to the table.

"In fact, I didn't have anything to bring to the table," admits Gordon.

But the next morning, he came across an interesting article in *Scientific American*. The article, in the magazine's March 1994 issue, is titled "The Quantum Physics of Time Travel." Written by two Oxford professors, it explains in mind-whirling detail how modern theory allows for the existence of "closed timelike curves": shortcuts in the space-time continuum that, if they do indeed exist, could someday enable us to flit back and forth between the present, the future, and the past. Old-fashioned physical theories, say the authors, prohibit individuals from time-traveling backward and altering history. The laws of quantum physics, however, do not.

He and his partner understood enough of all this, says Gordon, to finally get the wheels turning.

"I remembered that anecdote about J. Robert Oppenheimer, after he'd led the Manhattan project, coming into Harry Truman's office and complaining about the dropping of the atomic bomb he and his team invented. Well, what if Oppenheimer could have gone back into the past and 'uninvented' it?

"That led to another question: What would happen if we did know our future? I mean, life itself is about the unknown, and about finding out what lies ahead of us. But if everyone—or maybe just a few people—

knew what was going to happen, it would create a fresh set of horrors, and would have to be stopped."

Unfortunately, neither Gordon nor Greenwalt could figure out how to leapfrog ahead and take a look at their finished script. It took a week of fifteen-hour days—plus some important input from Shiban, Spotnitz, and Horton—to get the pretzel-shaped story line working properly. Gordon spent the weekend before shooting began in Vancouver frantically rewriting two important characters—one a Stephen Hawking-like wheelchair-bound scientist—out of the episode. "Those characters were useless, and this really tightened up the story, but on late Sunday night—the episode started on Tuesday—I really considered calling up Bob Goodwin and saying 'That's it, I've had my fill, I give up.'"

After that, it was a piece of cake.

Director Jim Charleston remembers happily that the scene where Dr. Yonechi (actually, stunt coordinator Tony Morelli in a protective suit) burst into flames went perfectly. "From the time his body was lit until the time the guys rushed in with fire extinguisher was exactly twelve seconds—no more, no less."

David Duchovny says, "I remember that we kept shooting makeup scenes, because obviously nobody could figure out whether the audience would understand what was going on. They would always be writing little one-page scenes where somebody would try to explain it."

Concludes Gordon: "I think it all came out pretty well in the end. But when it was all over I vowed I would never touch another time travel idea again as long as I lived."

Hiro Kanagawa previously appeared in "Firewalker" (2X09) as one of the scientists killed by the mysterious volcanic spores.

Ⓧ

episode: 4X20
first aired: April 20, 1997
written by: Vince Gilligan
editor: Heather MacDougall
directed by: Cliff Bole

small potatoes

Mulder and Scully investigate
several not-so-blessed events in
a small southern town.

guest stars:
Mitch Pileggi (AD Walter Skinner)
Darin Morgan (Eddie Van Blundht)
Christine Cavanaugh (Amanda Nelligan)
Lee de Broux (Eddie's Father)
Robert Rozen (Dr. Alton Pugh)
Paul McGillion (Angry Husband)
Jennifer Sterling (Angry Wife)
David Cameron (Deputy)
Forbes Angus (Security Guard)
Peter Kelamis (Second Husband)
P. Lynn Johnson (Health Department Doctor)
Carrie Cain Sparks (Duty Nurse)

principal settings:
Martinsburg, West Virginia;
Washington, D.C.;
Arlington, Virginia

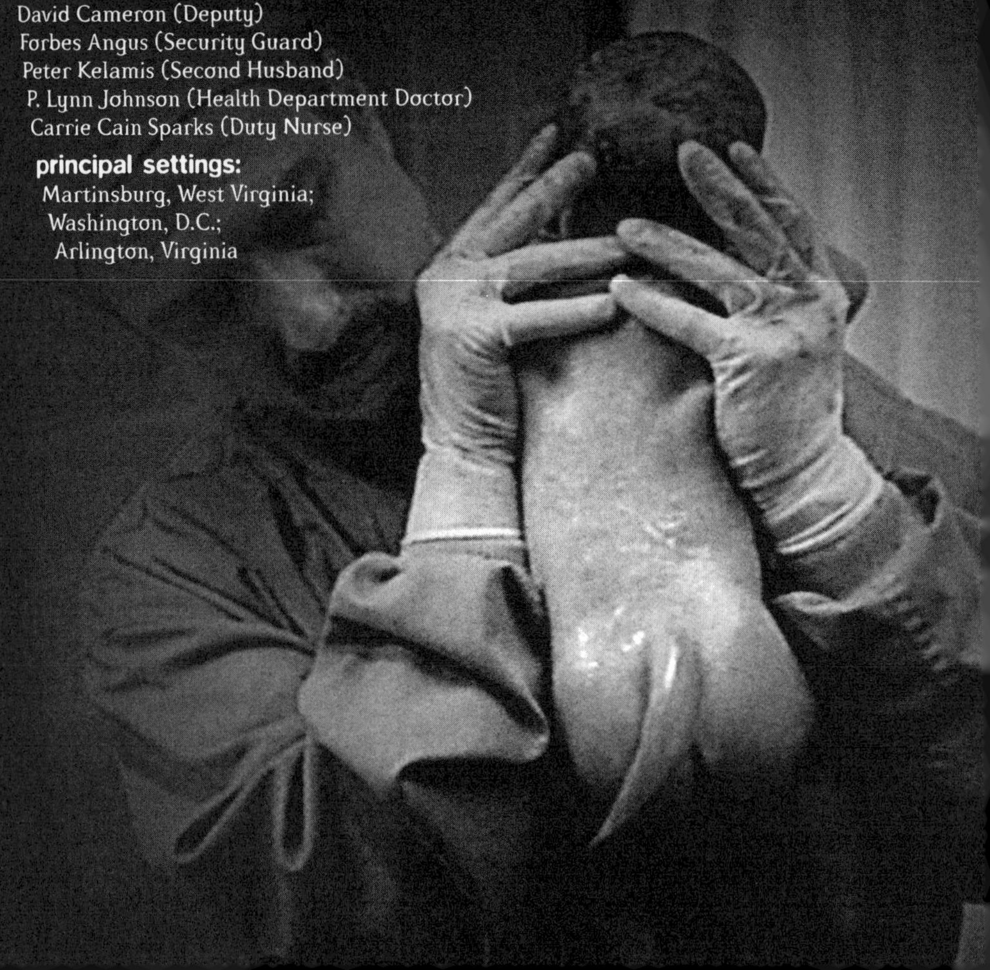

at Tablers Community Hospital in Martinsburg, a woman in labor is rushed toward the delivery room.

A duty nurse trots alongside her, taking down vital information.

"Ma'am, I'll need your full name and Social Security number," says the nurse.

"Amanda Nelligan. 545-02-0809," says the woman, in her mid-twenties.

"And your insurance carrier?"

"Atlantic Mutual."

"Great!" says the nurse. "Is there anyone you need us to contact? The father of the baby?"

"I'm not sure I know how to get a hold of him," says Amanda.

"Give me his name, and I can try," says the nurse.

"He's not from around here," says Amanda.

"Is he from out of state?"

"Another planet."

In the delivery room, Amanda screams in pain, pants, pushes, and delivers her newborn toward the arms of the attending OB-GYN.

"*There's* a cute face," says the doctor happily. "Uh-oh."

As the baby's body emerges, the doctor's expression changes to dismay. The attending nurse drops her forceps in shock.

The OB-GYN pulls himself together, cradles the newborn baby girl, and tells her mother—not too convincingly—that everything is "A-okay."

He takes the child, crying lustily, to a screened-off area. The baby looks perfectly healthy—except that it has a four-inch-long, pointed pink tail.

"Good lord," says the doctor wearily. "Not another one!"

A few days later, Mulder and Scully drive into town. The nature of the challenge they face is illustrated by the cover of a cheesy supermarket tabloid lying on the front seat. It reads: "Monkey Babies Invade Small Town!" and "Did West Virginia Women Mate with Visitors from Space?"

(Also in this issue: "Michael Jackson Held Captive by Exotic Pets!" and "ETAP Bigshot Busted!")

Mulder is obviously excited by the assignment. Scully, just as obviously, is not.

"What do you think, Scully?" says Mulder. "Children born with vestigial tails don't interest you?"

Scully replies evenly that although children are rarely born with vestigial tails, it is still a phenomenon well-known to medical science.

"Five times in the last three months?" counters Mulder. "All in a town of less than fifteen thousand people? I'd say that's a little more than a statistical anomaly."

"So would I," says Scully.

She concedes that it's a matter worthy of investigation—by the local health department.

"I called around," says Mulder. "They're already investigating."

"So, uh, what else about this interests you?" muses Scully, picking up Mulder's copy of the *National Informer*. "Could it be, um, 'visitors from space'?"

In Amanda Nelligan's hospital room, the agents question the new mother. Amanda appears to be in good spirits, considering.

"The doctor said my baby is gonna be fine," she says. "She's really healthy. Once she gets to be a few moths old, it's just a matter of—snip!"

"That's good to hear," says Mulder.

Scully asks Amanda if she had any complications during her pregnancy, or if she's taken fertility drugs.

"No," Amanda says with a chortle. "I wasn't *trying* to get pregnant. I guess you could just sorta say I'm a single mom now."

"When you were admitted," says Mulder, "you said that the father was 'from another planet.' What'd you mean by that, exactly?"

"Well, you know," she says, "he's not from *this* planet."

"Were you abducted?" asks Mulder.

"Huh?" Amanda takes a second or two to figure out what Mulder's talking about. "No, no," she says with a chuckle. "He dropped by my apartment one day, and one thing sorta led to another."

"But the baby's father *is* an alien?"

"No! I didn't say he was an alien. I said he was from another planet. His name is Luke Skywalker. He's what's known as a Jedi Knight."

Mulder's face sinks. He doesn't look at Scully—he doesn't want to give her the satisfaction. Scully remains deadpan.

"Did he have a light saber?" asks Scully.

"No," says Amanda. "He didn't bring it. But he did sing his song for me. Dum dum. Dum da da dum dum! Dum da da dum dum! Dum da da *dum*. . . ."

Scully gives a supportive nod.

"How many times have you seen *Star Wars*, Amanda?" she asks.

"Three hundred sixty-eight," says Amanda. "I should break four hundred by Memorial Day."

Mulder rises to his feet, nods farewell, and shuffles out the door. Scully, absolutely delighted, beams a friendly smile to Amanda. As Scully prepares to leave, Amanda remembers something that's been troubling her.

"Oh, wait a minute, wait!" she says. "These four babies born around here with tails? There isn't a chance that Luke could be the father—could there?"

Outside in the maternity ward, Mulder joins a crowd of people gawking at Amanda's baby—waving her tail contentedly—in the nursery. A round-faced man in a janitor's uniform seems particularly fascinated.

After taking a call on her cell phone, Scully rejoins her partner.

"Take your best shot, Scully," says Mulder. "But I think there's more going on here than Luke Skywalker and his light saber."

"I think you're right, Mulder," she says, heading out the door. "Coming?"

At the local health department, a doctor shows Scully chromosome charts of the babies. They prove that all five had the same father. In addition, all five had the same OB-GYN. And four of the five mothers—Amanda being the exception—had special insemination therapy in order to become pregnant.

At the office of Alton Pugh, M.D.—the OB-GYN in the opening scene—four angry couples confront the doctor. They accuse him of inseminating them improperly, to put it mildly. (One man, in the midst of this argument, calls his wife by her pet name, "Baboo.")

Pugh asks them all to relax.

"Don't you tell me to relax!" says an angry husband. "What the hell happened to my sperm?"

Another says, "I mean, it's bad enough having a boy with a tail. But then to find out he isn't even yours! For God's sake, Alton! How many of us are there?"

Scully and Mulder wade into the scene. Under questioning, Pugh tells the agents that, to solve a motility problem, he inseminated the women only with their husbands' sperm.

"The intrauterine process I used," he adds, "has about a 40 percent chance of success. I was surprised. It seemed to work all four times."

His eyes sweep across his female patients.

"Now, the only thing I can think of," he says, lowering his glance, "is that it never worked at all."

At this inflammatory juncture, accusations resume flying. Mulder hears a noise down the corridor and slips away to check it out. In a nearby examination room, a janitor, whom Mulder recognizes from the hospital, is fixing something under a sink.

"Hey," says Mulder.

"Hey," says the janitor, looking over his shoulder.

The man returns to his work underneath the sink. His pants slip a bit, showing his "plumber's moon."

Mulder notices something. "Excuse me," he says. "I'm an agent with the Federal Bureau of Investigation. I'd like to ask you a few questions."

The janitor stands up. "Uh, yeah. Okay," he says.

Then he bolts out the door and into the corridor. Mulder rolls his eyes and gives chase, hauling him down from behind in front of the crowd of squabbling inseminees.

Mulder grabs the back of the janitor's pants and pulls.

"Hey Scully, check it out!" he says.

There is a fading red scar where a tail might have been.

In a sheriff's department interrogation room, Scully tosses five file folders, each containing a paternity test performed on "Van Blundt, Edward H.," onto the table.

"Five out of five," says Scully.

"You spelled my name wrong," says the janitor. "It's Van Blundht with a silent 'h.' 'B-L-U-N-D-H-T.'"

"We'll get right on that," says Mulder.

"Lots of people get it wrong," says Van Blundht. "It's like, Dutch or something. Can I go now?"

"No sir, not yet," says Scully. "We'd like to clear up a few things first."

She asks him if he has any idea how five separate women came to be inseminated with his sperm.

"You make it sound so romantic," says Eddie.

Mulder's interest is stirred. "So you're saying there was romance involved?" he asks.

"Why is that so hard to believe?" says Eddie indignantly. "Just because I was born with a tail, no woman would want me? Maybe I got personality. You ever think of that?"

Scully changes the subject.

"You had sex with these women?" she asks. "How is it that none of them have any recollection whatsoever of that happening?"

"Look," says Eddie patiently. "I'm not saying anything one way or another. I'm just saying, hypothetically: If some woman wanted to have kids, and their husband wasn't capable, and everybody was happy, and nobody got hurt..."

Eddie shrugs. "Hypothetically," he whines, "where's the crime?"

Mulder accompanies his partner out of the interrogation room. He confesses that for once he has no coherent theory of events.

Scully says that she does. "On behalf of all the women in the world," she says, "I seriously doubt this has anything to do with consensual sex."

She suggests that Eddie administered "date rape" drugs to the women and then had his way with them. Eddie, she adds, could have identified the women through his janitorial job and followed them to a club or a bar.

"Those women don't look like the type to do a lot of solo drinking," says Mulder.

"I think," says Scully, "it's enough to keep him in custody while we check him out."

In the sheriff's department booking room later than night, a deputy types Eddie's name—without the silent "h"—into a computer. Eddie corrects him, then stares intently into the policemen's face. The cop looks back up Eddie.

"What the hell!?" he says.

A man looking very much like the booking cop smashes him over the head with a pig-shaped ceramic desk ornament. The cop tumbles to the floor.

"The 'h' is silent," says the fake deputy in a voice very much like its real owner's.

The next morning the real deputy, nursing a massive headache, tells Scully the strange nature of his braining. Mulder brings her the news that Eddie Van Blundht's clothing was found near the deputy's locker.

"I have a theory," says Mulder. "You wanna hear it?"

Scully says, "Van Blundht somehow physically transformed into his captor, then walked out the door leaving no one the wiser?"

Mulder beams. "Scully," he says, "should we be picking out china patterns or what?"

At Eddie Van Blundht's house, in a lower middle-class neighborhood, a man next door with a leaf blower watches the agents carefully as they walk to the front porch. Next to the front door, plastic letters spell out VAN BLUNDHT. The door opens suddenly. The letter "h" falls off, though no one notices.

An elderly man in a red bathrobe stands in the doorway. "What're you doing sneaking around my porch?" he says angrily.

The agents identity themselves. Mulder tells him they're looking for his son—Eddie, Jr.

"Eddie? What'd that moron do now?" the old man replies.

They tell him.

"Five women? Oh, lord! And what else?"

They tell him that, too. He leads them inside. On the wall of his living room is an old circus poster. It reads: "See Eddie the Monkey Man! Impressionist! Magician!" Below is a picture of a smiling young man with a tail poking out the back of his tuxedo pants.

Eddie, Sr., tells the agents that he hasn't seen his son in two days. Mulder stares at the poster.

"Is this you?" he asks.

"One and the same! Hey, you wanna see?" says Mr. Van Blundht, unbuttoning the work pants he's wearing underneath his robe.

"No! No thank you," says Scully quickly. Van Blundht's face registers hurt and disappointment. He shrugs it off and continues.

"My son had *his* removed when he was just a kid," he says. "He kept bugging me and bugging me until I finally let him do it. There you go."

Rummaging through a junk pile, Eddie, Sr., pulls out an old magazine. On the cover a team of surgeons surround an unhappy boy. One of the doctors holds up the youth's tail for the camera.

"I told him it was a mistake," the old man continues. "I said, 'Son, ya ain't much to look at. Ya ain't no athlete, and ya sure as hell ain't no Einstein. But at least you got that tail. Otherwise, you're just small potatoes.' But he didn't listen."

Mulder, struggling to absorb all this, asks Eddie, Sr., whether his son had any other unique medical conditions.

"Mr. Mulder," he replies, "that boy was born sickly. We used to have this condition down in the South called pellagra—"

Mulder interrupts. "Excuse me, sir," he says. "How did you know my name was Mulder?"

"She told me it was," says Van Blundht.

"No," says Scully. "Actually, I didn't."

Eddie Van Blundht, Sr. thinks for a split second—then turns and bolts through the

font door with amazing speed. Mulder and Scully realize what is happening. They follow him outside and see a normal neighborhood populated with normal, innocent-looking men. Everyone is wearing the same kind of pants as Eddie, Sr. Draped over a trash can is the red bathrobe.

"Pretty spry for an old guy, huh?" says Mulder.

"Eddie, *Junior*—not Senior," says Scully.

"Well, whichever one he is," says Mulder. "Wouldn't you say he's a man with a secret?"

In a somewhat nicer part of town, one of Alton Pugh's angry patients—no longer angry—diapers her baby. A gauze bandage just above the buttocks is the only reminder of the now excised tail.

The front door bursts open and the woman's husband rushes in. He locks the door and nervously looks behind him.

"Honey, what are you doing home so early?" asks the wife.

Her husband holds up a "wait" finger and dashes into the bathroom. He washes his face, and when he looks up a different person stares back from the mirror. He is, of course, Eddie Van Blundht, Jr.

His "wife" picks up the baby, walks down the hall, and stands outside the bathroom door.

"Fred?" she says. "Is everything okay?"

"Everything's fine," says Eddie.

"What happened to the clothes you were wearing this morning?"

"I'll explain later," says Eddie. "Just give me a little privacy. Okay . . . Baboo?"

"Okay—sugar patootie," she says, smiling winsomely.

Scully and Mulder search Eddie's house.

On the second floor, Mulder spots a trap door leading to the attic. He reaches up and gives it a tentative tug. A thin stream of white powder leaks down.

"It's quicklime," he tells Scully.

He pulls harder. A ghastly gray mummified corpse—complete with mummified tail—tumbles down and lies sprawled at their feet.

"Not so spry," says Mulder. "Think the fall killed him?"

At the house of the ex-angry couple, Eddie is still trapped in the bathroom. He hears a faint voice from elsewhere in the house.

"Baboo! I'm home!" it says.

"Oh, crap!" says Eddie.

The wife looks at her real husband—this one *is* wearing the clothes he left home with—in horror. The couple warily approaches the bathroom door. They touch the door handle—and it opens.

"All clear," says Special Agent Fox Mulder emerging.

At the health department Scully examines the corpse. She tells Mulder that besides having a tail, Eddie, Sr. had a thin sheet of voluntary muscle underlying the entire dermis layer of his skin. Mulder (who has accidentally broken the tail off the body) suggests that Eddie, Sr.—and now, Eddie, Jr.—could use this extra muscle to change the appearance of his body.

Scully is dubious. She suggests that Eddie simply has an identical twin.

"I'll check that out," says Mulder (who has been frantically trying to stick the tail back on). He moves quickly toward the exit.

"Where are you going?" asks Scully.

"Something about Van Blundht's MO

confuses me," says Mulder. "His victims were four married women who wanted to get pregnant—"

"And one single woman who didn't," says Scully.

(As Mulder exits, the tail breaks off again and clunks to the floor.)

In Amanda Nelligan's hospital room, feeding time is over and the duty nurse is taking Amanda's baby back to the nursery. Mulder enters.

"You know," Amanda tells him, "I thought they were letting me stay in the hospital so long because I have really great insurance. Turns out they're keeping me here because they think I'm kinda crazy. They want to make sure I'm safe to be around my baby."

"Free cable," says Mulder.

Amanda giggles. Mulder reaches into his pocket and pulls out a cheesy shopping mall studio portrait.

"I wanna ask you," says Mulder. "Do you recognize this man?"

"Oh, yes. *Eeew*," says Amanda. "That's Eddie Van Blundht."

"What can you tell me about him?"

"We went out all through high school," she says, rolling her eyes. "Oh, brother!"

"What?"

"Oh, nothing," giggles Amanda. "He's just sort of a loser. He's one of those guys you look back on and and go, 'Oh, my God? What was I thinking? *What* was I thinking?'"

Amanda laughs. Mulder's mood does not match her merriment, however.

"Uh, what specifically made him a loser?" he says somberly.

"I don't know! Everything! He had like one million annoying personal habits. You know, no sense of romance, no ambition, no direction. I mean, I hear he's like a janitor or something now."

She adds, "He had this weird family. His dad was in the circus or something, I don't know. He never let me meet him, thank God."

Mulder ponders this information gravely.

"He must have had some good qualities," he says.

"Yeah, sure," says Amanda. "Everybody's got a few. Yeah, we had some good times. He really loved *Star Wars*, so we used to go and see it every weekend. That was nice."

She chuckles warmly at the memory. "But he was no Luke—that's for sure."

She looks at Mulder quizzically. "Why do you want to know about Eddie?" she asks.

Mulder says sternly, "That's official FBI business."

"Wow!" says Amanda.

Mulder smiles and pulls a single red rose

out of his jacket. "I want to congratulate you on this blessed event," he says.

"Thank you," says Amanda. "May the Force be with you!"

Mulder leaves the room. Outside the door he slumps, emotionally spent. He looks down the corridor, sees another Fox Mulder, and scrams.

The other Mulder enters Amanda's room. "Seriously, though," Amanda says. "Why do you want to know about Eddie?"

Mulder's phone rings. It is the ex-angry husband, asking him whether it is now safe to enter their bathroom—and what exactly he's been doing with the charcoal suit he borrowed.

Mulder tells them he'll have to call them back. He stares at Amanda.

"I was just here," he says finally. "Where did I go?"

In the hospital corridor, Mulder asks a nurse if she's seen his look-alike. She directs him to the men's locker room. Inside, he sees two men—a half-naked security guard and Dr. Alton Pugh, who is wearing only a towel. He handcuffs both, then phones Scully and asks her to meet him at the hospital ASAP.

Mulder spots several fluorescent bulbs flickering in an overhead fixture. He cautiously pushes up a corner of the access hatch. Out of the ceiling comes a soft voice.

"You're a damn good-looking man," says Eddie.

He leaps down from the ceiling headfirst, landing directly on Mulder.

Afterward Mulder, nursing a sore head, tries rather ineffectually to explain to hospital officials why he thought that Pugh and the security guard might have been Eddie Van Blundht, Jr. Scully arrives at this chaotic scene.

"What the hell happened?" she asks.

"Van Blundht surprised me. He cold-cocked me, then he got away," says Mulder.

He tells his partner that he thinks the whole case is a big waste of time.

"You think there's no X-file here now?" she says.

"No," says Mulder. "I think the only thing here is small potatoes."

Scully is surprised by this, but seems willing to go along. The agents leave the building. Deep in the bowels of the hospital, past a thicket of grimy boilers and steam pipes, a man is locked behind an access door. He sticks his face against a tiny wire-mesh window.

"Hello! Hello!" shouts the real Fox Mulder. *"Get me out of here!"*

He kicks the door with his feet. Nobody can possibly hear him, but there's good news: Someone has thoughtfully left an apple, a can of soda, and a peanut butter sandwich for him to eat.

In his office at FBI headquarters, AD Skinner pages through a case report. The fake Mulder—actually, Eddie Van Blundht—and Scully sit opposite him.

"Which one of you wrote this?" says Skinner piqued.

"I did, sir," says Mulder.

"You spelled 'Federal Bureau of Investigation' wrong."

"It was a typo," says Mulder.

"Twice," says Skinner.

Mulder shrugs. Scully tells him that her tests reveal that Eddie Van Blundht, Sr., died of natural causes. Mulder adds with some confidence that Eddie, Jr., probably hid his dad's body in order to continue cashing his Social Security checks.

"So the son wasn't a murderer?" asks Skinner.

"Oh, no! Not at all," says Mulder.

Scully reports that she's entered Eddie's

215

name into the national sex offender database, the West Virginia state police are on the lookout, and an arrest should be made soon.

Mulder says breezily, "That about wraps it up."

On their way down to the basement, Mulder asks Scully, somewhat hopefully, what she's doing that evening.

"Well, seeing how it's Friday," she says, "I was thinking I could get some work in on that monograph I'm writing for *The Penology Review*. You know—'Diminished Acetylcholine Production in Recidivist Offenders.'"

"Oh," says Mulder, disappointed.

"But actually I might bag that, though," she adds.

"Really?" says Mulder with new hope.

"Yeah. I have to say, Mulder, the anomalous musculature in the corpse we found really has me intrigued. In fact, I think I'm going to go to Quantico and have some tissue samples run. I'll see you Monday."

The befuddled Mulder deflates once again. He tries most of the keys on his key ring until he finally finds the one that opens his office door. He flicks on the switch, walks to "his" desk, and picks up his name plate.

"'Fox,' he reads, rolling his eyes. *"Brother."*

He puts his feet up on the desk and leans way back in his chair, nearly tumbling backward in the process. Recovering, he notices the "I Want to Believe" poster and the wall full of UFO and Bigfoot clippings.

"Good *night*," he says. "This is where my tax dollars go?"

He pulls out "his" wallet and finds a driver's license.

"Where do I live?" he mutters.

At Mulder's apartment in Alexandria, Virginia, the fake Mulder lets himself in and gives himself the grand tour. He looks for a bedroom. In vain.

"Where the hell do I sleep?" he says.

He gives up and hits the PLAY button on the answering machine. He feeds the fish in his aquarium.

"Mulder? Langly," says a familiar voice. "You gotta see this. An on-line associate of ours—who will remain anonymous—has figured out a way to digitize the Zapruder footage so he can extrapolate a bird's-eye view of the Dealey Plaza at the exact moment of the assassination! You'll never believe where the third shot came from!"

In the background, Frohike breaks in. "Tell him about the cheese steaks," he says.

"Oh, yeah," says Langly. "Then Frohike, Byers, and me are going out for cheese steaks. Are you down with that? Erase this when you hear it."

"Geeks for friends," says Mulder disgustedly.

Message two of two: "Hello, Marty?" breathes a sultry female. "Chantal. It's been so-o-o-o long since we spoke, and I've been s-o-o-o lonely not hearing your sexy voice."

Mulder quickly reaches for a pencil and paper.

"Marty, just for you we've lowered our rates to forty cents a minute—two ninety-nine the first minute, all long distance rates apply. Do give me a call, lover man—I'll be waiting."

Disappointed that Chantal is a phone sex operator, Mulder tosses down the pencil and searches for other diversions. He looks into a full-length mirror and practices talking like a G-Man.

"FBI," he says, whipping out his ID.

He tries again. "F! B! I!"

He splits the difference.

"FBI!"

He practices gazing fearlessly at a nemesis.

"You lookin' at me?" he says. "There ain't nobody else here. You must be lookin' at me. You wanta piece of this?"

He draws Mulder's pistol, sending the bullet clip flying. He hastily rams it back home, holsters the sidearm, and looks back into the mirror.

"You're a damn good-looking man," he says.

At Scully's Washington apartment, the female FBI agent pores over some lab reports. There is a knock on the door and she looks through the peephole. It is

"Mulder." There is a wide smile of friendship on his face.

"Mulder, what's up?" says Scully, a little startled.

"Scully—is this a bad time?" says Mulder.

"No. No!" says Scully, a little confused.

Mulder produces a bottle of wine.

"For us," he says shyly.

Still baffled, Scully uncorks the bottle and fills two glasses—all the while expounding on some fascinating new data from the Van Blundht autopsy. Scully and Mulder finally settle on her couch.

"So seriously, Mulder," she says. "What's going on? You okay?"

"Yeah," says Mulder, his expression thoughtful. "I was just kinda knockin' around, and just thinking. We never really talk much, do we?"

"What do you mean?" says Scully. "Like *really* talk? No. No, we don't, Mulder."

"So what's stopping us?" says Mulder soulfully.

A bottle of wine later, things have loosened up considerably. There is a fire in the fireplace and Scully is deep into a hilarious story about her high school prom night.

"... they had tried to start this

campfire," she says, "and it went totally out of control, and so we all had to ride back on the, um, what do you call it?—the pumper truck!"

Mulder chuckles appreciatively.

"Yeah," says Scully. "Marcus was the twelfth-grade love of my life. I can't believe I'm telling you this."

"I can't believe you haven't told me before."

"I'm seeing a whole new side of you, Mulder," says Scully.

"Is that a bad thing?"

"I like it," she says coyly.

Mulder gets serious, showing an even more intimate side. "Do you ever wish things were different?" he says.

"What do you mean?" asks Scully.

"The person you wanted to be when you grew up—when you were in high school. How far off that did you end up?"

"Career-wise?" asks Scully. "Miles off target."

"Nah," says Mulder. "Not just that. Didja ever wish that you could go back and do it all differently?"

"Do you?" asks Scully.

They look deep into each other's eyes. Mulder

makes his move, leaning in to kiss her. Scully doesn't lean toward him, but she doesn't lean away, either. Time seems to stand still. Their lips get closer. And closer.

And—

Somebody kicks open the front door. It is Fox Mulder—the real one. He is dirty, disheveled, and gunless. With a little cry of panic, Scully leaps to her feet and pushing the ersatz Mulder away. Eddie morphs back to his real self with a sigh of resignation. Or is it regret?

One month later in the Cumberland Reformatory visitation room, a not particularly happy-looking Mulder sits facing Eddie Van Blundht, Jr. Eddie tells him that he's being treated with muscle relaxants so that he can't "make faces" anymore.

"Did you tell them to do that?" asks Eddie.

Mulder says nothing.

Eddie glances anxiously around the room. "Is, uh, Agent Scully here?" he says.

"What did you want to talk to me about, Eddie?" asks Mulder.

"I just think it's funny," says Eddie. "I was born a loser. But you're one by choice."

"On what do you base that astute assessment?" asks Mulder, annoyed.

"Experience," says Eddie, leaning forward. "You should live a little. Treat yourself. God knows I would, if I were you."

Mulder rises wearily and leaves. Scully is waiting for him outside. She has seen and heard the entire conversation on a prison video monitor.

"I don't imagine you need to be told this, Mulder," says Scully, sympathetically, "but you're not a loser."

"Yeah," he says. "But I'm no Eddie Van Blundht, either."

He glances at his partner meaningfully. "Am I?"

back story:

The legend of Darin Morgan continues. An able-bodied, intelligent man in his thirties, this irreproducible writer-performer matter-of-factly conceded to a reporter two years ago that his work as a story editor on *The X-Files* constituted his first real job of any kind. He wrote several of the series most bizarrely memorable episodes—including "Humbug" (2X20); "Clyde Bruckman's Final Repose" (3X04); "War of the Coprophages" (3X14); and "Jose Chung's *From Outer Space*" (3X20). He was also unforgettable as an actor, specifically as the genetically mutated Flukeman in "The Host" (2X02).

After the third season, he rested.

"I was tired of doing the show," says Morgan, who left the writing staff without a backward glance. "I didn't want to do it anymore. I'd only done four episodes, but that was more than enough for me. I wanted to stay home and maybe work on my own stuff."

Vince Gilligan, however, wanted Morgan to work on *his* stuff: specifically, an episode designed to change the mood around his *X-Files* office. "I was proud of 'Paper Hearts,'" says Gilligan, "but that script was exceedingly dark, and I didn't want to get a reputation for only writing about doom and gloom. You know, the funny thing is that I came to television from writing features, and six of the seven movies I've written have been comedies.

"So I went to Chris and said: 'You know, the season as whole has been great, but it's been kind of dark, especially with Scully getting cancer and all.' And he said, 'Absolutely.' He was very supportive."

As the character of Eddie Van Blundht took shape, Gilligan launched a telephone campaign to drag Morgan out of retirement. Morgan says, "He told me that the part was written with me in mind, and that I should just be myself. Then, a few minutes later, he called back. He said, 'The character's kind of a loser. I don't want you to think that you're a loser.'"

Morgan maintains adamantly that whatever acting ability he once possessed has long since evaporated. "Vince caught me on a good night," he says. "Immediately after saying yes, I thought: I should have said no."

Be that as it may, most everyone around the show maintains that he played the part perfectly. And, rather atypically for this bunch of perfectionists, most everyone involved in the production of "Small Potatoes" had at least a moment or two of pure enjoyment while making it.

"A great, great script. And it was fun to do," says Duchovny, whose favorite bit of business was the heaven-help-me eye roll—a last-take improvisation—that he threw in at the exact moment he realizes that he's going to have to chase Eddie through the corridors of a small-town gynecologist's office.

Gillian Anderson smilingly recalls leafing through a stack of prop department photos of Morgan as Eddie, choosing the proper one for "Mulder" to use in his scene with Amanda. "I mean, the props guy comes in with this stack of photos of Darin with all sorts of different expressions," she says. "And, of course, we're all sitting behind the video monitor going through them and laughing hysterically."

The actress also lights up at the memory of her hospital room scene with actress Christine Cavanaugh—who was the voice of Babe in the movie of the same name, which was why her unique voice sounded so naggingly familiar. When Amanda

reveals that she was impregnated by Luke Skywalker, it is one of the rare scenes where Scully's pragmatism triumphs over Mulder's zealotry.

"I also enjoyed singing the *Star Wars* theme song with her," says Anderson.

Shocking as it may seem now, in the first drafts of Vince Gilligan's script the very special babies of Martinsburg sprouted angels' wings instead of tails.

ⓧ

"I wondered if it was genetically possible to be born with something akin to wings," says the writer. "I had our researcher Jessica Scott look into it, and she said there's a condition that causes something like an extended scapula—which was fine except there was nothing cute about that. So we decided they'd look a lot cuter with tails, and we called them monkey babies instead of angel babies."

ⓧ

We discover that Mulder's home address (from his driver's license on screen) is 42–2630 Hegal Place, Alexandria, VA 23242. His license expires 3/31/99. It also confirms his height as 6 feet 0 inches.

ⓧ

zero sum

Walter Skinner makes a deal
with the devil—a.k.a. the
Cigarette-Smoking Man—in
an effort to prevent Scully
from dying of cancer.

episode: 4X21

first aired: April 27, 1997

written by:
Howard Gordon and Frank Spotnitz

editor: Michael S. Stern

directed by: Kim Manners

guest stars:
Mitch Pileggi (AD Walter Skinner)
William B. Davis (The Cigarette-Smoking Man)
Laurie Holden (Marita Covarrubias)
Nicolle Nattrass (Misty Nagata)
Paul McLean (Special Agent Kautz)
Fred Keating (Detective Roy Thomas)
Allan Gray (Entomologist)
Addison Ridge (Bespectacled Boy)
Don S. Williams (First Elder)
Lisa Stewart (Jane Brody)
Barry Greene (ER Doctor)
Christopher J. Newton (Photo Technician)
Morris Panych (The Gray-Haired Man)
Oscar Goncalves (Night Attendant)
Jason Anthony Griffith (Uniformed Officer)
Fred Keating (Detective Hugel)
Julia Body (Supervisor)
Allan Gray (Dr. Peter Valdespino)
John Moore (Second Elder)

principal settings:
Desmond and Crystal City, Virginia;
Washington, D.C.; Elsinore, Maryland;
New York City, New York;
Payson, South Carolina

in the main routing center of Transcontinental Express, an overnight package delivery company, two young woman—Jane Brody and Misty Nagata—work side by side sorting envelopes. Jane asks Misty to cover for her while she sneaks out for a cigarette break.

Jane goes AWOL to the women's rest room. She locks herself into a stall, takes out a magazine, and lights up. Angry bees drop out of the faucets of the rest room sinks. They fly across the rest room, swarm under the stall door, and attack the terrified worker.

Misty becomes alarmed at her companion's long absence. She leaves her work station, goes to the rest room, and finds Jane lying dead, slumped against the toilet tank, her face a mass of crimson sores and bumps. Nagata screams in terror.

Shortly afterward, an image of Jane Brody's body is displayed on a computer screen. In a darkened, otherwise unoccupied office, AD Skinner sits at a computer's keyboard. He systematically deletes the picture—in fact, the entire case file—from the FBI computer system. He stands up and leaves the desk at which he has been sitting. It is Fox Mulder's desk.

Later that evening Skinner—dressed in black and carrying an athletic bag filled with burglar tools—takes his home telephone off the hook, leaves his apartment, and surreptitiously enters the Desmond, Virginia, routing center. He peels the crime scene tape off the door and enters the rest room where Jane Brody died. He picks up cigarette butt from the floor and pockets it. Wielding a hand-held vacuum cleaner and a scrub brush, he cleanses the stall area of clues. He notes a sticky yellow substance at the junction of the wall and ceiling, takes a sample, and—after carefully reattaching the crime-scene tape—leaves.

He travels to the local county morgue. He picks the lock of an emergency exit, enters, and removes Jane Brody's body from a refrigerated drawer. He hides in the shadows until a suspicious morgue attendant passes, then carries the body out of the

building, drives to an unmanned industrial waste incinerator, and shoves the corpse into the open mouth of a roaring rotary kiln.

His final stop is the forensics lab of the Desmond police department.

"Brody, Jane L.," says the desk officer on duty. "Yeah, we've got the pathologist's work, but the techs haven't gone over the crime scene yet."

"Let me see what you've got," says Skinner, his face partially hidden now by the bill of a baseball cap.

"Your name?" asks the officer.

Skinner flashes an FBI ID. "Special Agent Fox Mulder," he says.

Skinner signs Mulder's name on the officer's clipboard and receives a plastic tray filled with forensic evidence. The cop turns his back. Skinner switches a vial of blood with an identical one from his pocket. He wipes his fingerprints off the pen, hands back the evidence tray, and leaves the lab. He crosses the parking lot and dumps the stolen evidence into a trash can.

Someone from inside the police station runs after him.

"Agent Mulder!" shouts a middle-aged man in a parka.

"Who are you?" asks Skinner coldly.

"Detective Thomas. Ray Thomas. I'm the one who contacted you. Who e-mailed the pictures to your office. I ran into Officer Robbins. He said you'd come down here to look at some of the forensic evidence."

"That's right," says Skinner, turning to leave.

Thomas, still breathing heavily, follows him.

"So? Does that mean you found something here? Something worth looking into?" asks Thomas.

"I'm afraid not," says Skinner curtly, walking quickly toward his car.

"No?" says Thomas, incredulous.

"I didn't find anything to recommend my further involvement in the case," says Skinner.

"But what about the woman?" asks Thomas. "How do you explain what happened to her? She walks into a bathroom, a minute later she turns up—"

Skinner bends down and inserts his key into the car door.

"You saw the pictures!" insists Thomas.

"I saw them," says Skinner dismissively.

Thomas is now confused—and angry. "I was told that you were part of something called 'The X-Files,'" he says. "That you looked into stuff like this. So if there's really nothing to this, why come down here in the middle of the night?"

Skinner pulls open his car door. "Just doing my job, detective," he says. "Same as you."

He climbs into his car and drives away. In another car, parked nearby, the Gray-Haired Man sits waiting.

Back inside his apartment, Skinner strips off his clothing and stuffs it into a trash bag. He puts his phone back on the hook. Trash bag in hand, he opens his front door—and sees Mulder standing in the hallway.

"Ah—you *are* home," says Mulder.

"Yeah," says Skinner, startled. "What are you doing here?"

"I was just trying to reach you. I think your phone's off the hook."

"I needed some sleep."

"That's why you were taking the garbage out at four in the morning?"

Skinner's eyes flash with annoyance. "What do you want, Agent Mulder?" he says.

"Some answers," says Mulder, brushing past him and into the apartment.

"Concerning?" asks Skinner.

"The unexplained death of a postal worker," says Mulder. "Which someone is apparently going to great lengths to keep unexplained."

Mulder hands Skinner a sheaf of photos. He explains that he'd been sent them by Detective Thomas. When he tried retrieving them from his computer, however, he discovered that the files had been hollowed out.

"So where did you get them?" asks Skinner.

"From his partner," says Mulder.

"When?"

"After he finished questioning me about the detective's death," says Mulder. "He was killed. Shot in the head execution-style. His body was found near the precinct two hours ago. Possibly by the same person who forged my name to get access to evidence from the forensics lab."

Skinner struggles to hide his shock and fear. "What do you want from me?" he asks.

"I want your help on this, sir," insists Mulder impatiently.

"What about Agent Scully?" asks Skinner.

Mulder hesitates for a second. His eyes flicker downward. "Agent Scully's in the hospital," says Mulder softly.

"Has something happened that I should know about?" Skinner asks, alarmed.

Mulder tells him that his partner is undergoing some imaging tests, because her oncologist suspects that her tumor may be metastasizing.

The mood changes. Mulder, his passion for the case drained away, asks Skinner to take a look at the photos. The AD agrees to do it first thing in the morning. Mulder walks toward the door and nods at Skinner's trash bag.

"Want me to dump this on the way out?" he asks.

"No," says Skinner, still stunned. "I've got it."

Late that night, Skinner descends into the parking garage underneath his apartment building. Headlights beam out of the darkness toward him; a large gray car screeches to a halt just inches from where he's standing. The passenger door opens and the Cigarette-Smoking Man steps out.

The enraged Skinner glances through the car's windshield. The Gray-Haired Man sits expressionless behind the wheel.

"Was it you? Did you pull the trigger?" asks Skinner, furious. "Or did you have him do it for you?"

Cancer Man takes a drag of his cigarette. "I'm not here to answer your questions," he says.

Skinner grabs his adversary by the lapels and lifts him off his feet. "You murdered him! You killed an officer of the law!"

"I suggest you keep your voice down, Mr. Skinner," says the Cigarette-Smoking Man with steely calm. "Unless you want your neighbors to know the hours and the company you keep."

Skinner releases him. "I won't be a party to murder," he says.

The Cigarette-Smoking Man says, "I wouldn't get too comfortable on your moral high ground, Mr. Skinner. This only happened because you left your job unfinished."

Skinner says angrily, "I handled him just like I've handled everything else you've asked me to do! I've followed your instructions!"

"You failed to neutralize a potentially compromising situation," sneers the Cigarette-Smoking Man.

"You didn't have to kill him," says Skinner. "He didn't have to die."

"You're in no position to question the terms of our arrangement."

"Then we have no arrangement," says Skinner, turning away.

Cancer Man smiles smugly and addresses Skinner's retreating figure. "You'll find that it's not that easy to walk away from, Mr. Skinner," he says.

Skinner whirls and glares. "No?" he says.

"When a man digs a hole," says his tormentor, "he risks falling into it."

At eight that morning Skinner—sprawled out on the couch in his apartment—is wakened by his ringing phone. It is Mulder, reporting that Jane Brody's body has been stolen and that the forensic evidence has been tampered with by the man impersonating him.

"How do you know?" asks Skinner.

"I had them run a test," says Mulder. "The blood sample in the police forensics lab is B-positive, as is the postal worker's. But she suffered from a mild form of anemia characterized by a folic acid deficiency. The blood sample in the forensics lab showed a normal folate serum level."

Skinner, realizing that Mulder is close behind him, is rattled. "Are there any suspects?" he asks.

"No," says Mulder, "but I do have a place to start. The gun that killed Detective Thomas—ballistics has identified it as a Sig Sauer P228."

The news hits Skinner like a kidney punch.

Mulder continues, "I've got ballistics running comps on all weapons registered to federal agents and local officers."

Cradling the phone, Skinner walks to his desk and sees that a locked drawer has been forced. Inside the drawer is an empty holster. Realizing the worst, he crumples it in his fist.

"Sir?" says Mulder, perplexed by his boss's silence.

"Let me know what you find," says Skinner, finally.

Shortly afterward, a phone rings inside a nondescript office. A hand casually lifts the receiver.

"Yes?" says the Cigarette-Smoking Man.

"You can't do this!" says Skinner.

Nearly out of his mind with anger and guilt, Skinner demands to know if his gun was used to kill Detective Thomas. Teasingly, the Cigarette-Smoking Man suggests he report his suspicions to the police.

"Oh, don't think I won't!" says Skinner.

"Then why are you calling me?" says the Cigarette-Smoking Man with feigned innocence.

Skinner says nothing.

"Perhaps," says Cancer Man in a mocking tone, "because you realized you'd be admitting to obstruction of justice, criminal conspiracy, destruction of evidence."

He adds: "The consequences can be very serious for you—even in the unlikely event you could persuade the authorities you didn't kill the detective."

Skinner demands to know what he's been helping to cover up. The Cigarette-Smoking Man tells him that the less he knows the better.

"I need to know what that man died for," says the FBI man.

"He died for you, Mr. Skinner," says the Cigarette-Smoking Man. "He died so you could have what you wanted—a cure for Agent Scully. Isn't that what you want?"

"Agent Scully is in the hospital," says Skinner. "If you can do anything for her, I want it done now!"

The Cigarette-Smoking Man says airily that he is fully aware of Scully's condition.

"If anything happens to her," says Skinner threateningly, "I will expose you. I don't care what happens to me."

With only a slight darkening of his tone, the Cigarette-Smoking Man conveys effortlessly an equal—or greater—threat. "Agent Scully stands to live a long and healthy life," he says. "I would hope the same for you, Mr. Skinner."

At the Transcontinental facility, a supervisor leads Skinner through the sorting area and into the ladies' room where Jane Brody was killed. Skinner stares at the spot near the ceiling from which the sticky substance is still oozing. He reaches up and rubs it between his fingers.

"I need a hammer," he says.

He pounds a large hole in the wall. Behind the wallboard is a massive honeycomb, covered completely with rancid honey and dead bees.

Later that day, Skinner visits the Maryland home of Peter Valdespino, an entomologist. They enter an extensive home laboratory. Valdespino carries a container; inside it is a section of the honeycomb.

"Is there any reason you're not running this through the FBI lab?" asks Valdespino.

"This evidence is classified," says Skinner. "We've had some controversy over security at the Bureau. I'd appreciate your discretion."

"Certainly," says the scientist.

Skinner asks him if he can determine what kind of bees made the honey.

Valdespino says that it's hard to tell from just the comb, but he might be able to find the answer. The scientist opens the container and scrapes a honey sample from the comb.

"Huh. We're in luck," he says.

He tells Skinner that the sample contains royal jelly, used to feed the colony's larvae. Under a lighted magnifying glass, a tiny egg sac is visible. Once the eggs pupate, he says, he'll be able to give Skinner a definitive answer.

He also tells Skinner that six months ago he'd gotten a call from another FBI agent asking him about killer bees.

"Who was it?" asks Skinner.

"Name was Fox Mulder. I wondered if there was any connection."

"No," says Skinner.

He leaves.

Later that day, the assistant director enters Mulder's empty office, opens a file folder, and examines the photos of the Canadian apiary seen in "Herrenvolk" (4X01). He leafs through Mulder's Rolodex and copies Marita Covarrubias's phone number.

"Sir?" says Mulder.

He is standing in the doorway, watching Skinner.

"You looking for me?" asks the agent.

"I was just writing you a note," says Skinner, recovering. "Where've you been?"

With a definite tinge of suspicion, Mulder tells him that he's been at the First Nations Bank of Virginia—a branch directly across from Desmond police headquarters. He hands Skinner a sheaf of photos taken by the bank's surveillance camera. One of them is a grainy image of a now-familiar scene.

"That man there—that's Detective Thomas," says Mulder. "This man in the baseball cap? He was identified by the officer on duty at the forensics lab as 'Agent Mulder.'"

The picture of Skinner is too dark and indistinct to be recognized. The AD struggles to hide his anxiety.

"Can you get a usable image of this?" he asks.

Mulder asks, "I'm handing it over to Special Photo right now. What did you want to talk to me about?"

Lost in worry, Skinner doesn't reply.

"You were writing me a note," says Mulder.

"I was just checking on your progress," says Skinner.

Under Mulder's searching gaze, he leaves.

From his office, Skinner phones Marita Covarrubias at the UN. He asks her for information about the Canadian agricultural project. She insists—just as she told Mulder in "Herrenvolk"—that her investigation turned up no evidence of beehives or bee husbandry.

"What if I told you," says Skinner, "I had access to that evidence."

"You have access to these bees?" asks Covarrubias, startled.

"I may, soon," says Skinner. "Very soon."

In his home in Maryland, Peter Valdespino enters his lab and flips a wall switch. The lights do not go on. He switches on a desk lamp and looks at the honeycomb sample. The top of the container is broken. He hears a faint scratching noise and points the lamp at a window near the ceiling. The inside of the glass is covered by an angry, undulating wall of bees.

Attracted by the light beam, the bees fly off the window and swarm onto Valdespino. He tries to brush them off, but it is hopeless. The bees sting every inch of exposed flesh. He beats his fists in vain against the locked window.

At the morgue of a nearby hospital, Skinner joins Mulder, who has already examined Valdespino's corpse.

"I wanted you to get a look at this body before somebody tried to steal it," says Mulder.

He adds, "See these pocks and blisters? They're the same we saw in the photo of the deceased postal worker."

"Symptoms of what?" asks Skinner.

"Smallpox," says Mulder. "The first reported case in over seven years."

Mulder explains that Valdespino was infected by an especially virulent mutation of the disease. The infection entered his body via the bees' stingers and venom—in fact, says the agent, he'd already consulted with Valdespino about this scenario.

"You mean you've seen this before?" asks Skinner.

"Yeah, but I've never had any hard evidence," says Mulder. "Not until now. I think that's what somebody has gone to great lengths to prevent."

"Why?" asks Skinner.

"I can only guess," says Mulder. "But I think that somebody is trying to engineer a method of delivery—for a disease that has killed more people throughout history than any contagion known to humankind."

"Can they be stopped?" asks Skinner.

"How can we stop them?" asks Mulder. "We don't even know who these people are. And we won't, until we know the identity of that shooter."

"How close are you?" asks Skinner in agony.

"Hopefully, very," says Mulder firmly.

In a break room at the Transcontinental facility, Misty Nagata, depressed and alone, unwraps a candy bar. Skinner enters and flashes his credentials.

"I need to talk to you, Misty," he says. "About your coworker."

Nagata flinches. She protests that she's already told the police everything she knows.

"Everything?" asks Skinner, looking deeply into her eyes.

He tells her that Jane Brody's death was not an accident. She fights back her fear and tells him that Jane was her best friend—and that the men investigating her death threatened her with the loss of her job if she talked about her to anyone else.

"Did these men say who they were?" asks Skinner.

"No. And I didn't ask," says Misty. "They just wanted the package."

"What package?"

Misty explains that damaged packages are routed to the facility for inspection before they're reshipped. Skinner, starting to see the bigger picture, gazes at her even more intently.

"The place where these damaged packages are kept: How close is it to the rest room where you found Jane?" he says.

"It's just the next door down the hall. They've got a storage room," says Misty.

"The damaged package they wanted. Do you remember where it was being sent?"

"No. Not offhand."

"Is there any way of finding out?"

"I can look up the tracking number," says Nagata.

"That would be a big help for me, Misty," says Skinner. "And maybe to Jane."

At the Special Photo lab, Mulder peers over the shoulder of an FBI photo technician. The man has digitized the surveillance picture; as he repeatedly enhances the image, the face of "Mulder" becomes clearer. A final pass reveals a grainy but unmistakable picture of Walter Skinner.

Mulder is shocked—and momentarily staggered. "I need you to print out a hard copy of that for me," he says finally.

At the New York City headquarters of the Shadowy Syndicate, the Cigarette-Smoking Man and two Elders contemplate a glass vial containing the body of a dead bee.

"This is the last remaining specimen," says the Cigarette-Smoking Man. "The bees from the scientist's house have been contained and destroyed."

"And the body?" says the First Elder.

"It also has been sanitized."

The First Elder presses for details of the mishap, but the Cigarette-Smoking Man is evasive. "You'll have to trust my assurance," he says, "that any other breaches have been handled."

"Handled by whom?" says the First Elder.

"We have a man in place," he says. "A man with no other choice but to succeed."

The Elder says, "What assurance can you give us that he can be trusted?"

The Second Elder breaks in. "We can't risk even the slightest exposure!" he says.

"He has nothing to expose," says the Cigarette-Smoking Man coolly. "Except his own duplicity."

"Should we assume, then," says the first Elder, "that the trial run is proceeding as planned?"

Cancer Man takes a deep drag of his cigarette, picks up the vial, and turns to leave. "It's already begun," he says.

In the schoolyard of the JFK Elementary School in Payson, South Carolina, a class of third graders are playing under the watchful eye of their teacher, Mrs. Kemper. Unnoticed, a bee flies down toward a jungle gym. It lights on the hand of a small boy, who cries out in pain and drops to the ground.

"Mrs. Kemper!" says one of his pals, a bespectacled ten-year-old. "Billy got stung by a bee!"

Mrs. Kemper is already tending to a little girl who's been stung. Other crying children run toward her. Dozens of bees light on her, and she swats at them ineffectually.

"Everyone get inside! *Everyone inside!*" shouts the teacher.

Screaming, the children run into the school building—all except the bespectacled boy, who drops his glasses in the midst of a small cloud of bees and scrambles to recover them. Mrs. Kemper runs

back into the yard and pushes him to safety. She is swarmed under by the frenzied insects.

In a hospital emergency room, the children in Mrs. Kemper's class are being treated for the their injuries. Skinner arrives and locates the physician in charge. He tells the physician that the bee-stung children must be inoculated immediately against smallpox. The doctor looks at Skinner as he would a madman, tells him that smallpox has been eradicated, and adamantly refuses.

"Mr. Skinner?" says a woman's voice. It is Marita Covarrubias.

"What are you doing here?" asks Skinner.

She tells him that his call about the bees set in motion her own inquiries.

"Into what?" asks Skinner nervously.

"Seven packages that were sent from Canada to a P.O. box in Payson, South Carolina," she says. "I came here to find out what was in those packages."

Skinner glances around at the stricken children. "You're a little late to do anything about it," he says.

"So are you, apparently," replies Covarrubias.

Invoking her sworn duty to advise and inform the UN Secretary General, she presses him to tell her what he knows about the matter. Skinner struggles with his conscience and finally speaks.

"I think it's some kind of experiment," he says. "Using bees as carriers."

"Have you told Agent Mulder this?" asks Covarrubias.

Skinner grimaces. "I can't," he says, and lapses into a tortured silence.

"Are you involved in this, Mr. Skinner?" demands Covarrubias. "No? Then what are you doing here?"

Skinner still says nothing.

"What aren't you telling me, Mr. Skinner?" she insists. "If you know who's behind this, you have to come forward. No one else can."

That night, the AD enters his apartment, picks up the telephone, prepares to dial—and stops. He looks into his desk drawer. The pistol has been returned to its holster. He picks it up.

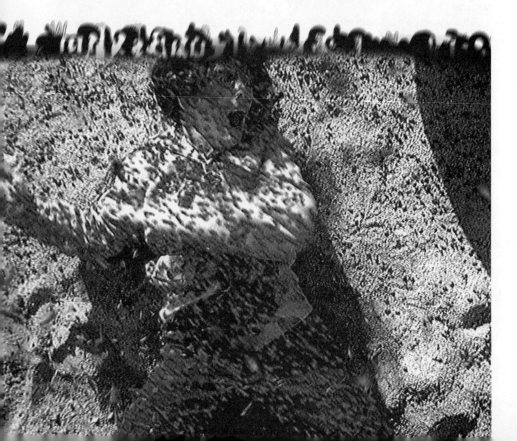

"Put the gun down," says Mulder, stepping forward from the shadows.

He holds his own gun trained at Skinner's head.

"I was just calling you," says Skinner.

"I said—put the gun down!"

Skinner complies. "You don't understand," he says wearily.

"I do now," says Mulder, spitting out the words. "Is this the gun you used to kill the detective?"

"No," says Skinner.

Mulder says, "How does it feel to shoot an innocent man in the head?"

"I didn't kill that—"

"You're a liar!" shouts Mulder. "You've been working with the Smoking Man all along! You knew when they had my father killed. And you knew when they took Scully!"

"Listen to me!" says Skinner. "He set me up! He stole my gun and then he put it back! Which means the police are probably on their way right now."

"I don't believe you," says Mulder.

"Look at my desk drawer, Agent Mulder. "Look at it! Why would I force my own lock?"

Skinner adds, "If I lied to you—I have lied to you. And I won't make excuses for those lies. But there was a reason I did what I did. One I think you're in a unique position to understand."

Mulder's gun hand wavers. But he does not put the weapon down.

"I advised you against a certain course of action some time ago—concerning Agent Scully. I didn't follow my own advice."

Mulder says, "Give me the gun."

Skinner's Sig Sauer P228 fires six times—into a water tank at the FBI ballistics lab by Special Agent Kautz, last seen in "Anasazi" (2X25). Kautz wears goggles and protective earphones, as does Mulder and Skinner, standing nearby.

Kautz uses a magnifying device connected to a video monitor to compare one of the newly fired slugs with the bullet that killed Detective Thomas. On the screen, the rifling patterns are identical.

"So this is definitely the murder weapon?" asks Mulder.

"If I were called to testify," says Kautz, "I'd say without a doubt."

He turns to Mulder and Skinner.

"So where'd you find it?" he says.

Skinner bows his head. Nobody speaks.

"In a sewer grate," says Mulder finally. "Around the corner from the crime scene."

Skinner looks searchingly at Mulder.

"Sometimes you get lucky," says Mulder.

"Sometimes you don't, right?" replies Kautz.

Mulder says, "What do you mean?"

"The serial number. It'd been filed clean off. Now, unless forensics pulls a print, this gun is virtually untraceable."

That night, the Cigarette-Smoking Man enters a darkened apartment. He reaches for the light switch.

"Leave it off," says Skinner, "I'm starting to get used to the dark."

Skinner is sitting at the Cigarette-Smoking Man's desk and pointing his gun at his tormentor.

"Is this part of our deal?" smirks the Cigarette-Smoking Man.

"We never had a deal," says Skinner. "No?"

"Agent Scully is dying," says Skinner. "And you haven't done a damn thing about it."

The Cigarette-Smoking Man's smirk widens.

"You think that's funny?" says Skinner, his gun hand shaking with rage.

"I'm just enjoying the irony, Mr. Skinner," says Cancer Man. "Only yesterday you said you wouldn't be a party to murder. And here you are."

His tone becoming menacing.

"Yours isn't the first gun I've had pointed at my face, Mr. Skinner. I'm not afraid to die. But if you kill me now, you'll also kill Agent Scully."

"You have no intention of saving her. You never did," says Skinner.

"Are you certain?" says the Cigarette-Smoking Man. "I saved her life once before—when I had her returned to Agent Mulder. I may save her again. But you'll never know if you pull the trigger, will you?"

The phone rings loudly.

"Now, unless you intend to kill me," he says tensely, "I'd like to answer my phone."

Skinner says nothing. The phone rings again. He fires his gun once, twice, three times. He turns and leaves the apartment.

The Cigarette-Smoking Man stands erect. Only his eyes betray how deeply he's been rattled.

He crosses to the desk and picks up the phone.

"Yes?" he says.

Fingers quivering slightly, he pulls out a Morley and places it between his lips.

"He was just here," he says. "He threatened to kill me. I'm sure Mulder will be contacting you. He'll want to know if Skinner has seen all there is to see."

At the other end of the line is Marita Covarrubias. A shadowy figure stands behind her. "I'll tell him what you want me to tell him," she says.

The Cigarette-Smoking Man strikes a match, lights up, and inhales. "Tell him," he says, "what he wants to hear."

back story:

"'Zero Sum,'" says Frank Spotnitz, "was a fortunate accident."

That's the short version of the story. The long version, complete with a typical (for *The X-Files*) semi-desperate struggle to surmount a formidable creative obstacle, begins with the mid-season news that Gillian Anderson would be gone for a week in March, filming her part in a theatrical movie called *The Mighty* with Sharon Stone.

Spotnitz says, "We needed to construct the story without her, and it didn't seem fair to make David work like a dog while she had the week off. So we tried to keep him light while still involving him in the story to some degree."

The solution: Bring in Assistant Director Walter Skinner—and the now-annual tradition of writing an episode around Mitch Pileggi's recurring character. Bring in, too, executive producer Howard Gordon, the on-staff Skinner specialist with "Avatar" (3X21) under his belt, as cowriter.

"After all," says Spotnitz, "Skinner had already made his Faustian bargain with the Cigarette-Smoking Man in 'Memento Mori'

[4X15]. This was a logical time to see it played out. It was also a good place to bring back the bees, which were introduced at the beginning of the season in 'Herrenvolk,' but which had never really been explained.

"What we wanted to stay away from," Spotnitz adds, "was taking the liberty of having something paranormal happen to Skinner. We'd done that once before—in 'Avatar'—and there's no reason for it to happen twice in a lifetime to a person."

Gordon has a slightly different take on the episode. Beating out a story without Scully and with only a minimal amount of Mulder, he recalls, was like working "with one hand tied behind our backs." He also remembers, with a weary shake of his head, that he and Spotnitz did the difficult deed over a marathon weekend writing session, during which his previous script, "Synchrony," was in the throes of a difficult shooting schedule.

"What we were trying to do, basically," he says, "was preserve Skinner's integrity as a character *while* he makes his deal with the devil, and at the same time allow us to better understand his character and his relationship with Mulder and Scully by taking him into the gray area between right and wrong. I mean, to what level is he willing to sacrifice himself—and his integrity—for them? Where does he draw the line?"

Where indeed?

"Who knows?" says Mitch Pileggi good-naturedly. "Nobody tells anybody anything on this show."

The actor reports that, as usual, no explanation whatsoever was offered to him for his character's on-screen behavior. Indeed, Pileggi got only a few days' notice that he would be appearing before the American public in his underwear—wearing jockey shorts instead of boxers. This gave him just enough time to hit the weight room and whip his physique into shape, but nowhere near enough to brace himself for the screen grab that *TV Guide* subsequently published.

"That was not," says Pileggi, "a happy moment for me."

Neither was the news that *The X-Files'* most unloved recurring characters would be returning. By this time, everyone even loosely connected with show knows that the word "bee" in a script is synonymous with "trouble"—and "Zero Sum" was no exception. As always, the insects were hard to handle on the set and showed up poorly on film. As always, too, the problem had to be fixed by the visual effects wizards in postproduction. "Laurie Kallsen-George had basically nine days to create full-blown bee sequences—a job that for a feature film would take months," says Howard Gordon. "But she was unflinching. I think in that entire period she logged in maybe a dozen hours of sleep."

Laurie Holden, who plays Marita Covarrubias, notes that her final scene in "Zero Sum" gave her at long last *some* indication of where her character's loyalties lay—although all that may change, of course, when and if the U.N. operative returns during Season Five.

Kim Manners, who directed, seems to be the only person—except for Anderson, of course—who remained serenely above the struggle. "This was really a good show for me," he says, "because I had not got a chance to work Mitch. And they wrote a great script, you know? It was really something he could sink his teeth into and he just did a great job. Bill Davis was fabulous in that show, too."

This is the second episode to be filmed entirely without Agent Scully. The first was "3"(2X07), and she appeared only in flashback in "Musings of a Cigarette-Smoking Man."

ⓧ

episode: 4X22
first aired: May 4, 1997
written by: John Shiban
editor: Jim Gross
directed by: James Charleston
guest stars:
Steven M. Porter (Harold Spüller)
Alex Bruhanski (Angelo Pintero)
Sydney Lassick (Chuck Forsch)
Nancy Fish (Nurse Innes)
Daniel Kamin (Detective Hudak)
Lorena Gale (Attorney)
Mike Puttonen (Martin Alpert)
Christine Willes (Karen Kosseff)
Ken Tremblett (Uniformed Officer)
Gerry Nairn (Sergeant Conneff)
Fawnia Mondey (Blond Bowler)

principal setting:
Washington, D.C.

elegy

Several young women have been
murdered on Mulder and Scully's
home turf. Their prime suspect is a
mentally disabled man, Harold Spüller,
who has been beset by a series of
frightening apparitions.

at Angie's Midnight Bowl, a bowling center in Washington, D.C., the sixtyish proprietor, Angelo Pintero, prepares to lock up for the night. He collects the empty soda cups and beer bottles and returns them to the snack bar. He circles back to the shoe counter—where he is surprised to find Harold Spüller, a squat, emotionally disabled man in his forties. Harold is laboriously shelving returned rental shoes.

"Aw, gosh. Go home, Harold!" says Angie.

"Not done yet," murmurs Harold, concentrating fiercely on his job.

"Harold, you hear me?" says Angie wearily. "You shoulda gone home already."

"Not done yet!" says Harold.

"Aw, for crying out loud, Harold! This ain't so difficult!" says Angie.

Pintero walks around the counter and begins tossing the shoes into their slots. His job usurped, Harold watches with growing anxiety.

"*I'm not done yet!*" he cries with frantic anger.

Angie catches himself and looks at Harold with sympathy. He lays his hands on the little man's shoulders and looks him in the eye.

"Harold, it's past your bedtime," he says. "The doctors'll be worried about you. You did a good job today. Now, you go home. C'mon!"

Harold calms down somewhat and walks to the exit, muttering to himself what sounds like a series of random numbers.

Pintero turns and scans the empty bowling alley. To his surprise, the automatic pinspotter on Lane Six is recycling endlessly. He walks to that lane and presses the reset button. A bowling ball shoots out of the ball return. When it comes to rest, he reaches for it—and recoils. Its finger holes are overflowing with blood.

"What the hell . . . ?"

Pintero walks up Lane Six and kneels down in front of the bowling pins. They are standing in a poll of blood. He peers up into the pinspotting machinery. A young blond woman is suspended in the mechanism, her throat cut. She tries to speak, but no words come out.

"Oh, my God! Oh, my God! I'll get help!" says Pintero, horrified.

He runs to the front desk and dials 911. A police car, its lights flashing, has already pulled up across the street. Pintero runs outside.

"Officer! Officer!" he says.

"This don't involve you," says the cop, shooing him away.

Angie, breathing heavily, struggles to speak.

"A woman inside! She's bleeding . . . !"

He glances down past the cop. A young blond woman lies sprawled in the street. She is covered with blood. Her throat has been cut.

"Oh, my God!" says Pintero. "That's her—that's the girl I saw!"

The next day the bowling alley—except for Lane Six—is in full operation.

Lying flat on his stomach at the far end of the lane, Pintero shows Mulder and Scully how the weight of the murdered woman has bent the pinspotting mechanism. He also tells them that when he returned inside with the policeman, both the woman and the blood were gone.

Scully shoots Mulder a skeptical glance, not unnoticed by Pintero. He slides out from under the pinspotter and faces the agents.

"Look, I'm not makin' this up!" insists Pintero.

"No one's suggesting that you are, Mr. Pintero," says Mulder. "Can I ask you a favor? Can I get a soda, a cola, something like that?"

"Sure. Yeah," says Angie, puzzled.

He heads for the snack bar.

"What *is* that look, Scully?" says Mulder, walking with his partner up the lane to the foul line.

"I'd have thought that after four years you know exactly what that look meant," she replies.

"What?" says Mulder. "You don't believe in ghosts?"

"You're saying that what this man saw was the victim's ghost," says Scully.

"Sounds more like a disembodied soul," says Mulder. "According to Mr. Pintero, this one was trying to communicate. She was speaking to him, as if she was trying to

tell him something. Sounds more like a death omen."

"A death omen?"

"Yeah. A spirit being that arrives as a harbinger of death."

Mulder interrupts his colloquy to coolly fling a cobalt blue ball down the alley—rolling a strike, of course. He continues:

"This is the third reported sighting in as many weeks. And as many murders. Each time the victim appearing near the crime scene—trying to communicate, to say something."

"To communicate what?" asks Scully.

"I don't know yet," says Mulder. "But if you hold on a second I might have an answer for you."

Angie Pintero arrives with Mulder's soft drink. The FBI agent walks back toward the pinspotter and spills the bubbly liquid on the site of the bloodstain. It pools up on the polished hardwood surface in an unusual pattern.

"'She Is Me,'" says Mulder.

"What?" says Scully.

"'She Is Me,'" says Mulder. "Written onto the wax. Look at this."

Scully stares at the evidence, speechless.

Inside a District of Columbia station house, a beefy homicide detective named Hudak displays several crime-scene slides and explains to a dozen-cop task force that three women, all approximately the same age and weight with the same hair and eye color, have been murdered within as six-block area.

"Our FBI profiling model," he says, "suggests a while male, late twenties, early thirties. His victims were probably strangers to him—symbols representing other women in his life, perhaps all women."

At the back of the room, Mulder leans over and whispers to Scully.

"Hey, you!" says Hudak. "In the back—are we boring you?"

"No, not at all," says Mulder. "Actually, I have something to add. I think that following the FBI model in this case will not only fail to turn up the killer, but will undoubtedly lead to more victims and more deaths."

"You wanna tell us who you are and what you base this on?"

"I'm Special Agent Mulder and this is Agent Scully. We're from the FBI. We've been following up on a lead that seems to have been dropped. The statement made by the proprietor of the bowling alley."

What Pintero saw, says Mulder to a skeptical Hudak, was an apparition—what the Irish call a fetch, but which is more commonly known as a wraith.

Mulder asks, "Were there any written messages in these other cases? Do the words 'She Is Me' have any meaning to you?"

Struggling to hide his surprise, Hudak tells him that these were the last words of a murder victim named Penny Timmons, according to a 911 call they received the night of her death.

"Who made that call?" asks Mulder.

"A nut," says Hudak.

He adds, "There *were* no dying words. Penny Timmons's larynx was severed. She couldn't cry for help even if there was help to cry for."

"And no one followed up on this lead?" asks Mulder.

"No," sneers Hudak. "But I'll have someone get you the number and you can follow up on it."

At the New Horizon Psychiatric Center, the agents wait while Martin Alpert, a good-natured and soft-spoken occupational therapist, and Nurse Innes, a rather gruff middle-aged psych nurse, assemble the two dozen or so emotionally disabled residents. Harold Spüller is one of them.

"Hi," says Mulder gently. "I wanted to ask if anyone here used the pay phone out in the hallway there on Friday night? Because somebody called the police and reported a murder."

Silence. Harold Spüller hangs his head.

Alpert whispers toward Mulder. "Sloppy Joe night," he says.

"That was Sloppy Joe night," says Mulder.

"Oh! That was me!" says a patient, an older man with thick glasses. "I did it! I admit it, I did it! I'm just a human being, after all!"

Alpert looks at him reprovingly. "Chuck, tell the truth," he says.

"Nah," says Chuck. "I'm sorry. I didn't mean it. I lied. I lied—but I'm just a human being!"

Addressing the patients respectfully but firmly, Alpert asks if any of them used the pay phone to call the police. The patients look at him blankly—except for Harold, who sits, rocking back and forth, in obvious distress.

Mulder holds up a graduation photo of Penny Timmons, the woman killed near the Midnight Bowl.

"Does anybody recognize this woman?" he asks.

All the patients except Harold raise their hands.

"That's the lady that got murdered!" says Chuck.

Scully holds up a copy of *TV Guide* with a picture of Jay Leno on the cover. "Does anybody recognize this man?" she says.

"Yes!" says a male patient. "He did it!"

"He did it!" says a pretty young female resident.

"He's the murderer!" says another patient.

"He's a very funny man!"

"He smiles a lot!"

Once again, Harold is the only patient who remains silent. Mulder smiles ruefully and asks Alpert about him.

"He has a tendency to get a little worked up," says the therapist.

"Can I talk to him?" asks Mulder.

"Sure," says Alpert.

In the corridor of the psychiatric center, Scully carefully studies photos of the three crime scenes. Mulder joins her; she tells him that in each murder the killer removed a ring from the victim's left hand and placed it on her right. It is, she adds, a classic symptom of a syndrome called ego-dystonia—a form of obsessive-compulsive behavior that rarely escalates to murder.

"Not ordinarily," says Mulder, "unless there's a more complex psychology at work—like pronounced mental illness."

He adds, "I'm not sure that the killer is here. But certainly the person who made that phone call is. And I think his name is Harold Spüller."

"Did he cop to making the call?" asks Scully.

"No," says Mulder, "but he's about to."

Harold Spüller sits despondently on the edge of the bed in the room he shares with Chuck. Mulder and Scully stand next to him. Nurse Innes is at the other end of the room, listening.

"I don't know anything!" says Harold, rocking. "I didn't do anything! Leave me alone!"

"You made that phone call, didn't you, Harold?" says Mulder.

"No," says Harold.

"Did you say the words 'She Is Me'?"

"No."

"Have you ever heard those words?"

"No!"

Mulder pauses.

"Have you ever seen a ghost, Harold?"

Harold stops rocking. He hesitates several seconds before answering.

"No," he says. "*No. No! No! No! No! No! No! No!* Nonononononono . . . just leave me alone!"

He is keening hysterically. Nurse Innes steps in to comfort him.

"Well," says Scully to Mulder, half admiringly and half reproachfully. "When you're right, you're right."

She leaves. Mulder looks back at Harold, eyeing him with more concern than certainty.

Harold is rocking very rapidly now.

He says: "Seventeen, thirty, thirty-seven, forty-five, fifty-three. . . ."

In the New Horizons recreation room, Scully pores over a thick file of medical records. Mulder joins her.

"Harold Spüller," says Scully. "He suffers from Pervasive Developmental Disorder. It's what is sometimes called Atypical Autism. He's spent his entire life in and out of facilities just like this one."

She adds, "He has been medicated, he has received shock therapy, and besides his other disabilities, he has been diagnosed with severe ego-dystonic obsessive-compulsive disorder. Which would explain the switching of the victims' rings."

"But why all of a sudden?" asks Mulder.

"You mean, what made him snap?" asks Scully. "I think his outburst showed clearly a frustrated impulse toward violence when he was put in a challenging situation."

Mulder shakes his head. "That outburst didn't come," says Mulder, "until after I asked him if he'd ever seen a ghost."

Mulder contends that Harold's condition explains neither the apparitions seen by Angie Pintero or the phrase "She Is Me." Scully tells him that she has found a partial explanation: Harold's IRS 1040 form, which lists him as earning wages working at Angie's Midnight Bowl. As she leans over the table, a drop of blood hits the form.

"Oh, Scully. . . ." Mulder, who's seen this before, says, concerned.

"Yeah," says Scully, wiping a thin trickle of blood from her nostril. "It's okay."

"You sure?" says Mulder.

"Yeah. It's just—I'm fine. I just need to find a washroom."

Not looking fine at all, Scully enters the ladies' room and presses a wet paper towel to her nose. She looks up from the wash basin: "She Is Me" is written in dripping blood on the mirror.

Shaken, Scully scans the room. In another corner stands a young woman wearing a college sweatshirt. Her face is pale—almost gray. Blood runs down from a long gash on her neck. The woman tries to speak, but cannot. Scully stares at her, horrified.

There is a knock on the door.

"Scully?" says Mulder.

Scully looks again. Both the woman and the bloody writing are now gone.

"Scully? Are you in there?"

"Yeah," gasps the agent.

Mulder enters.

"They found another victim," he says. "A college student with her throat cut. Just about half a block from here."

In a dark alley near the psychiatric center, Scully examines the body of a woman—the same woman she saw in the washroom. Scully appears dazed—or perhaps numb.

"Her name was Lauren Heller, age twenty-one," says Mulder. "She's single. Apparently she was on her way home from a bar that she part-timed at after school. She had a ring on her left hand—switched to her right-hand pinkie finger. She was dead less than an hour when she was found."

Scully emerges from her reverie, at least partially. She says, "That would rule out Harold Spüller as a killer, huh?"

"No, actually it doesn't," says Mulder. "Harold's not at the home. He's nowhere to be found. His nurse locked him in his room after we left, but he managed to escape unnoticed."

Mulder adds that they should be the ones to find him first—if only to find what "She Is Me" means.

Scully hesitates, then speaks. She gestures toward her nose.

"Mulder, I think I'm going to let you take care of that. I'm going to get this checked out, just to be safe."

Mulder offers to drive her to the hospital, but she refuses.

"I'm fine, Mulder, really. I've had the doctors keep a close watch. It's just a precaution."

"You're sure?" asks Mulder.

"I'm fine," says Scully.

She walks toward her car, shoulders hunched against the chill.

In a dark room somewhere nearby, Harold Spüller mutters more series of numbers to himself. He pastes a bowling score sheet onto a wall—next to dozens of other score sheets. He looks up to the top of the wall. "She Is Me" is written on an old score sheet in blood.

"No," Harold moans. "No! I just want to be left alone!"

Scully sits silently in a hospital examin-

ing room while a nurse pumps a blood sample from her arm. Shortly afterward, she sits in the office of Karen Kosseff, the L.C.S.W. introduced in "Irresistible" (2X13).

"We've spoken about your fear," says Kosseff. "You've been afraid to express it to others. To Agent Mulder."

"This is different," says Scully.

"How?"

Scully tells the therapist what we already know: She has been diagnosed with a non-operable cancer, but thus far the effect on her health has been minimal. The therapist's eyes shine with real concern.

"I'm sorry," she says. "You've kept working?"

"Yes," says Scully. "It's been important to me."

"Why?"

Scully falls silent, perhaps having never before considered the question.

"Agent Mulder has been concerned," she says. "He's been very supportive through this time."

"Do you feel that you owe it to him to continue working?" asks the therapist.

"No," says Scully, shaking her head.

Another long pause.

"I guess I just never realized how much I relied on him before this. His passion—he's been a great source of strength that I've drawn on."

Kosseff says, "What happened last night, Dana?"

Scully shudders and forces herself to face her demons.

"I saw something," she says.

She adds, "I don't know what to trust. If I saw it because of the stress—because the image had been suggested to me—or if it was a suggestion of my own fears."

"Your fear of failing him?"

"Maybe," says Scully, near tears.

"What did you see?" asks the therapist.

"I saw a woman who had recently been murdered. It appeared as if she was trying to tell me something."

"Do you know what?"

"No," says Scully quickly.

"Are you sure?" says Kosseff, her gentle gaze locked into Scully's own.

At the bowling center, Mulder finds Angie Pintero working at the shoe counter. He tells the proprietor that Harold Spüller is wanted for the murder of Penny Timmons. Angie shakes his head in disbelief.

"Harold's worked for me for ten years," he says. "He might be crazy, but he couldn't kill anyone. He's a sweet kid."

"You know where he is now?" asks Mulder.

"He was here this morning when I arrived, arranging the shoes."

"He has a key?"

"Nah. He has some damn way of getting in from an abandoned building next door."

From his hiding place, a frantic-looking Harold peers out at Mulder talking to Pintero.

"You ever get Lane Six working?" asks Mulder.

"No. Not since I saw the girl," says Pintero.

Mulder glances over his shoulder toward Lane Six—just as a lone bowling pin falls onto the lane from the mechanism above. He runs toward the spot. Harold, who'd dislodged the pin, scrambles back into the crawl space behind the pinsetting machines.

"Harold! Harold! Harold, I just want to talk to you!" shouts Mulder.

He ducks under the pinspotter and follows Spüller through the dark, noisy area. He finds Harold slumped in a corner in a near-catatonic state. He is repeating a single phrase over and over.

"She is me," says Harold. "She is me she is me she is me she is me."

In a D.C. police interrogation room, Harold Spüller sits rocking and muttering. His court-appointed attorney, a formidable-looking woman, spars with Hudak. The detective is determined to treat Harold as an ordinary murder suspect; she is just as determined to stop him.

"Tell me why you did it, Harold, huh?" says Hudak. "Tell me why you killed those women!"

Harold rocks faster. The lawyer threatens to end the interview.

Mulder has been standing in the background. He steps forward.

"Harold?" he says. "Harold, you knew those women who were murdered, didn't you? That's why you're scared. You're afraid they've come back to visit you."

Harold keeps rocking. His attorney, perhaps a little frightened herself, looks at Mulder quizzically.

"Penny Timmons," says Mulder.

"Eight, seventeen, thirty, thirty-seven," says Harold. "Fifty-three, seventy-one, eighty, ninety-two, ninety-nine, one hundred and eight."

"Risa Shapiro?" says Mulder.

"Fourteen, twenty-nine, thirty-eight, fifty-seven, seventy-one, seventy-nine, eighty-eight, one hundred and one, one hundred and seventeen."

"Michelle Chamberlain."

"Seventeen, thirty-two, forty-nine, sixty-

nine, seventy-eight, eighty-seven, ninety-nine—"

Mulder cuts Harold off. "What was her shoe size?" he says.

"Six and a half," sobs Harold.

"There you have it!" says Hudak triumphantly.

Harold's attorney objects. "This is not a confession!" she says.

Hudak is undeterred. "He killed 'em!" says the detective. "He stalked 'em, he fixated on 'em, and he slit their pretty little throats!"

Harold rocks and counts to himself. Mulder speaks to him forcefully, but not unkindly.

"Harold," he says, "there are people who think you murdered these woman. I'm not one of them. But I need your help for me to prove it. Do you think you can do that? I think you can."

At the bowling center that night, a small procession of individuals—Mulder, Hudak, Harold, his attorney, and two uniformed cops—stops at Angie Pintero's shoe counter. Mulder asks the owner's permission to search the building.

"Sure," says Pintero. "You okay, Harold?"

"Your shoes are out of order, Mr. Pintero. I'm sorry," says Harold.

Angie squeezes the little man's shoulder affectionately. "It's okay, buddy," he says. "Don't you worry about it. You get things straightened out with these folks, then you come back and keep me in line."

Harold leads the group into the dark space behind the machinery.

"He's going to show us something that's going to exonerate him?" says Hudak skeptically.

"I think so," says Mulder.

"Here!" says Harold, stopping in front of a wall we've seen before.

Fixed in Hudak's flashlight beam is a huge collage of bowling score sheets—three have the names "Penny T.," "Risa S.," and "Michelle C." penciled on them.

"Oh, my God!" growls Hudak. "They're all here. Every victim."

"This proves nothing," says the attorney.

"Choose a name," says Mulder. "Pick a name. Pick any name up there."

Though puzzled, Hudak does so. "Craig Graham," he says.

"Seventeen," says Harold. "Forty-two, sixty-seven, eighty-eight, hundred and seven, hundred and twenty-two, hundred and thirty-one, hundred and sixty, hundred and seventy-eight, two hundred and one."

"Two hundred game," says Mulder. "Not bad."

He adds that Harold has memorized all the scores—including the victims'.

"You said this proves his innocence," says the attorney. "How?"

"I'm not sure exactly," says Mulder, "but I think that—"

"No!" moans Harold. "No! No no no!"

Spüller sees Angie Pintero standing in a corner, his skin a shade of bluish white. Pintero's mouth moves, but no words come out. Harold bolts through the crawl space and back to the front of the bowling alley. The others run after him.

They catch up to him at the front desk. Harold, kneeling over the prostrate body of Angie Pintero, keens loudly. His employer is being given CPR by the uniformed officers.

"He just keeled. Fell right over," says one of them. "We done what we can. Must've been a heart attack."

Harold Spüller wails inconsolably.

Later that night Scully, dressed in her bathrobe, is deep in thought. Mulder knocks on her apartment door and Scully lets him in.

"I need your help on something," says Mulder. "I need your medical expertise."

"On what?" asks Scully.

"Harold Spüller—oh, I'm sorry. I didn't even ask you. What did your doctor say?"

Scully insists that she is fine. Mulder hesitates, then decides not to push it. He tells her of Angie Pintero's death of natural causes—congestive heart failure.

"That's what you need my medical opinion on?" asks Scully.

"No," says Mulder. "Harold Spüller had a premonitory vision of his boss's death. Harold saw an apparition. What may have been Angie Pintero's disembodied soul at the moment or just prior to his death."

"How do you know?"

"Because I was standing right there when he saw it."

"But you didn't see it yourself?"

"No. I don't have that facility—the connection to the victims that would make it possible."

"What was Harold Spüller's connection?" asks Scully.

"I don't know it's exact nature," says Mulder. "But I think it has something to do with his autism. Harold experienced a profound attachment to these victims, but because of his disability, he was unable to express the depth and power of these relationships. So somehow, a psychic or preconscious bond was formed that went beyond the temporal."

Harold met all the victims, adds Mulder, at the bowling alley.

Scully shakes her head. It still doesn't quite make sense. "Even if what you're saying is true," she says, "Harold wasn't the only one who claims to have seen these apparitions."

"No. But he does have something in common with those who had the visions that is quite powerful in its own right."

"Which is what?" asks Scully.

"They were all dying," says Mulder. "One of emphysema, one of cancer, and now Angie Pintero."

Scully is rocked by this information, although she tries to keep Mulder from seeing her distress.

"Harold Spüller is dying, too?" she says.

"That's what I need your medical opinion on," says Mulder.

Scully says, "Well, what if he isn't?"

"I would be very surprised," says Mulder. He adds, "What is a death omen if not a vision of our own mortality? And who

among us would most likely be able to see the dead?"

At the psychiatric center, Chuck peeks out from behind a door. His roommate Harold is being escorted into the facility. Inside an examining room, Martin Alpert holds a cup containing several pills.

"Still have to take your meds, though, Harold," says Alpert, with a not unpleasant air of institutional cheerfulness. "Keeps you flying straight and level."

Harold quietly mutters numbers to himself.

"C'mon," says Alpert, smiling. "It's the way we always do it."

Nurse Innes enters, and Harold visibly tenses up. Alpert hands his patient over to her, smiles again at Harold—who is too scared to respond—and leaves. Nurse Innes faces Harold. She looks at him with contempt.

"Take your poison, Harold," she sneers. "Go on!"

Harold, rocking rapidly, grimaces in anguish.

"Whadaya got to live for now, huh?" she says. "What did you tell them, Harold? Did you tell them about your little girlfriends? Did you tell them how you were in love?"

"No!" cries Harold.

"Did you show them your pictures?"

"No!"

Innes curls her thin red lips into a smirk. "What do you think those girls thought of you, Harold? Do you think they loved you back? No one could love you, Harold. Look at yourself!"

She grabs Harold's neck, pulls him over to a metal towel dispenser, and forces him to look at his reflection.

"They looked at you and saw an ugly toad. A retard!"

In the corridor, Mulder confers with Alpert about having Scully examine Harold. They hear a woman's scream, and run toward it. In the examining room, Nurse Innes lies on the floor, dazed and with a small gash on her forehead. Harold is nowhere to be seen. Mulder looks on intently as Alpert tends to Innes. Scully arrives and stands next to him.

"He just went wacko," says Innes, pressing a compress to her forehead. "I was trying to get him to take his meds and he went berserk. He jumps me. He starts pounding me like he wanted to kill me."

"Did he say anything?" asks Mulder.

"No, he just started screaming like a lunatic," says Innes. "Something's gone wrong with him. I think he's lost it for good. And I'll be damned if I'm gonna take care of him anymore."

Innes asks for a few moments alone to settle her nerves. Mulder tells Alpert to call Hudak and tell him to get a search started for Harold. Alpert nods gravely and leaves.

"Maybe you were wrong," says Scully.

"Well, that's a superficial head wound, Scully," says Mulder. "He didn't mean to kill her or maim her. It's not the work of murderer, if you ask me."

Chuck peeks around his bedroom door at the agents. Mulder spots him.

"There's somebody you can talk to about it," says Mulder. "Why don't you talk to his roommate and I'll see what I can do about finding Harold."

In the examining room, Nurse Innes sits alone, fingering a wicked-looking scalpel. Scully enters a bedroom. She gently closes the door behind her.

"Oh, hi!" says Chuck nervously.

"Is your name Chuck?" says Scully.

"Yes! Yes, it is!" he replies. "Chuck Forsch. F-O-R-S-C-H. Chuck Forsch."

Chuck tells Scully that Harold is his friend as well as his roommate.

"Do you know where he is?" asks Scully.

"He's dying, isn't he?" says Forsch. "Harold. He's dying."

For obvious reasons, this answer rattles Scully.

"Why do you say that?" she asks.

"Nurse Innes," says Chuck. "She was trying to poison him."

"Who told you that?"

"Harold. He said she told him she was putting poison in his meds."

Scully says, "Harold hasn't been taking his medication?"

Chuck shakes his head. "I don't know," he says. "I don't know everything. I'm only a human being. But I do know that Harold's my friend. He wouldn't hurt anybody. He really loved them."

"Who?" says Scully.

Harold smiles, walks over to a dresser, opens the top drawer, takes out graduation pictures of Penny Timmons, Risa Shapiro, and Michelle Chamberlain, and shows them to Scully.

"Harold gave them to me," says Chuck. "He was afraid."

"Does anybody else know about these pictures, Chuck?" asks Scully.

"Nurse Innes," he replies.

Scully crosses the hall and enters a rest room. Nurse Innes is facing the sink, gulping water from a paper cup. She turns, startled by the FBI agent's entrance.

"How are you feeling?" asks Scully.

"I'm, you know, shaky," says Innes.

"Understandable," says Scully, nodding.

"Working with these people drives you crazy, too," says Innes. "I'm just looking forward to getting home."

"Will your family be a comfort?"

"I live alone."

"No children?"

"Just the one my husband ran off with."

Scully nods, glancing down at Innes's left hand. Unconsciously, the nurse is rubbing her thumb against her empty ring finger. Several capsules—Harold's meds—fall from her grasp.

Scully puts two and two together.

"Nurse Innes," she says, "I'm going to have to ask you step out into the hall."

For a split second, the woman stands silent. Then she reaches into her pocket, pulls out her scalpel, and with an animal-like cry launches a vicious attack on Scully.

Scully desperately fends off the bigger woman's slashing scalpel. She grabs her wrist and forces her to drop the instrument, but in her drug-fueled frenzy, Innes manages to fling Scully off her and onto the rest room floor. She recovers the scalpel and advances toward Scully.

"Stay where you are!" shouts Scully, drawing her gun. "Drop it! Let it go!"

Innes doesn't. She raises the blade and advances. Scully fires.

Elsewhere in the building, Mulder hears the gunshot and runs toward the rest room. He enters with Alpert behind him. Innes lies on the floor with a gunshot wound in her shoulder; Scully kneels and tends to her.

Mulder looks worriedly at a small slash wound on Scully's hand, then picks the nurse's scalpel off the floor.

"You'll want to bag that," says Scully. "I'm pretty sure it's the murder weapon."

Several paramedics wheel Innes, strapped onto a gurney, toward an ambulance. Mulder and Scully follow her down the corridor.

"She been taking Harold's meds," explains Scully. "Clonazepam and clonizine—the unregulated effects of which can be violent and unpredictable behavior."

"But why do you think she killed those women?" says Mulder.

"I don't know," says Scully. "Maybe in some drug-addled way she was trying to kill happiness—Harold's happiness, his love for those women. Maybe she was trying to destroy something she felt she'd never had."

"'She Is Me,'" says Mulder.

Scully shakes her head, still troubled by it all.

"Have they found Harold?" she asks.

"Yeah," says Mulder, his expression clouded.

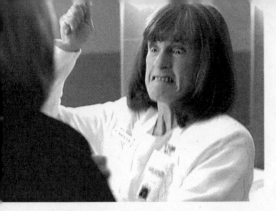

He stops, then turns to face his partner.

"They found him in an alley a few blocks from here, facedown on the pavement. They worked on him for twenty minutes, but they couldn't revive him."

"What happened?" says Scully, shocked.

Mulder tells her that the preliminary diagnosis was apnea—respiratory failure. He looks at his partner intently while she struggles to speak.

"I saw something, Mulder," she says finally. "The fourth victim. I saw her in the bathroom before you came to tell me."

"Why didn't you tell me?" says Mulder softly.

"Because I didn't want to believe it," she says. "Because I don't want to believe it."

Mulder nods. "Is that why you came down here?" he says. "To prove that it wasn't true?"

"No. I came down here because you asked me to."

Mulder frowns. "Why can't you be honest with me?" he says.

"What do you want me to say?" says Scully angrily. "That you're right? That I believe it, even if I don't? I mean, is that what you want?"

"Is that what you think I want to hear?" asks Mulder.

Scully looks inward for a moment.

"No," she says.

"You can believe what you want to believe, Scully," says Mulder forcefully. "But you can't hide the truth from me—because if you do, you're working against me. And yourself."

Scully stares at her partner. Mulder's tone softens.

"I know what you're afraid of," he says. "I'm afraid of it, too."

"The doctor said I was fine," says Scully, her voice breaking.

"I hope that's the truth," says Mulder, compassion mixed painfully with fear and doubt.

There is a long silence.

"I'm going home," whispers Scully.

She turns and walks away. In the parking lot, she unlocks her car, slips behind the steering wheel, and begins to silently cry.

An ambulance, siren wailing, passes through the darkened streets nearby. In her rearview mirror, Scully sees the face of Harold, calm and very pale. She turns and checks the seat. It is empty.

back story:
"Haunted Bowling Alley."

That was all that was written on the index card that clung tenaciously to story editor John Shiban's bulletin board for an entire year. "It just seemed right, somehow," says Shiban of his cryptic story idea. It blossomed into a full-blown story line only after the filming of "Memento Mori"— the episode in which Scully's battle with cancer is established.

"My wife reminded me of something we'd seen happen ten years ago," says Shiban. "Her father, Jerry Tanner, was dying of lung cancer. Janet and I weren't married yet, but we were going together, and we went to visit him in his hospital room. This was near the end, and he was very sick. Jerry kept looking away from us, then at Janet, and then he said, 'How many people are in the room?' My wife said, 'There's just me and John.' And he looked over to the other side of the room, then looked back to us, and finally just said, 'Okay'"

Shiban adds, "That incident—and the idea that a dying person might be able to

look through the cracks, so to speak, into the next world—really stuck in my mind. So just before Christmas break, when Chris asked me what I was going to do next, I told him that I had this idea about an apparition that only the dying can see. And when he heard that he said, 'Yes. That's a perfect idea for Scully.'"

The episode's obvious fascination with the retro-tech world of bowling and mechanical pinspotting can be traced back to John R. Shiban, the writer's father. Mr. Shiban had worked in a bowling alley as a young man and had regaled his son with tales of that experience. The part of "Angie's Midnight Bowl" was played by the Thunderbird Bowling Center, a venerable North Vancouver fun spot staked out by locations manager Louisa Gradnitzer and rented for several days of filming. Cast and crew were under strict instructions to preserve the bowling surfaces; all those who arrived too late to grab an empty pair of bowling shoes were required to shuffle alone with paper booties on their feet.

The other main story element—the mentally disabled and institutionalized character Harold Spüller—was inspired by Shiban's love for the 1975 movie One Flew Over the Cuckoo's Nest. In fact, Chuck Forsch, Harold's friend and roommate, is played by Sydney Lassick, the actor who portrayed Jack Nicholson's "challenged" sidekick Cheswick in the movie all those years ago. (Not at all coincidentally, Chuck Forsch is also the name of Chris Carter's LA-based assistant.)

Steven M. Porter, the experienced (and totally nondisabled) character actor who played Harold Spüller, was invited to audition for The X-Files by an old college friend from UCLA, Frank Spotnitz. A member of the well-known Actor's Gang theater troupe, he had previously played a part similar to Spüller in one of the troupe's productions, an original play called Asylum.

Porter remembers pulling out all the stops when he read for Chris Carter: "After I left the room I thought, I've either made a great impression or a complete fool of myself." Many of the gestures and tics

Porter used in the episode were products of his research, in several mental hospitals and adult group homes, for Asylum. In fact, he says, a certain flapping-hand movement became so vital to his portrayal of Harold that he kept doing it even when looping some dialogue in the recording studio after filming had wrapped.

Despite all the splits and spares, Gillian Anderson remembers "Elegy" as being a particularly challenging—and emotionally draining—episode. "There were some very good, very real transactions between Mulder and Scully," says Anderson.

For David Duchovny, "Elegy" was memorable for a different reason. "I realized how old I am," he deadpans. "The day after we did the bowling scenes, I was sore. And when you get sore from bowling, it's time to start thinking about your life and where it's going."

Never mind all that, says the episode's director, Jim Charleston, who bowled several "friendly" games with Duchovny between camera setups.

"Tell him that he still owes me $80," says Charleston, phoning from a Utah location of a TV movie—about killer ants—that he's shooting for Fox.

"That's $80 Canadian," replies Duchovny. "I owe him a lot less than he thinks."

This is the second time Scully has asked for counseling related to her job; the first time was with the same therapist in "Irresistible" (2X13). Karen Kossoff, playing therapist Christine Willes, also appeared in "The Calusari" (2X21).

Ⓧ

Mulder asks Harold Spüller about one of the victims, a woman named "Risa Shapiro." The real Risa Shapiro is David Duchovny's agent.

Ⓧ

Harold's lawyer is played by Lorena Gale, who played a nurse in "One Breath" (2X08) and a medical examiner in "Shadows" (1X05).

Ⓧ

episode: 4X23

first aired: May 11, 1997

written by: R. W. Goodwin

editor: Heather MacDougall

directed by: Kim Manners

After experiencing a series of blackouts and seizures—and what might be the recovery of repressed memories—Mulder gains new insights into his younger sister's abduction. However, while taking his inner journey, he may also have murdered two people.

guest stars:

Jay Acovone (Detective Joe Curtis)
Mike Nussbaum (Dr. Charles Goldstein)
Chris Owens (Young Cigarette-Smoking Man)
Rebecca Toolan (Mrs. Mulder)
Andrew Johnston (Medical Examiner)
Terry Jang Barclay (Officer Imhof)
Vanessa Morley (Young Samantha)
Eric Breker (Admitting Officer)
Rebecca Harker (Housekeeper)
Shelley Adam (Young Mrs. Mulder)
Dean Aylesworth (Young Bill Mulder)
Alex Haythorne (Young Fox Mulder)

principal settings:

Quonochontaug, Massachusetts;
Providence, Chepachet, and
Warwick, Rhode Island;
Greenwich, Connecticut

demons

a flash of blinding white light. A muffled rhythmic pounding, like the beating of a heart. Lying in his childhood bed, Mulder awakens to a cacophony of voices. A dark-haired young girl kneels over him.

"Fox! Wake up! Fox!" she says.

"Samantha?"

"Shhh! They'll hear you," she says.

Samantha turns and leaves him. Mulder is in a weirdly distorted world, filled with flashing lights and muffled, hollow sounds. Mulder follows his sister through a small sleeping loft. In the corner, he sees himself at age twelve.

Samantha peers down from the loft to the living room. On the couch sits young Bill Mulder and young Teena Mulder, her parents. They are arguing furiously, their voices unintelligible.

"I'm afraid, Fox!" says Samantha. "I'm afraid."

The adult Mulder jerks awake in the darkness. He is in a motel room; he is sweating profusely, and his face is covered with two days' growth of beard. The agent struggles unsteadily to a sitting position.

A phone rings in yet another bedroom. A woman's hand reaches out to pick up the receiver.

"Hello?"

"Scully . . ." says Mulder.

"Mulder—what time is it?" says his partner.

"I don't know," says Mulder.

Scully looks at her bedside clock.

"It's almost five A.M. Is anything wrong?"

"I think so," says Mulder.

"Where are you?"

Mulder scrabbles around his night stand and picks up a key with a plastic tag. He reads it.

"I think I'm in a motel room in Providence," he says. "Rhode Island."

"What are you doing there?" says Scully.

"I don't know," he replies worriedly. "There's blood all over me."

"Are you hurt, Mulder?"

"I don't think so," says Mulder with a slight trembling in his voice. "I don't think it's my blood."

Scully's car screeches to a halt in front of Hansen's Motel, a nondescript but well-maintained motor court. She knocks on the door to Room 6. It is unlocked. She pushes her way inside. The shower is running and the bathroom door is ajar.

"Mulder?" she says.

"Yeah," he replies weakly.

She asks him if he's all right.

"I can't get warm," he says.

Scully pulls open the shower curtain. Mulder sits naked on the floor of the shower, his knees drawn up to his chest, hot water cascading over him.

"You're in shock," says Scully.

She turns off the water, wraps Mulder in a towel, and fetches a blanket to cover him. She asks him if he feels sick, nauseous, or dizzy.

"No," says Mulder, "but I woke up on the floor with a pounding headache."

Scully rests her palm on his forehead, checks his pupils, and has him track her finger with his eyes.

"Were you here alone?" she asks.

"I think so. I don't know. I don't remember anything."

"Do you know what day it is?"

"No. What day is it?" he says, teeth chattering.

"It's Sunday," says Scully. "What was the last thing you remember?"

"I was in my apartment," says Mulder. "We were talking on the phone."

Scully says, "That was Friday."

Pushing back her fear, Scully scans the room and notices Mulder's overnight bag. She asks him if he's received a blow to his head or taken any drugs.

"No," says Mulder, still shaking.

She retrieves his blood-covered shirt from the bathroom.

"Are you sure you didn't cut yourself?"

"Yeah," says Mulder.

"Where's your weapon?" asks Scully.

Mulder turns away from his partner, dismayed. "I don't know," he says.

Scully reaches into Mulder's overnight bag, finds Mulder's gun in its holster, pops out the clip, and examines it.

"Two rounds have been fired," she says.

"I don't remember that," says Mulder, stunned.

Scully worriedly urges Mulder—who, she says, may be suffering from a cerebral aneurysm or encephalitis—to go with her immediately to a hospital.

"If there was a crime committed," murmurs Mulder, "I have to find out what happened."

Over Scully's strong objections, he stands up, sheds his blanket, and examines the top of the dresser. He holds up a key ring.

"Are these your keys?" he says.

"No," says Scully.

Mulder looks more carefully at the key ring. A brass plate engraved with the name "Amy" is attached to it.

After a visit to the motel manager's office, Scully returns to Room 6. She tells Mulder that he checked in around noon Saturday, made no calls from his room, had no visitors, and listed the license plate number of a stranger's car on his registration form.

That car is parked outside. As Mulder—now dressed in jeans and a white undershirt—looks on, Scully peers through the driver's side window.

"There's blood on the steering wheel, Mulder," she says.

Using Amy's keys, Scully unlocks the car and finds a registration slip in the glove compartment. The car is owned by a Providence resident named David Cassandra.

"Who's Amy?" asks Mulder.

"That's what I'm going to find out, Mulder," says Scully. "But first I'm going to check you out—because you have no business even walking around here."

"No, Scully," says Mulder. "If I've shot someone, if my weapon was used in a crime, I need to know."

"You are taking a big risk, Mulder. I feel strongly about this," says Scully.

"I know you do," says Mulder. "But it's my risk."

An unidentified apartment at an undisclosed location is filled with photographs: normal-looking snapshots except for the fact that many have been painstakingly altered. Only round holes remain where faces once had been. A balding young man, trembling, sits at a table slicing up more photographs with an X-Acto knife. He is bleeding from a head wound above his hairline. Blood drips steadily onto the photos.

At the address listed on the car registration, a young female housekeeper—startled to see the keys in Mulder's hand—tells the agents that the house's owners, Amy and David Cassandra, aren't home. Mulder peers into the hallway and spots a painting on a wall. It is of a white clapboard house surrounded by lush gardens of shrubs and flowers.

"That painting behind you," says Mulder. "Do you think I can take a look at it?"

While a puzzled Scully waits outside, Mulder enters the house and stares intently at the painting.

"Who painted this?" asks Mulder.

"Amy," says the housekeeper.

"I know this house," says Mulder.

"How?" says Scully.

"I don't know," he says. "I've seen it before."

He turns to the housekeeper. "Does this house have any special meaning for Amy or David?"

"I know it's her favorite subject," says the housekeeper. "It's the house she grew up in."

Prompted by Mulder's fierce interest, she opens a door and leads Mulder and Scully into the living room. Every available wall surface is covered with paintings of the same white clapboard house.

"I've been to this house," says Mulder. "I don't know when, but I've been there."

The housekeeper tells him that the house is located in Chepachet.

"Where's that?" Scully asks.

Mulder answers. "It's about twenty miles from here, on Route Eight," he says. "On Route Eight. My parents had a summer house out there when I was a kid. In Rhode Island."

A short time later, Mulder and Scully stand in front of the white clapboard house—undoubtedly the cottage in the paintings, but run-down, neglected, and forlorn. The gardens are weed-filled and overgrown.

"If you've been here, Mulder," says Scully, "I don't think it was any time recently."

Mulder stares at the house—then winces and grabs his temples. He falls to his knees in excruciating pain.

A flash of blinding white light. Scully frantically calls out her partner's name. Her voice echoes hollowly inside his head, then fades away.

Mulder is in the same house—and the same surreal universe—from his previous vision. Down a dark hallway a door is slightly ajar. Behind it, his parents' heated, muffled argument continues.

Now it is the young Fox Mulder who is watching. His father glares at his son and closes the door in his face. Another adult figure, silhouetted against the light, approaches from the other end of the hall.

"You're a little spy," smirks the man.

It is the Cigarette-Smoking Man, in his early thirties. Young Mulder looks at him fearfully. He hears a female voice. It is Scully's.

"Mulder! Mulder, can you hear me?" she says. "What happened?"

The adult Mulder, lying on the lawn in front of the white cottage, slowly regains consciousness.

"I remember what I saw," he murmurs. "A very vivid flashback to my childhood. Except that I was there."

"Anything else?" says Scully.

"Just that it was very real," he says, struggling to get up.

Scully presses her finger to his neck and takes his pulse. It is racing, she says; in her opinion, he has suffered some kind of brainstorm or disturbance and should see a specialist immediately.

"I feel really good right now," says Mulder, looking at the house.

"Mulder, you are *not* really good," insists Scully.

Mulder ignores her. He stands up and walks toward the house. Amy's key unlocks the front door. The living room is dark and deserted.

"I think I've been here before," says Mulder.

"When? In your childhood?" says Scully, following behind him.

"Maybe," says Mulder.

Scully says, "I don't think anybody's lived here in a long time."

Mulder tells Scully that he's going to check upstairs. Scully drifts through sheet-shrouded furniture to the dining area.

"Mulder," she says, stopping short.

Her partner joins her. Lying on the floor is a blood-covered female corpse. A man's body, splayed below a curtained window, lies a few feet away.

"There's a gunshot wound to her heart," says Scully. "I think this must be Amy Cassandra. And her husband."

Mulder kneels beside the dead man and rolls him over. The bearded face is unfamiliar. Mulder looks up at his partner beseechingly.

A short while later, the cottage is swarming with policemen. The Cassandras' bodies are loaded into a coroner's wagon.

Mulder sits slumped in the front passenger seat of a police car. Scully, after talking briefly with two detectives, joins him.

She says, "They'd like to ask you some questions. I told them about your condition. You don't have to speak to them if you don't want to."

"You mean not without my attorney present?" says Mulder.

Scully says firmly, "Mulder, I refuse to believe that you had any part in this."

Mulder looks away, then turns back and speaks briskly. "I had those people's blood on my shirt, Scully. I was missing for two days. I have no recollection of my actions during those two days. There were two rounds discharged from my gun. I had the keys to this house, the keys to their car. Do the words Orenthal James Simpson mean anything to you?"

As he says this, one of the detectives, an intense-looking man named Curtis, walks over.

"How are you feeling, Agent Mulder?" he says with an accusatory edge.

"A little confused," says Mulder.

Curtis listens skeptically as the FBI agent explains the circumstances that brought him to the cottage. His expression indi-

cates that Mulder's FBI badge earns him only a limited amount of slack. Perhaps just the opposite.

Curtis says, "We got plenty of prints on that house—some with blood on them. We're going to run those prints, Agent Mulder. Is that the story you want to stick with?"

"For now," says Mulder.

Curtis requests that Mulder come to the station house and give a statement. Scully interrupts and insists that Mulder first go directly to a hospital.

"Okay," says Curtis, with a tight smile. "But we're all going down there together. Agent Mulder, I'd like you to ride with us."

Mulder gets out of the car. Scully, her apprehensions clearly visible, steps in front of him.

"Mulder, I'd advise you not to say anything more," she says. "Not until I take a look at those bodies and the forensics reports."

At the coroner's autopsy bay, the body of Amy Cassandra lies on a table. A medical examiner dictates his autopsy notes; Scully stands and watches him closely.

"Amy Ann Cassandra, Caucasian female," says the ME. "Birth records indicate her age

at sixty-two years. The subject is one hundred sixty-five pounds. Sixty-seven inches in height. Preliminary exam indicates cause of death due to gunshot wound to the chest. Powder burns and flashing at point of entry, approximately four inches below the clavicle, indicating the shot was delivered at point-blank range."

Scully steps forward and examines the body. She pushes away the hair at Amy's hairline, exposing a dark brown scab.

"A preexisting superficial puncture wound," says the ME.

"Do you mind?" asks Scully.

She removes the scab carefully with a pair of forceps, peers at the small puncture wound with a magnifying glass, and asks the ME to conduct two additional tests: a craniotomy and a histological examination.

"I think it's clear what killed these people," says the ME, slightly miffed.

"Yeah, I think it is, too," says Scully. "But what I'm more interested in right now is why they died."

In a police interrogation room, an unshaven Mulder sits in deep thought. A piece of gauze is taped to the spot on his arm from which blood has been drawn. Detective Curtis enters, holding a paper bag. He places it on the table in front of Mulder.

"Have you jogged your memory at all, Agent Mulder?" says Curtis. "Do you want to change your story?"

"No. Why?" says Mulder.

"Because I have evidence here," Curtis replies, "that contradicts what you told us."

Mulder leans back and folds his arms. "Well," he says, "I haven't really told you anything."

Curtis continues his by-the-numbers interrogation. He repeats what Mulder has told him: He didn't know the Cassandras and he hadn't been in or near their house since childhood.

"And you're telling me," says Mulder, fully aware of the trap that Curtis is laying, "that what's in that bag is evidence that I'm a liar?"

"I'm not saying that you're a liar," says Curtis, aware himself that Mulder knows

where he's going. "I believe that this memory lapse is real. That you murdered these people in some fit of blind insanity."

"What's in the bag?" says Mulder evenly.

"It's not your gun," says Curtis coolly.

He says that preliminary ballistics tests have shown that Mulder's gun was the murder weapon. Then he pauses for a second.

"Is any of this coming back to you, Agent Mulder?" he says, a hint of contempt in his tone.

"No," says Mulder. "Can I look in the bag now?"

"Be my guest," says Curtis.

Mulder pulls out a bloody shirt. Curtis tells him that two blood types were detected— one matching Amy Cassandra's, the other David Cassandra's.

"Is that your shirt, Agent Mulder?" asks Curtis.

"Yes," says Mulder, closing his eyes wearily.

"Can you explain to me how the blood of two people you claim not to know got on your shirt?"

"No," says Mulder. "What about the prints in the house? Were they my prints?"

Curtis says nothing.

"Look," says Mulder forcefully. "You're not going to get a confession out of me. Because I can't answer your questions. Because I don't remember."

Curtis stares back at Mulder for a long second—then almost without inflection, reads the FBI agent his Miranda rights.

Curtis escorts Mulder—now handcuffed and wearing an orange jail jumpsuit—into the police lockup. Scully intercepts them.

"Mulder," she says, "I'm going to get you out of here."

Mulder says, "You're a doctor, not a lawyer."

"Did you make a confession?" she asks.

"No," he says. "Only to my own ignorance."

Scully turns to Curtis and tells him what she's found: Amy Cassandra's blood contained evidence of ketamine, a fast-acting veterinary anesthetic known to produce hallucinations in humans. Mulder's blood, she adds, also contained traces of the substance.

"Given by whom?" says Curtis impatiently.

"I don't know," says Scully. "But the presence of such a powerful drug could explain his memory loss or the blackouts."

"Given the weight of all the other evidence," says Curtis skeptically, "I think that's all it explains."

Curtis turns toward the admitting desk. Mulder, much of his fight gone, turns to Scully. "You don't have to do this," he says.

"Mulder, you have to help me out," she pleads. "There's nothing here that points directly to your guilt. Unless somebody can show me with absolute certainty that you were holding the weapon that killed those two people, the rest of the narrative is far too convenient and suspect. The drug in your system already suggests other explanations."

"What? That I was partying with a few senior citizens?"

Exasperated, Scully addresses Curtis, who has returned. "You're jailing an innocent man," she says.

"Yeah, well," says Curtis, "this way he won't get lost for two days and do something else he won't remember."

Scully watches helplessly as Curtis leads Mulder to his cell. A jail admitting officer—the same man who we'd seen feverishly mutilating photographs—emerges from an office and enters an empty cell. He pulls out one of his curiously altered snapshots, stares at it, and unholsters his service revolver. There is the sound of a gunshot.

Every officer in the building runs toward it. The admitting officer lies slumped on the floor. Scully pushes her way through the crowd.

"I'm a doctor! Call the paramedics!" she shouts.

Scully examines his head wound. "He's dead," she says.

She probes a small patch of skin above the hairline—and finds a small brown scab.

"I need to speak to Detective Curtis," she says. "Right now."

Scully and Curtis enter the dead admitting officer's apartment. Altered photographs cover every horizontal surface.

Scully asks, "Did this officer have a history of depression or mental illness?"

Curtis shrugs and tells Scully that the man had been removed from a beat and given a desk assignment a year ago—he had a reputation for erratic behavior and lying.

"The man we're talking about," says Curtis, "had become something of a joke on the force. One of those guys who believes in—you know, extraterrestrials, stuff like that."

Scully hides her reaction. She looks at the photograph with the bloodstains on it. The face that has been removed is that of a police officer—the admitting officer's. She points out the bloody photos to Curtis.

"Does this mean anything to you?" she says.

"Should it?"

"I think it speaks to a pronounced mental illness," she says. "The compulsive and repetitive act of removing his own image from these photos leads me to believe that he not only believed these stories, but was traumatized by them."

Curtis looks at her, irritated. "I thought you told me this was going to explain something about your partner's crime?" he says.

Scully says nothing, but looks intently at a coffee table in the corner of the room. On it is a magazine. It's title is *Abductee*. A woman's picture is on the cover. It is Amy Cassandra.

Lying on his cot in his jail cell that night, Mulder suffers another seizure. Amid the

flashing lights, he is back in the hallway. He watches the young Cigarette-Smoking Man argue with his father. The door is slammed in his face again. Panicked, he climbs a ladder to his sleeping loft. Samantha, terrified, huddles in her bed.

He peers over the edge of the loft and sees his mother arguing with the young Cigarette-Smoking Man. She beats him on his chest while his father looks on guiltily.

"No! No! My baby!" shouts young Mrs. Mulder.

Mulder regains consciousness, lifts himself off his cot, and grips the bars of his cell.

"Guard! Guard!" he shouts. "I need to talk to someone! *Guard!*"

The next morning, Scully and Curtis walk toward Mulder's cell. Curtis gives Scully permission to talk to Mulder alone.

"I didn't kill those people, Scully," says Mulder.

"I know that," she says. "And I think I've gathered enough proof and evidence to get you out of here."

Scully explains that according to the forensics report, the blood-spatter patterns on his shirt doesn't match the victims' entry wounds. Instead, the evidence points to a murder-suicide.

"But I was there," says Mulder. "And I still don't remember why."

Scully says, "I think I have an idea about that, too."

She explains that Amy Cassandra claimed to be an alien abductee—and that she had found a way to remember the details of that event. Mulder nods.

"And I contacted her," he says.

"Yes, apparently," says Scully. "According to an article I read on Amy, she had begun psychiatric treatment that was effectively recovering her past. The repetitive behavior exhibited in those paintings that we saw was an expression of that treatment."

"But why would she kill herself and her husband?" says Mulder.

"I can't say definitively," says Scully. "But judging from an almost identical suicide of a police officer who was receiving the same psychiatric care, I believe that the victims were suffering from something called Waxman-Geschwind syndrome—the symptoms of which are trancelike states leading to vivid dreams about the past, dreams more vivid than the conscious mind can recall. It's also called Dostoevsky syndrome, because the Russian novelist suffered from it."

Mulder shakes his head. "What was I doing there, Scully?" he says. "And why wasn't I doing anything to stop it?"

"I can't explain that," says Scully.

She tells him that she's arranged for his arraignment in one hour. By that time, she and Curtis will have gathered enough forensics data to have him released.

"I still need, though," says Mulder, "to know why."

Later that day, the agents pull up to the Warwick office of Dr. Charles Goldstein, a psychologist. Mulder's car is parked across the street from his clinic. Its doors are locked and it is covered with a thick layer of dust.

"It's been here a few days," says Scully.

Dr. Goldstein is an elderly gray-haired man. He receives the FBI agents in his office. Mulder introduces himself and asks if they've ever met.

"I don't believe so," says Goldstein politely.

Scully tells him that they're investigating the deaths of Amy and David Cassandra and that according to their information Amy was a patient of his.

"I was very upset to learn about Amy," says Goldstein sadly. "She was a troubled woman who struggled through an unfortunate period of darkness in her life."

Scully says, "Are you referring to her belief that she was an abductee?"

Goldstein skirts the issue. Without admitting that he believed her stories, he says that he used "aggressive" methods—including a therapy that stimulates electrical impulses in the brain—to help Amy recover her memories of the event.

Scully says, "Did you also use this same treatment on a police officer named Michael Fazekas?"

"Yes. Why?" says Goldstein.

"Mr. Fazekas shot himself in the head yesterday."

Goldstein seems shocked by the news. Under questioning by Scully, however, he defends his techniques as being within the bounds of accepted medical practice. Scully appears highly skeptical of his claims. She takes another tack.

"Are you familiar with Waxman-Geschwind syndrome, Dr. Goldstein?" she says accusingly. "Did you know that Amy Cassandra suffered from it?"

Goldstein becomes defensive. "Waxman-Geschwind, if you know anything about it," he says, "is not necessarily a destructive condition. In fact, Amy, after undergoing treatment, experienced periods of extreme happiness and creativity."

He denies indignantly that there were indications that any of his patients were suicidal.

"I've been in practice for over forty years," he says. "I have a very good ethical and professional record, if you care to check."

"No, that won't be necessary," says Mulder, leaving.

Scully says contemptuously, "*I* know what you do."

Mulder waits for Scully outside Goldstein's office.

"I have been here before, Scully," he says. "I met Dr. Goldstein with Amy Cassandra."

Scully says, "This man is lying about more than that. I think that he administered the ketamine to Amy and to you. I think that you were treated by him, and I think that your blackouts, your seizure, were a result of that."

Mulder agrees. Scully asks him why he underwent such a dangerous procedure. Before he can answer, Mulder doubles over with pain. The bright light signals a brief seizure; Mulder sees the young Cigarette-Smoking Man grabbing his mother in anger—or perhaps with passion. The vision ends.

When he comes to, Scully once again insists that he go to a hospital. Once again, he refuses. He walks to her car and asks for the car keys. She refuses, saying forcefully that he shouldn't be driving—or doing anything else, for that

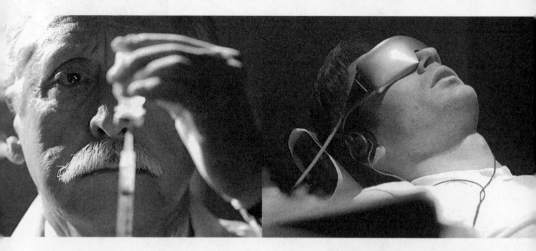

matter—until his symptoms go away. Mulder turns to his partner.

"Scully, I don't *want* them to go away," he says. "Whatever's happening to me, whatever treatment I've received, is allowing me to go back into my subconscious. The truth is in there, recorded, and I've gotten access to it. What happened to my sister, the reason she was taken, is becoming clearer to me.

"I need to know that. Now give me the car keys."

Several hours later, they pull up in front of Mulder's mother's house in Greenwich, Connecticut. Mulder storms inside.

"I need to speak to you," says Mulder to his mother.

"What's happened, Fox?" says Mrs. Mulder. "Why did you come here?"

"You've kept things from me," he says. "You've kept secrets from me. You told me when they took Samantha it was because you had to make a choice. But that's not how it happened. It wasn't your choice to make."

"What do you want to hear from me?" says Mrs. Mulder.

"I want to know what happened that night on Quonochontaug—and I want to speak to you privately."

They move away from Scully and into the living room.

"You had some kind of relationship with him," says Mulder angrily.

"Who?" says Mrs. Mulder, baffled.

"You know who. The man who worked with my father. The man who came to you that night when I was twelve and forced you to choose Samantha. You betrayed my father—your husband!"

"Never!" says Mrs. Mulder.

"How far back did it go?" asks Mulder.

Mrs. Mulder slaps him. It is her turn to be angry.

"How dare you!" she says. "How dare you come here and accuse me!"

"Who is my father?" says Mulder, forcing out the words.

Mrs. Mulder says, "What do you want? To kill him again?"

"Just answer the question, Mom! *Just answer the question!*"

"*I am your mother,*" she says bitterly. "*And I will not tolerate any more of your questions.*"

She sets her jaw defiantly. "You're bleeding, Fox," she says.

She turns and walks up the stairway. Mulder wipes the blood from his wound. It is near his hairline. He leaves the house, climbs into the car, and drives away alone.

At 9:25 P.M., Dr. Goldstein is exiting his clinic carrying armloads of files. As he loads them into his car trunk, Mulder pulls to a halt behind him.

"What did you do to me?" demands Mulder.

Goldstein, frightened, says nothing.

Mulder says, "You treated me. I asked you to treat me to recover my past."

"I did nothing wrong!" protests Goldstein. "You put a hole in my head!"

"A slight electrical stimulation," says the psychologist.

"It triggered my memory," says Mulder grimly. "Now I want you to finish the job."

In his darkened office, Goldstein fills a syringe with ketamine. He injects Mulder in the hip and leads him to a recliner.

"I want to remember," says Mulder groggily.

Goldstein places headphones over Mulder's ears and a pair of opaque metallic wraparound glasses over his eyes. He adjusts a switch on a console. The glasses strobe brightly into Mulder's eyes. The flashes trigger the white lights inside Mulder's mind—brighter and more powerful than ever.

The visions are faster and more fragmented. There are slices of moments from that weekend at Quonochontaug: Samantha crying out in alarm; the young Cigarette-Smoking Man calling him a little spy; his parents arguing; young Mrs. Mulder embracing the Cigarette-Smoking Man; doors slamming in his face; the markers on Samantha's Stratego board vibrating wildly.

In Goldstein's office, Mulder's body is shaking and he is breathing in short gasps. The psychologist immobilizes Mulder's arms with Velcro straps.

More fragments: his parents arguing; Samantha crying; the Stratego pieces

shaking; a white light shining through the window of the country house; a doorknob turning.

Goldstein fits a small, sharp bit into a high-speed medical drill. He switches it on and lowers it toward Mulder's forehead.

Outside the clinic, several Providence police cars skid to a stop. Detective Curtis gets out of one, strides inside Goldstein's office, and tells the psychologist that he's under arrest. He glances at the restraints on the recliner. They are empty.

"Where is he?" says Curtis.

Goldstein says nothing.

Scully arrives outside in her own car—just as Goldstein, under arrest, is being driven away. She runs toward the squad car, yells for it to stop, and yanks open the back door.

"What did you do to him?" shouts Scully. "Look—I know he came back here. This is the only place he would have gone. Did you treat him? *Damn it! Answer me!*"

"Yes," says Goldstein weakly.

"Where is he now?"

"I don't know where he went."

Scully says, "What was the last thing he said to you?"

"He said," says Goldstein pathetically, "he was going to exorcise his demons."

At the Mulders' old summer home at Quonochontaug, local police have already thrown up a cordon. When Scully arrives, a local cop tells her that they've seen lights and movement inside the house.

"All right," says Scully. "That man in there is armed. He is a federal officer in dire need of medical attention. He is not himself. Now, I am going in there. If at any time he should flee that house, you should tell your officers not to shoot."

Alone, Scully enters the house. Mulder is sitting, his eyes closed, in agony. He is holding his gun.

"Mulder, it's me," says Scully.

"Scully, leave me alone," he says.

Mulder is wracked by a new jolt of seizures and visions. One of them is the young Cigarette-Smoking Man giving a fatherly embrace to Samantha.

"It's all falling into place," groans Mulder in a kind of ecstasy.

"Mulder, put down the gun," says Scully.

"Oh, no. Try to stop me," he says, pointing it at his mouth.

Scully inches toward him. "Please, Mulder," she says.

Another flash of light. This time Mulder sees Samantha being drawn into bright light, crying after him.

"I'm afraid, Fox," says Samantha. "I'm afraid."

This vision shatters like a broken mirror—revealing the young Cigarette-Smoking Man.

Scully takes a chance and moves toward him, but Mulder emerges from the seizure too quickly.

"Get away!" he says, pointing the gun at her.

"Are you going to shoot me?" says Scully, fighting her fear. "Is that how much this means to you?"

Mulder nods feverishly.

"Mulder, listen to me. You have been given a powerful hallucinogen. You don't know that these memories are yours. This is not the way to the truth, Mulder. You've got to trust me."

"Shut up!" shouts Mulder.

"Put down the gun," says Scully.

Mulder's hand wavers.

"Let it go," whispers Scully.

Mulder fires—then fires again and again, seven times in all. Outside, the policemen rush the building. Mulder lowers his gun. Scully stands, untouched, behind him. He begins to cry. She comforts him.

Later, Scully sits in FBI headquarters typing her case notes. She writes:

Although cleared of any wrongdoing in the deaths of Amy and David Cassandra, Agent Mulder still has no recollection of the events that led to their deaths. His seizures have subsided, with no evidence of permanent cerebral damage. But I am concerned that this experience will have a lasting effect. Agent Mulder undertook this treatment hoping to lay claim to his past—that by retrieving memories lost to him he might finally understand the path he's on. But if that knowledge remains elusive, and if it's only by knowing where he's been that he can hope to understand where he's going, then I fear Agent Mulder may lose his course. And the truths he is seeking from his childhood will continue to evade him—driving him more dangerously forward in impossible pursuit.

back story:

Early in the 1996–97 season, Bob Goodwin had a vision. "I saw Mulder waking up in a strange place having no idea how he got there," says the executive producer. "I fleshed it out a bit, told the story to Chris—who needed scripts and had been asking me for a while to write one—and the next thing I knew it was on the schedule."

Goodwin, who heads the Vancouver production office of *The X-Files* and directs the first and last episodes of each season, has written many TV and feature film scripts, but the last one was for the NBC series *Mancuso, FBI*, which went off the air in 1990. So he swallowed hard, he says, and carved out the time to write "Demons" by sacrificing six weeks of whatever home life his demanding job affords him.

Goodwin admits cheerfully that he lifted several of the major plot devices for "Demons" from *An Anthropologist on Mars*, a book of short essays by the writer-neurologist Oliver Sacks. In a case study titled "The Landscape of Dreams," Sacks tells the story of Franco Magnani, an Italian-born resident of San Francisco whose life is driven by the strange ability—at least partly attributable to "Waxman-Geschwind" or "Dostoyevsky" syndrome—to recall every sight, sound, and smell of his childhood. Magnani's meticulously accurate paintings of Pontito, his native village in Tuscany, have been the subject of several medical symposia and art exhibitions.

The on-screen notion that Waxman-Geschwind syndrome can be induced by drugs and/or electrical impulses is a bit of creative license; so are the opaque flashing eyeglasses applied to Mulder by the self-righteous Dr. Goldstein. "They were based on this New Age 'brain stimulator' that we bought," says Goodwin. "They were supposed to help you to relax and improve your creativity, but I found them disconcerting; they freaked out my twelve-year-old completely, and my wife [actress Sheila Larken, who plays the recurring role of Margaret Scully] couldn't sleep for days."

Neither, after watching the episode, did some viewers, for rarely are such realistic and nauseating levels of pain inflicted on the stars of prime-time TV shows. But Chris Carter felt, says Goodwin, that the episode was a good bridge between Scully's near-death sentence in "Elegy" and the apocalyptic events of the season finale to come.

Compared to Mulder's debilitating brain seizures, the actual filming was comparatively painless. The part of the picturesque cottage that Amy Cassandra compulsively painted, then died in, was played by a run-down farmhouse on a piece of swampy flatland in South Surrey—not far from the horse farm in "Tunguska" and the Peacocks' hovel in "Home."

The house was owned by an absentee landlord, a Maryland woman who had inherited it from her grandmother. It was scouted and rented by Todd Pittston's locations crew, then completely restored, refurbished, and replanted by Graeme Murray's art department, Rob Maier's construction department, and head greensman Frank Haddad.

The "Wisteria Cottage" does not appear in the episode in its restored state, however, only in preproduction photographs taken by art director Gary Allen. These photos were scanned by computer playback technician Sally Hudson. She manipulated the images, using two computer programs—Adobe Photoshop and Fractal Painter—to produce dozens of laser-printed "paintings" for Amy Cassandra's living-room wall. Then, before actual filming began, the house and garden were completely trashed, bringing it right back to the sorry state in which Mulder and Scully first see it.

During the filming of Mulder's dream sequences, the shutter mechanism of the camera was continuously stopped and started to create the "out-of-time" feeling on the final print. However, most of the weird, dystemporal nature of Mulder's flashbacks was created in postproduction:

The sequence's colors were altered during film development, the negative was hit with strobe lights during the printing process, and the recorded dialogue and background noise was filtered and otherwise altered by coproducer Paul Rabwin's small army of editors and mixers.

For his part, says David Duchovny, the hardest task was to somehow connect the two disparate elements of the script. "Here I was, having holes drilled in my head, and these brainstorms," he says, "and at the same time I was walking around trying to solve the case. The challenge was to make both the seizures and the recovery realistic."

This is not Gillian Anderson's favorite episode. "'Mulder, get to the hospital!' 'Mulder, get to the hospital!'" she says. "I kept having to play the same thing over and over again."

As for Goodwin, although he's proud of "Demons," he doesn't exactly envision becoming an X-Files staff writer—or even whispering another story idea in his boss's ear anytime soon.

"It became a real strain on the family," he says. "Mostly what I remember is taking everybody up to Whistler, the ski resort north of Vancouver, for a three-day vacation to celebrate one of my son's sixteenth birthday. My wife and kids skied and played and all stayed in one condo. I stayed in a condo right next to them—and spent the entire time writing."

This is the only episode written by Vancouver producer R. W. Goodwin, and only the second time a director or crew member has written an episode (the other was "Wetwired" (3X23), written by X-Files special effects maven Mat Beck).

X

The time stamp "9:25" is the birthday of Gillian Anderson's daughter—September 25.

X

Characters Amy and David Cassandra are named after the Greek prophetess Cassandra, who was cursed by the god Apollo. Not unlike Mulder, everything Cassandra said was true, but no one ever believed her.

X

During a scene between Agent Scully and Detective Curtis in the apartment of a police officer who has committed suicide, careful observers can see the moving shadow of a crew member on the wall behind Scully.

X

Andrew Johnston returns as the medical examiner, having previously appeared as Colonel Budahas in "Deep Throat" (1X01) and as Agent Weiss in the two-parter, "Colony/End Game" (2X16 and 2X17). Jay Avocone, playing Detective Curtis, was a series regular on Beauty and the Beast, which was produced by X-Files executive producer Howard Gordon.

X

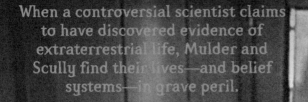

When a controversial scientist claims
to have discovered evidence of
extraterrestrial life, Mulder and
Scully find their lives—and belief
systems—in grave peril.

episode: 4X24
first aired: May 18, 1997
written by: Chris Carter
editor: Michael S. Stern
directed by: R. W. Goodwin

guest stars:
Matthew Walker (Arlinsky)
James Sutorius (Babcock)
Sheila Larken (Mrs. Scully)
Pat Skipper (Bill Scully, Jr.)
John Finn (Michael Kritschgau)
John Oliver (Rolston)
Charles Cioffi (Section Chief Scott Blevins)
Steve Makaj (Ostelhoff)
Nancy Kerr (Agent Hedin)
Barry W. Levy (Vitagliano)
Arnie Walters (Father McCue)
Rob Freeman (Detective Rempulski)
Craig Brunanski (Saw Operator)

gethsemane

principal settings:
Boston, Massachusetts; St. Elias
Mountains, Yukon Territory, Canada;
Washington, D.C.; Arlington and
Sethsburg, Virginia

at Boston University in 1972, a panel of preeminent American scientists, including Carl Sagan, have come together to answer a most pressing question: What would happen if we learned there was other sentient life in the universe?

The astronomer Richard Berendzen speaks:

"Each passing year has seen our estimate of the probability of life in space increase along with our capabilities of detecting it. More and more scientists feel that contact with other civilizations is no longer something beyond our dreams, but is a natural event in the history of mankind that will perhaps occur within the lifetime of many of us. The promise is now too great either to turn away from it or to wait much longer before devoting major resources to a search for other intelligent beings. In the long run, this may be one of science's most important and most profound contributions to mankind and to our civilization."

It is early morning in Mulder's apartment, which is swarming with uniformed officers, detectives, and forensic techs. Scully enters, flashes her FBI ID, and pushes her way through the crowd. An Arlington PD detective named Rempulski greets her grimly. He leads her to a sheet-covered body lying face down between the couch and the coffee table, and lifts a corner of the sheet.

"It him?" he asks.

"Yeah," whispers Scully.

She turns on her heels and walks away.

In a large conference room at FBI headquarters, a high-level investigative committee, chaired by Section Chief Scott Blevins, is assembled. Scully enters and is asked by Blevins to take her seat. She does so.

"Agent Scully, we've had a brief discussion," says Blevins. "But will you restate the matter we're here to put to rest."

"Yes, sir," says Scully.

She braces herself and—without referring to notes—begins:

"Four years ago, Section Chief Blevins assigned me to a project you know as the X-Files. As I am a medical doctor with a background in hard science, my job was to provide an analytical perspective on the work of Special Agent Fox Mulder, whose investigations were fueled by a personal belief that his sister had been abducted by aliens when he was twelve."

Her voice begins to waver.

"I come here today, four years later, to report on the illegitimacy of Agent Mulder's work. That it is my scientific opinion that he became, over the course of these years, a victim. A victim of his own false hopes—and of his belief in the biggest of lies."

A jet helicopter skims over the snow-covered peaks of the St. Elias Mountains, in northwestern Canada. Seated behind the pilot, wearing cold-weather climbing gear, are two anthropologists, Arlinsky and Babcock. They converse via headsets over the chopper's intercom system.

"We're meeting the guide at base camp," says Arlinsky. "He'll take us to the site."

"Has he seen it?" asks Babcock.

"Oh, yeah," says Arlinsky. "He says it's unbelievable."

The helicopter sets them down at a base camp in a snowy clearing. With their guide, a man named Rolston, they begin the long and arduous trek upward. By nightfall, they reach the narrow entrance of a large, vaulted snow cave. A team of experienced climbers is waiting inside; they exchange solemn handshakes and advance further into the cave.

Flashlights beaming into the darkness, they reach a wall of ice. A small, round window has been carved out of its opaque surface. Arlinsky peers into it.

"My God," says the scientist. "It's beautiful!"

Not more than a foot below the surface is the entombed body of an alien being. Its sightless black eyes stare back at the men who have discovered it.

In the FBI conference room, the hearing continues.

"Agent Scully," says Blevins. "I presume you have a reason for this break from Agent Mulder."

"Yes, sir," says Scully. "Recent events have shed new light on the factual and physical evidence that would serve to prove the existence of extraterrestrial life—which is the foundation of Agent Mulder's consuming devotion to his work."

"What factual evidence?" asks Blevins.

"Agent Mulder," she says, "was recently contacted by a man whose pursuit of this evidence seemed to coincide with his own. In his intense desire to believe, Agent Mulder was duped by this man. He was fooled by an act of scientific sleight of hand calculated to perpetuate false truths. The larger lie."

She adds, "I am here today to expose this lie, to show the mechanism of the deception that drew him—and me—into it, and to expose Agent Mulder's work for what it is."

At Margaret Scully's large, well-appointed house, a dozen or so guests—the youngest is her daughter Dana—enjoy cocktails before dinner. A late arrival is Bill Scully, Jr., a U.S. Navy Lieutenant Commander. He embraces his younger sister. She thanks him for sending her a birthday card.

"Well, once a decade," he says.

At the front door, Mrs. Scully welcomes a sixtyish Catholic priest, Father McCue. Scully watches this with some suspicion.

"How are you feeling, Dana?" says her brother, his mood turning serious.

"I'm fine," she says quickly. "Let's get some dinner, huh?"

At the candlelit dinner table, Scully has been seated between her brother and Father McCue. As the table is cleared, Bill, Jr., rises, leaving Scully alone with the priest.

"I feel awkward sitting here," he says. "I'm sure you do, too."

"No. I'm sorry," says Scully.

Father McCue says, "I've known your family for so many years. Your mother asked me to come, that I might have a word with you."

Scully glances accusingly at her mother.

The priest continues, "I know it's been some time since we've spoken ourselves, since you drifted from the church—"

"Father McCue," says Scully gently.

"—but in a time of personal crisis, a threat to your health, turning back to your faith is important and essential."

"Father McCue," sighs Scully, "I appreciate my mother's concern. And yours. But I'm being treated for my cancer. And I'm taking every precaution—"

"Faith can make you stronger," says McCue.

"I haven't felt a need," says Scully. "I have strength. And I'm not going to come running back now. It's just not who I am. I'd be lying to myself and to you."

Their exchange is interrupted by Bill Scully, who tells his sister that she has a phone call. She takes it in another room. It is Mulder.

Her partner apologizes for interrupting her dinner, then tells her that he needs her

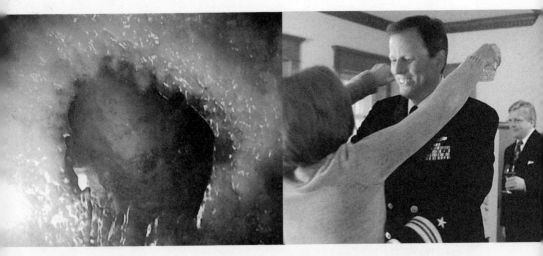

help. Arlinksy has contacted him from his office at the Smithsonian.

"Contacted you about what?" says Scully.

"About something he found on a mountain in Canada. I'd rather not talk about it on the phone. I just need you to meet me at the Smithsonian."

"When?"

"Right away."

Scully turns and catches her brother looking at her disapprovingly.

"I'm on my way," she says to Mulder.

As the agents climb the circular marble staircase to Arlinsky's office, Mulder tells Scully that the anthropologist is a man whom he has been corresponding with for four years. He adds that Arlinsky was involved in an embarrassing UFO photo enhancement scandal several years ago, but still maintains his innocence.

"What am I coming to see?" asks Scully.

"I'm not going to tell you," says Mulder. "I want you to decide for yourself."

In Arlinsky's cluttered office, the agents view a series of projected transparencies of the trapped alien.

"The body you're looking at," says the scientist, "is over two hundred years old."

"It looks perfectly intact," says Mulder.

"Yes," says Arlinsky.

"That doesn't make sense," says Mulder, pouncing. "There would have been signs of predation."

Arlinsky explains that at that altitude, the

dead alien might have been swallowed up by the glacier too fast to be carrion for a passing wild animal. While Mulder continues to probe for holes in his story, Arlinksy explains how geological evidence—as well as ice core samples taken to prove the site hasn't been disturbed—supports his scenario.

The body, he says, was found by a Canadian geodetic survey team working with his colleague Babcock. They are all still up on the mountain.

"Who else knows about this?" asks Mulder.

"No one," says Arlinsky.

Mulder looks at him skeptically.

Arlinsky says, "I know what your first thought was. But the St. Elias Range? That's a long way to go for a hoax."

"If you're gonna go, why not go all the way?" says Mulder.

Arlinsky protests that ice core samples can't be faked. He offers to let the agents test the ones he's brought back with him.

Mulder says, "You go public with this and nobody is going to believe you. You also risk never knowing for sure, because the same people who've buried the truth so assiduously will be in charge of its authentication."

"That's why I came to you," says Arlinsky excitedly. "I need to get the specimen out so that I can authenticate it."

He pauses.

"This body means everything to you, Agent Mulder. You're going to have the proof in your hands!"

"And what do you want?" asks Mulder.

"We just want the credit."

On their way downstairs, Mulder asks Scully what she thinks of Arlinsky's claims. She tells him that she has no opinion.

"You have no opinion?" says Mulder, incredulous.

"This is *your* holy grail, Mulder," she says. "Not mine."

"What is that supposed to mean?"

"It just means," says Scully evenly, "that proving to the world the existence of alien life is not my last dying wish."

"How about Santa Claus or the Easter Bunny?" says Mulder.

Scully grimaces. Mulder also frowns—at her reaction.

"This is not some selfish pet project of mine, Scully," he says. "I'm as skeptical of that man as you are. But proof? Definitive proof of sentient beings sharing time and existence with us? That would change everything. Every truth we live by would be shaken to the ground. There is no greater revelation imaginable. No greater scientific discovery."

"You already believe, Mulder," says Scully. "What difference will it make? What will proof change for you?"

Mulder says, "If someone could prove to you the existence of God, would it change you?"

"Only if it had been disproven."

"Then you accept the possibility that faith in God could be a lie?"

"I don't think about it, actually," says Scully. "And I don't think it can be proven."

Mulder says, "But what if it could be? Wouldn't that knowledge be worth seeking? Or would it just be easier to go on believing the lie?"

Scully looks, thinks, then disengages from his argument.

"I can't go with you, Mulder," she says.

"Then can you at least take a look at those core samples," says Mulder, "and tell me if they're a lie? That's all I'm asking."

In the FBI conference room, Scully continues her report.

"What I couldn't tell Agent Mulder," she says, "what I had only just learned myself, was that the cancer which had been diagnosed in me several months earlier had metastasized. And the doctors told me, short of a miracle, it would continue to aggressively invade my body, advancing faster each day toward the inevitable."

Section Chief Blevins looks at her with obvious sorrow.

Inside the snow cave, one of the climbers, wielding a large chain saw, is cutting the alien—or rather, the block of ice containing the alien—out of the wall. Elsewhere in the cave, Babcock sits inside his tent and loads a large handgun.

"What's that for?" says Rolston, the guide.

"I don't know these men well," says Babcock. "Do you?"

Babcock puts the gun aside. The head of the working party kneels down at the tent entrance.

"I think you'd better have a look at this," he says.

He shows Babcock a curious anomaly in the ice—evidence, perhaps, of a man-made pour hole or casting channel. The workers'

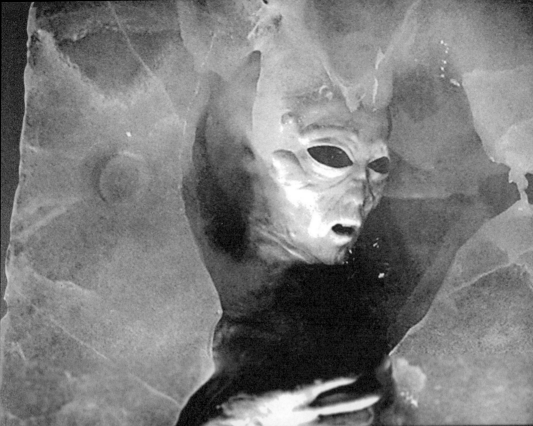

faces betray their confusion. Rolston makes an effort to hide his own fears.

"We'll never know," he says loudly, "until we get it out of there."

Behind him a chain saw roars into life. Shortly afterward, Rolston treks down the mountain, retracing his steps of the day before.

In the paleoclimatology lab at American University in Washington, a scientist named Vitagliano tells Scully that the ice core samples he's tested generally support Arlinsky's scenario. However, he's also found some anomalous hybrid cells—chimeras—that he'd like to analyze under an electron microscope.

"Yes, please," says Scully, intrigued.

At the summit that night, a dark figure, snow crunching lightly under his feet, enters the cave. The climbers are bedded down inside their tents. The intruder pulls out an exotic shotgun pistol, cocks it, and fires again and again through the fabric walls. Babcock scrambles out of his sleeping bag and flings open the tent flap. Another shotgun blast rings out.

The next morning, the helicopter alights briefly to deposit Mulder and Arlinsky at the base camp. To Arlinsky's surprise and dismay, the site is deserted.

"I thought you said there was someone meeting us," says Mulder.

"Yes," says Arlinsky, "a guide named Rolston."

Mulder checks inside the main base camp tent. The cooking stove is cold and the satellite phone is dead. Mulder's expression turns grim; the pair sets out to follow Rolston's tracks up the mountain. Halfway up the mountain, they spot a man in climbing gear forty meters ahead of them. He is lying by the side of the path.

"Funny place to take a nap," says Mulder.

They run toward the motionless figure. It is Rolston, shot dead, his blood oozing onto the snow. Arlinsky is terrified. Mulder leads him upward.

That night, Scully enters the lab at American University. The only other person in sight is a tall, nondescript man in a dark suit.

"Excuse me. I'm looking for Dr. Vitagliano," says Scully.

The man, fumbling with something on a lab bench, does not respond.

"Dr. Vitagliano? Is he here?"

"No, I'm afraid not," says the man. "Sorry."

He snatches up a cylindrical metal tube—of the type used to hold Arlinsky's core samples—and leaves. Scully looks at the glass-sided refrigerator where the core samples are stored. Its door stands open.

Scully turns and runs into the corridor. The door to a stairwell is just clicking shut. She enters the dark passageway and checks another door leading from it—which opens abruptly and violently, knocking her to the floor. The dark-suited man, holding the core sample, emerges from behind the door. Scully rises and grapples with him. He flings her aside. She tumbles painfully down the staircase.

At nightfall, Mulder and Arlinsky enter the snow cave. Mulder draws his gun. Their flashlights probe inside the tents. They find more dead men—including, apparently, Babcock, who lies motionless in his sleeping bag.

"The body!" says Arlinsky.

He runs to the ice face. Mulder follows close behind him. Where there was once an alien body there is now a rectangular hole in the ice.

"It's gone! They took it!" says Arlinsky.

Mulder grabs the scientist's arm. In the background is the faint sound of a man moaning.

"Someone's still alive," says Mulder.

It is Babcock.

"Give him some water," says Mulder. "Looks like he took a shotgun hit. But it didn't open him up too badly. The bleeding's stopped."

"Who did this?" says Arlinsky to his associate.

Babcock shakes his head.

"They took the body, Babcock," says Arlinsky angrily.

"No," rasps Babcock. "I buried it."

"Where?"

Mulder holds Babcock in his arms, moving him out of the tent. Arlinsky lifts the lightweight structure, pushes it aside, and scrapes the snow off the ground on which it stood. Not more than six inches below the surface is a rectangular block of ice. The alien's body is inside it.

In a hospital in Washington, a battered and bruised Scully, her clothes still bloody from the previous night's incident, prepares to check herself out and go home.

The door to her room opens. It is Bill Scully, Jr.

"Bill? What are you doing here?" says Scully.

"I picked up the phone when you called Mom's," he says. "They said you could use a change of clothes."

"Thank you," says Scully. "Where's Mom?"

"I didn't tell Mom what happened," says her brother uncomfortably. "So—what did happen?"

"I was knocked down a flight of stairs," says Scully. "But I'm okay. Luckily."

Bill Scully looks at his sister with a mixture of distress, sympathy, and disapproval.

"You're not okay, Dana," he says. "I know about your cancer."

Scully says unhappily, "I told Mom not to tell you."

"Why?"

"Because it's very personal," she says. "Because I don't want sympathy."

Bill Scully shakes his head, frowning. "You think you can cure yourself," he says. "Mom tells me that you've gotten worse. That the cancer's gotten into your bloodstream. What are you doing at work getting knocked down, beaten up? What are you trying to prove? That you're going to go out fighting?"

He adds angrily, "Do you know what Mom is going through? Why do you think I didn't tell her when you called?"

Now Scully flares into anger. "What should I be doing?" she asks.

"We have responsibilities!" says her brother. "Not just to ourselves, but to the people in our lives!"

"Hey, look!" says Scully. "Just because I haven't bared my soul to you, or to Father McCue, or to God, it doesn't mean that I'm not responsible to what's important to me!"

Bill Scully says, "To what? To who? This guy Mulder? But where is he, Dana? Where is he through all this?"

Scully pauses, thinks, and chokes back whatever it is she means to say.

"Thank you for coming," she says finally.

She takes the clothes from her brother and leaves.

At a darkened warehouse, a truck backs up to a loading dock. Mulder and Arlinsky lift out a large wooden crate and pry it open with a crowbar. The ice-entombed alien is lowered by forklift into a fiberglass tub filled with a warm liquid solution.

Mulder and Arlinsky gaze down at the rapidly melting ice block.

"We should be able to do a good enough examination of the body right here—to remove any doubt," says Arlinsky eagerly.

Mulder says firmly, "We won't know for sure until we do a carbon-dating test."

Arlinsky says, "I'm anticipating his physiology alone is going to be telltale."

"The Piltdown Man hoax," says Mulder through gritted teeth, "wasn't uncovered for forty years, until it failed a carbon-dating test. And that wasn't even very good."

Babcock, his shoulder bandaged and his arm in a sling, approaches behind them.

"If this were a hoax, would we have six dead men up on that mountain?" he says. "Somebody other than us sure believes it's not."

At the FBI Sci-Crime lab, a female agent named Hedin runs a fingerprint, lifted from the lab at American University, through her computerized matching system. There are no hits.

"Try the federal database," says Scully, looking over her shoulder.

Agent Hedin types in a few commands, then waits.

"I'll be damned," she says, astonished. "How'd you know he'd be a government employee?"

"Where does he work?" asks Scully.

"Right here in Washington," says Hedin. "Michael Kritschgau, formerly of the U.S. Army, now attached to the Pentagon's research division in Virginia."

Hedin pulls up Kritschgau's personnel file, including an attached photo. It is of the man who attacked Scully.

At the makeshift autopsy bay in the ware house, Mulder examines a series of alien

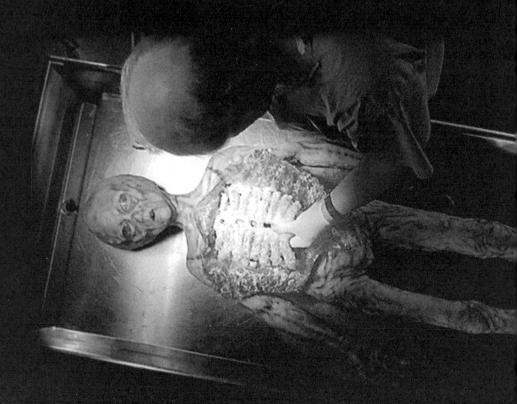

X-rays on a light board. Arlinsky dissects the alien corpse and dictates his case notes. Babcock videotapes the proceedings. Arlinsky says:

"Body is one hundred forty-seven centimeters long, weighing twenty-four kilograms deliquesced. Derma is hairless gray with an elephantine texture, with no odor. There are some small eruptions on the surface of the skin, most likely to the presence of iron phosphate in the ice. Otherwise, there appears to be no scarring, no identifying marks. The circumference of the head is sixty-four centimeters. There are four digits on each hand, three on each foot. Sex is indeterminate. The eyes are lidless, black, covered in a thin membrane, which I am removing. The tissue underneath is semi-gelatinous, with a fine network of veins running throughout."

Arlinsky, who is wearing surgical scrubs and a surgical mask, glances up at Mulder before making an incision in the alien's chest cavity. He continues:

"Examination of the chest cavity confirms the presence of what appears to be a cardiopulmonary system; heart and lungs, all identifiable within a mass of white, stringlike tissue that doesn't appear to correspond to human physiology."

Scully sits in her parked car across the street from an office park in Sethsburg, Virginia. She watches a stream of workers leaving an office building. Michael Kritschgau, wearing a black raincoat and carrying a briefcase, appears among them and heads into an underground parking structure. Scully starts her car, drives into the garage, and intercepts him—stopping just inches from where he's standing. Kritschgau spots Scully through the windshield, turns, and flees. Scully gets out the car and draws her gun.

"Stop! Federal agent!" she shouts.

Scully runs after the tall, balding man. He reaches his car and tries to drive to freedom, but she cuts him off by sprinting up the parking structure stairs. Standing between his speeding car and the exit ramp, she points her gun through the windshield at his head. He surrenders.

"Please don't shoot," says Kritschgau. "I didn't mean to hurt you. I had no choice."

Scully spread-eagles Kritschgau against the car and frisks him.

"If you arrest me," insists Kritschgau, "they'll kill me."

"I don't know what you're talking about!" says Scully.

"They're the same people who are trying to kill you," he replies. "The people who gave you your cancer."

At the warehouse facility, Arlinsky weighs an unidentifiable alien on a digital scale. He turns to Mulder.

"There's tissue culturing to be done," he says. "DNA sequencing and analysis. And we'd be wise to run a gas chromatograph and that carbon dating you suggested. But—if this isn't alien, I don't know what it is."

With his one good arm, Babcock brushes a layer of crushed ice over the alien's eviscerated body. Mulder's cell phone rings, and he answers it.

Scully continues her narrative for the FBI investigative committee.

"I had reached Agent Mulder in a warehouse just outside of Washington in Sethsburg, Virginia," she says. "They had managed the frozen corpse by helicopter down the side of the mountain, and across the Canadian border in a refrigerated truck. After conducting a limited physical examination, Agent Mulder was ready to believe that the body was that of an extraterrestrial biological entity. That he had finally found the proof which had eluded him. Which would confirm not only the existence of alien life, but of his sister Samantha's abduction."

Section Chief Blevins says, "But this man Kritschgau had convinced you otherwise. How?"

Scully says, "He told me a story which detailed point by point the systematic way in which Agent Mulder had been deceived and used. And how I, as his partner, had been led down the same path, losing a

family member due to my allegiance and contracting a fatal disease which I was being told was being engineered by the men who were responsible for Agent Mulder's deception."

"Were you able to convince Agent Mulder of these facts?" asks Blevins.

"I was only able to convince him to meet me—so that he might hear the story the way I had."

Mulder exits the warehouse, moving to his car. Waiting in another car nearby is a dark figure. He cocks his shotgun pistol and watches Mulder drive away. Inside, Arlinsky and Babcock continue their work. The rolling door at the loading dock lifts. The dark figure, whose name is Ostelhoff, advances toward them.

"Who the hell is this?" says Arlinsky.

"Right there, pork," says Ostelhoff, pointing his shotgun at him.

Ostelhoff turns to Babcock. "How's the wound?" he asks.

"I'll live," Babcock replies.

Arlinksy turns to his fellow scientist, realizing.

"Get the door," says Ostelhoff to Babcock.

Ostelhoff fires one shotgun blast into Arlinksy, then walks over to Babcock.

"Where did Mulder go?" he asks.

"He got a call," says Babcock.

"Is he a believer?"

"Oh, yeah."

"Then we're the only ones who know," says Ostelhoff.

"Right," says Babcock, nodding.

In Mulder's apartment that night, Kritschgau sits across from the agent. Scully stands, arms folded, near the door. Mulder is slumped on his sofa, eyeing them defiantly.

Kritschgau says, "The lie you believe— that they have cleverly led you to believe, Agent Mulder—is that there is intelligent life other than our own, and that we have been in contact with these life forms."

Mulder says, "So you're saying that this has all been orchestrated. A hoax."

"Which you've been used to perpetuate," says Kritschgau.

"You come by this knowledge how?"

"Working for the DOD," says Kritschgau. "Watching a military-industrial complex that operated unbridled and unchecked during the Cold War create a diversion of attention from itself and its continued misdeeds by confabulating enough believable evidence to convince adepts like yourself that it really could be true."

"And just by chance you run into Agent Scully?" says Mulder sarcastically.

"That's just like you, Agent Mulder," says Kritschgau, with a tight smile. "Suspicious of everything but what you should be."

He adds, "I ran the DOD's agitprop arm for a decade. I can show you records of disinformation dating back to before the Korean War—before you were even born."

"Why come to me now? Why not four years ago?"

Kritschgau pauses. "I have a son who's very sick," he says sadly. "He served in the Gulf War."

Kritschgau closes his eyes and frowns.

"The lies are so deep," he says. "The only way to cover them is to create something more incredible. They invented you. Your regression hypnosis; the story of your sister's abduction; the lies they fed your father. You want to believe so badly—and who could have blamed you?"

"The thousands of UFO sightings?" says Mulder.

"Above top-secret military aircraft," says Kritschgau. "Concept designed to feed hysteria."

"Evidence of alien biology?"

"Unclassified. But naturally occurring biological anomalies science will eventually explain."

"The body that was found?"

"Meticulously constructed out of biomaterials," says Kritschgau. "Created through the hybridization of differentiated cells—what are called chimeras. Frozen into place over the course of years, using sediment and materials that would bear out its age, poured though a small channel drilled in the rock above."

Mulder says, "They would have known the body would be carbon-dated. That it would be proved a fake."

"The body will never be tested, Agent Mulder. You were only meant to see it. To make you believe the lie. So you might finally commit—go public with the news."

Mulder looks at Scully. "This man is a liar," he says.

Scully says nothing.

"You can see for yourself, Agent Mulder," says Kritschgau. "The body is already long gone."

Mulder gets up and walks out the door.

Mulder enters the warehouse, calling Arlinsky's name. No answer. The body is gone.

Scully enters behind him. Mulder stops in his tracks and kneels. "It's Arlinsky," he says. "He's dead."

"So is this man," says Scully.

In the thawing tank lies Babcock, a thin scum of his blood floating on the surface. Mulder looks at him and walks briskly toward the door.

"Who did this, Mulder?" asks Scully.

No answer.

"Mulder?"

"What we had here was proof, Scully," says Mulder, walking very fast. "There's no way it could be anything else."

Scully says, walking rapidly behind him, "You said it yourself. Mulder! More tests needed to be run."

"The ice core samples checked out. If the ice hadn't been tampered with, how could the body within it be a fake?"

"Cellular material found in the ice core samples were a direct match for what this man Kritschgau described. Hybrid cells—chimeras within the matrix."

"Do we know for sure that those cells are not extraterrestrial?"

"Mulder! Everything this man described—you just can't guess at the details. I'm sorry, but the facts here completely overwhelm any argument against them."

"Facts overwhelmed by the lies created to support them!"

"Mulder, the only lie here is the one you continue to believe!"

Mulder stares at Scully, seething. "After all I've seen and experienced, I refuse to believe it's not true!"

"Because it's easier to believe the lie," says Scully. "Isn't it?"

"What the hell did that guy say to you to make you believe his story?"

Scully says, "He said the men behind this hoax, behind these lies, gave me this disease to make you believe."

Mulder stares at her, stunned, and walks away.

At the Boston University conference, the anthropologist Ashley Montagu is speaking. He says:

"It is highly probable that there are such intelligent forms of life in other galaxies in the universe. And it is even more probable that many of these forms are vastly more intelligent than we."

The next speaker is the biologist George Wald. He says:

"I think that there's no question but that we live in an inhabited universe that has life all over it."

Mulder sits on the sofa in his apartment, staring intently at the TV screen on which the tape of the conference is playing. He is not visibly emotional, but something fundamental about him appears changed. The next speaker is Carl Sagan:

"By finding out what the other planets are like, by finding out whether there are civilizations on planets of other stars, we reestablish a meaningful context for ourselves."

Ashley Montagu:

"I don't think we should wait until the encounter occurs, but that we should do all in our power to prepare ourselves for it."

Now Mulder is clearly in pain. He closes his eyes as if something inside of him has died. George Wald:

"I can conceive of no nightmare as terrifying as establishing such communication with a so-called superior or more advanced technology in outer space."

Upon hearing this, Mulder's expression becomes one of infinite sadness. Tears run down his cheeks.

In the FBI conference room, Scully's own eyes are welling with emotion.

"Early this morning," she says, "I got a call from the police asking me to come to Agent Mulder's apartment. The detective asked me—he needed me to identify a body."

She cannot go on.

"Agent Scully?" says Blevins softly.

Scully's voice trembles as she forces herself to finish her report. She says, "Agent Mulder died late last night—of an apparent self-inflicted gunshot wound to the head."

back story:

Twenty-one degrees below zero. Fahrenheit.

That's what the thermostat read inside the windowless warehouse in Burnaby, just east of Vancouver. Inside a cavernous seventy-by-twenty-by-thirty-foot storage space, the members of the *X-Files* cast and film crew fought for verisimilitude—and to keep from losing their extremities in the cause of art.

In order to give viewers and actors alike the feeling that the action was indeed taking place in a frigid wilderness, an entire set—one of the most expensive and elaborate in *X-Files* history—was built by Rob Maier's construction crew inside a refrigerated building originally designed to hold pork loins and TV dinners. Several truckloads of lumber went into the construction of the set; the entire framework was covered with 10,000 square feet of Styrofoam and "ice dressed" by spraying the whole assemblage with water.

"Um, I think I left a couple of toes on that soundstage," jokes David Duchovny of the several days he spent filming his snow cave scenes.

Everyone involved in the shooting was required to dress *very* warmly (see memo). But nobody anticipated that the company's two carefully frozen ice blocks (one a spare) containing Toby Lindala's latex aliens—intended, of course, to be dug out of the ice by the mountain climbers—would literally explode from the extreme cold. As a fallback, director Bob Goodwin substituted a urethane plastic-enclosed alien, designed for the warm-bath autopsy scenes, built by David Gautier's special-effects crew.

The other major logistical challenge posed by "Gethsemane" was the filming of its outdoor mountain scenes. To producer J. P. Finn's extreme frustration, the shooting schedule had to be juggled repeatedly because stormy weather and whiteouts around nearby Mount Seymour hindered visibility, mobility, and helicopter operations. (This was in early May, a season when melting snow and bare ground seemed a more likely problem.)

Compounding these difficulties was the fact that "Gethsemane" was the last episode of the season. Since the actors and most of the other personnel would be released at an agreed-upon date, adding additional filming days was extremely difficult.

Also worthy of several Extra Strength Excedrin: the fact that the lead actors, facing only a brief vacation before filming of the *X-Files* motion picture was to begin, were nearly exhausted. Although no one knew it at the time, David Duchovny—whose secret fiancée Téa Leoni visited him on the set during the filming of "Gethsemane"—was only a week away from his wedding day. Some of the dialogue of the scientists in the opening and closing scene was indistinct—but could not be easily rerecorded, because most of the people in those archival scenes were dead.

T H E (X) F I L E

MEMO

DATE: April 28, 1997

TO: Department Heads of the Shooting Crew

FROM: Louisa Gradnitzer

RE: Filming "Summit Cave" set at subzero temperatures
Location: 6228 Bereford Street, Burnaby, BC

Please be advised that our cave set is extremely cold with temperatures n
0° to -15° F.

Here is a list of recommended protection from the elements:

Goretex or Similar Shell Clothing, Jacket and Pants
Fleece or Wool Clothing Underneath
or
Warm Winter Ski Suit
Extra Insulated Jacket, Sweater, or Vest
Wool Hat
Warm Gloves or Mitts
Thin Working Gloves (glove liners)
Winter Boots ("Sorrels", etc...)

Also, please help to keep the snow clean. So please do not:
- wear muddy boots to and from set
- smoke, eat or drink on set
- throw confetti on set

Spelunking is not advised due to harsh weather conditions and please do
reflector boards.

Enjoy the trek!

The unfortunate actor James Sutorious, playing dead in the alien autopsy bath, had to lie motionless underwater for more than a minute. Visual effects supervisor Laurie Kallsen-George had to painstakingly erase his tiny air bubbles in postproduction. (She also digitally added a thin scum of blood to the surface of his bathwater.)

The first cut of "Gethsemane" was twelve minutes too long. "We took out a lot of hiking through the mountains," says story editor John Shiban. As mentioned previously, "Gethsemane" was also completely reedited by Chris Carter just two days before its air date.

But apparently *something* went right: The season-ender earned one of the highest ratings of the season—and, amazingly, set off a nationwide buzz of speculation as to whether Mulder was really dead.

For instance: an article in the *Wall Street Journal* (headline: "The Truth Is Out There, And So Are Some of These Fans") chronicled fans' theories as to the method behind Mulder's alleged madness. A few weeks later a cartoon that ran in *The New Yorker* showed a deeply depressed man lying on a psychiatrist's couch. "I see no problem with a limited period of grief," says his bearded shrink, "as long as you keep in mind that Agent Mulder was a fictional character."

Even Chris Carter was amazed by the response. He's not complaining, though. He sees it all as a good sign that viewers will tune in *en masse* to the two-parter (or three-parter, if you count 4X24) that will begin the fifth season. In other words: The bait has been swallowed and the hook has been set.

"The whole plot line of 'Gethsemane' revolved around a hoax," says Carter, "but there are actually huge revelations in this show. And it's an amazing thing that we could get people to believe that Mulder could actually kill himself because his belief system was stolen from him."

He adds: "We'll see this theme continued at the beginning of next season."

The tagline was changed to "Believe the Lie."

Ⓧ

"Gethsemane" is a particularly evocative title, coming directly from the Bible. On the night before he was crucified, Jesus retired to the Garden of Gethsemane to pray and keep vigil, and to struggle with his fate. It was here that Judas Iscariot betrayed him.

Ⓧ

Although Dana Scully's brothers have been mentioned occasionally, and we saw them as teenagers in a flashback in "Beyond the Sea"(1X12), this is the first time one of them has put in an appearance. Scully's sister, Melissa, was killed in the third-season episode "The Blessing Way" (3X01).

Ⓧ

A chimera, mentioned by Scully as a hybrid cell of two organisms, takes its name from a Greek myth about a fire-breathing monster, described as having a lion's head, a goat's body, and a serpent's tail. Another meaning of the word is "an impossible and foolish fancy."

Ⓧ

Michael Kritschgau is named for a former drama teacher of Gillian Anderson's.

Ⓧ

Scully mentions the Law of Occam's Razor. This is a scientific principle that states that other things being equal, the simpler of two explanations is usually the correct one.

Ⓧ

"Gethsemane" marks actor Charles Cioffi's (Section Chief Blevins) first appearance since the pilot episode.

Ⓧ

redux

After faking his own suicide to shake off Syndicate and FBI surveillance, Mulder secretly searches for the cause of—and cure for—Scully's terminal cancer.

episode: 5X02

first aired: November 2, 1997

written by: Chris Carter

editor: Heather MacDougall

directed By: R. W. Goodwin

guest stars:
Mitch Pileggi (AD Walter Skinner)
William B. Davis (The Cigarette-Smoking Man)
John Finn (Michael Kritschgau)
Steve Makaj (Scott Ostelhoff)
Ken Camroux (Senior Agent)
Charles Cioffi (Section Chief Scott Blevins)
Barry W. Levy (Vitagliano)
Don S. Williams (Elder)
Bruce Harwood (Byers)
Tom Braidwood (Frohike)
Dean Haglund (Langly)
Julie Arkos (Holly)
John D. Sampson (Sentry)

principal settings:
Washington, D.C.; Alexandria and Sethsburg, Virginia

In a brief flashback to 4X24 ("Gethsemane"), Mulder is seated on the sofa in his apartment, staring intently at the TV screen.

A videotape of the 1972 conference on the possibility of extraterrestrial life is playing. Mulder is racked with guilt over Scully's illness and his own dashed hopes over the revelation that the alien body he discovered was a fake. Everything he's believed in and worked to prove has been revealed to be false.

The action moves forward: Mulder reaches for his weapon, checks that it is loaded, and turns off the television. His telephone rings. It is Kritschgau, the Defense Department operative who has previously told him that he, Scully, and the X-Files were pawns in a massive program of government deception. Kritschgau implies obliquely that he has more information for Mulder.

Mulder will have none of this. "Did they give Agent Scully this disease?" he demands. "Did they do this because of me?"

"They may be listening, Agent Mulder," cautions Kritschgau. "They may be watching everything you do and say."

Mulder glances upward and spots a dark pinhole next to a light fixture on the ceiling.

Somewhere nearby, a shadowy figure is looking at a video monitor. The door to this location bursts open and Mulder, gun in hand, pushes through. He confronts Scott Ostelhoff, the man whose shotgun pistol silenced over half a dozen men in the previous episode, and who is lighting flash paper that he has tossed into a metal wastebasket.

"Back away!" shouts Mulder, overturning the wastebasket and trying to stamp out the fire with his foot. Ostelhoff lunges for his shotgun pistol. One shot rings out.

Later that night, a weary Scully enters her darkened Washington apartment and begins to take off her clothes.

"Keep going, FBI woman," says Mulder, who has been lying in wait for her.

After Scully recovers from her shock, Mulder shows her Ostelhoff's government ID card. He tells her these facts: his apartment had been under surveillance for at least two months; Ostelhoff, like Kritschgau, worked for the Department of Defense; the assassin is now dead from "a bullet wound to the face"; Mulder has reported the death to no one; and, since phone records he found in Ostelhoff's apartment included at least a dozen calls to the FBI telephone exchange, the Bureau is somehow connected to the hoax described by Kritschgau.

"How long has this been going on?" asks Scully.

"Maybe since the beginning," says Mulder. "Since you joined me on the X-Files."

Scully says, "That would mean that for four years we've been nothing more than pawns in a game. That it was a lie from the start." She blinks away tears of anger and frustration.

"These men," she adds, "you give them your trust. You're supposed to trust them with your life."

"There are those who are to be trusted," says Mulder. "What I want to know is who among them is not. But I won't let this treason prosper. Not if they've done this to you."

"We can't go to the Bureau making these accusations," says Scully.

"No," says Mulder. "But as they lie to us, we can lie to them. A lie to find the truth."

On a laboratory workbench, an unseen scientist performs an unspecified test, placing drops of clear liquid into a segmented glass container.

Another flashback from 4X24: It is early the next morning in Mulder's apartment, which is swarming with uniformed officers, detectives, and forensic techs. Scully enters, flashes her FBI ID, and pushes her way through the crowd. An Arlington PD detective named Rempulski greets her grimly. He leads her to a sheet-covered body lying facedown between the couch and the coffee table—and lifts a corner of the sheet.

"Is it him?" he asks.

"Yeah," whispers Scully.

Back to 5X02: In the hallway outside Mulder's apartment, Scully is intercepted by AD Skinner. She confirms her "identification" of Mulder. Skinner tells Scully that Section Chief Blevins, the man who originally assigned her to the X-Files, wants to talk to her.

"He believes you have information you haven't come forward with," says Skinner, who appears to have some unanswered questions himself.

At the Defense Department's Advanced Research Project Agency facility—where Scully tracked down Kritschgau in 4X24—Mulder walks through the main lobby and enters a secure area by swiping an ID card through the guard gate.

At FBI headquarters later that day, Scully enters Blevins's office. Skinner enters behind her. A senior FBI agent—who was also with Blevins in the pilot episode—is also in the room.

"From all reports," says Blevins to Scully, "your work on the X-Files brought you very close to Agent Mulder."

"Yes, sir," says Scully.

Blevins says, "There are those in the Bureau who believe that you came to share his belief in the paranormal, and in the existence of extraterrestrial life."

"No, sir," says Scully. "That couldn't be further from the truth."

Blevins tells Scully that she is being questioned because the FBI has learned that a Department of Defense employee had contacted her and passed her classified information shortly before Mulder's "accident."

"He had information about the discovery of what Agent Mulder believed was an alien corpse," says Scully. "He said the body was part of a hoax."

"He provided evidence of this?" says Blevins.

"He provided us with no hard evidence," says Scully unconvincingly.

Blevins presses Scully for the informant's name. Scully remains silent. Blevins tells her that she will have to reveal whatever she's withholding at a special FBI panel he has convened for that evening. Scully still says nothing.

Skinner stands and pulls a surveillance photo from a manila envelope.

"Is this the man? Michael Kritschgau?" he asks accusingly.

"Yes," says Scully reluctantly.

At the DARPA facility, Kritschgau intercepts Mulder among a morning crush of employees. "How did you get in here? You can't bypass security," asks the astonished DOD man.

"You can with The Card," says Mulder, showing him Ostelhoff's identification.

"Put that away. Put it away!" says Kritschgau frantically.

Mulder coolly pockets the card. "You knew my apartment was being surveilled," says Mulder. "How?"

An extremely nervous Kritschgau hustles Mulder into his office. He tells Mulder that he was followed from Mulder's apartment after their first meeting. Mulder tells him that Ostelhoff had had contact with someone at the FBI. Kritschgau asks how he got Ostelhoff's card.

"I found it on a dead man," says Mulder.

Understanding exactly what the agent means by this, Kritschgau tells Mulder that Ostelhoff's ID gives him top-security clearance.

"You have access to everything, Mr. Mulder," he says. "Things I don't. Things I can only tell you about."

"I need to know who did this to Scully," says Mulder.

Kritschgau says, "What you can have—what you may find—is so much more than that. What you want most desperately of all."

"The cure for Scully's cancer?"

Kritschgau nods, then asks Mulder who else knows that Ostelhoff is dead.

"Only Agent Scully," says Mulder.

"Then you have only until they learn what's happened to him. If they run a scan on his card, they'll know you're inside."

Later that morning, someone picks the lock on Mulder's apartment. The door swings open and the Cigarette-Smoking Man steps inside. He appears shaken. He looks sadly at the tape outline of a body on the floor and gazes at an old framed photograph of young Mulder and his sister Samantha. A beam of light hitting the floor leads his eye to the ceiling. He spots the pinhole for the surveillance camera—and seems genuinely surprised.

On the laboratory bench we've seen previously, the unseen scientist removes a drop of liquid from the segmented vessel, places it into a petri dish, and places it under an electron microscope. A single cell floats in the pinkish media.

In the X-Files office at FBI headquarters, Scully picks up the phone, reaches a woman—Holly (seen previously in "Pusher" [3X17])—in the Bureau's communications unit, gives her the dates and times of Ostelhoff's calls to the FBI exchange, and asks her to trace them internally.

"I've got five calls," says Holly, "match-

ing those times and dates to an executive level extension."

"Whose?" says Scully.

"It's a branch extension. It could be anyone at that level."

"Would Assistant Director Skinner be on that branch extension?" asks Scully.

"Yes," says Holly.

Scully hangs up the phone. It rings immediately, startling her. It is the paleoclimatologist Vitagliano (from "Gethsemane" [4X24]), who reminds her that she had asked him to examine the ice-core samples gathered near the alien burial site.

"Right. I'm sorry I haven't gotten back to you," says Scully.

"I think you might want to come to the lab," says the scientist. "There's something I know you're going to want to see for yourself."

At the DARPA facility, Kritschgau leads Mulder out of his office and toward an even higher-security area.

"What am I looking for?" asks Mulder.

"Level Four is a biological quarantine wing," says Kritschgau. "It houses a series of labs and medical facilities, and an elaborate system for the storage of mass quantities of DNA."

"DNA from whom?" asks Mulder.

"Virtually every American born since 1945. Every immigrant, every indigenous person who's ever given blood or tissue to a government doctor."

Mulder realizes the significance of this immediately. As Kritschgau leads the shaken agent toward Level Four, he explains what he knows about the project.

This is his explanation:

"This is the hoax into which you have been drawn. The roots go back fifty years, to the end of World War II. Playing on a virulent national appetite for bogus revelation and a public newly fearful of something called the atom bomb, the U.S. military command began to fan the flames of what were being called 'flying saucer stories.' There are truths which can kill a nation, Agent Mulder, and the military needed something to deflect attention away from its arms strategy: global domination through the capability of total enemy annihilation. The nuclear card was fine as long as we alone could play it, but pointed back at us the generals and politicos knew what they couldn't win was a public relations war.

"Those photos of Nagasaki and Hiroshima were not faces Americans wanted to see in the mirror. Oppenheimer knew it, of course, but we silenced him. When the Russians developed the bomb, the fear in the military was not for safety at home, but for armistice and treaties. The business of America isn't business, Agent Mulder. It's war. Since Antietam, nothing has driven the economy faster.

"We need a reason to keep spending money, and when there wasn't a war to justify it, we called it war anyway. The Cold War was essentially a fifty-year public-relations battle. A pitched game of chicken against an enemy we did not much more than call names. The Communists called us a few names, too. 'We will bury you,' Khrushchev said, and the public believed it. After what McCarthy had done to the country, they ate it with a big spoon. We squared off a few times, in Korea and Vietnam. But nobody dropped the bomb. Nobody dared."

Mulder interrupts him. "What's any of that have to do with flying saucers?" he asks.

Kritschgau continues: "The military saw a good thing in '47 when the Roswell story broke. The more we denied it, the more people believed it was true. Aliens had landed—a made-to-order cover story for generals looking to develop the national war chest. They opened official investigations, with names like Grudge and Twinkle, Project Blue Book and Majestic 12. They brought in college professors and congressmen and fed them enough bogus facts, enough fuzzy photos and eyewitness accounts, that they believed it, too. They even hooked Doug MacArthur, for God's sake.

"I can't tell you how fortuitous the timing of it all was. Do you know when the first supersonic flight was, Agent Mulder? 1947. Soon every experimental aircraft being flown was a UFO sighting. And when the abduction stories started up, it was too perfect. We'd almost gotten caught in Korea. An ambitious misstep. China and the Soviets knew it. The U.N. got all worked up about it."

Mulder looks at Kritschgau. "Germ warfare," he says finally. "We were accused of using it on the Koreans."

Kritschgau nods. "It was developmental then," he says. "Nothing like what we or the Russians have now. The bioweapons used in the Gulf War are so ingenious as to be almost undetectable. Developed right here in this very building."

Mulder says, "Then all these accounts of abductions—you're saying they've all been lies?"

"Not lies, exactly," says Kritschgau. "But unsuspecting citizens taken and tested. A classified military project above top secret. And still ongoing."

"But I've seen aliens. I've witnessed these things," says Mulder.

Kritschgau, leading Mulder into an elevator, says, "You've seen what they've wanted you to see."

"Then why a hoax?" asks Mulder.

"The body you found is so good, so believable, that only a directed scientific examination would have proven the fraud."

Mulder says, "Scully would have known."

"The timing of the hoax," replies Kritschgau, "was planned so that Agent Scully wouldn't be alive to do an examination."

The elevator door opens, but Mulder blocks Kritschgau's path. "You went along with all this," says the agent accusingly.

"I've paid the price, Agent Mulder. When my son came home from the Gulf War, it was my retribution. I'm helping you now, but not unselfishly."

"You believe there's a cure for him in there, too," says Mulder.

Kritschgau says, "I have to think there is."

Mulder and Kritschgau arrive at a security door to Level Four. Mulder swipes his card through a reader, the door opens, and he walks through. Kritschgau turns and heads back. He is accosted by two armed sentries.

"DOD is detaining you for questioning," says one of them. "Would you come with us, Mr. Kritschgau, sir?"

At an otherwise empty racetrack, the Elder sits in a box in the grandstand and watches a horse and rider complete their workout. In a seat just a short distance away, another man sits quietly.

The Cigarette-Smoking Man arrives, takes a seat next to the Elder, and complains bitterly that he hadn't been informed of Ostelhoff's surveillance of Mulder. He asks if the operation was run out of the Defense Department. The Elder coolly disclaims all knowledge of the project. They both know that he is lying.

"e always kept Mulder in check," says the Cigarette-Smoking Man. "I put this whole thing together. I created Mulder."

"Agent Mulder is dead," says the Elder flatly.

"You know that for a fact?" challenges the Cigarette-Smoking Man.

"Our FBI source confirmed it this morning. Mulder killed himself," says the Elder.

He adds, "Mulder was an asset. But without his partner, you may have underestimated his fragility."

Replies the Cigarette-Smoking Man, "I never underestimated Mulder. I still don't."

At the American University paleoclimatology lab, Dr. Vitagliano tells Scully that he's finished testing the cells in the ice-core sample. He reports that the cells were unclassifiable—neither plant nor animal—and that he placed them in a nutrient media. The cells began to divide.

"But they didn't just multiply," adds Vitagliano. "They began to go through the stages of morula, blastula, gastrula—"

"They began somatic development," says Scully, astonished.

Vitagliano nods, rises from his chair, and leads Scully to his microscope. She peers at the rudimentary creature.

"The beginning of a life-form," says Vitagliano. "Growing into what, I don't know."

Inside the DARPA research facility, Mulder cautiously explores a Level-Four corridor—until he spots the two sentries,

searching frantically for him. He picks the lock of a door leading off the hallway, enters a dark room, and waits there until his pursuers are safely past. He flips a light switch. The room is filled with metal hospital gurneys, lined in rows. On each

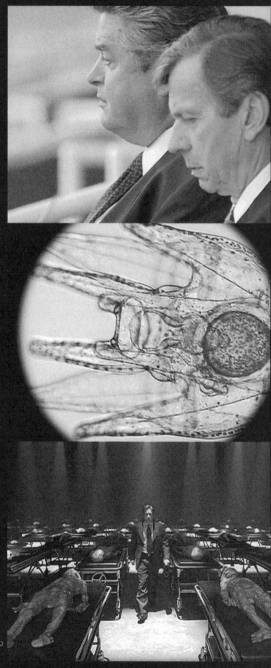

gurney is an alien body, exactly like the one found in the ice cave in 4X24. A strobing light begins to illuminate the room. It is flashing through a small, square window on a door at the far side of the room. Mulder opens the door, which leads to a long, dark corridor. The strobing light is emitting from another door at its far end. Mulder walks toward it.

At the American University lab, Vitagliano is drawing blood from Scully's arm. He tells her that he's not sure what she's asking him to do.

"I want you to do a Southern Blot, to run the culture you've shown me against my own DNA," says Scully. "You said when you looked at the unclassified cells under the EM they were full of virus."

"Right," says Vitagliano. "What are you looking for?"

"A match. And I need it before seven."

"Tonight? Not going to happen," says Vitagliano.

"It's got to happen," says Scully. "Everything in my life depends upon it."

Scully turns and looks toward the window in the lab door. Skinner is peering through at her. She quickly exits the lab in pursuit, but the assistant director is gone. She turns a corner in the corridor—and finds herself face to face with him.

"You followed me here. Why are you following me?" asks Scully. "Is this more dirty work you're doing for the DOD?"

Skinner says, "Why don't you tell me something, Agent Scully? Why don't you tell me what you're doing here?"

Suspicious of Skinner's ultimate allegiance, Scully discloses nothing.

"Your lie is on the record, Agent Scully," says Skinner.

"And yours?" says Scully.

"On my desk," says Skinner, "I have the pathology and forensics reports for the body found in Agent Mulder's apartment."

He adds, "You have to answer for yourself in five hours. As you compound the lies, you compound the consequences for them."

Scully says, "All lies lead to the truth, don't they?"

"And what about your lie?" replies Skinner. "What does it lead to?"

Inside DARPA Level Four, Mulder puts his face to the window. On the other side of the door is an operating theater; a woman lies on an operating table, eyes open. Her hands and feet are bound down with Velcro cuffs. A hose protrudes out of her greatly expanded abdomen. Suspended over her is a lighting grid, from which an intense blue geometric pattern of light is projected.

Mulder moves away from the door, heading back into the hall from which he spotted the sentries. He enters a long, seemingly endless tunnel, which finally ends at an emergency evacuation door. Mulder swipes his card and enters a warehouse—which appears to be the repository for all the alien-related odds and ends that the Cigarette-Smoking Man has taken from Mulder over the years. At one end of the building are floor-to-ceiling cabinets filled with small drawers. Index cards labeled alphabetically are attached to each drawer; Mulder finds the ones that start with the letter "S."

Reaching for the handle on one of them, he pulls it out as far as it goes, revealing a series of small index cards, which he begins to finger through rapidly. He draws out one card.

It reads: DANA KATHERINE SCULLY.

At the American University lab, Scully, wearing gloves and goggles, performs a Southern Blot: a complicated test designed to isolate DNA—the genetic building blocks of life—from blood. The test has several steps; after finishing them, Scully places tiny samples of her DNA in gel-filled glass containers.

At the DARPA facility, Mulder looks at Scully's index card, which is covered with several lines of letters and numbers. In the bottom right-hand corner is an index number that begins with the letters SEP. Mulder opens another drawer and finds the card that reads: MICHAEL LEE KRITSCHGAU. The card behind it reads: MICHAEL LEE KRITSCHGAU, JR. That card is empty except for the name on the top.

In a photographic darkroom, Scully shines a UV light on her genetic material, which reacts by glowing a fluorescent pink. She lays a special paper towel atop the gel, onto which she soaks blue dye. Scully takes the paper off the gel, placing it in a liquid-filled Ziploc baggie. To the liquid in the baggie Scully adds more liquid poured from a test tube. She takes the paper from the baggie, carefully placing it on a piece of X-ray film.

Mulder moves through a different part of the DARPA warehouse; it is stacked with cardboard boxes floor to ceiling. He finds a box with the same index number as on Scully's card. Inside it is a series of small metallic vials, arranged in a special holder.

In the darkroom Scully removes the paper from the X-ray film. It is 6:37 P.M. Dr. Vitagliano enters just as Scully turns on a white-light spot lamp. We see the X-ray film has a series of black strip lanes on it.

"There it is," says Scully, eyeing a pair of lanes not like any of the others, because they are paired. "My DNA hybridized with the viral DNA from the cell culture."

"Yes," says Vitagliano, amazed. "But that means that the material in the ice-core sample—you'd have to have DNA from the unclassified chimera cells in your own body."

"I know," says Scully gravely.

"But how? And how did you know?"

"I believe I was exposed to this material," says Scully. "And it is responsible for giving me a serious illness."

"What kind of illness?"

"One which cannot be cured."

In the DARPA warehouse, Mulder lifts a vial out of its holder. He looks carefully at it, considering the life-giving substance that might be contained inside. At 7:07 P.M., he leaves the warehouse.

Another flashback—this time with small but significant additions—to "Gethsemane" (4X24): In a large conference room at FBI headquarters, a high-level investigative committee, chaired by Section Chief Scott Blevins, is assembled. Scully enters and is asked by Blevins to take her seat. She does so.

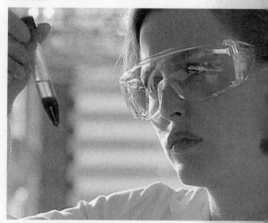

"Agent Scully, we've had a brief discussion," says Blevins. "But will you restate the matter we're here to put to rest."

"Yes, sir," says Scully.

She braces herself, and—without referring to notes—begins:

"Four years ago," she says, "Section Chief Blevins assigned me to a project you know as the X-Files. As I am a medical doctor with a background in hard science, my job was to provide an analytical perspective on the work of Special Agent Fox Mulder, whose investigations were fueled by a personal belief that his sister had been abducted by aliens when he was twelve."

In the DARPA facility, Mulder retraces his steps through the Level-Four facility. He

scans the area carefully, looking for the two sentries who had pursued him earlier.

In the FBI star chamber, Scully's voice begins to waver. "I come here today, four years later, to report on the illegitimacy of Agent Mulder's work," she says. "That it is my scientific opinion that he became, over the course of these years, a victim. A victim of his own false hopes—and of his belief in the biggest of lies."

Mulder reaches the security door. A light on the device is red. He swipes his ID card. The red light goes out—and comes back on again.

Scully says: "Recent events have shed new light on the factual and physical evidence that would serve to prove the existence of extraterrestrial life—which is the foundation of Agent Mulder's consuming devotion to his work."

She adds, "I am here today to expose this lie, to show the mechanism of the deception that drew him, and me, into it, and to expose Agent Mulder's work for what it is. And what it was."

The Senior Agent, last seen in Blevins's office, addresses Scully: "You were contacted by a man who claimed he worked for the Defense Department," he says. "A Michael Kritschgau. Who told you Mulder was taken in by a hoax. By a body found in the Yukon."

Scully replies: "They had managed the frozen corpse by helicopter down the side of the mountain, and across the Canadian border in a refrigerated truck. After conducting a limited physical examination, Agent Mulder was ready to believe that the body was that of an extraterrestrial biological entity. That he had finally found the proof which had eluded him. Which would confirm not only the existence of alien life, but of his sister Samantha's abduction."

Blevins says, "But this man Kritschgau had convinced you otherwise. How?"

Scully says, "He told me a story which detailed point by point the systematic way in which Agent Mulder had been deceived and used. And how I, as his partner, had been led down the same path. Losing a family member due to my allegiance, and contracting a fatal disease which I was being told was being engineered by the men who were responsible for Agent Mulder's deception."

"Were you able to convince Agent Mulder of these facts?" asks Blevins.

At the DARPA facility, Mulder swipes his card again—with the same results.

In the FBI conference room, Scully continues her report. "What I couldn't tell Agent Mulder," she says, "what I had only just learned myself, was that the cancer which had been diagnosed in me several months earlier had metastasized."

Mulder reaches down and tries the door, but it is locked. He turns back to see the two sentries rounding the corner in the background, moving quickly toward him.

Scully says, "And the doctors told me

short of a miracle it would continue to aggressively invade my body, advancing faster each day toward the inevitable."

The sentries continue to advance upon Mulder.

Scully says, "These facts—these revelations—once learned were devastating to Agent Mulder. Early this morning," she says, "I got a call from the police asking me to come to Agent Mulder's apartment. The detective asked me—he needed me to identify a body."

She cannot go on.

"Agent Scully?" says Blevins softly.

Scully's voice trembles as she forces herself to finish her report. She says: "Agent Mulder died late last night—of an apparent self—inflicted gunshot wound to the head."

Scully looks up from the table and sees Skinner entering the room with a file folder in his hand. Their eyes meet. He levels her with a judgmental gaze.

At the DARPA facility, a desperate Mulder, the sentries bearing down on him, swipes his card a third time. The light turns green and the door pops open. Mulder escapes into the crowded central facility.

The Cigarette-Smoking Man, taking a drag, is standing nearby behind two seated sentries.

"It's okay," he says with a thin smile. "Let him go."

In the FBI star chamber, Skinner, having caught Scully in a lie, stares her down. She turns away.

"Agent Scully," says Blevins. "Those accusations that you made that you were given a disease—these are extremely serious charges."

"Yes, sir," says Scully, holding up a file folder. "But I have proof. Of the men behind this. Of the lies I believed."

She pulls the X-ray film from her folder, stands, and declares angrily: "What I have here is proof undeniable that the men who gave me this disease were also behind the hoax. A plot designed to lead to Agent Mulder's demise—and my own. Planned and executed by someone in this room."

The conference room erupts in alarm and confusion.

Scully continues, "What I have in my hand is scientific evidence—"

Several drops of blood fall on the X-ray film. They are from Scully's nose. She dabs at her nose with her finger, then suddenly gets woozy. She begins to fall. Skinner leaps forward and catches her.

"You—" says Scully.

"Somebody get a doctor," says Skinner.

In another location, somebody is pouring a small amount of liquid from the metallic vial that Mulder had procured into a complicated scientific instrument—a mass spectrometer. It is Byers. The other Lone Gunmen—Frohike and Langly—are with him. Mulder also watches the procedure intently.

The instrument's meters and readouts flash. Byers looks away, catching the eyes of Frohike and Langly.

"What? What is it?" says Mulder.

Byers can hardly bring himself to speak.

"It's deionized water," he says finally. "Nothing more than that."

To be continued...

redux II

While Scully, dying from cancer, undergoes
the desperate treatment her partner has
stolen for her, Mulder penetrates the inner
circle of the Syndicate-FBI conspiracy.
He finds many of the truths that have long
eluded him—as well as disillusionment,
despair, and danger.

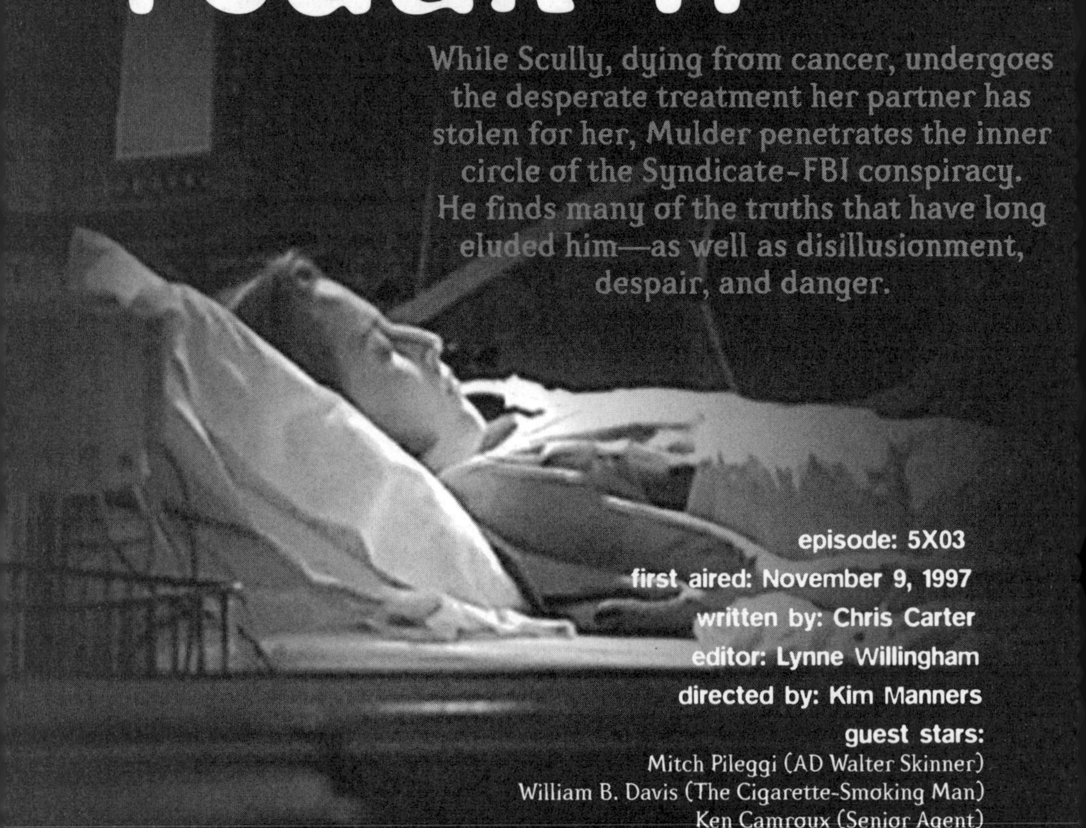

episode: 5X03
first aired: November 9, 1997
written by: Chris Carter
editor: Lynne Willingham
directed by: Kim Manners

guest stars:
Mitch Pileggi (AD Walter Skinner)
William B. Davis (The Cigarette-Smoking Man)
Ken Camroux (Senior Agent)
Charles Cioffi (Section Chief Scott Blevins)
Don S. Williams (Elder)
Megan Leitch (Samantha Mulder)
Bruce Harwood (Byers)
Tom Braidwood (Frohike)
Dean Haglund (Langly)
Sheila Larken (Mrs. Scully)
Pat Skipper (Bill Scully, Jr.)
John Finn (Michael Kritschgau)
Robert Wright (Dr. Zuckerman)
Arnie Walter (Father McCue)
Willy Ross (Silent Assassin)
Brent Shepard (Doctor)
Erin Fitzgerald (Waitress)
Catherine Barroll (Secretary)

principal setting:
Washington, D.C.

It is 5:13 in the morning at the emergency medical unit of Trinity Hospital in Washington. Fox Mulder storms in, asks directions to Dana Scully's room, and raises hell when the information is not immediately forthcoming. An intimidated doctor tells him that Scully is in the ICU; Mulder is about to go there when Walter Skinner—accompanied by other FBI agents—arrives. Mulder brushes past Skinner, who in "Redux" (5X02) he suspected might be part of the FBI-Defense Department conspiracy. The assistant director turns and pursues him.

"Moving well for a dead man," says Skinner.

"Yeah," says Mulder curtly.

"You've got a lot to answer for, Agent Mulder," says Skinner.

Mulder doesn't respond. He enters the ICU and, looking through a large window, spots Scully lying in a bed. She is hooked up to a ventilator.

"What happened to her?" says Mulder.

Skinner says, "She went into hypovolemic shock. She's lost a lot of blood."

"Due to what?" asks Mulder. Skinner does not answer.

"*Due to what?*"

"She's dying," says Skinner finally. "Let's go."

"I'm staying here," says Mulder.

Skinner says, "There's nothing you can do for her."

He takes Mulder's arm. Mulder pulls away angrily and starts toward the door leading into Scully's room.

"Get the hell away from me!" says Mulder. But Skinner restrains him, surprising Mulder with his force.

"I don't want to have to arrest you," says Skinner.

"Let me go, damnit!"

But Skinner doesn't let him go. Mulder struggles to escape. The other agents appear and look through the window at the two struggling men. They enter, help Skinner wrestle Mulder under control, and drag him back into the hallway. The anguished Mulder turns his head to get a last glimpse of his unconscious partner.

Mulder is escorted, more or less forcibly, to the FBI office of Section Chief Blevins. Skinner is also present, as is the Senior Agent from the similar scene in 5X02 in which Blevins questioned Scully.

Blevins smoothly tells Mulder that the revelation that he is still alive "reshapes" the investigation into the murder in Mulder's apartment building. He asks the agent to help them identify the dead man. Mulder remains silent.

"Agent Mulder," says Blevins. "We're here informally to give you the chance to help yourself."

"Help myself how?" asks Mulder.

"By allowing any facts or details which might serve to let us go ahead with this inquiry in a more informed matter."

"That helps you," replies Mulder. "How's it help me?"

Under Skinner's accusatory gaze, Mulder continues treating Blevins's questions with scorn.

"Agent Scully lied to us," says Blevins. "Why?"

No answer.

"Who is protecting whom?" asks the section chief.

Silence.

"Your choice is your own," says Blevins, "but your failure to answer will reflect poorly on the record in a formal inquiry."

"Are we finished here, then?" says Mulder curtly.

He gets up and leaves the room. Skinner also exits and intercepts him in the hall. Surprisingly, he tells Mulder to continue withholding information from his superiors.

"Thanks, buddy," says Mulder sarcastically.

"Right now you need a buddy," says Skinner. "You need any help you can get."

Mulder says, "You should have mentioned it down at the hospital when you were hauling my ass off."

"I saved your ass, Agent Mulder," says Skinner.

The AD adds, in an angry whisper, "I've been withholding forensic evidence about the body on your apartment floor. Until you showed up last night, I was the one keeping

your secret. I had no choice but to bring you in. Scully'll verify all that."

"That's a good place to lay it," he says with a thin smile. "Considering her condition."

"You want me to lay it where it belongs, Agent Mulder? Pathology turned up two gunshot wounds on the dead man in your apartment. One fired point blank through the left temple with a handgun. The second a post-mortem wound to the face to remove the man's identity. I'd be happy to verify the ballistics on the first shot."

Mulder is cornered, and he knows it. "How can you help me?" he asks.

"Tell me why Scully lied for you," says Skinner.

Mulder tells him that her disease was given to her by a mole inside the FBI.

"Who?" asks Skinner.

Mulder says dejectedly, "I failed to find out. I failed in all respects."

Skinner nods, relieved. "You don't want to forget who your friends are, Agent Mulder," he says. "To remember who you can trust."

At the same racetrack at which he was seen in 5X02, the Elder—accompanied by the silent man we'd also seen there before—watches a televised congressional hearing on the ethics of human cloning. The Cigarette-Smoking Man arrives.

"Mulder is alive," says the Elder.

The Cigarette-Smoking Man nods, unable to hide his satisfaction at the news. "As I said, he is not to be underestimated."

"Yes. As you said," says the Elder. "Though I hear he has you to thank, in some part, for his new freedom."

"Yes," says the Cigarette-Smoking Man.

The Elder says sternly, "We're too vulnerable. Our man in the FBI is exposed. Now we have even further risk to the project. What Mulder may have seen would expose our plans."

The Cigarette-Smoking Man says, "What Mulder saw only serves us, only serves to insure our plans."

The Elder stares at his underling with obdurate disbelief.

The Cigarette-Smoking Man adds, "Mulder is in trouble. He needs help. We can give it to him."

"In exchange for?"

"His new loyalty. To us."

The Elder gives the Cigarette-Smoking Man the same stone-faced look as before.

"As I've said all along," adds the Cigarette-Smoking Man, "he's so much more valuable to us alive."

He turns and walks away, watched for several moments by the Elder. Then the Elder looks toward his silent associate.

"You can proceed now," he says. The other man nods.

At the hospital, Scully, her condition somewhat improved, has been moved from the ICU into a regular room. Mulder arrives and tells his partner that he is going to testify about everything he knows about the FBI–Defense Department conspiracy. Scully warns him that if he does so, Skinner will reveal his forensic evidence.

"Mulder, Skinner is dirty," she says. "He's not your friend."

"I don't believe that," says Mulder.

Scully says, "If you testify, he's going to use it to ruin you. He's been in a position to know everything. Everything we've done for the last four years."

Mulder insists that the evidence he's gathered will expose the conspiracy no matter what any of the conspirators do or say.

"You've got to be sure," says Scully. "If you can't bury them absolutely, they're going to bury you. They'll make you into a murderer with an unbelievable alibi."

Mulder says, "If I don't testify now, Scully, they'll begin to bury the truth."

Scully squeezes his hand tightly, nodding. "Then you've got to lay it on me," she says. "Tell them I killed that man."

"Scully. I can't," says Mulder.

"You can," says Scully. "If I can save you, then let me. Let me at least give what's happened to me some meaning."

Mulder shakes his head. As he does so, Scully's mother enters. She sees his hands in hers; he greets her awkwardly and leaves. Scully's older brother, whom we've seen in "Gethsemane" (4X24) but whom Mulder has never before met, greets the agent in the hospital corridor.

"Mr. Mulder," says Bill Scully, Jr. "I know something about you—what Dana's been

through with you. Leave the work away from here, okay? Let her die with dignity."

Without waiting for Mulder's reply, he turns and walks into his sister's room.

In a stairwell at the top of a multi-storied parking structure, a door opens and the Elder's quiet companion enters. He is carrying a molded fiberglass suitcase; he opens it, revealing a disassembled sniper's rifle.

Mulder leaves the hospital the way he came in. As he does so, he sees the Cigarette-Smoking Man heading toward Scully's room.

"Please tell me you're here for severe chest pains," says Mulder, blocking the other man's path.

The Cigarette-Smoking Man says, "You should be glad for why I'm here. To pay you some respect—"

"Go to hell," says Mulder.

"—for your cleverness and resource. What you've managed to do for Scully."

"What are you talking about?"

"Breaching the security at the Defense Department facility. Finding the cure for her disease."

Mulder says, "What I found was useless."

"On the contrary," says the Cigarette-Smoking Man. "It is essential to her survival."

At a workbench we've seen before, Mulder pours the last of the deionized water out of the metallic vial he liberated in 5X02. To the astonishment of Mulder and the three Lone Gunmen gathered around him, a tiny microchip remains inside.

"This is the cure for cancer?" says Frohike.

"For Scully it may be," says Mulder.

"How?" asks Byers.

Mulder says, "Some time after her abduction, she found a small metallic chip implanted subcutaneously on her neck. Not long after she had it removed her cancer developed."

Langly says, "I know you're preaching to the choir here, Mulder—but I've never heard of such a thing."

"Scully met a group of women, all with similar abduction stories," explains Mulder. "Each had a chip removed from her neck. And all died from cancer."

The following day, the FBI investigative committee has reconvened. The witness is Michael Kritschgau. Under questioning from Blevins, he admits that he came to Mulder and Scully and gave them classified information shortly before Scott Ostelhoff's death.

"What motivated this?" asks the section chief.

Kritschgau says, "My knowledge of government involvement in a conspiracy against the American people."

This causes a minor commotion in the star chamber. The Senior Agent cuts in. "Before we get into any specifics on that subject," he says, "I'd like to ask you a more pointed question. Do you know who killed Scott Ostelhoff?"

"No, I don't," says Kritschgau, after a long pause.

Blevins asks, "Are you aware of any connection between his death and agents Mulder and Scully?"

"No," he answers. "I'm aware of one death in connection, though. My son, who died this morning."

Kritschgau fights back his emotions. He's given a moment to recover. The Senior Agent asks the next question.

"Mr. Kritschgau—you are employed by the Department of Defense, is that correct?"

"Technically," says Kritschgau.

He pauses again, then adds, "Part of my remuneration has come from another source. A congressional lobbying firm. Something called Roush."

Skinner speaks up for the first time. "Roush? Any idea what that is?" he says.

"No, sir," says Kritschgau. Blevins and the Senior Agent exchange glances.

In Scully's hospital room, Mulder tries vehemently to convince Mrs. Scully and Bill Scully that implanting the stolen microchip in her body is worth a try. Scully's oncologist, a Dr. Zuckerman, watches silently.

"This is crazy. Just crazy," Bill Scully tells Mulder.

"Crazy in what sense?" replies Mulder. "That it might save your sister's life?"

Bill Scully says, "You're not a doctor. You've got no place even suggesting this science fiction."

Mulder turns to Zuckerman. "Would she have to stop with her conventional treatment?" he asks.

"To be honest," says Zuckerman, "at this point the only approach I have left with her particular cancer is quite unconventional."

All eyes are on Scully as she fingers the metallic vial.

"I'd like to try this," she says. She holds out the vial to Zuckerman. He steps over and takes it from her.

"I don't suppose it came with instructions," he says with mock consternation. Scully smiles at him.

In the stairwell, the quiet assassin meticulously assembles his sniper's rifle. He then affixes a small laser sight, loads several rounds of ammunition, sights down the barrel, and checks his watch.

In the corridor outside Scully's room, Mulder sits alone. Bill Scully emerges and walks past him, then stops. He retraces his steps.

"You really believe this crap, don't you?" he says.

"What crap is that?" says Mulder.

Bill Scully stares at Mulder, then shakes his head. "She's your big defender. But I think the truth is, she just doesn't want to disappoint you."

"If it works," says Mulder, "I don't care what you think she thinks."

"You're a real piece of work. You know that, Mr. Mulder?"

"Why?" says Mulder. "Because I'm not playing by your rules? Because I'm not part of the family tragedy?"

"You're the reason for it," says Bill Scully flatly. He adds, "I've already lost one sister to this quest you're on. Now I'm losing another. Has it been worth it? I mean, for you. Have you found what you've been looking for?"

For a few horrible moments, Mulder doesn't answer. "No," he says finally.

"No? You know how that makes me feel?"

Mulder says painfully, "In a way I do. I lost someone very close to me—a sister. And then my father. Because of the things I've been looking for."

"These what? Little green aliens?" says Bill Scully.

"I don't know anymore," says Mulder, miserable.

Bill Scully stares at Mulder, who seems to have lost all the fight in him.

"You're one sorry sonofabitch," says Scully's brother. "Not a whole lot more to say."

Mulder watches him round the corner, then sits by himself for several painful moments. His cell phone rings.

"How's our patient?" says a voice Mulder knows only too well. "You did find the chip, didn't you?"

"Yes," says Mulder.

The Cigarette-Smoking Man says, "I can imagine there was some question to its medical value."

"There still is."

"So I have yet to earn your trust, in spite of my gesture."

"You could say that."

"Well," says the Cigarette-Smoking Man, "I have something else to offer you. To cement our bond."

"Gonna take a lot of cement," says Mulder.

"I've arranged a meeting I think you'll want to be at, Mr. Mulder," the Cigarette-Smoking Man replies.

In a small diner that night, Mulder sits with a coffee cup in front of him, watching the waitress. Her arms laden with condiment bottles, she walks over to where he sits.

"Tabasco. Cures anything," she says.

"I'll keep that in mind," says Mulder.

Just after 9:30 a car, headlights blazing, pulls up in front. Two people are seated in the front seat; they remain inside with the motor running. Curious, Mulder stands and looks outside through the window. The headlights are finally turned off and Mulder recognizes the occupants immediately: they are the Cigarette-Smoking Man and a grown woman—last seen in "End Game" (2X17)—in the passenger seat.

"You know them or something?" asks the waitress.

"Yeah. I think that's my sister," says Mulder.

Mulder leaves the diner and walks toward the car. It is indeed Samantha Mulder. With tears in her eyes, she exits and joins her brother.

She is the first to speak. "I was afraid I'd never see you again," she says. "He always told me something had happened to you that night."

"Who?" says Mulder. "Who told you that?"

"My father," says Samantha. She gestures toward the Cigarettes-Smoking Man sitting behind the wheel.

In the diner later that night, Samantha and Mulder sit facing one another.

"I never really knew what happened," says Samantha. "I could never put the memories all back together, but as much as I tried to remember, I tried more to forget."

"Why?" asks Mulder, stunned.

"I was eight years old," says Samantha. "I was eight years old. I was frightened to death. They told me I was an orphan."

Mulder stares at her as if she were an apparition. Outside, the Cigarette-Smoking Man sits in the car, smoking.

"But you called this man your father," says Mulder.

Samantha says, "Some time later, I don't know how long, my foster parents took me to a hotel room and said I was going to see my father."

"But you knew who your father was."

"I thought I knew. But he told me that it had all been a secret. That he and Mom hadn't told anyone to protect the family."

"And you believe that?" says Mulder incredulously.

Samantha nods and explains that the man who called himself her father was kind to her and that is all she can remember about the night she disappeared.

"You were abducted, Samantha," says Mulder forcefully. "I can help you. I can help you to remember."

"I don't want to, Fox. I don't."

"Then why come here at all?"

"My father told me he'd found you," she says, "and that you wanted to see me very badly—that you'd been looking for me a long time. Is it true?"

"Yes," says Mulder. She reaches out and takes his hand.

"Samantha," says Mulder. "You have to listen to me. What you've been told—

what this man has told you—it may not be true."

Samantha refuses to believe him. Mulder asks her to come with him to see their mother. Samantha is surprised that she is still alive, but she shakes her head.

"Why can't you?" asks Mulder.

"This is too much," says Samantha. "I didn't want to come here at all, Fox. I was afraid to see you. I have my own life. I have children of my own."

Mulder begs her to stay with him, or at least tell him where she can be reached. She stands up from the table, then pulls her hand away from his.

"Please let me go," she says, then walks toward the door as Mulder watches helplessly. "Please. I promise you I'll think about it."

In the hospital, Dr. Zuckerman injects Scully with a cancer-fighting substance, flurodeoxy deoxyglucose.

"If you're making any progress," he says. "I'm hoping it might show up on the PET scan."

"You're not holding your breath, though, are you?" says Scully.

Zuckerman looks up at her, unsurprised by the question.

"I'm going after your cancer as aggressively as I know how, Dana," he says patiently. "If I can jump-start your immune system, if I can get your cytolytic cells to recognize your tumor as something to attack, then there's a chance."

Scully says, "My cancer—nasopharyngeal—I'm well aware it has a very poor response to treatment."

"You're doing everything you can," says Zuckerman.

"Am I?"

"And then some," he says ironically.

Scully watches him take the spike out of her arm, then forces herself to say what's on her mind.

"Have you ever witnessed a miracle, Dr. Zuckerman?" she says.

"I don't know that I have. But I've seen people make recoveries, come back from so far gone I can't explain it."

"Isn't that a miracle?"

Zuckerman says, "There was something from my religion I learned as a boy. Whoever destroys a single life is as guilty as though he had destroyed the entire world, and whoever rescues a single life earns as much merit as though he had rescued the entire world. Maybe they are miracles, but I don't dare call them that."

Scully smiles up at him. "Thank you," she says.

Mulder walks down a Washington, D.C., sidewalk. He is in the crosshairs of a rifle sight. The silent assassin stands at a corner of the parking structure, aiming outward and downward. Mulder reaches a street corner and stands impatiently next to a brick building. He is joined by the Cigarette-Smoking Man, and—still tracked by the assassin—they walk together through a busy Georgetown street.

"What do you want from me?" asks Mulder.

"Want from you?" says the Cigarette-Smoking Man mockingly.

Mulder says, "You give me these things—the only things I've ever wanted. You have no other reason to do this."

"It's true," says the Cigarette-Smoking Man. "No act is completely selfless. But I've come today not to ask, but to offer. To offer you the truth you so desperately sought. About the project, and the men who have conspired to protect it."

Mulder counters that he already knows the truth.

"What have you seen?" says the Cigarette-Smoking Man. "You've seen but scant pieces of the whole."

"What more can you show me?" says Mulder.

The Cigarette-Smoking Man tells him that Kritschgau has lied about the nonexistence of extraterrestrial life, that only he can tell Mulder the real story.

"In exchange for what?" asks Mulder.

"Quit the FBI. Come work for me. I can make your problems go away."

"No deal."

The Cigarette-Smoking Man chuckles. "After all I've given to you—"

Mulder erupts in rage. "What have you given me?" he says angrily. "The claim of a cure for Scully. Is she cured? You bring my sister to me, only to take her back. You've given me nothing!"

The Cigarette-Smoking Man says, "What is given can be taken away. I intend to keep my promises. I just need something from you."

The furious Mulder gets right up into the Cigarette-Smoking Man's face. "You murdered my father," he says. "You murdered Scully's sister. And if Scully dies, I will kill you. I'll put you down. I don't care whose father you are."

"You certainly are capable of that, from what I'm told," says the Cigarette-Smoking Man coolly. "I understand you have a hearing tomorrow where you'll have to testify to these murderous impulses of yours."

In the parking structure, the quiet assassin sights his rifle and prepares to shoot. But Mulder and the Cigarette-Smoking Man are so close together that it would be hard to shoot one and not the other. Mulder walks away. The assassin pulls his gun back. He has missed his shot.

In her hospital room, Scully, her condition unchanged, rests on her bed. Her mother enters; she has sent for her, Dana says, to tell her something important. She begins to cry; her mother embraces her.

"I fight and I fight, but I've been so stupid," she says. "I've been so wrong."

"What? What is it?" says Mrs. Scully.

"I've come so far in my life on simple faith," says Scully. "And now when I need it most I push it away."

Scully breaks away from her mother, grasps at the chain around her neck, and pulls out the small Christian cross she wears. "Why do I wear this?" she says. "I'll put something I don't understand on the skin of my neck. I'll subject myself to these crazy treatments. I tell myself I'm doing everything I can, but it's a lie."

"You haven't lost your faith, Dana," says Mrs. Scully.

"But I have, in a way," says Scully. "When you asked Father McCue to dinner [in "Gethsemane" (4X24)] to minister to my faith, I just blew him off."

Mrs. Scully tries to calm her.

"I'm not getting better, Mom," says Scully. "My PET scan showed no improvement."

"I know you're afraid, Dana," says her mother. "And I know you're afraid to tell me. But you need to tell someone."

Scully nods.

"He's been praying for you," says Mrs. Scully.

"Father McCue?" says Scully. "Would you call him for me?"

"Of course," says Mrs. Scully, nodding.

In the Syndicate headquarters room that night, the Elder sits watching the congres-

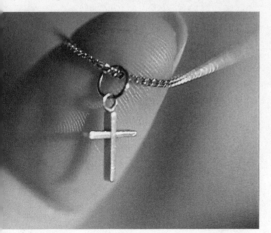

sional hearing. As the TV camera pans the spectators' gallery, it finds Assistant Director Walter Skinner talking to another man. Seeing this, the Elder quickly reaches for his phone and punches in some numbers.

"Turn on your television. Are you watching the hearings? Do you see who's there? Who he's there talking to? He's gathering information. For who?"

Whoever is at the other end replies. The answer is indistinct, but whatever it is, the Elder is not satisfied.

"Our colleague was supposed to have fixed the FBI problem," he says. "You will fix it now, do you understand me? Then I will fix it for good." He hangs up the phone angrily.

In her hospital room that night, Scully is asleep. Mulder enters quietly and stands watching her for a quiet moment, torn over something, debating with himself about waking her to share his thoughts. Then he bends to one knee and lays his head on the side of her bed in quiet, private anguish.

The next day Mulder, depressed and

nearly expressionless, enters Blevins's FBI office. The section chief holds up a file folder—the same one that Skinner had brought into the star chamber in 5X02—and tells him that he has forensic evidence indicating he was the man who shot Ostelhoff.

"Where did you get it?" asks Mulder.

"I'm not at liberty to say," says Blevins. "But unless you can offer up someone else who might have fired the kill shot, everything points to you as this man's murderer."

Mulder says nothing.

Blevins says, "Are you prepared to give testimony that you are not the man who fired that shot?"

Mulder ignores this. "Why am I here?" he says.

Blevins tells him accusingly something Mulder already knows: the dead man worked for the Department of Defense.

"This man was spying on me!" says Mulder.

"Do you know for whom?" asks Blevins.

Again Mulder is silent.

Blevins says, "Agent Scully was prepared to name the man at the FBI who was involved in the plot against you and her. We believe she was about to name Assistant Director Walter Skinner—who we've just now learned has been working inside the FBI with a secret agenda."

"I refuse to believe that," says Mulder.

"We have accumulated substantial evidence against him," says Blevins.

"Show it to me."

Blevins does not. Instead, he shifts tactics and offers to exonerate Mulder from murder charges if he names Skinner as the traitor.

"That's what I've called you here to recommend," says Blevins. "As a friend."

Mulder stands up to leave. "I'll see you at the hearing," he says.

At the hospital later that day, a drawn and tired Scully receives her partner. He tells her of his visit the night before; she asks him what he wanted to discuss with her.

"I was lost last night," says Mulder, "but as I stood there I thought I'd found my way. I was offered a deal. A deal that would save my life in a way. And although I'd refused this deal earlier, I left here with my mind made up to take it."

"A deal with who?" says Scully.

"It doesn't matter now. I'm not taking that deal. I'm not taking any deal. Not after this morning."

"What happened this morning?"

Mulder tells Scully about Blevins's promise to clear him if he testifies against Skinner.

"Are you going to name him?" asks Scully.

"No."

"Then they'll prosecute you," says Scully.

Mulder nods. "They have evidence against me," he says. "They know I killed that man."

Scully says, "Even with ballistics evidence, I could still be the shooter—"

Mulder shakes his head. "I can't let you take the blame. Because of your mother, and your brother. And because I couldn't live with it."

He adds, "To live the lie you have to believe it, like these men who deceive us. Who gave you this disease. We all have our faith, and mine is the truth. I've been looking for it so long I don't know any other way."

Scully regards Mulder with a respectful sadness.

"Why come here," she asks, "if you'd already made up your mind?"

Mulder replies: "I knew you would talk me out of it if I was making a mistake."

She takes his hand and squeezes it tightly. They both turn in reaction to the door opening. It is Father McCue.

"You'll be in my prayers," says Scully to Mulder. Mulder turns away from her and leaves.

In the FBI star chamber later that day, Blevins waits impatiently. The Senior Agent is also present. Skinner sits next to him. Mulder arrives and apologizes for the delay.

"Agent Mulder," says Blevins, "the assembled members of this review panel first convened to address your reported death, only to find out shortly this report had been a lie. That you were indeed very much alive, and that the body found in your apartment, believed to be yours, was a murder victim—killed with a weapon issued by the FBI and registered to you—"

Mulder interrupts. "Respectfully, sir," he says, "I'd like to set the record straight today—so that the process which you have begun can be completed, and the guilty parties named."

Skinner jumps in and asks for a short adjournment, but Mulder ignores him.

"Go on, Agent Mulder," says Blevins.

This is Mulder's testimony:

"Four years ago, working on an assignment outside the FBI mainstream, I was paired with Special Agent Dana Scully, who I believed was sent to spy on me, to debunk my investigations into the paranormal. That Agent Scully did not follow these orders owes more to her integrity as an investigator, as a scientist, as a person. She's paid greatly for this integrity—"

Blevins jumps in. "Agent Mulder," he says. "Agent Scully lied straightfaced to this panel about your death."

Mulder stops to refute him: "She lied because I asked her to. Because of evidence I had of a conspiracy at work. A conspiracy against the American people—and a conspiracy to destroy the lives of those who might reveal its real purpose."

In the parking garage, the quiet assassin is again at his post. Through his scope he tracks the Cigarette-Smoking Man walking down the street. It's an imperfect shot due to trees, lampposts, and the other people on the street, but the Cigarette-Smoking Man remains in the crosshairs until he disappears into the front entrance of the brick building.

In the hearing room, Mulder continues.

"To conduct experiments on unwitting victims to further a secret agenda for someone within the government, working at a level without restraints of responsibility. Who deceive as they pretend to honor. The price of this betrayal: the lives and reputations of the deceived."

In Scully's room, Father McCue is at her bedside, praying with her.

"Agent Scully is lying in hospital right now, diagnosed with terminal cancer—a victim of these same tests, conducted without her consent or knowledge by these same men who as they try to cover their tracks, try to suborn and prosecute those who they've used in the plot. I will now call by name—"

Now the Senior Agent jumps in. "Agent Mulder!" he says. "Did you or did you not shoot the man found dead in your apartment—"

"I will answer that question—" begins Mulder, but the Senior Agent cuts him off.

"Did you shoot Scott Ostelhoff, employee of the Department of Defense—"

"I will answer that question—" repeats Mulder.

In the hospital room, Scully, tears now streaming down her face, continues praying with Father McCue.

Inside his apartment, the Cigarette-Smoking Man exhales a cloud of smoke and studies a photograph. It is of Mulder and his sister Samantha. Through the Cigarette-Smoking Man's open window is the parking structure.

"I will answer that question," says Mulder, "after I name the man responsible for Agent Scully, the same man who directed my apartment be surveilled by the DOD. A man who I want prosecuted for his crimes. Who is sitting in this room as I speak."

"Agent Mulder!" says the Senior Agent. "The section chief has asked you a question. You are going to answer it."

"I can't do that, sir," says Mulder, "because the section chief is the man I am about to name." The room erupts at this announcement.

In the apartment, the Cigarette-Smoking Man is still looking at the photograph. He notices something that causes him alarm— a red laser dot on the center of his chest. He looks up and out the window and sees the quiet assassin firing his weapon.

In the FBI hearing room, Section Chief Blevins is up on his feet, shouting something at Mulder. His words cannot be heard above the din. Mulder sits calmly in his seat. Skinner stares at him. The Senior Agent leaves the room quickly and hurries down an empty corridor.

The photograph of Mulder and Samantha—now blood-spattered and the glass in its frame shattered by a bullet— lies on the floor of the apartment. The Cigarette-Smoking Man lies on his stomach nearby. For a moment, he appears dead; then his eyes blink and his hand reaches out feebly to find the photo. When his hand touches the frame, only then do his eyes close.

Inside Blevins's FBI office, the Senior Agent talks into the phone, his manner urgent, but his words hushed and unintelligible. A panicky-looking Blevins enters; the Senior Agent turns and raises a handgun. A shot rings out; Blevins falls; the Senior Agent steps over his body and exits.

In the hospital corridor, Mulder is sitting outside Scully's room. Skinner appears at the end of the hall, approaches, and with a nod sits down on the bench next to him.

"The Smoking Man is dead," says Skinner.

"How?" asks Mulder.

"Shot through his window."

Skinner hands Mulder the photo of himself with his sister. "Forensics found it at the scene," he says. "We're assuming it's his blood."

"Assuming?" says Mulder, confused.

"No body was found, though there was too much blood loss for anyone to have survived."

Mulder stares at Skinner, unconvinced. He looks back at the photo.

Skinner says, "This afternoon, when you named Blevins. How did you know?"

"I didn't," says Mulder. "I guessed."

"Hell of a guess," says Skinner. "Blevins had been on payroll for four years to a biotechnology company called Roush, which is somehow connected to all this."

"I'm sure whatever connection has already been erased."

Skinner nods. "They're cleaning up, taking everything away."

"Not everything," says Mulder. "Agent Scully's cancer has gone into remission."

Skinner is stunned. "That is unbelievable news," he says after a moment.

"That is the best news I can ever imagine," says Mulder, trying—with limited success—to restrain his emotions.

Skinner asks Mulder what treatment turned her disease around.

"I don't know," says Mulder. "I don't know if we'll ever know."

Skinner says, "Can I see her?"

Mulder nods. "I know she'd like to see you. She's in with her family."

Skinner gets up, moves to the door, and opens it. Inside, Scully is lying in bed, her mother and brother by her side. Dr. Zuckerman and Father McCue are there, too. She sees Skinner and her face beams.

Mulder remains seated, alone. He looks down again at the photograph—at his family photograph—and surrenders to his emotions at last.

awards and honors

1996–97

PRIME-TIME EMMY AWARDS
—Winner, Outstanding Lead Actress in a Drama Series—Gillian Anderson

—Winner, Outstanding Art Direction for a Series—Graeme Murray, Gary P. Allen, Shirley Inget for "Memento Mori"

—Nominee, Outstanding Sound Editing for a Series—Thierry J. Couturier, Stuart Calderon, Ira Leslie, Maciek Malish, Debby Ruby-Winsburg, Chris Fradkin, Jay Levine, Chris Reeves, Susan Welsh, Jeff Charbonneau, Gary Marullo, Mike Salvetta for "Tempus Fugit"

—Nominee, Outstanding Drama Series

—Nominee, Outstanding Lead Actor in a Drama Series—David Duchovny

—Nominee, Outstanding Writing in a Drama Series—Chris Carter, Vince Gilligan, John Shiban, Frank Spotnitz for "Memento Mori"

—Nominee, Outstanding Directing in a Drama Series—James Wong for "Musings of a Cigarette-Smoking Man"

—Nominee, Outstanding Makeup for a Series—Laverne Basham, Toby Lindala for "Leonard Betts"

—Nominee, Outstanding Music Composition for a Series (Dramatic Underscore)—Mark Snow for "Paper Hearts"

—Nominee, Outstanding Single Camera Picture Editing for a Series—Jim Gross for "Terma"

—Nominee, Outstanding Single Camera Picture Editing for a Series—Heather MacDougall for "Tempus Fugit"

—Nominee, Outstanding Sound Mixing for a Drama Series—Michael Williamson, David J. West, Nello Torri, Harry Andronis for "Tempus Fugit"

GEORGE FOSTER PEABODY AWARDS
—Winner, Excellence in Broadcasting

GOLDEN GLOBE AWARDS
—Winner, Outstanding Drama Series

—Winner, Outstanding Performance by an Actor in a Drama Series—David Duchovny

—Winner, Outstanding Performance by an Actress in a Drama Series—Gillian Anderson

SCREEN ACTORS GUILD AWARDS
—Winner, Best Performance by an Actress in a Dramatic Series—Gillian Anderson

—Nominee, Best Performance by an Ensemble in a Dramatic Series

—Nominee, Best Performance by an Actor in a Dramatic Series—David Duchovny

TELEVISION CRITICS ASSOCIATION (TCA) AWARDS
—Nominee, Program of the Year

—Nominee, Drama of the Year

—Nominee, Best Performance of the Year—Gillian Anderson

GOLDEN SATELLITE AWARDS
—Winner, Best Drama Series

—Winner, Best Actor in a Drama Series— David Duchovny

—Nominee, Best Actress in a Drama Series—Gillian Anderson

PRODUCERS GUILD OF AMERICA AWARDS
(GOLDEN LAUREL AWARDS)
—Nominee, Outstanding Series

WRITERS GUILD OF AMERICA AWARDS
—Nominee, Outstanding Writing in a
  Drama Series—Darin Morgan for "Clyde
  Bruckman's Final Repose"

AMERICAN SOCIETY OF
CINEMATOGRAPHERS AWARDS
—Nominee, Outstanding
  Cinematography—John Bartley for
  "Grotesque"

MOTION PICTURE SOUND EDITORS
GOLDEN REEL AWARDS
—Nominee, Outstanding Music Editing for
  "Syzygy"

—Nominee, Outstanding ADR Editing for
  "Hell Money"

CINEMA AUDIO SOCIETY AWARDS
—Nominee, Outstanding Sound Mixing for
  "Tunguska"

SCIENCE FICTION AND FANTASY
SATURN AWARDS
—Winner for Outstanding Television
  Series

worldwide broadcast outlets

During the 1996-97 season, *The X-Files* was
televised in the following countries:

Argentina
Australia
Austria
Bali
Belgium
Bolivia
Borneo
Brazil
Brunei
Canada
Chile
Colombia
Denmark
Ecuador
El Salvador
Fiji
Finland
France
Germany
Greece
Greenland
Hong Kong
Iceland
Indonesia
Ireland (Eire)
Israel
Italy
Jamaica
Lebanon
Luxembourg
Malaysia
Malta
Mexico
Nassau
Netherlands
New Zealand
Nicaragua
Norway
Paraguay
Peru
Philippines
Portugal
Puerto Rico
Singapore
South Africa
South Korea
Spain
Sri Lanka
Sweden
Switzerland
Taiwan
Thailand
Trinidad and Tobago
United Kingdom
United States
Uruguay
Venezuela

ratings: season 4

AIR DATE	EPISODE	RATING/SHARE	VIEWERS (in millions)
10/4/97	Herrenvolk	13.2/23	21.11
10/11/96	Home	11.9/21	18.85
10/18/96	Teliko	11.3/20	18.01
10/27/96	Unruhe	11.7/18	19.10
11/3/96	The Field Where I Died	12.3/18	19.85
11/10/96	Sanguinarium	11.1/16	18.85
11/17/96	Musings of a Cigarette-Smoking Man	10.7/15	17.09
11/24/96	Tunguska	12.2/18	18.85
12/1/96	Terma	10.6/15	17.34
12/15/96	Paper Hearts	10.7/16	16.59
1/12/97	El Mundo Gira	13.3/19	22.37
1/26/97	Leonard Betts*	17.2/29	29.15
2/2/97	Never Again	13.0/19	21.36
2/9/97	Memento Mori	11.5/17	19.10
2/16/97	Kaddish	10.3/15	16.56
2/23/97	Unrequited	10.9/16	16.56
3/16/97	Tempus Fugit	11.9/18	18.85
3/23/97	Max	11.6/18	18.34
4/13/97	Synchrony	11.3/18	18.09
4/20/97	Small Potatoes	13.0/20	20.86
4/27/97	Zero Sum	11.7/17	18.60
5/4/97	Elegy	10.6/16	17.10
5/11/97	Demons	11.8/18	19.10
5/18/97	Gethsemane	12.7/19	19.85

Each rating point equals 970,000 homes, or 1 percent of all households in the United States. Share is based on the percentage of TV sets in use within the time period. Total viewers for each episode is measured by Nielsen's people-meter rating service, which draws its figures from a small sample designed to represent all television viewers in the United States.

Source: Nielsen Media Research

*The post–Super Bowl episode won the highest rating, share and total audience in The X-Files history.

appendix

SEASON ONE

PILOT 1X79
FBI Agent Dana Scully is paired with maverick agent Fox Mulder, who has made it his life's work to explore unexplained phenomena. The two are dispatched to investigate the mysterious deaths of a number of high school classmates.

DEEP THROAT 1X01
Acting on a tip from an inside source (Deep Throat), Mulder and Scully travel to Idaho to investigate unusual disappearances of army test pilots.

SQUEEZE 1X02
Mulder and Scully try to stop a mutant killer, Eugene Tooms, who can gain access through even the smallest spaces and awakens from hibernation every 30 years to commit murder.

CONDUIT 1X03
A teenage girl is abducted by aliens, compelling Mulder to confront his feelings about his own sister's disappearance.

JERSEY DEVIL 1X04
Scully and Mulder investigate murders thought to be the work of the legendary man-beast living in the New Jersey woods.

SHADOWS 1X05
Mulder and Scully investigate unusual murders committed by an unseen force protecting a young woman.

GHOST IN THE MACHINE 1X06
A computer with artificial intelligence begins killing in order to preserve its existence.

ICE 1X07
Mulder and Scully and a small party in the Arctic are trapped after the unexplained deaths of a research team on assignment there.

SPACE 1X08
A mysterious force is sabotaging the United States space shuttle program and Scully and Mulder must stop it before the next launch.

FALLEN ANGEL 1X09
Scully and Mulder investigate a possible UFO crash site, which Mulder believes the government is covering up.

EVE 1X10
Two bizarre, identical murders occur simultaneously on different coasts, each involving a strange young girl.

FIRE 1X11
Mulder and Scully encounter an assassin who can start fires with the touch of his hand.

BEYOND THE SEA 1X12
Scully and Mulder seek the aid of a death row inmate, Luther Lee Boggs, who claims to have psychic abilities, to help them stop a killer who is on the loose.

GENDERBENDER 1X13
Scully and Mulder seek answers to a bizarre series of murders committed by one person who kills as both a male and a female.

LAZARUS 1X14
When an FBI agent and a bank robber are both shot during a bank heist, the robber is killed but the agent begins to take on the criminal's persona.

YOUNG AT HEART 1X15
Mulder finds that a criminal he put away who was supposed to have died in prison has returned, taunting him as he commits a new spree of crimes.

E.B.E. 1X16
Scully and Mulder discover evidence of a government cover-up when they learn that a UFO shot down in Iraq has been secretly transported to the United States.

MIRACLE MAN 1X17
The agents investigate a young faith healer who seems to use his powers for both good and evil.

SHAPES 1X18
Mulder and Scully travel to an Indian reservation to examine deaths caused by a beastlike creature.

DARKNESS FALLS 1X19
Mulder and Scully are called in when loggers in a remote Pacific Northwest forest mysteriously disappear.

TOOMS 1X20
Mulder becomes personally involved when Eugene Tooms, the serial killer who extracts and eats human livers, is released from prison.

BORN AGAIN 1X21
A series of murders is linked to a little girl who may be the reincarnated spirit of a murdered policeman.

ROLAND 1X22
Mulder and Scully investigate the murders of two rocket scientists apparently linked to a retarded janitor.

THE ERLENMEYER FLASK 1X23
Working on a tip from Deep Throat, Mulder and Scully discover that the government has been testing alien DNA on humans with disastrous results.

SEASON TWO

LITTLE GREEN MEN 2X01
With the X-Files shut down, Mulder secretly journeys to a possible alien contact site in Puerto Rico while Scully tries to help him escape detection.

THE HOST 2X02
Mulder stumbles upon a genetic mutation, the Flukeman, while investigating a murder in the New Jersey sewer system.

BLOOD 2X03
Several residents of a small suburban farming community suddenly turn violent and dangerous, prompted by digital readouts in appliances telling them to kill.

SLEEPLESS 2X04
Mulder is assigned a new partner, Alex Krycek, and they investigate a secret Vietnam-era experiment on sleep deprivation that is having deadly effects on surviving participants.

DUANE BARRY (PART 1 OF 2) 2X05
Mulder negotiates a hostage situation involving a man, Duane Barry, who claims to be a victim of alien experimentation.

ASCENSION (PART 2 OF 2) 2X06
Mulder pursues Duane Barry in a desperate search for Scully.

3 2X07
Mulder investigates a series of vampiresque murders in Hollywood and finds himself falling for a mysterious woman who is a prime suspect.

ONE BREATH 2X08
Scully is found alive but in a coma, and Mulder must fight to save her life.

FIREWALKER 2X09
Mulder and Scully stumble upon a deadly life form while investigating the death of a scientist studying an active volcano.

RED MUSEUM 2X10
Mulder and Scully investigate a possible connection between a rural religious cult and the disappearance of several teenagers.

EXCELSIUS DEI 2X11
Mulder and Scully uncover strange goings-on in a nursing home after a nurse is attacked by an unseen force.

AUBREY 2X12
Mulder and Scully investigate the possibility of genetic transferring of personality from one generation to another in connection with a serial killer.

IRRESISTIBLE 2X13
A psycho who collects hair and fingernails from the dead steps up his obsession to killing his soon-to-be collectibles himself.

DIE HAND DIE VERLETZT 2X14
Mulder and Scully journey to a small town to investigate a boy's murder and are caught between the town's secret occult religion and a woman with strange powers.

FRESH BONES 2X15
Mulder and Scully journey to a Haitian refugee camp after a series of deaths, finding themselves caught in a secret war between the camp commander and a voodoo priest.

COLONY (PART 1 OF 2) 2X16
Mulder and Scully track an alien bounty hunter who is killing medical doctors who have something strange in common.

END GAME (PART 2 OF 2) 2X17
Mulder tracks an alien bounty hunter who has taken Scully prisoner while discovering that his sister may not be who she seems.

FEARFUL SYMMETRY 2X18
Mulder and Scully investigate animal abductions from a zoo near a known UFO hot spot.

DOD KALM 2X19
Mulder and Scully fall victim to a mysterious force aboard a Navy destroyer that causes rapid aging.

HUMBUG 2X20
Mulder and Scully investigate the bizarre death of a retired escape artist in a town populated by former circus and sideshow acts.

THE CALUSARI 2X21
A young boy's unusual death leads Mulder and Scully to a superstitious old woman and her grandson, who may be possessed by evil.

F. EMASCULATA 2X22
When a plaguelike illness kills ten men inside a prison facility, Scully is called to the quarantine area while Mulder tracks two escapees.

SOFT LIGHT 2X23
An experiment in dark matter turns a scientist's shadow into a form of instant death.

OUR TOWN 2X24
Mulder and Scully investigate a murder in a small Southern town and its strange secrets surrounding a chicken processing plant.

ANASAZI 2X25
Mulder's and Scully's lives are jeopardized when an amateur computer hacker gains access to secret government files providing evidence of UFOs.

SEASON THREE

THE BLESSING WAY 3X01
With the Cigarette-Smoking Man pursuing the secret files that prove the existence of alien visitation and experimentation, and Mulder still missing, Scully finds her own life and career in jeopardy.

PAPER CLIP 3X02
Mulder and Scully seek evidence of alien experimentation by Nazi war criminals while Skinner tries to bargain with the Cigarette-Smoking Man for their lives.

D.P.O. 3X03
Mulder and Scully investigate a series of deaths related to a teenage boy who can control lightning.

CLYDE BRUCKMAN'S FINAL REPOSE 3X04
Mulder and Scully enlist the help of a man who can see when people will die while searching for a serial killer who prays upon fortunetellers.

THE LIST 3X05
A death row inmate makes good on his promise to return from the dead and kill five people who wronged him.

2SHY 3X06
Mulder and Scully track a serial killer who preys on lonely overweight women via the Internet.

THE WALK 3X07
A suicide attempt and subsequent murders at a military hospital bring Mulder and Scully into contact with a quadruple amputee veteran who may have the power of astral projection.

OUBLIETTE 3X08
The abduction of a young girl prompts Mulder to seek the help of a woman who was kidnapped by the same man years

earlier and who has the ability to feel what the victim feels.

NISEI 3X09
Video of an alien autopsy puts Mulder and Scully on the trail of a conspiracy involving Japanese scientists that may shed light on Scully's abduction.

731 3X10
Mulder is caught on board a speeding train with what might be alien cargo and a government killer while Scully seeks her own solution to the conspiracy.

REVELATIONS 3X11
Mulder and Scully seek to protect a young boy who displays wounds of religious significance from a killer, causing Scully to question her own faith while being cast in the role of the boy's protector.

WAR OF THE COPROPHAGES 3X12
A number of deaths seemingly linked to cockroaches cause widespread panic in a small town.

SYZYGY 3X13
Two high school girls born on the same day are involved in a series of deaths thanks to an odd alignment of planets that causes strange behavior in all the towns-people, as well as Mulder and Scully.

GROTESQUE 3X14
A serial killer maintains that an evil spirit was responsible for his actions, as Mulder's own sanity comes into question when the murders persist.

PIPER MARU 3X15
A French salvage ship finds mysterious wreckage from World War II that unleashes a strange force causing radiation sickness and leading Mulder into a web of intrigue.

APOCRYPHA 3X16
Mulder pursues Krycek and the mystery of the sunken World War II wreckage, while the shooting of Skinner brings Scully new clues to her sister's murder.

PUSHER 3X17
Mulder and Scully investigate a man possessing the power to bend people to his will who engages Mulder in a scary battle of wits.

TESO DOS BICHOS 3X18
The unearthing of an ancient Ecuadorian artifact results in a series of deaths potentially linked to a shaman spirit.

HELL MONEY 3X19
The deaths of several Chinese immigrants missing internal organs leads Mulder and Scully to a mysterious game with potentially fatal consequences.

JOSE CHUNG'S *FROM OUTER SPACE* 3X20
A novelist interviews Scully about a rumored UFO abduction of two teenagers that seems open to a number of different interpretations.

AVATAR 3X21
In the midst of a marital breakup Skinner becomes a murder suspect, while a clue to the case may lie in the form of a strange woman who appears to him in dreams.

QUAGMIRE 3X22
Mulder and Scully investigate a series of deaths that may be linked to a lake monster known by the locals as Big Blue.

WETWIRED 3X23
Mulder and Scully discover a conspiracy involving mind control through television signals that's responsible for a series of murders in a small town and begins causing Scully herself to behave strangely.

TALITHA CUMI 3X24
Mulder and Scully search for a mysterious man with the power to heal, whose existence risks exposing a conspiracy involving the presence of aliens on Earth, while various forces seek a strange weapon that comes into Mulder's possession.